Christiane Trüe | Vera de Hesselle | Lydia Scholz [eds.]

Green Deal II – on track for 2030 and 2050?

Political, Economic and Legal Issues

Nomos

The Deutsche Nationalbibliothek lists this publication in the Deutsche Nationalbibliografie; detailed bibliographic data are available on the Internet at http://dnb.d-nb.de

1st Edition 2026

Published by
Nomos Verlagsgesellschaft mbH & Co. KG
Waldseestraße 3–5 | 76530 Baden-Baden
www.nomos.de

Production of the printed version:
Nomos Verlagsgesellschaft mbH & Co. KG
Waldseestraße 3–5 | 76530 Baden-Baden

ISBN 978-3-7560-3115-3 (Print)
ISBN 978-3-7489-5456-9 (ePDF)

DOI https://doi.org/10.5771/9783748954569

Onlineversion
Inlibra

Introduction

The European Green Deal appears to have lost some of its impetus: with a new European Parliament and a new Commission, even if the previous Commission's president is also its current president, Ursula von der Leyen, political priorities have changed. Rather than ‚greening' EU policies across the board in order to ‚become the first climate-neutral continent by 2050', as Commission President von der Leyen put it in December 2019, competitiveness, resilience and less bureaucracy now seem to have become the topics of the day, even used as arguments to reverse achievements of the Green Deal. However, mitigating climate change as much as still possible, and adapting to the unavoidable, have lost none of their importance. To the contrary, they are even more important, as confirmed by various constitutional courts; in particular, failure to act now risks imposing a disproportionate and unlawful burden upon the young generation. In addition, greater resilience against the uncertainties of our time is not only economic, in terms of access to cheap energy and other resources, but depends a lot on suitable environmental conditions, the availability of workforce, and good and stable international relations. Challenges to our resilience will be the greater the more climate change takes effect.

The stocktake offered by this Volume after the end of the Green Deal strategy period is thus very timely in order to establish where we stand in the light of the Green Deal legislative program, and whether we can really afford to shift the focus to other priorities. The contributions are mostly based on papers given at the conference ‚Green Deal II – on track for 2030 and 2050?' held in Bremen in 2024, which have been developed into full academic articles, and added to by further relevant contributions.

Chapter 1 addresses the deficits and dynamics of the Green Deal. The first contribution, by Shazia Wülbers, begins with exactly the crucial and sensitive points, in querying the extent and the effectiveness of measures taken under the Green Deal. She shows that in various respects the EU might and must be doing more, and that a holistic approach would ensure much more effectiveness over the fragmented approach addressing individual policy areas. This should include improving citizen participation for democratic legitimacy, and involving the rest of the world in the further development of addressing climate change.

The second chapter deals with taxation as a means of promoting the aims of the Green Deal. The first contribution here, by Célia Maria Silva Carvalho and Vera de Hesselle, is a comparative piece on consumer tax law, exploring the differences and similarities between the Brazilian and German approaches to ecological transformation. It examines to what extent the Brazilian approach can provide valuable insights for Germany, particularly with regard to the changed perception of the financing and steering function of tax law and the need for an interdisciplinary approach to promote sustainable behaviour. The second contribution, by Marco Antonio Veríssimo Teixeira, explores the theory used to justify extra-fiscal taxation, as well as the details of the newly introduced excise tax in Brazil, which is a selective tax on specific goods harmful to health or the environment. This may serve as a proof of Brazil's commitment to promoting health and environmental protection, including mitigating climate change, to other regions of the world, namely the European Union, and offer a model for the EU, or its Member States, for using taxation as a means to influence behaviour.

Chapter 3, on players of the Green Deal, namely private enterprises and policy makers, offers two contributions. The first, by Ralf Schlemminger, explores sustainability management and reporting in the EU, and thus focusses on the framework for the private sector, for which sustainability management is increasingly developing into a "licence to operate". This contribution looks at the globally established standards for sustainability management, the increasing transparency of corporate sustainability practices and, in particular, the Corporate Sustainability Reporting Directive (CSRD) in the EU. It is argued that such reporting, as well as the structures of sustainability management and controlling the value-setting within companies, must be developed further.

The second contribution in this chapter, by Beate Zimpelmann, looks at the sub-state level's role in transposing the Green Deal, explicating the Bremen model based on the Bremen Parliamentary Commission of Enquiry into climate issues (Bremen Climate Enquete Commission) and the transposition of its conclusions into practice. She elaborates where, due to EU and federal competences and responsibility, Bremen does not have much room for manoeuvre, and where the local level could use its powers. As for Bremen, she sets out the relevant priorities according to the Climate Enquete Commission's findings, but remains sceptical as to whether Bremen is moving swiftly and effectively enough to meet its targets, namely climate neutrality by 2028.

The fourth chapter is devoted to resources, or more specifically to their protection under the Green Deal. This is exemplified by Rainer Lisowski's contribution to this Volume, on the political options and impediments to implementation of the Green Deal, looking at 'Biodiversity and the question of political power'. Considering biodiversity protection against the background of political theory he analyses which political forces work in which way at municipal level regarding biodiversity, showing that EU regulation may not always be effective at municipal level, and seeking stakeholder co-operation may be more efficient than mere law enforcement.

Chapter 5 continues the focus on implementation issues, looking in particular at smart specialisation, green growth and the workforce. The first contribution in this chapter, co-authored by Sergejs Stacenko and Tatjana Muravska, looks at the EU Cultural and Creative Industries ecosystem as a catalyst for sustainable development, driving green growth and innovation, in particular in Latvia. They regard the EU Industrial Strategy as a vital engine for innovation, economic competitiveness and societal advancement, generating employment opportunities and creating value. They elaborate that the Cultural and Creative Industries (CCIs) have a unique role in promoting green growth and sustainable competitiveness, thereby enhancing their contribution to economic development and addressing pressing environmental challenges. The article emphasises the importance of ensuring synergy between the CCIs ecosystem and competitiveness of the EU. The authors conclude that the EU policy framework for the CCIs ecosystem development should be integrated into Member States' national programmes with a focus on promoting green growth and sustainable practices.

The second contribution in this chapter, by Girts Jirgensons and Tatjana Muravska, adds another facet of Green Deal implementation, namely the effects of the Green Deal in healthcare. On this count, the Green Deal encourages medical practitioners to adopt sustainable practices that result in a healthier environment, leading to better overall public health. In particular, health risks related to pollution and climate change must be managed. At the same time, EU law provides for free movement of persons, including medical doctors and personnel. Considering both aspects, the article specifically considers EU labour mobility and the outflow of medical practitioners from Latvia in the context of sustainable healthcare.

The third contribution in this chapter, by Radu-Ioan Popa, continues the theme of mobility, by analysing the impact of climate change on the workforce and migration and particularly addressing the vulnerabilities of the ingroups and outgroups in a climate change context. Given that climate change is set to continue for years to come, and what can be done is mitigating and adapting to it rather than preventing it for the foreseeable future, the importance of this topic cannot be underestimated. Whilst historically greenhouse gas emissions have occurred non-negligently, without knowledge of the consequences on the climate, this is no longer the case for the last several decades. Will societies in countries which remain habitable be prepared to help, and, more particularly, be prepared to face responsibilities? The article considers the decisive parameters which will be relevant to policy-making in this area.

The final Chapter 6 considers hydrogen, an issue lying between Green Deal implementation and competitiveness, thus coming back to the question raised in the beginning, namely whether climate neutrality or competitiveness should be prioritized. This contribution, by Nils Schuckenberg, explores the market ramp-up of renewable hydrogen in the area of conflict between climate protection and competition, offering a competition law assessment of the promotion through auction procedures of the European Hydrogen Bank.

The hope of the contributors and editors of this volume is, as with the first volume, to thereby stimulate further discussion, with the aim of achieving the Green Deal targets in an economically and legally effective manner, uniting competitiveness and resilience with climate neutrality.

Vera de Hesselle　　Lydia Scholz　　Christiane Trüe

Inhaltsverzeichnis

Chapter 1
Deficits and Dynamics of the Green Deal

Dr. Shazia Aziz Wülbers[1]

What European Green Deal does not do

Abstract

The European Green Deal (EGD) is the European Commission's answer to the climate crisis that is faced by the entire Earth. Under the aegis of the EGD, the European Union aims to be climate neutral by 2050 and aims to reduce carbon emissions by 55 % in 2030. It should be noted that this 55 % decrease is measured from the carbon emissions levels in 1990. Although the EGD makes progress in greening the industry it does not go far enough to tackle the multifaceted aspects of the climate crisis which go far beyond green economics. This article attempts to critically analyse the EGD, present its limitations and propose tangible improvements that could lead to better and more holistic results to our response to the climate crisis.

Keywords – European Green Deal, climate change, climate crisis, green economy, European Union, European Commission

1. Introduction

Antonio Guterres, the Secretary General of the United Nations, famously said at the Climate Action Summit 2019 that when it comes to climate change, it is a race that we are losing but it is a race that can be won. The European Green Deal (EGD) is the European Commission's response to the looming climate crisis that this generation is struggling with and the future generations will probably continue to struggle with if changes are not made right now in the way we deal with the crisis.

The EGD is definitely a step in the right direction. "And indeed, it seems that with this Commission, the period of reduced environmental ambition ended. In contrast to the development of the 1990s, the EU's environmental agenda was advanced with a clear and prominent strategy with the EGD."[2] Ursula von der Leyen, the president of the European Commission, called

1 City University of Applied Sciences Bremen, Faculty 3.

2 Jan Pollex and Andrea Lenschow, "When talk meets actions – return to Commission leadership in EU environmental policy-making with the European Green Deal", in Journal of European Public Policy, Open Access, 2024, pp. 1–26, p. 21.

EGD the 'man on the moon' moment. To a certain extent, she was right because it was the most significant achievement of the EU in the field of environment policy and sustainability. Europe has finally put the money and its policies where its mouth is.[3]

Some of the positive changes that the EGD has brought about are **firstly;** it concretises the European climate change mitigation strategy through an array of laws and regulations. Some of these laws and regulations were regrouped in the EU's Fit for 55[4] strategy; they are legally binding. The European Climate Law stipulates that, by 2050, the European Union will be climate neutral, and every five years the member states have to submit national energy and climate plans, which will be then published as a part of Climate Action Progress Report.[5] The Land Use, Land Use Change, and Forestry (LULUCF) Regulation legally requires EU member states to balance GHG emissions from land use with carbon removals from forestry and agriculture.

Secondly, it takes a bold leap into clean energy transition where the renewable energy directive (RED) sets a target of 32% renewable energy share by 2030 for all the EU member States. It is not just about clean energy expansion but also about energy efficiency aiming for 32,5% improvement in buildings, industry and transport through the energy efficiency directive (EED) and energy innovation where the EU Green Deal Investment Plan[6] is designed to mobilize €1 trillion in sustainable investments by 2030 to finance the innovation required for energy transition. Decarbonizing the transport sector and promoting electric vehicles plays an important role in the EU's calculations. They even envisage carbon capture and storage.

Thirdly, the EGD attempts to invigorate sustainable and circular economy and tries to make it the rule and not the exception. The Circular Economy Action Plan,[7] which is unfortunately not an EU regulation or directive, aims to improve waste management of electronics, textiles, plastics and construction. Implementing legislation introduces legally binding targets for recycling and waste management of specific materials and setting standards for product design to facilitate reuse and recycling, for example the single use

3 Donald Blondin , et al., (2022) "The International dimension of the European Green Deal: How the EU can enable a fair transition for the whole planet", in Policy Brief, European Policy Institute, Open Society Foundations.

4 Fit for 55 https://www.consilium.europa.eu/en/policies/fit-for-55/.

5 Climate Action Progress Report 2023, https://climate.ec.europa.eu/eu-action/climate-strategies-targets/progress-climate-action_en.

6 European Green Deal Investment Plan https://ec.europa.eu/commission/presscorner/detail/en/qanda_20_24.

7 Circular Economy Action Plan, https://environment.ec.europa.eu/strategy/circular-economy-action-plan_en.

plastics directive.[8] Through this directive, plastic waste can be reduced and recycling can be increased, helping to close the loop in the circular economy.

These steps are taken to make Europe the first climate neutral continent of the world and are an enormous effort towards decarbonisation of the economy. This looks like a rather rosy picture of a continent that is doing its best to counter the climate crisis and is spending a lot of money in the form of investments in green economy.

However, are these steps enough? In spite of the European Green Deal and the Fit for 55 goals, only a 41 per cent reduction will be achieved by 2030.[9] What does the EGD ignore? What does the EGD not do but needs to be done for a sustainable future, not just for Europe but also for the world?

What the European Green Deal does not do

One of the most important deficiencies in the European Green Deal approach is the missing holistic dynamics to the environment. The EU is wearing blinkers and imagines that its transition to a green economy is happening in an isolated context. The framework continues to operate within the silo mentality, where the EU focuses primarily on its own internal issues without sufficiently addressing the **global context** of climate change, particularly the involvement of the Global South. Climate change cannot be tackled effectively without considering the international dimension, including the socio-economic challenges faced by countries outside of Europe. A case in point is its insistence on e mobility. In the future, it will increase Europe's footprint on resources like lithium, rare earths, aluminium and steel, which are often extracted and produced outside the EU, where the carbon footprint associated with their extraction and processing can be much higher. This oversight creates a contradiction in the Green Deal's environmental goals, as it focuses on the end-product but neglects the embedded carbon emissions associated with the materials and manufacturing processes needed to produce these vehicles.

The transition to decarbonisation and electrification also raises concerns about the potential for a new era of extractivism. While the EGD seeks to reduce emissions, it may inadvertently increase the demand for certain raw

8 Directive (EU) 2019/904 of the European Parliament and of the Council of 5 June 2019 on the reduction of the impact of certain plastic products on the environment, https://eur-lex.europa.eu/eli/dir/2019/904/oj.

9 European Environment Agency, Trends and Projections in Europe 2022 (Publications Office, 2022).

materials, thus driving further exploitation of resources in regions already vulnerable to environmental degradation. This shift could deepen extractive practices in countries outside Europe, raising ethical and environmental concerns about the global distribution of benefits and burdens.

On the global stage, the EU lacks the diplomatic tools needed to make the European Green Deal relevant in the future. The geopolitical instability, such as the Russian invasion of Ukraine, has created challenges in advancing European green policies and highlighted the need for a stronger, more cohesive international approach. Although the EU remains committed to being a global leader in green industries, its strategy for accelerating the global climate transition remains unclear.

The EGD's merger of industrial, green, and climate policies does show a commitment to integrating sustainability with industrial development. However, the EU still faces challenges in using its clean economy transformation to accelerate global climate action and strengthen resilient international partnerships.[10] As one key challenge, the EU faces a dilemma in designing a carbon pricing mechanism that promotes industrial decarbonization without undermining international competitiveness.[11]

Although mentioned in the EGD as one of the cornerstones of the European Union economy, **circular economy** is not the pivot on which the economic system stands. EGD is about greening its economic strategy.[12] "The main purpose in the EGD is the top-down management of the mitigation of climate consequences of free market economy".[13] The European Green Deal merged the European Industrial, green and climate policies.[14] Even though the EGD lays emphasis on a transition to cleaner industries, its focus on

---

10 Ignacio Velasco, et al., "European Green Deal diplomacy toolbox: Partnerships to shape the global clean economy transition" in 2023, pp 1– 11, p 2.

11 Stuart Evans, et al., (2021) "Border carbon adjustments and industrial competitiveness in a European Green Deal, in Climate Policy, , 21:3, 307–317, DOI: 10.1080/14693062.2020.1856637.

12 Zainab Usman, et al., "The European Green Deal: A Vision to Combat Climate Change: What Does the European Green Deal Mean for Africa? Published by Carnegie Endowment for International Peace, 2021.

13 Katarzyna Molek-Kozakowska (2024) The hybrid discourse of the 'European Green Deal': road-mapping economic transition to environmental sustainability (almost) seamlessly, Critical Discourse Studies, 21:2, 182–199, DOI: 10.1080/17405904.2023.2197607.

14 Andrea Prontera, (2024) "The European Union The Would-Be Green Leader: From energy markets to climate leadership and technological sovereignty", in Green Superpowers, Oxford University Press, DOI: 10.1093/9780191987304.003.0004, p. 104.

growth and industrial production contradicts the principles of circular economy, which advocates for sharing, recycling, and reusing resources.[15]

These crucial elements of resource management do not receive the attention they deserve in the EGD framework, leading to an imbalance in how Europe manages its resource consumption and waste production. Waste management aspects of the Green Deal remain largely unaddressed, even though waste prevention is an essential component of climate change mitigation. The EGD's approach to waste management often leads to the outsourcing of waste-intensive activities to countries with less stringent environmental regulations, undermining global sustainability efforts and further perpetuating inequality.

Another area where the EGD is lacking is in the area of **democratic participation.** The EU's approach often prioritizes market-driven solutions over democratic participation, with citizens being treated more as consumers than active participants in the decision-making processes. "This approach falls short of the deliberative democratic governance needed for transformational change"; it is because EGD portrays climate change as a scientific or a political and economic phenomenon and removes the need for democratic participation in the policy-making.[16]

The Green Deal also lags behind in gender inclusivity in its climate policy. While **gender considerations** have gained prominence in climate change literature, the European Green Deal remains largely gender-neutral.[17] Climate change disproportionately affects marginalized communities, especially women, yet the EGD does not sufficiently address this disparity. The Green Deal's focus on enterprise-driven solutions overlooks the need for a more inclusive, equitable transformation that accounts for the needs and vulnerabilities of all sectors of society. "A just transition requires protecting and assisting communities most affected by the transition".[18]

In addition to that, the EGD falls short of **cohesion and integration** with other major EU policies such as European Agricultural Policy, European Trade Policy, and Intellectual Property Rights (IPR), among others. The Green

---

15 Kalina Arabadjieva, Sanja Bogojevi, (2024) "The European Green Deal: climate action, social impacts and just transition safeguards", in Yearbook of European Law.

16 Feyyaz Barış Çelik (21 Jan 2025): Unpacking democratic participation in the European Green Deal: the case of Climate Pact, Journal of European Integration, DOI:10.1080/07036337.2025.2455688.

17 Joanne Flavel (2024) "From Gender-Blind to Gender Bind: Foregrounding Gender in the History of the UNFCCC." Global Environmental Politics 24 (1): 31–51. https://doi.org/10.1162/glep_a_00717.

18 Francesca Colli, "A transition for the citizens? Ensuring public participation in the European Green Deal", in European Policy Brief, n. 68, Egmont Institute, 2021.

Deal, as a standalone framework, lacks the necessary synergies and vision with these key policy areas, which limits its ability to deliver on its broad ambitions and dilutes its potential impact across the world in general and in the EU in particular. For example, the lack of a clear connection between the EGD and CAP undermines efforts to promote sustainable farming practices. While the Farm to Fork Strategy under the Green Deal emphasizes the need to make food systems more sustainable, it does not provide enough coherent policy guidance to shift CAP away from practices that are resource-intensive and unsustainable.[19] In relation to trade policy, EU's trade agreements prioritize economic growth and market access over environmental protection and sustainability. As a result, green tariffs, carbon border adjustment mechanisms,[20] and other measures aimed at promoting sustainable trade are only now beginning to be explored and are not yet deeply integrated into EU's broader trade frameworks.[21] The lack of a cohesive strategy that links trade policy with the EGD means that the EU may not be using its trade negotiations to push for greener global standards and greener supply chains—two factors that can act as a catalyser for global transition toward sustainability.

Finally, while the EGD provides a foundation for a more sustainable future, its implementation reveals several critical gaps that need to be addressed. To ensure the EGD's success, Europe needs a more cohesive strategy for global climate leadership, stronger diplomatic engagement, a more inclusive and participatory governance model, democratic participation of its people and a greater focus on de-growth, circular economy principles, and social equity.

What can be done

To improve the EGD and ensure that it comes closer to achieving its ambitious environmental and sustainability goals, several key actions could be taken: **Firstly,** an increase in the carbon price could be a crucial step in driving the decarbonization of industries across Europe.[22] A higher carbon price

19 Andrea Zappalaglio, (2023)"The law of geographical indicator at the centre of European Green Deal", in Journal of Intellectual Property Law & Practice, Vol. 18, No. 8, pp. 557–558.

20 Carbon border adjustment mechanism, https://taxation-customs.ec.europa.eu/carbon-border-adjustment-mechanism_en.

21 Jennifer Tollmann, and Lea Pilsner, "Paris-Aligned EU External Action: European Green Deal Diplomacy for accelerating global action to achieve the Paris Agreement goals", in E3G, 2021.

22 Moritz Scherleitner, and Edoardo Traversa, "Will It Be FINE-for-EU? A Proposal for a Mechanism Funding Pan-European Green Investment to Promote the EU (Still) Meet-

would provide stronger incentives for businesses to reduce their emissions and invest in cleaner technologies, helping to accelerate the transition to a greener economy.

Secondly, the EGD could evolve into a platform for broader environmental discussions, rather than simply dictating EU priorities to the rest of the world. It can go beyond a top-down approach and become a forum where international collaboration and dialogue on environmental policies take place. The EU could engage more actively with other countries, take into account diverse viewpoints and present best-practices that support global sustainability goals. This would signal the EU's commitment not only to its own climate goals but also to fostering global cooperation on environmental issues. Europe could leverage its environmental leadership and diplomatic channels to set global environmental standards and strengthen international partnerships.

Thirdly, the EGD and the Corporate Sustainability Due Diligence Directive (CSDDD) should not be treated as separate policies. These frameworks are both critical for ensuring sustainability and addressing corporate accountability, and their integration would lead to a more cohesive and comprehensive approach. The Green Deal could provide the overarching framework for sustainable industry, while the CSDDD could ensure that businesses operating within the EU meet strict environmental and social responsibility standards.

Fourthly, the challenges posed by the Trump presidency could also be reframed as an opportunity for Europe to fuel its diplomacy and assert its global leadership. The EU could position itself as the leading proponent of global climate action, using this period of crisis to build stronger alliances and promote the EU's green agenda.

Conclusions

There is no doubt that EGD represents a commendable step towards addressing the climate crisis. But it remains just that – a step in the right direction. If and when the lack of a holistic approach to global environmental dynamics, insufficient integration with other key EU policies, and absence of critical elements such as democratic participation and gender inclusivity are addressed and steps towards solving these issues are taken, it can go towards fulfilling its potential. The focus on industrial growth, carbon pricing, and

ing Its Climate Goals", in Cambridge Yearbook of European Legal Studies, 2025, pp, 1–23, p. 2.

clean energy transition is no doubt important but needs to be balanced with an emphasis on circular economy principles, resource management, and the social and environmental impacts of resource extraction globally.

To enhance the EGD's effectiveness, it is important for Europe to adopt a globally-oriented approach. This includes strengthening green diplomacy, ensuring that the EGD aligns with other critical EU policies such as agriculture, trade, and intellectual property, and integrating frameworks like the Corporate Sustainability Due Diligence Directive under its aegis. By building bridges with the Global South, ensuring equitable transitions for marginalized communities, and fostering democratic participation, the EU can reshape the Green Deal into a truly transformative force that not only addresses its internal climate goals but also sets the stage for global climate action.

References

Arabadjieva, K., Bogojevi, S., "The European Green Deal: climate action, social impacts and just transition safeguards", in Yearbook of European Law, 2024, pp. 1–22.

Blondin D., et al., "The International dimension of the European Green Deal: How the EU can enable a fair transition for the whole planet", in Policy Brief, European Policy Institute, Open Society Foundations, 2022.

Çelik, F. B., (2025) "Unpacking democratic participation in: The European Green Deal: the case of Climate Pact", in Journal of European Integration, pp. 1–20.

Circular Economy Action Plan, https://environment.ec.europa.eu/strategy/circular-economy-action-plan_en

Climate Action Progress Report 2023, https://climate.ec.europa.eu/eu-action/climate-strategies-targets/progress-climate-action_en

Colli, F., "A transition for the citizens? Ensuring public participation in the European Green Deal", in European Policy Brief, n. 68, Egmont Institute, 2021.

Directive (EU) 2019/904 of the European Parliament and of the Council of 5 June 2019 on the reduction of the impact of certain plastic products on the environment, https://eur-lex.europa.eu/eli/dir/2019/904/oj

European Environment Agency, Trends and Projections in Europe 2022 (Publications Office, 2022).

European Green Deal Investment Plan https://ec.europa.eu/commission/presscorner/detail/en/qanda_20_24

Evans, S., et al., "Border carbon adjustments and industrial competitiveness in a European Green Deal, in Climate Policy, 2021, 21:3, 307–317, DOI: 10.1080/14693062.2020.1856637

Fit for 55 https://www.consilium.europa.eu/en/policies/fit-for-55/

Flavell, J. 2024. "From Gender-Blind to Gender Bind: Foregrounding Gender in the History of the UNFCCC." Global Environmental Politics 24 (1): 31–51. https://doi.org/10.1162/glep_a_00717.

Gray E. K. and McArdle, R. "Communities and the European Green Deal: opening 'sites of struggle' for a democratic energy transition, in Journal of European Integration, 2025. DOI: 10.1080/07036337.2025.2455683

Molek-Kozakowska, K., "The hybrid discourse of the 'European Green Deal': road-mapping economic transition to environmental sustainability (almost) seamlessly, Critical Discourse Studies, , 21:2, 182–199, DOI: 10.1080/17405904.2023.2197607,.

Pollex, J. and Lenschow, A, (2024) "When talk meets actions – return to Commission leadership in EU environmental policy-making with the European Green Deal", in Journal of European Public Policy, Open Access, pp, 1–26.

Prontera, A:, "The European Union The Would-Be Green Leader: From energy markets to climate leadership and technological sovereignty", in Green Superpowers, Oxford University Press, 2024 DOI: 10.1093/9780191987304.003.0004.

Scherleitner, M. and Traversa, E., (2025) "Will It Be FINE-for-EU? A Proposal for a Mechanism Funding Pan-European Green Investment to Promote the EU (Still) Meeting Its Climate Goals", in Cambridge Yearbook of European Legal Studies, 1–23.

Tollmann, J. and Pilsner, L., (2021) "Paris-Aligned EU External Action: European Green Deal Diplomacy for accelerating global action to achieve the Paris Agreement goals", in E3G.

Usman, Z., et al., (2021) "The European Green Deal: A Vision to Combat Climate Change: What Does the European Green Deal Mean for Africa? Published by Carnegie Endowment for International Peace.

Velasco, I., et al., (2023) "European Green Deal diplomacy toolbox: Partnerships to shape the global clean economy transition" in, pp 1– 11.

Zappalaglio, A., "The law of geographical indicator at the centre of European Green Deal", in Journal of Intellectual Property Law & Practice, 2023, Vol. 18, No. 8, pp. 557–558.

Chapter 2
Taxation

Prof. Dr. Célia Maria Silva Carvalho,[1]
Prof. Dr. Vera de Hesselle, Germany[2]

The New Excise Tax in Brazil – an Example for Germany?

Abbreviations

BRASIL:

ABC:	Low Carbon Agriculture Plan
ANNEL:	National Electric Energy Agency
BNDES:	National Bank for Economic and Social Development
CBS:	Contribution on Goods and Services: Goods and Services Tax (GST) and Harmonized Sales Tax (HST)
CG-IBS:	National Committee for the Tax on Goods and Services
CIDE:	Contribution on Intervention in the Economic Domain
CNBA:	National Basic Food Basket
COFINS:	Contribution to Social Security Financing
DETER:	Real-Time Deforestation Detection System
EC:	Constitutional Amendment
GST:	Goods and Services Tax and Harmonized Sales Tax (HST)
HST:	Harmonized Sales Tax
IBAMA:	Brazilian Institute of the Environment and Renewable Natural Resources
IBS:	Goods and Services Tax
ICMBio:	Chico Mendes Institute for Biodiversity Conservation

1 Professor of the Professional Doctorate Program in Economics at the Federal University of Ceará, Brazil, President of the State Finance Managers Group, President of the Ibero-American Forum on Budgetary and Fiscal Intergovernmental Coordination.

2 Professor of Tax Law and Business Law at City University of Applied Sciences Bremen (HSB), Vice Dean of the Faculty of Business Administration, Vice Academic Director of Research, International Graduate Center (IGC).

ICMS:	Tax on the Circulation of Goods and Services
INPE:	National Institute for Spatial Research
INSS:	National Social Security Institute
IOF:	Tax on financial transactions
IPI :	Tax on industrialized products
IPTU:	Urban Property Tax
IPVA:	Motor Vehicle Ownership Tax
IR:	Income Tax
IS:	Excise Tax
ISS:	Tax on Services
ITBI:	Real Estate Transfer Tax
ITCMD:	Tax on Causa Mortis Transmissions and Donations of Any Goods or Rights
IVA:	Value Added Tax
LC:	Complementary Law
PASEP:	Public Servant Asset Formation Program
PIS:	Social Integration Program
PLP:	Complementary Bill
PNMC:	National Policy on Climate Change
PRODES:	Project to Monitor Deforestation in the Legal Amazon by Satellite
SECINT:	Special Secretariat for Foreign Trade and International Affairs
SNUC:	Conservation Units
STN:	National Tax System
UNFCCC:	United Nations Framework Convention on Climate Change
ZFM:	Manaus Free Trade Zone

GERMANY:

BEHG:	Fuel Emissions Trading Act
BGBl:	Federal Law Register
BVerfGE:	Federal Constitutional Court
CDU:	Christian Democratic Union of Germany

CO2:	Carbon dioxide
CSU:	Christian Social Union in Bavaria
DSTR:	Deutsches Steuerrecht, Journal
EnergieStG:	Energy Tax Act
ff:	following
GG:	Basic Law, German Constitution
p:	page
Rn:	Margin number
SPD:	Social Democratic Party of Germany
STROMSTG:	Electricity Tax Act
UStG:	Value Added Tax Act
VAT:	Value added tax
WWF:	World Wide Fund For Nature

Abstract

As a country with enormous biological diversity and important resources such as the Amazon rainforest, Brazil plays a key role in the ecological transition. This article examines the new consumption tax reform in Brazil and its potential impact on sustainability and social justice.

Particular attention is paid to the newly introduced excise tax (IS) and its function as an instrument for steering environmentally harmful behavior. In addition, existing environmental taxes such as the ecological ICMS, Green IPTU, Green ISS, etc. are analyzed, as well as reform proposals to include environmental variables in the national tax system (STN).

The differences and similarities between the Brazilian and German approaches to ecological transformation are also considered in the context of German tax legislation. The extent to which the German tax system can learn from the Brazilian experience is examined. To what extent the Brazilian approach can provide valuable insights for Germany, particularly with regard to the changed perception of the financing and steering function of tax laws and the need for an interdisciplinary approach to promote sustainable behavior, will be discussed. The role of incentive taxes and the importance of integrating environmental values into the legal system to promote a profound social transformation towards more sustainability, will also be emphasized.

1. Introduction

The simplification of the environment to an object or resource destined exclusively for economic purposes, without considering its complexity, intrinsic value or essential role in maintaining the balance on this planet, has sparked a real environmental crisis. This instrumental view sees nature only as a means to meet the demands of production and consumption, ignoring its ecological and cultural importance. This negligence of society to recognize the limits of the environment has been observed.

Environmental degradation includes problems such as deforestation, pollution, loss of biodiversity and climate change, which are the direct result of unsustainable production and consumption practices. The unbridled exploitation of natural resources exceeds the limits of nature's regenerative capacity, creating severe imbalances. Nature has a limited capacity to regenerate and withstand impacts, and its vulnerability increases as those limits are exceeded, resulting in damages that can often be irreversible.

An economic model which encourages excessive consumption and continuous production, often disconnected from society's real needs, must be curbed. This system, fueled by economic growth at any cost, contributes to the intensive exploitation of natural resources, often without planning or concern for sustainability. The impact of this predatory view of the environment not only affects nature, but also the quality of life of human beings.

Problems such as climate change, scarcity of resources and ecological disasters have led society and the State to reflect on their practices. The "environmental issue" has become a central theme in global discussions, leading to questions about the behavior adopted and the need for a new attitude towards the environment. It is a reflection on the need for society and the State to change their behavior in order to build a more balanced and sustainable relationship with nature, respecting its limits and vulnerabilities.

From this perspective, the law, in an interdisciplinary approach, must use economic instruments to guide practices that will impact the environment, promoting sustainable activities and discouraging those that are detrimental to the environmental balance.

It is essential to connect environmental protection, legal values and social transformation as pillars for achieving both sustainability and the realization of fundamental rights. Achieving a balanced environment, recognized as a fundamental right, and promoting sustainable development will only be possible if there is effective integration of the legal system. This means that all areas of law need to incorporate environmental values into their basis, as a way of stimulating profound social change.

These changes include re-educating society about more sustainable practices and transforming behavior so that human actions are linked to the preservation of the environment. This joint effort is essential to ensure sustainability, which presents itself as an indispensable condition to guarantee a healthy quality of life and preserve human dignity.

Tax law plays a fundamental role in environmental protection and promoting sustainability, by using taxes with an extra-fiscal function to encourage environmentally conscious practices that are compatible with economic development. In Brazil, environmental taxation is applied both through existing taxes with environmental components, as for example, the Ecological ICMS, Green ISS, Green IPTU, etc. as well as through reform proposals which incorporate environmental variables into the National Tax System (STN).

Constitutional Amendment 132, enacted on December 20, 2023, has as its main objective the reform of consumption taxation in Brazil. This reform seeks to replace current taxes with new ones, to establish the distribution of the new revenues among the federal entities and to define the transition to the new tax system.

Among the changes introduced, the following stand out:

- The creation of the Tax on Goods and Services (IBS): this unifies state and municipal taxes, like ICMS and ISS, with the aim of simplifying tax collection and harmonizing taxation on the consumption of goods and services throughout the country.
- The implementation of the Contribution on Goods and Services (CBS): replaces federal taxes such as PIS, COFINS and IPI, with the aim of simplifying the tax system and increasing its efficiency.
- The introduction of the Excise Tax (IS), which will be discussed in the next section, is levied on products and processes that are harmful to the environment or public health, such as cigarettes and alcoholic beverages, promoting environmental sustainability and encouraging healthier practices.
- The establishment of cashback mechanisms, which return part of the taxes collected to low-income families, with the aim of reducing social inequalities and correcting the regressive nature of the Brazilian tax model.

The reform also anticipates the simplification and digitalization of the tax system, allowing companies to direct their efforts towards innovation and wealth generation, rather than dealing with complex tax regulations.

In summary, Constitutional Amendment 132/2023 seeks to modernize the Brazilian tax system, making it fairer, more efficient and in line with the goals of environmental sustainability and reducing social inequalities.

The Brazilian approach can also provide valuable insights for Germany, with its altered perception of the financing and the steering functions of tax laws. The interdisciplinary approach of using economic incentives in the fiscal sector deserves to be reconsidered in order to steer environmentally relevant behavior. The Brazilian approach promotes sustainable activities and discourages those that harm the ecological balance. Considerations such as those in Brazil could inspire the German discussion of a German or European ecological financial reform to protect the natural foundations of life.

2. The concept of taxes in the light of the current ecological transformation in Brazil and Germany

2.1 Short introduction to taxes, fees and improvement contribution

The theory of taxes, fees and contributions is based on the tax system, which seeks to finance the State and guarantee the provision of essential public services. Each of these categories has distinct characteristics and purposes, and understanding their differences is essential for a more informed debate on taxation and its role in society.

It is a branch of Tax Law and Public Finance that seeks to explain and regulate the different tax types and their objectives. In Brazil, the 1988 Federal Constitution establishes a threefold classification of taxes: taxes, fees and contributions. Each one has different characteristics and purposes.

Taxes are levied by the state without the need for a direct benefit to the taxpayer. In other words, the amount collected is not linked to a specific service, but rather to the financing of general public activities. Examples in Brazil include the Income Tax (IR), the Tax on the Circulation of Goods and Services (ICMS) and the Urban Property Tax (IPTU) and now, after the tax reform, the IBS, the CBS and the Excise Tax. Their function can be both revenue-raising and regulatory, as in the case of taxes on products that affect public health or the environment, with the aim of discouraging harmful behavior. The revenue is used to finance general government activities such as health, education and security. The tax base is normally based on economic facts such as income, assets and consumption.

Also in Germany, levies are divided into three categories: taxes, fees and contributions. Levies are unilaterally imposed, public-law payment obligations that accrue to an authority with sovereign power (e.g. federal, state, municipal) and at least also serve to generate income for the community. This means that citizens are obliged to pay levies if they fall under the scope of the individual laws, e.g. the individual tax laws or the fee or contribution regulations.[3]

Fees, unlike taxes, are binding. They are charged in return for a specific public service or the exercise of administrative police power. For example, a garbage collection fee, an environmental inspection fee or a fee for issuing a passport. They reflect a more direct relation between the taxpayer and the service provided by the state. The calculation basis is related to the cost of the service or state activity.

Contributions, such as social or improvement contributions, have a more limited purpose, usually linked to specific actions of collective interest or to the development of certain economic sectors. For example, social security contributions (such as the National Social Security Institute – INSS) are intended to finance social security, social assistance and health. Improvement contributions, on the other hand, are related to public works that increase the value of private property. The calculation basis varies according to character and purpose.

Incentive taxes, on the other hand, are fiscal tools designed to stimulate behavior or investments that the state considers beneficial for society. They go beyond simple collection: they play a strategic role in inducing desirable behavior on the part of companies and citizens. They can play a crucial role in accelerating the transition to a more sustainable and resilient economy.

These taxes can be used to: a) promote economic development in less favored regions; b) stimulate technological innovation and; c) encourage sustainable and ecological practices. Examples in Brazil include IPI reductions or exemptions for the purchase of electric or hybrid vehicles; ICMS credits for companies that adopt circular economy practices; tax benefits for companies that invest in reforestation or environmental preservation projects, etc. It is important to assess how Brazil has positioned itself in relation to climate change, which will be dealt with in the following topic.

In contrast to the Brazilian constitution, in Germany, not all competencies arise directly from the Basic Law. Rather, only the tax legislative competencies are described; the other types of levies are not mentioned directly.[4]

The German constitution does not contain an exhaustive list of permissible types of tax, but it does set out a framework of fiscal principles, fundamental rights and budgetary law within which the legislature may levy taxes

---

3 Kirchhof in: Isensee/Kirchhof, Handbuch des Staatsrechts, § 119 Nichtsteuerliche Abgaben, Rz. 17.

4 Cf. Müller-Franken in: Höfling/Augsberg/Rixen, Berliner Kommentar zum Grundgesetz, 2024, Art. 105 GG Rn. 84.

or create new ones.[5] According to Article 104a of the German Basic Law, the federal government and the states governments shall bear the expenditure resulting from the tasks respectively assigned to them.

However, Germany does not have what are known as "improvement contributions". The entire tax code is part of the German general tax code, which also includes the law on fees and contributions.

2.2 Ecological transformation in Brazil – an overview

The ecological transformation in Brazil reflects the country's efforts to balance economic development with environmental preservation and tackle climate change. Brazil has a strategic position in this debate, as it is home to most of the Amazon rainforest, vast water resources and one of the greatest biodiversity on the planet. However, it also faces significant challenges, such as deforestation, environmental degradation and pressure from agribusiness and mining.

The ecological transformation seeks to change economic, social and cultural practices, promoting a transition to a sustainable development model that is resilient to climate change. This transformation is based on principles like reducing greenhouse gas emissions, preserving natural resources and strengthening vulnerable communities.

Given the growing awareness of the climate crisis, tax incentives play a key role in the ecological transition, promoting a low-carbon and sustainable economy. In Brazil, the ecological transformation can be driven by the following initiatives:

Green Taxation (**Green Taxes**) refers to charges on activities or products that cause damage to the environment, such as the use of fossil fuels, carbon emissions or industrial pollution. The idea is to discourage harmful practices and encourage more sustainable alternatives by imposing higher taxes or rates on polluting activities, such as greenhouse gas emissions, and applying tax benefits to companies that adopt sustainable practices. Examples in Brazil include the Ecological ICMS, Green IPTU, Green ISS and Green IPVA.

Carbon taxes aim to introduce a levy on carbon emissions, with the proceeds going towards investments in green infrastructure and clean technologies. In Brazil, there is still no carbon tax implemented in a specific and comprehensive way, but there are tax instruments and initiatives that are moving in the direction of pricing carbon emissions or encouraging the reduction of

5 Kirchhof in: Isensee/Kirchhof, Handbuch des Staatsrechts, § 119 Nichtsteuerliche Abgaben, Rz. 18.

emissions. Here are some examples and related discussions: CIDE-Combustíveis (CIDE-Fuels), which is levied on the commercialization of fossil fuels such as gasoline, diesel and aviation kerosene. Although its collection is not directly linked to emissions mitigation, it is a tool that can be adjusted to encourage a reduction in fossil fuel consumption.

The Green ICMS on fuels, which in some states has a differentiated rate of ICMS in order to encourage the use of biofuels, like ethanol, which emit less carbon. Carbon Credits in the Tax Sector are instruments which companies participating in voluntary or compulsory carbon markets can use to offset taxes or as part of strategies to reduce tax costs. There are also discussions about carbon emission taxes through bills currently before the National Congress, such as PL 528/2021, which proposes a carbon tax system associated with a regulated carbon market.

Tax Incentives for Renewable Energies (exemptions or tax benefits) aim to provide tax reductions or exemptions for companies that invest in clean technologies, circular economy, renewable energy or environmental conservation projects. For example, tax incentives for buying electric vehicles or installing solar panels. Or the reduction of taxes on solar, wind and biomass energy equipment and tax benefits for energy transition projects in rural communities. In Brazil, there are various tax incentives aimed at promoting the development and use of renewable energies. They include exemptions, rate reductions and special regimes applicable to equipment, projects and clean energy sources such as solar, wind and biomass.

Examples in Brazil include: a) ICMS Agreement 101/1997, which reduces or exempts ICMS on the purchase of equipment and components used to generate wind, solar, biomass and hydroelectric power. Some Brazilian states, such as São Paulo, Minas Gerais and Rio de Janeiro, exempt or reduce ICMS on solar panels, inverters and batteries. There is also Distributed Generation (which is covered by ICMS Agreement 16/2015, exempting ICMS on electricity generated by solar systems installed on buildings, provided that the energy generated is offset against consumption by the electricity grid, as regulated by ANEEL Normative Resolution 482/2012.

Regarding the IPI, there is a reduction or exemption for equipment used to generate renewable energy, such as: photovoltaic modules; wind generators or solar thermal system components. The benefit is provided for in decrees issued by the federal government which place these products under reduced or exempted tax rates. Products used to generate renewable energy, like photovoltaic modules and inverters, can have a zero rate for PIS/Pasep and Cofins, with the aim of making it cheaper to import and sell these products on the domestic market. Equipment for generating renewable energy, as solar panels and wind turbines, can be imported with exemption or reduction in the import tax rate, depending on the classification and type of project. SECINT Ordinance No. 220/2019 offers a reduced rate for products destined for clean energy projects.

BNDES offers financing for renewable energy projects at subsidized rates, such as the Finem Energia Renovável (Renewable Energy) program, allowing easier conditions for purchasing equipment with tax exemptions. Some private banks offer credit lines for residential solar energy systems, and these projects can benefit from tax benefits already applied to the sector. And companies located in the Manaus Free Trade Zone (ZFM) that manufacture components for renewable energy systems (solar and wind) enjoy benefits such as IPI exemption, ICMS reduction and PIS/Cofins exemption, among others.

Promoting the Bioeconomy through tax incentives for sustainable economic activities in the Amazon and other biomes, such as sustainable forest management and the production of bioactive compounds. **Tax credits can be granted for environmental preservation,** which are instruments to reward rural or urban landowners for practices such as reforestation, preservation of areas of native vegetation or recovery of degraded ecosystems.

The role of Social and Environmental Justice is structuring fiscal policy to reduce inequalities and promote social inclusion, ensuring that the ecological transition benefits vulnerable communities and respects the rights of populations, especially indigenous peoples.

2.3 Ecological transformation in Germany – an overview

The ecological financial reform in Germany emerged from the ecological movement in the 1970s. Due to the social and ecological deficits, the Green Party was founded in 1980, and by 1983 it had 29 representatives in the Bundestag.[6]

In 1998, the Green Party, along with the Social Democratic Party of Germany (SPD), was part of the government after winning the election, and the first steps towards an ecological financial reform emerged. The introduction of an electricity tax as an excise duty of DM 20.00 per megawatt hour in 1999 was intended to mark the beginning of an ecological tax reform. The revenue

6 BÜNDNIS 90/DIE GRÜNEN, The founding of the Greens, self-portrayal, https://www.gruene.de/unsere-gruene-geschichte [access: 10.02.2025]. After German reunification, it merged with the civil rights movement in the GDR and was renamed BÜNDNIS 90/DIE GRÜNEN.

from the eco-tax is used primarily to reduce pension insurance contributions or to limit their increase.[7]

The electricity tax has been increased in several ways to date and has remained unchanged at 20.50 euros per megawatt hour since 2003.[8] Furthermore, a decision was taken in 1999 to gradually increase the already existing mineral oil tax (also as an excise duty) on motor fuels, gas and heating oil.[9]

In addition to the mineral oil tax, a CO2 tax has been levied since 2021 as the basis for pricing CO2 emissions from fossil fuels, including natural gas, heating oil and petrol. It amounted to €45.00 per ton in 2024 (Section 10 (2) (Fuel Emissions Trading Act – BEHG) and will increase to €55.00 per ton from 2025. Companies that market fossil fuels (e.g. energy supply, mineral oil supply, production or disposal companies) or that have a permit under the Energy Tax Act[10] are defined as tax debtors under Section 3 no. 3 BEHG. The tax rate is based on the CO2 emissions, which are based on estimates according to scientifically recognized methods.[11]

In the coalition agreements of the subsequent governments, reference is repeatedly made to ecological financial reform and the sustainable development of the society. The coalition agreement between the SPD and the Greens in 2002, for example, refers to ecological financial reform, but remains vague in its stipulations. It is to be examined, for example, whether and how taxation can be further developed from an ecological point of view. Incentive programs are to be created, sales tax is to be levied on flights within Europe, and

7 Knigge/Görlach, Die Ökologische Steuerreform – Auswirkungen auf Umwelt, Beschäftigung und Innovation, Forschungsprojekt im Auftrag des Umweltbundesamtes, Oktober 2005, Kap. 3.2.

8 § 3 StromStG 1999, the electricity tax was then gradually increased, from DM 25.00 on January 1, 2000, to DM 30.00 on January 1, 2001, to €17.90 on January 1, 2002, and has remained unchanged at €20.50 since March 1, 2003; cf. Art. 1 of the Act on the Introduction of an Ecological Tax Reform of March 24, 1999, BGBl I, 1999 (No. 14), 378 et seq.; section 3 as amended by Art. 2 No. 2 of the Act on the Continuation of the Ecological Tax Reform of December 16, 1999, BGBl. I 1999, 2432 (2438); § 3 as amended by Art. 2 no. 2 of the Law for the Further Development of the Ecological Tax Reform of December 23, 2002, BGBl. I 2002, 4602 (4604).

9 Art. 2 des Gesetzes zum Einstieg in die ökologische Steuerreform vom 24. März 1999, BGBl I, 1999 (Nr. 14), p. 378 (p. 380).

10 Energiesteuergesetz (EnergieStG) vom 15. Juli 2006, BGBl. I 2006, 1534; 2008 I, 660, 1007, zuletzt geändert durch Artikel 3 des Gesetzes vom 27. März 2024, BGBl. 2024 I Nr. 107.

11 Cf. Juhrich in Umweltbundesamt (Hrsg.), CO2 Emissionsfaktoren für fossile Brennstoffe, Climate Change 27/2016, p.10.

the federal government wanted to advocate kerosene taxation at European level.[12]

In 2005, the government changed and the coalition agreement between the Christian Democratic Union of Germany (CDU), the Christian Social Union in Bavaria (CSU) and the Social Democratic Party of Germany (SPD) and as of November 11, 2005, no longer includes the continuation of the ecological financial reform. However, the ecologically and economically "sensible" expansion of renewable energies was agreed upon. To protect the domestic energy-intensive industry, eco-taxes should not be increased any further.[13] At the same time, further measures were taken, such as the introduction of tax exemptions for combined heat and power plants and reduced tax rates for natural gas vehicles.

All in all, it can be said that in the years in which social democratic and green parties were in government, ecological financial reform was always given more weight than in the years in which Christian democratic and liberal parties were in government.[14]

In their 2019 study on the environmental impact of the eco-tax, Kemfert et al. assume that the current eco-tax has a limited effect. Emissions trading is considered to be more effective.[15]

2.4 Challenges and prospects for Brazil

Despite the potential, the adoption of taxes to encourage ecological transformation faces challenges, for example, political and economic resistance, the

---

12 SPD and Bündnis 90/Die Grünen, Coalition Agreement from SPD and Bündnis 90/Die Grünen from 16.10.2002, Erneuerung – Gerechtigkeit – Nachhaltigkeit. Für ein wirtschaftlich starkes, soziales und ökologisches Deutschland. Für eine lebendige Demokratie p. 21.

13 CDU, CSU and SPD, Gemeinsam für Deutschland – mit Mut und Menschlichkeit, Coalition agreement between the CDU, CSU and SPD of 11.11.2005, p. 41 ff.

14 For example Coalition agreement between the CDU, CSU and FDP of 26.10.2009, "Wachstum. Bildung. Zusammenhalt", https://archiv.cdu.de/sites/default/files/media/dokumente/091215-koalitionsvertrag-2009–2013-englisch_0.pdf [Abruf 13.01.2025]; Coalition agreement between the CDU, CSU and SPD of 16.12.2013, Deutschlands Zukunft gestalten, https://archiv.cdu.de/sites/default/files/media/dokumente/koalitionsvertrag.pdf [access: 13.01.2025]; Coalition agreement between the SPD, the Greens and the FDP of 24.11.2021, Mehr Fortschritt wagen, Bündnis für Freiheit, Gerechtigkeit und Nachhaltigkeit, https://www.bundestagswahl-bw.de/koalitionsvertrag-2021 [access: 10.01.2025].

15 Kemfert/Schill/Wägner/Zaklan, Umweltwirkungen der Ökosteuer begrenzt, CO2-Bepreisung der nächste Schritt, DIW Wochenbericht 2019, p. 216 (p. 218).

need for a wide-ranging tax reform that considers fiscal and environmental justice, besides weaknesses in the supervision and execution of environmental policies.

In Brazil, the establishment and expansion of incentive taxes in the context of the ecological transformation is fundamental, especially in light of international commitments, such as the Paris Agreement, and domestic challenges, like deforestation in the Amazon and the climate crisis. However, as mentioned above, this approach faces practical and political challenges, including institutional challenges, fiscal justice, education and awareness-raising, and multisectoral coordination.

The institutional challenges stem from the need to reformulate the Brazilian tax system to better integrate environmental objectives, reducing bureaucracy and promoting greater efficiency. Along these lines, Brazil's tax reform approved in 2024 created the Excise Tax (IS), also known as the "Sin Tax", which is included in the calculation base for consumption taxes. The tax seeks to reduce the consumption of products that have a negative impact on health, like cigarettes and alcoholic beverages, or that cause damage to the environment. The next chapter will be dedicated to explaining the composition, functioning and scope of the IS in Brazil.

We cannot abstain from fiscal justice, which aims to ensure that the resulting tax burden is socially fair, avoiding overburdening vulnerable populations and promoting equity. Education and awareness-raising are essential because seeking a greater understanding in society of the importance of green taxes and incentives can increase acceptance of those measures.

Finally, there is the need for multi-sectoral coordination, which is no easy task and involves aligning governments, the private sector and civil society organizations, and is essential if ecological taxation is to produce the expected results.

Taxation, far from being just a collection mechanism, can become a powerful lever for shaping behavior and catalyzing structural change. In the Brazilian case, with its rich biodiversity and central role on the global environmental stage, the integration of incentive taxes into an ecological agenda is not only desirable, but essential for a more sustainable and just future.

2.5 Challenges and prospects for Germany

In Germany, the current development is very similar to that in Brazil; there is also political and economic resistance in Germany, especially since Donald Trump took over the presidency in the USA on January 20, 2025.

As a result, there is currently little progress in ecological financial reform in Germany as well. Agreement between politics, business and society is also a lengthy process that will need to be coordinated further in the future.

A new Bundestag will be elected in Germany on February 23, 2025. According to the World Wide Fund For Nature (WWF), most parties fall short of the necessary climate protection measures when comparing the election manifestos for the 2025 Bundestag elections.[16]

The WWF's analysis shows that the major parties CDU, CSU and SPD have significantly scaled back their ambitions compared to the last general election.

Bündnis 90/Die Grünen have presented the most ambitious program, which includes a comprehensive concept for the energy, building and transport transition as well as the establishment of a circular economy. However, they have been the subject of sustained criticism due to a poorly designed heating law from 2023, which many felt was unfair. The CDU/CSU is mainly focusing on the CO2 price and wants to abolish the Building Energy Act, while the SPD is committed to climate targets, but remains vague on specific measures.

For a successful climate and environmental policy, it is crucial that it is socially just. A poorly designed environmental policy can lead to an overburdening of vulnerable population groups and reduce the acceptance of the measures. The WWF emphasizes that a government that promotes the phase-out of fossil fuels and invests heavily in renewable energies is necessary. The integration of social justice into climate policy is crucial to increase the acceptance and effectiveness of the measures. This requires a comprehensive reform of tax and social policies to ensure that the costs of the transformation are distributed fairly.

3. Constitutional basis for the introduction of new excise taxes

3.1 Brazil

The coexistence of federal and state taxes in Brazil is structured by the principles and provisions established in the 1988 Federal Constitution. The Brazil-

16 WWF, WWF Zukunftswahl-Check analysiert Wahlprogramme zur Bundestagswahl https://www.wwf.de/2025/januar/wie-zukunftsfit-sind-die-parteien-in-deutschland; WWF Zukunftswahl-Check zur Bundestagswahl 2025 https://www.wwf.de/themen-projekte/politische-arbeit/bundestagswahl-2025/wwf-zukunftswahl-check-2025, published 30.01.2025 [access: 05.02.2025]

ian tax organization, based on the federative model, seeks to harmonize the financial autonomy of the federative entities (Union, States, Municipalities and Federal District) with the exercise of their constitutional powers. The constitutional foundations that support this coexistence are highlighted below.

Federative Principle and Financial Autonomy: The 1988 Constitution organizes Brazil as a federation, according to article 1, main section, article 18. This federative structure recognizes the political, administrative and financial autonomy of the federative entities. Financial autonomy is guaranteed by the power to institute taxes of their own, according to the tax powers established in Article 145 of the Constitution. The states have their own competence to institute state taxes, regardless of prior authorization from the Union or the municipalities, guaranteeing their independence.

Allocation of Tax Responsibility: Article 153 of the Constitution lists the taxes that the Union can institute, while article 155 defines those of state responsibility, article 156 deals with municipal taxes and article 156-A creates a new tax of shared responsibility between states and municipalities. This separation seeks to avoid tax overlap and conflict between federal entities, ensuring balance in the federative pact. Examples of state taxes include: the Tax on the Circulation of Goods and Services (ICMS); the Tax on the Causa Mortis Transmission and Donation of Any Goods or Rights (ITCMD); and the Motor Vehicle Ownership Tax (IPVA). Regarding federal taxes, we can mention, for example: Income Tax (IR); Tax on Industrialized Products (IPI); Social Contributions, such as Cofins and PIS/Pasep, etc. and in relation to municipal taxes, the Tax on Services of Any Nature (ISS), Urban Property Tax (IPTU) and Real Estate Transfer Tax (ITBI), are some examples.

The Constitution ensures that part of the revenue collected by the Union and the states is to be shared between the federated entities, according to articles 157, 158 and 159. This mechanism guarantees the redistribution of resources, especially to entities with lower tax collection capacity, promoting federative balance. The tax reform approved in Brazil brought significant changes to federal, state and municipal taxes. Implementing this new model will require a great deal of cooperation and coordination from the federated entities. Below we will discuss some of the main aspects of this reform.

3.1.1 The recent Tax Reform approved in Brazil

Constitutional Amendment 132/2024 promoted a significant reform of the Brazilian tax system, with its focus on simplifying and modernizing the tax on goods and services. This amendment created a dual VAT: the IBS and the CBS and also created a tax of an extra-fiscal nature called the Selective Tax. The IBS (Goods and Services Tax) replaces state and municipal taxes related to consumption. The taxes replaced by the IBS are: ICMS (Tax on the Circulation of Goods and Services) – a state tax, and ISS (Tax on Services of Any Nature) – a municipal tax.

The IBS tax base operates on the IVA (VAT–Value Added Tax) model, taxing goods and services at all stages of the production chain with the right to tax credits. The tax will be shared between states and municipalities, with a gradual transition by 2033.

The other tax created by the amendment was the CBS (Contribution on Goods and Services), which is levied on companies' gross revenue, calculated using the credit and debit model (similar to the IBS, but restricted to the federal level). It will be implemented before the IBS and will be levied from 2027, while the taxes it replaces are being gradually phased out. It replaces PIS (Social Integration Program) and Cofins (Contribution to Social Security Financing), two exclusively federal taxes.

The following taxes were also abolished: IOF/Insurance: discontinued for financial transactions and insurance, and IPI, which will remain only for the Manaus Free Trade Zone and specific industrialized products. The transition from the old system to the new tax model will take place progressively between 2026 and 2033, to ensure that the federal entities adapt to the new revenue distribution. These new taxes reflect an attempt to simplify the tax system, reducing cumulativeness and promoting greater collection efficiency. The proposal is inspired by international VAT models, adjusted to the characteristics of the Brazilian federative pact.

The Excise Tax, which we will deal with in a specific section, aims to act on certain goods and services, especially those considered harmful to health or the environment, or whose production or consumption has a negative social impact. The tax seeks to discourage the consumption of those goods and services.

On January 16, 2025, the Congress approved Complementary Law 214, the first regulation of the tax reform. The new law simplifies the co-billing of taxes on consumption (goods and services). The text originates from the Complementary Bill (PLP) 68/2024, approved in December by the National Congress. Twenty-eight sections were vetoed, including those that benefited certain financial and information security services.

The main change brought about by the new law are the rules for implementing Value Added Tax (IVA/VAT), which is levied only on the value added at each stage of production, discounting what has already been taxed at previous stages. This avoids the cumulative collection of taxes along production chains.

The implementation of the new system will be gradual. In 2026, CBS and IBS will be tested nationally but will not actually be collected. For these tests, companies will have to issue an invoice with a value that corresponds to the new taxes. This will be the time for the public administration to check the viability of the new model and make the necessary adaptations. The transition to the new system will not be completed until 2033. Every five years, parliamentarians will make a new assessment of the effects of the reform.

The standard rate, which will be established in a future law, should be around 28%[17] of the price of the product or service consumed. The text stipulates that the Executive Power will adopt measures to bring the rate below 26.5% by 2030. As a rule, the standard rate will be charged equally for any product or service, which simplifies the current system. In addition, the effective tax rate should only be applied to final consumption, and not to the production sector.

The regulation provides for a tax reduction, a reduced list, for example, of services and products related to national security and information, with 40 items that will have a 60% tax reduction. Exemption for the basic food basket, where food from the National Basic Food Basket (CNBA) will not pay CBS or IBS. The list includes essential foods such as rice, beans, milk, bread and meat. Cashback is a form of tax refund that will be given to families with an income of up to half the minimum wage per capita – which currently amounts to R$706 per family member.

A regulation will define the method of calculation and refund, but the text already defines that for expenses with internet and telephone, gas, electricity, water and sewage, 20% of the IBS and the entire amount paid in CBS will be refunded.

Regarding the tax benefit for the Manaus Free Trade Zone (ZFM), it was vetoed by the Executive Power on the grounds that it would create favorable treatment that does not exist today. It involves presumed credits – a mechanism that allows a "discount" on tax debts – for certain products from the region which, according to the government, currently "no longer have a competitive advantage over the rest of the country". The decision was based on the constitutional provision that the tax reform will maintain the ZFM current competitive advantages. The Free Trade Areas, which offer tax benefits to other cities in the Northern Region, will also receive incentives

17 Conjunturaonline, https://www.conjunturaonline.com.br/noticia/economia/brasil-tera-nova-tributacao-sobre-consumo-a-partir-do-proximo-ano [access: 10.02.2025].

under the reform. The same goes for special customs regimes. Some parliamentarians claim that if it were not for maintaining the advantages of the Manaus Free Trade Zone and the free trade areas established in Roraima, Amapá, Rondônia and Acre, a large part of this population would be destined for hunger and poverty. Or worse: to drug trafficking and criminal gangs.

Another important approval was the creation of the temporary and independent Management Committee, which will last until the end of 2025, for the sole regulation of the IBS during its time of existence. The idea is that the procedures needed to implement the initial tests, starting in 2026, could be delayed, since Bill 108/2024, which effectively creates the Committee, is still being analyzed.

PLP 108 proposes the creation of the Goods and Services Tax Management Committee (CG-IBS), the body responsible for coordinating the collection, inspection, charging and distribution of the IBS among Brazilian states and municipalities. The CG-IBS will be made up of representatives from all federal entities, ensuring shared and harmonious management of the new tax. The structure of the CG-IBS includes a Superior Council, made up of 54 members: 27 appointed by the state governments and the Federal District, and 27 elected to represent the municipalities and the Federal District. This council will be the highest decision-making body within the committee.

Internationally, there are similar structures aimed at coordinating the administration of value-added taxes (VAT) in federal systems. For example, in the European Union, the VAT Committee acts as a consultative forum made up of representatives of the member states and the European Commission. This committee discusses the uniform application of VAT guidelines and promotes cooperation between member countries to ensure harmonized implementation of the tax.

Another example is the VAT Harmonization Council in Canada, which coordinates the administration of the Goods and Services Tax (GST) and the Harmonized Sales Tax (HST) between the federal government and the participating provinces. This council facilitates collaboration between the different jurisdictions to ensure consistent application of VAT- related tax policies. These international examples demonstrate the importance of management committees in the efficient administration of consumption taxes in federal systems, promoting cooperation between different levels of government and ensuring uniformity in the application of tax laws.

3.1.2 The Excise Tax

A federal tax, the IS is extra fiscal in nature, i.e. its main function is to discourage the consumption of products considered harmful to health or the environment, as well as correcting negative externalities associated with these goods. The tax will replace part of the collection of the Tax on Industrialized Products (IPI) and will be levied only once on each product, without the possibility of using tax credits from previous or future transactions.

Complementary Law 214/2025 indicates general categories of products that should be taxed by IS, including: cigarettes and other tobacco derivatives; alcoholic beverages; sugar-sweetened beverages; motor vehicles; mineral goods, i.e. products that cause significant environmental impact. These items should receive this additional tax, which will be levied only once on the penalized product. The rates still need to be defined in the future, in specific ordinary laws. But the new rule already stipulates that the maximum rate for minerals will be 0.25%.

According to the text, the IS tax will apply to the following items: vehicles, except trucks; boats and aircraft; smoking products; alcoholic beverages; sugary drinks, such as industrialized juices and soft drinks; mineral goods; and online betting (prediction contests and fantasy sport). However, there will be no tax on vehicles with specific technical characteristics for operational use by the Armed Forces or Law Enforcement agencies. The tax is not levied on transactions involving electricity and telecommunications and on goods and services whose rates are reduced under the terms of § 1 of art. 9 of Constitutional Amendment no. 132, of December 20, 2023.[18]

The rate bands will be progressive, varying according to the product's impact on health or the environment. For example: Products such as cigarettes or fossil fuels may have higher tax rates, while other harmful goods may be in lower bands. The law allows for the adoption of specific rates, differentiated by product category, providing flexibility in taxation.

IS does not form its own calculation base and neither does it include IBS and CBS, nor ICMS and ISS during the transition until 2032. On the other hand, the reciprocal is not true, as IBS and CBS will have IS in their calculation base.[19]

Article 414 of LC 214/2025 establishes the different calculation bases for the IS, which vary according to the time criterion established in article 412.

---

18 Presidência da República, https://www.planalto.gov.br/ccivil_03/constituicao/emendas/emc/emc132.htm [access: 10.02.2025].

19 Source: CF/1988 – Complementary Law 214/2025.

We would like to point out that according to Article 414(III)(b), the basis for calculating the IS will be "the reference value for extracting the mineral asset.

The legislation provides for two main ways of defining the tax base, depending on the type of good or service being taxed:

3.1.2.1 Ad Valorem Calculation Basis – art. 415

The tax base is the monetary value of the transaction, i.e. the sale price of the good or service. The tax rate is applied as a percentage of this value. Generally used for goods and services whose impact varies in proportion to the value of the item. For example: for luxury products with environmental impacts (such as highly polluting vehicles), the tax is applied as a percentage of the final price. Alcoholic drinks or cigarettes can have the tax calculated in this manner, based on the sales price. The advantage of using this calculation basis is that it adapts to price variations in the market and makes it easier to adjust the tax on products with higher or lower prices. However, there is the challenge that products with artificially low prices can be under-taxed, reducing tax efficiency.

3.1.2.2 Specific Calculation Basis

It is defined by the physical quantity traded, such as volume, weight or unit of the good, regardless of its monetary value. Indicated for goods whose environmental, social or health impact is proportional to the quantity consumed, not the price. Examples include fossil fuels, which could be taxed based on the volume consumed (in liters). Cigarette tax could be levied per pack or unit. The advantage of this type of calculation basis is that it guarantees taxation proportional to the physical consumption of the good, regardless of price variations, and it also directly encourages the reduction in the consumption of taxed items. However, it can disregard differences in quality and environmental impact between similar products.

Collections arising from the Excise Tax will be allocated to specific funds and programs, with the aim of: a) financing public health policies – for example: public health funds and initiatives aimed at reducing the impact of tobacco, alcoholic beverages and sugary drinks; b) promoting environmental preservation actions in the case of products with a significant environmental impact, such as fossil fuels and combustion-powered cars; and c) mitigating the negative effects caused by the consumption of taxed products.

According to the Federal Constitution, the Excise Tax (IS) is not levied on exports. Complementary Law (LC) No. 214/2025 – reflecting constitutional immunity, listed in item I of article 413 the non-incidence of IS on exports, alongside immunities on transactions with electricity and telecommunications and transactions with goods and services whose IBS and CBS rates are reduced. However, when the bill was sanctioned, the Executive Power vetoed item I of article 413, which provided for the complete exemption of exports from the Selective Tax on the sale of mineral goods. This means that such operations will be able to charge the aforementioned tax levied on extraction, regardless of the destination of the mineral product. According to § 2 of art. 422 of LC 214/2025, the rate cannot exceed 0.25 %, calculated on the market value of the product. Had the Executive Power not vetoed the bill, the export of minerals would have resulted in the return of credits from the Selective Tax levied on extraction.

3.2 Germany

3.2.1 Justification of incentive taxes

Each state refinances the fulfillment of its tasks, e. g. public services, defense, social tasks, essentially by levying taxes on all those who live in that state or are otherwise connected to it.

However, like any imposed pecuniary charge, tax payments trigger avoidance behavior in citizens. They therefore always have a behavioral effect. With this knowledge, tax payments can also be associated with a behavioral purpose. Section 3 (1), 2nd half-sentence of the German Fiscal Code (AO) explicitly states that the generation of revenue can also be an ancillary purpose of tax collection, i. e. the main purpose can be another, e. g. rewarding desirable behavior through tax reductions or sanctioning undesirable behavior through tax increases.

The German legal system thus explicitly allows taxes to be waived for non-fiscal reasons, but the main purpose must still be to generate revenue.

This means that tax laws are allowed to create incentives that (may) have a behavior-guiding function. Insofar as such non-fiscal objectives are pursued by law, such promotion or guidance objectives must be clearly supported by legislative decisions. In this way, the generation of revenue takes a back seat to another purpose – usually behavior guidance. In addition to fiscal objectives, the focus of taxation can therefore also include distributional aspects, as well as social, economic, fiscal or even ecological objectives. However, the fundamental principles of taxation must always be observed, such as the principle of equality (ability to pay principle), the principle of legality, the prohibition of excess or the principle of the social state.[20]

The **ability-to-pay principle** concerns the effect of the tax burden and applies to all levies. It is derived from the principle of equality enshrined in Article 3, paragraph 1 of the German constitution. Tax payments must be based on the taxpayer's ability to pay, i.e. their financial means.[21]

One example of the application of the ability-to-pay principle is the progressive income tax rate, which means that taxpayers with higher incomes not only pay more taxes, but also pay a higher tax rate than taxpayers with lower incomes.[22] It is well known that people with a higher income pay more tax. However, due to the increasing tax rate (from 14% to 42%), they also pay a higher proportion of their income than people with a lower income.

The **principle of legality**[23] The principle of legality means that taxation must be lawful and results from Article 20, paragraph 3 of the German Basic Law. Tax collection must strictly adhere to the requirements of the law and the Basic Law. The relevant laws must be clear and unambiguous, and they must not have a retroactive effect on closed cases (known as the prohibition of retroactivity). According to section 85 of the German Fiscal Code (AO), the tax authorities must assess and collect taxes uniformly in accordance with the law. Taxes may not be reduced, levied wrongly, and tax refunds and rebates may not be wrongly granted or denied. Furthermore, contracts between the state and citizens are prohibited under tax law. This principle ensures that state power is organized and exercised in accordance with the provisions and within the limits of the law, and does not occur arbitrarily, thus enabling the abuse of power.[24]

The **prohibition of excess** is an expression of the principle of proportionality enshrined in Article 20, paragraph 3 of the German constitution. It is based on the idea that state measures may not, in principle, be unlimited and unfounded, and that tax obligations, too, may not be disproportionate.[25]

---

20 Cf. Gersch in: Klein AO, § 3 Rn. 9.

21 Cf. Gersch in: Klein AO, § 3 Rn. 14. It also refers to the effect of a tax burden and includes the principle that it must be payable from disposable income, which varies according to financial possibilities.

22 Cf. the interesting article on the current political discussion of the efficiency principle by Eichfelder/Knaisch/Nicolai in: DStR 2021, S. 2168.

23 Vgl. Grzeszick in: Dürig/Herzog/Scholz, GG Kommentar, Rn. 1.

24 Vgl. Küpper/Booß in: Zugmaier/Nöcker, Abgabenordnung, § 227 AO, Rn. 58.

25 BVerfGE v. 8.7.2021 – 1 BvR 2237/ 14, 1 BvR 2422/ 17, Rn. 117; BVerfG v. 5.4.1978 – 1 BvR 117/ 73 –, BVerfGE 48, 102 juris Rn. 35 ff.

They must not be allowed to strangle the taxpayers; their property must be spared, and families must be protected. This applies to every tax, including ecologically motivated taxation.

The **welfare state principle** is enshrined in Article 20, Paragraph 1 of the German Constitution. The state is obliged to ensure a fair social order and bears fundamental responsibility for the protection of the socially weak by redistributing wealth from the financially strong to the financially weak.[26] The legislation implements the principle of the welfare state through tax exemptions for basic needs, progressive taxation in the income tax law and the deductibility of individual pension costs.

With regard to an ecological financial reform, this means that it can be further developed with a sense of proportion and that, like all other tax laws, it must be in line with the principles outlined.

3.2.2 Legislative competence

Germany also has a decentralized system, set out in the federal principle of Art. 20 of the German Basic Law.

The German federal state is a special manifestation of federalism. It is a principle of political organization in which political units are territorially divided into political subsystems that are linked politically and legally at different levels. Sovereignty and legislative powers are divided among regional authorities, and the Basic Law defines the respective powers, particularly in tax matters.[27]

The basic rule for the distribution of legislative competence in the federal state between the federal government and the federal states is derived from Article 70, paragraph 1 of the Basic Law. In Germany, only the federal government and the federal states can be considered as legislative associations, but not the municipalities; the setting of standards by other associations, such as the enactment of municipal statutes, does not constitute "legislation" within the meaning of Article 70, paragraph 1 of the Basic Law.[28]

In this respect, there is a significant difference between the German system and the Brazilian system, in which there are municipal taxes regulated by the constitution. In deviation from Article 70 of the Basic Law, Article 105

---

26 Grzeszick in: Dürig/Herzog/Scholz, GG Kommentar, Art. 20 Rn. 1.

27 Graf von Kielmansegg in: Höfling/Augsberg/Rixen, Berliner Kommentar zum Grundgesetz, 1. Ergänzungslieferung 2024, Art. 20 GG, Rn. 49 ff.

28 Herbst in: Höfling/Augsberg/Rixen, Berliner Kommentar zum Grundgesetz, 1. Ergänzungslieferung 2024, Art. 70 GG, Rn. 4.

of the Basic Law, as a lex specialis, regulates the distribution of legislative powers in the area of taxation between the federal government and the states.

According to Art. 105 of the German Basic Law (GG), the federal government has exclusive legislative authority over customs duties and financial monopolies. A state financial monopoly is to be understood as the state's exclusive right to offer a particular good or service on the market. Today, the only remaining monopoly is the spirits monopoly, which, however, has not generated any income for the federal government since the liberalization of the markets and the former import monopoly. It is even subsidized from tax revenues to protect small and medium-sized distilleries from foreign competition.[29]

The Federation shall have concurrent legislative power over real property tax and other taxes if it is entitled to all or part of the revenue from these taxes. The rule of concurrent legislation means that the federal states have legislative competence as long as and to the extent that the federal government has not legislated. In other words, if the federal government regulates an issue by law, the federal states have no legislative competence for this issue and this scope or period. This is also known as the blocking effect.[30] By contrast, the states are responsible for legislation on local consumption and excise taxes. However, they may not levy any taxes if these are similar to the taxes regulated by federal law. In this respect, German tax legislation differs greatly from the Brazilian legal situation.

3.2.3 Limits to tax creation

Article 106 of the German Basic Law (GG) serves as the final regulation for the distribution of tax revenue between the federal government, the federal states and the municipalities. This means that Article 106 GG describes exactly what proportion of one of the types of tax mentioned there is due to the federal government, the federal states or the municipalities.

While Article 105 of the Basic Law regulates legislative sovereignty, Article 106 of the Basic Law provides precise instructions for the revenue sovereignty over various taxes and financial monopolies. It distinguishes between federal taxes, state taxes, municipal taxes and community taxes. In the case of

29 Cf. Müller-Franken, Sebastian in: Höfling/Augsberg/Rixen, Berliner Kommentar zum Grundgesetz, 2024, Art. 105 GG Rn. 196.

30 Cf. Herbst in: Höfling/Augsberg/Rixen, Berliner Kommentar zum Grundgesetz, 2024, Art. 72 GG, Rn. 25.

joint taxes, the revenues are due jointly to the federal government and the federal states according to a percentage share. The exhaustive list in Article 106 of the Basic Law means that only the taxes listed there are recognized as such, and new taxes must be assigned to one of the types mentioned.

The federal and state governments have no legislative competence for taxes or types of tax that are not explicitly mentioned in Article 106 of the Basic Law (GG). However, the legislator has a great degree of freedom within the type concepts defined by Article 105 and Article 106 of the Basic Law. The ordinary legislature does not have a free right to introduce new taxes, which is also referred to as the blocking effect of the financial constitution. The taxes and types of tax listed in Article 105 and Article 106 of the Basic Law are type concepts; new taxes must therefore be examined to determine whether they correspond to the type of a conventional tax. The assignment of a tax to a competence title of Article 106 of the Basic Law is based on the essential structural characteristics of the tax. These include the debtor (subject), the object of taxation (object), the scale of assessment and the method of collection. The decisive factor is whether two taxes materially siphon off the same source of economic performance. The taxes listed in Article 106 of the Basic Law can be fundamentally restructured. New types of taxes can also be introduced, provided they can be assigned to one of the tax types listed in Article 106 of the Basic Law.

Furthermore, the legislator has no free right of tax invention. This therefore means that the introduction of a new type of tax, such as a selective tax based on the Brazilian model, requires an amendment to the Basic Law, for which a two-thirds majority of the German Bundestag is required.[31]

3.2.4 Excise Tax

The **Value Added Tax** is the most important excise tax in Germany, with the highest revenues, and plays a central role in the German tax system. It is levied on the sale of goods and services and is a transaction tax that targets the sales process itself and the consideration for the service.

The legislative power for value added tax lies with the federal government, Article 105, para. 2 of the Basic Law, because it is entitled to a portion of the revenue.

The revenue from value added tax is divided between the federal government and the states. Pursuant to Article 106, paragraph 3 of the Basic Law, the

31 Compare to all this Kempny in: Höfling/Augsberg/Rixen, Berliner Kommentar zum Grundgesetz, 2024, Art. 106 GG.

revenue from the VAT accrues jointly to the Federation and the states. The distribution of the value added (or turnover) tax revenue is based on a fixed scale, which is adjusted annually to ensure that the Federation and the Länder can cover their necessary expenditure (coverage ratio principle). This principle ensures a flexible distribution of revenues to meet the changing financial needs of the Federation and the federal states.

With the exception of the import turnover tax, the administrative competence for the turnover tax lies with the federal states. This means that the federal states collect and administer the turnover tax on behalf of the federal government. This division of administrative competence enables the tax to be collected efficiently, since the federal states have the necessary structures in place to carry out the tax collection.[32]

German tax law is less complex than the Brazilian system. In Germany, the regulations of Articles 105 and 106 of the Basic Law, as described above, prohibit the federal states from levying a tax similar to the VAT, so called Ban on similarity.[33] The federal government has concurrent legislative authority over taxes, which means that it has the power to legislate on important taxes such as VAT (Article 105 paragraph 2a GG). VAT is a shared tax, which is split between the federal and state governments (Article 106 paragraph 3 GG). The taxable base for VAT in Germany is the consideration that an entrepreneur receives for his deliveries or services (Section 10 (1) UStG). This means that the VAT is calculated on the net price of the delivery or service, with the VAT itself not being part of the tax base. In Germany, there are two main tax rates: a standard tax rate of 19% and a reduced tax rate of 7% for certain goods and services.[34]

4. Future granting of the new excise taxes in Brazil

Brazil has a good track record with green fiscal transfers. The Federal Constitution stipulates that states must transfer 25% of the revenues from the Tax on the Commercialization of Goods and Services (ICMS) to municipalities, but part of these transfers can be sent to municipalities according to criteria established by the state, which include environmental criteria. The tax has become known as the ecological ICMS.

32 Deutscher Bundestag, Steuerkompetenzen von Bund und Ländern, Verfassungsrechtliche Regelungen der Gesetzgebungs-, Ertrags- und Verwaltungskompetenzen für Steuern (2022), WD 4 – 3000 - 020/22, p. 13.

33 Jachmann-Michel/Vogel in: Huber/Voßkuhle, Grundgesetz, 8. Auflage 2024, Article 105 Rn. 66ff.

34 Korn in: Bunjes, Umsatzsteuer, 23. Auflage 2024, R. 4ff.

Currently, another 18 states[35] make transfers to their municipalities based on environmental criteria. This is a tool to reward/encourage municipalities with ecological assets or relevant environmental performance. The states have the autonomy to establish their transfer criteria, which change in terms of importance (from 1% to 13% of the total ICMS transfer) and criteria used to evaluate the municipalities, such as protected areas, sewage treatment, garbage, etc. However, as the ICMS will cease to exist with the tax reform, a solution was needed for the ecological transfers.

In this sense, the new Tax on Goods and Services (IBS), established by Constitutional Amendment 132 of 2024, stipulates that up to 5% of the IBS passed on to municipalities can be linked to environmental criteria. Some are already calling it Green IBS. This measure aims to continue encouraging sustainable practices in municipalities, like what already happens with the Ecological ICMS. The Green IBS creates an opportunity for states to review their transfers in order to adjust them to today's environmental realities.

However, IBS-Green will be even more effective if states also have incentives to seek results in the environmental area. In addition, states that have not yet adopted the ICMS transfer will need to implement this mechanism within the IBS. According to World Bank estimates, the new criteria will increase the volume of transfers linked to environmental criteria to municipalities by 60%.

The value of the environmental portion: up to 5% of the funds passed on to municipalities from the IBS can be distributed based on compliance with environmental indicators and targets. The aim is to encourage local initiatives for environmental preservation, conservation of natural resources and sustainability actions. The application criteria include: a) the existence of Conservation Units (UCs) or protected areas in the municipalities; b) effective environmental management, such as solid waste and basic sanitation policies; c) the recovery or maintenance of water sources and permanent preservation areas (APPs) and d) the promotion of renewable energy and climate change mitigation projects.

Although the IBS replaces the ICMS as a state and municipal tax, the logic of the Ecological ICMS will be adapted to ensure that environmental criteria remain relevant. This adaptation seeks to preserve the incentive for sustainable practices in municipalities, ensuring a smooth transition to the new tax

---

35 Mahdi, Shireen, Reforma tributária e sustentabilidade: uma nova era para as transferências fiscais ecológicas https://www.worldbank.org/pt/news/opinion/2025/01/16/reforma-tributaria-e-sustentabilidade-uma-nova-era-para-as-transferencias-fiscais-ecologicas [access: 10.02.2025].

regime. We emphasize that the ICMS will be completely abolished in 2033, when the Ecological ICMS will also be abolished.

The detailed regulation of the environmental portion of IBS transfers will be done through state and federal laws, which will define the indicators and mechanisms for monitoring environmental impacts and calculating the transfer to municipalities. The application is scheduled to take place gradually, as part of the transition to the new unified tax system. This mechanism reflects Brazil's commitment to sustainable development and the alignment of tax practices with environmental objectives.

One important aspect is that it is essential to align incentives between the three spheres of government. Alignment allows objectives to be achieved more efficiently and in an articulated manner between the federated entities. This is what is known as **climate federalism:** a concept that explores the role and responsibilities of the different levels of government in a federation (national, state and municipal) in tackling climate change. It seeks to articulate competencies to mitigate environmental impacts and promote effective climate adaptation policies in a coordinated manner, respecting the autonomy of the federative entities and taking advantage of their particularities.

Climate Federalism has several characteristics, among which we would like to highlight the following: Firstly, the division of competencies, where responsibilities for combating climate change are shared between federal entities, depending on their capacity to act and the local impact of the policies. Sub-national governments (state and municipal) are usually closer to local problems and can lead specific initiatives, such as clean energy programs or resilient infrastructure. Secondly, Intergovernmental Coordination, which involves the creation of coordination mechanisms between governments to guarantee integrated and coherent actions, avoiding conflicts between national, state and local climate policies. Thirdly, Climate Policy Instruments with the adoption of tools such as climate funds, tax incentives, emission targets, environmental regulation and intergovernmental agreements. And finally, Flexibility and Regionalization, which allow climate actions to be adjusted to regional characteristics, such as biomes and specific vulnerabilities.

Practical examples of Climate Federalism in some countries and in the EU include: In the Brazilian case, the Brazilian climate federalism is seen in the implementation of sub-national climate policies, such as the states of the Legal Amazon adopting strategies to combat deforestation, and cities joining the Global Covenant of Mayors for Climate and Energy; and instruments such as the Ecological ICMS also reflect federal initiatives focused on sustainability.

In the United States, states have taken a leading role in the fight against climate change, such as California, which has implemented stricter standards for vehicle emissions and clean energy targets, even at times when national policies have been set back. In the European Union, although not a federation in the classic sense, the EU coordinates climate efforts between member states, combining national policies and continental targets, such as the commitment to reduce greenhouse gas emissions.

Finally, I must mention that Brazil has implemented a series of initiatives and public policies to make progress on climate change. Some of the main actions include participation in international agreements such as the Paris Agreement (2015), in which Brazil made international commitments to reduce greenhouse gas emissions, with targets of cutting emissions by 37% by 2025 and 43% by 2030 (compared to 2005 levels). Also, Brazil has been actively participating in The United Nations Framework Convention on Climate Change (UNFCCC), in its global climate conferences e.g. Cops, defending the importance of climate finance for developing countries. Below, we list a few examples.

- The development of National Plans and Climate Policies, such as the National Policy on Climate Change (PNMC), which establishes guidelines for mitigating the impacts of climate change and integrating sustainability into government planning. The Low Carbon Agriculture Plan (ABC), aiming to reduce agricultural emissions through sustainable practices such as the recovery of degraded pastures, no-till farming and crop-livestock-forest integration systems. The National Energy Plan promotes the transition to renewable sources like wind, solar and biomass energy.
- Regarding Environmental Protection and Conservation, the creation of the National System of Conservation Units (SNUC) guarantees the protection of natural areas and biodiversity through conservation units. Deforestation monitoring with programs as PRODES and DETER, operated by the National Institute for Space Research (INPE), monitor and provide data on deforestation.
- As for the promotion of Renewable Energies, the country is a leader in clean energies as it has a predominantly renewable energy matrix, especially hydroelectric, wind and solar energy. In recent years, the country has made progress in expanding photovoltaic solar energy and wind farms.
- Concerning the fight against deforestation, the country has the Amazon Fund, which is financed by international donations, such as those from Norway and Germany, which supports projects aiming to reduce deforestation and promote sustainable development in the Amazon. It also has environmental inspection efforts: operations carried out by agencies like IBAMA and ICMBio which are intended to combat illegal deforestation and other predatory practices.

5. Improvement

Brazil has the potential to lead the global ecological transformation due to its natural wealth and experience in renewable energies. Some measures that can strengthen progress include reforestation and recovery of degraded areas with ecosystem restoration projects, such as the commitments under the Bonn Challenge, which can capture carbon and recover biodiversity. Deforestation and fires are a particular challenge in the Amazon and the Cerrado, driven by agricultural expansion, illegal mining and land speculation.

Economic incentives through fiscal and tax policies, such as subsidies for clean technologies and green taxes, can encourage sustainable practices. Even with political and economic pressures given that the tension between economic development and environmental preservation is an ongoing obstacle.

Empowering local (indigenous and traditional) communities to conserve forests and ecosystems is an essential strategy for combating socio-environmental inequality. Indigenous and traditional populations face constant threats to their land and culture. Technology and innovation that correspond to investments in research, development and low-carbon technologies can transform sectors such as agriculture, transportation and energy.

A fundamental aspect is meeting climate objectives. There are gaps in the monitoring and implementation of public policies that guarantee the fulfillment of climate commitments. All the actions mentioned above are necessary for both the Excise Tax and the green IBS to be successfully implemented.

Although the Excise Tax is an important mechanism to promote sustainability, public health and social justice, its implementation can be improved in several aspects to achieve better results. Below we list some suggestions for improvement.

- It is essential to clearly define which products are taxed. The challenge lies in the lack of clear criteria for determining which goods and services should be taxed and which can lead to doubts and legal disputes. The ideal would be to create a detailed and updatable list of products subject to the tax, with objective criteria such as environmental impact, public health or negative externalities.
- Improve transparency in the allocation of resources, because without a clear destination, the funds collected can be used for purposes that do not meet the objectives of the tax. In this sense, it is important to ensure that the revenues are compulsorily applied to specific public policies, such as investments in health, environmental education and green infrastructure.
- Establish criteria to mitigate regressive effects because taxed products, such as fuels, can disproportionately affect low-income families. One solution

would be to implement compensation mechanisms, such as cashback or targeted subsidies, to protect vulnerable populations from excessive impacts.

- Seek technological evolution and make regular adjustments because the impact of certain products can change over time, like advances in less polluting technologies. To this end, it is important to periodically review the scope of the tax, considering new scientific information, changes in the market and technological innovations.
- Integrate with education and sustainability policies, as the tax alone may not be enough to change consumption habits. The ideal is to complement the excise tax with awareness campaigns about the benefits of sustainable practices and the impacts of taxed products.
- Seek Regional Equity, i.e. states or municipalities that depend on the production of taxed items, such as fossil fuels, may suffer disproportionate economic impacts. It is therefore essential to create revenue redistribution mechanisms or incentives to support economic transition in the most affected regions.
- Promote efficient inspection, as the absence of an effective system for monitoring and enforcing tax can lead to fraud or tax evasion. In this sense, investment should be made in monitoring technology, such as digital systems, to ensure that taxation is applied fairly and efficiently.
- Alignment with global policies: the excise tax needs to be aligned with international commitments on sustainability and trade. Seek to harmonize tax rates and regulations with global practices, avoiding friction in trade agreements and promoting international cooperation.
- Encourage climate federalism, which strengthens environmental governance by combining the actions of all tiers of government, taking advantage of both the scope of national policies and the local focus of sub-national actions. This is essential for tackling a challenge as complex and interconnected as climate change.

The success of the excise tax depends not only on its technical implementation, but also on its integration with social, economic and environmental policies. Improving aspects such as transparency, fairness and enforcement can maximize its positive impact and minimize unwanted side effects.

The ecological transformation in Brazil is currently a multifaceted process that requires political commitment, social engagement and economic investment. Despite the progress made, it is important to intensify efforts to tackle climate change and consolidate Brazil as a leader in sustainability and environmental preservation. This transition is crucial not only for the well-being of the Brazilian population, but also for global climate balance.

6. Conclusion

The instrumental view of the environment as a mere resource for economic purposes has led to an environmental crisis. Environmental degradation, climate change and scarcity of resources require a rethink and a reorientation towards more sustainable development. Law, in particular tax law, can play a significant role in guiding behavior and promoting environmentally friendly conduct.

Brazil has introduced a new special consumption tax, the so-called selective tax (IS). This tax is levied on products and processes that are harmful to the environment and/or public health, such as cigarettes and alcoholic beverages, as well as other products. The aim is to promote environmental sustainability and more environmentally friendly behavior.

Although the tax systems in Brazil and Germany are very different, the taxation of fossil fuels, the levies on CO2 emissions and tax incentives for investment in environmentally friendly technologies are comparable.

The interdisciplinary use of economic incentives in the tax area deserves to be reconsidered in Germany as a way of influencing environmentally relevant behavior. Brazilian ideas such as these could stimulate the German discussion on a German or European ecological financial reform for the protection of the natural environment. Greater consideration of environmental aspects in the entire tax code could provide a major incentive for a sustainable change in behavior. Brazilian experiences should also be incorporated into the German and European discussion on the further development of ecological financial reform.

Bibliography

CARVALHO, Cristiano. *In* GAETA, Flávia Holanda (Coordenadora). Comentários à EC 132/2023– Reforma Tributária. São Paulo: Thomson Reuters, 2024.

Conjuntura online, Brasil terá nova tributação sobre consumo a partir do próximo ano, 17.01.2025, https://www.conjunturaonline.com.br/noticia/economia/brasil-tera-nova-tributacao-sobre-consumo-a-partir-do-proximo-ano [access: 10.02.2025]

Mahdi, Shireen, Reforma tributária e sustentabilidade: uma nova era para as **transferências fiscais ecológicas, 16.01.2025, Worldbank,** https://www.worldbank.org/pt/news/opinion/2025/01/16/reforma-tributaria-e-sustentabilidade-uma-nova-era-para-as-transferencias-fiscais-ecologicas [access: 10.02.2025]; https://www1.folha.uol.com.br/colunas/shireen-mahdi/2025/01/reforma-tributaria-e-sustentabilidade-uma-nova-era-para-as-transferencias-fiscais-ecologicas.shtml?pwgt=l8o3kjd4pyq879jcb9uqasx8v9hknfvbj9q740espmtxek1u&utm_source=whatsapp&utm_medium=social&utm_campaign=compwagift [access: 10.02.2025]

MONTERO, Carlos E. Portela. O fundamento e a finalidade extrafiscal dos tributos ambientais. InMOTTA, Maurício (Coord.). Fundamentos teóricos do direito ambiental. Rio de Janeiro: Elsevier: 2008, pág. 272.

NABAIS, José Casalta, O dever fundamental de pagar impostos. Coimbra: Almedina, 1998.

PRATES, Pamela Varaschin, Tributação do Pecado no Brasil. Belo Horizonte: Forum: 2024, pág. 113e 114.

QUINTANILHA, Gabriel Sant'Anna, Reforma tributária brasileira – tributos sobre o consumo. Rio de Janeiro: GEN/Atlas/Forense, 2024.

VENTURA/ABEL, Cesta básica, cashback, Imposto Seletivo: entenda a regulamentação da Reforma Tributária; texto vai a sanção, https://oglobo.globo.com/economia/noticia/2024/12/17/cesta-basica-cashback-imposto-seletivo-entenda-a-regulamentacao-da-reforma-tributaria-texto-vai-para-sancao-de-lula.ghtml

VIEIRA FERREIRA DE MELLO JUNIOR, NILSON, Imposto seletivo: o desenho equivocado de um tributo regulatório, O risco de termos mais um tributo de caráter meramente arrecadatório, apesar da roupagem extrafiscal, 19.12.2024, https://www.jota.info/artigos/imposto-seletivo-o-desenho-equivocado-de-um-tributo-regulatorio [access: 10.02.2025]

GERMANY:

BÜNDNIS 90/DIE GRÜNEN, Die Gründung der Grünen, Eigendarstellung, https://www.gruene.de/unsere-gruene-geschichte [access: 10.02.2025]

BUNJES, UStG Umsatzsteuergesetz, Kommentar, 23. Auflage 2024, C.H.BECK-Verlag

CDU, CSU AND FDP, Koalitionsvertrag zwischen CDU, CSU und FDP vom 26.10.2009, „Wachstum. Bildung. Zusammenhalt", https://archiv.cdu.de/sites/default/files/media/dokumente/091215-koalitionsvertrag-2009–2013-englisch_0.pdf [Abruf 13.01.2025];

CDU, CSU AND SPD, Gemeinsam für Deutschland – mit Mut und Menschlichkeit, Coalition agreement between the CDU, CSU and SPD of 11.11.2005, https://webarchiv.bundestag.de/archive/2006/0202/aktuell/archiv/2005/koalition/index.html [access: 09.12.2024]

CDU, CSU AND SPD, Koalitionsvertrag zwischen CDU, CSU und SPD vom 16.12.2013, Deutschlands Zukunft gestalten, https://archiv.cdu.de/sites/default/files/media/dokumente/koalitionsvertrag.pdf [access 13.01.2025];

DEUTSHCER BUNDESTAG, Steuerkompetenzen von Bund und Ländern, Verfassungsrechtliche Regelungen der Gesetzgebungs-, Ertrags- und Verwaltungskompetenzen für Steuern (2022), WD 4 – 3000 - 020/22, p. 8, https://www.bundestag.de/resource/blob/886622/2d86e5c3efa84a48dcccda0d9ee61347/WD-4–020-22-pdf.pdf [access: 10.02.2025]

DÜRIG/HERZOG/SCHOLZ, Grundgesetz Kommentar, 105. Auflage. 2025, C.H.BECK-Verlag

EICHFELDER/KNAISCH/NICOLAI, Orientieren sich die steuerlichen Reformvorschläge der Parteien zur Bundestagswahl *2021* am Leistungsfähigkeitsprinzip?, DStR 2021, S. 2168

HÖFLING/AUGSBERG/RIXEN, Berliner Kommentar zum Grundgesetz, 2024, juris

HUBER/VOßKUHLE, Grundgesetz, 8. Auflage 2024, C.H.BECK-Verlag

ISENSEE/KIRCHHOF, Handbuch des Staatsrechts, 3. Aufl. 2007, C. F. Müller-Verlag

JUHRICH, in: Umweltbundesamt (Hrsg.), CO2 Emissionsfaktoren für fossile Brennstoffe, Climate Change 27/2016, 10 https://www.umweltbundesamt.de/sites/default/files/medien/1968/publikationen/co2-emissionsfaktoren_fur_fossile_brennstoffe_korrektur.pdf [access: 06.12.2024]

KEMFERT/SCHILL/WÄGNER/ZAKLAN, Umweltwirkungen der Ökosteuer begrenzt, CO2-Bepreisung der nächste Schritt, DIW Wochenbericht 2019, 216, https://www.diw.de/documents/publikationen/73/diw_01.c.617676.de/19-13-1.pdf [access: 09.12.2024]

KLEIN, Abgabenordnung: AO, Kommentar, 18. Auflage. 2024, C.H.BECK-Verlag.

KNIGGE/GÖRLACH, Die Ökologische Steuerreform – Auswirkungen auf Umwelt, Beschäftigung und Innovation, Forschungsprojekt im Auftrag des Umweltbundesamtes, Oktober 2005, https://www.umweltbundesamt.de/sites/default/files/medien/publikation/short/k2810.pdf [access 09.12.2024

SPD AND BÜNDNIS 90/DIE GRÜNEN: Coalition Agreement from SPD and Bündnis 90/Die Grünen from 16.10.2002, Erneuerung – Gerechtigkeit – Nachhaltigkeit. Für ein wirtschaftlich starkes, soziales und ökologisches Deutschland. Für eine lebendige Demokratie, https://www.spd.de/fileadmin/Dokumente/Beschluesse/Bundesparteitag/koalitionsvertrag_bundesparteitag_berlin_2002.pdf [access: 10.02.2025].

SPD, GRÜNEN AND FDP, Koalitionsvertrag zwischen SPD, Grünen und FDP vom 24.11.2021, Mehr Fortschritt wagen, Bündnis für Freiheit, Gerechtigkeit und Nachhaltigkeit, https://www.bundestagswahl-bw.de/koalitionsvertrag-2021 [access 10.01.2025].

WWF, WWF Zukunftswahl-Check analysiert Wahlprogramme zur Bundestagswahl https://www.wwf.de/2025/januar/wie-zukunftsfit-sind-die-parteien-in-deutschland; WWF Zukunftswahl-Check zur Bundestagswahl 2025 https://www.wwf.de/themen-projekte/politische-arbeit/bundestagswahl-2025/wwf-zukunftswahl-check-2025, published 30.01.2025 [access: 05.02.2025]

ZUGMAIER/NÖCKER, Abgabenordnung, online-Kommentar, 2025, nwb-Verlag

Marco Antonio Veríssimo Teixeira[1]

Tax Reform in Brazil: Taxation on Activities Harmful to the Environment

Abstract

The purpose of this article is to present an important point of the tax reform approved by the National Congress in December 2024: the introduction of a selective tax that aims to tax goods that are harmful to health or the environment.

The theory used to justify extra-fiscal taxation is initially presented, involving the discussion on the intervention of the state in the economic domain and the compatibility of the extra-fiscal tax rule with the principle of taxable capacity.

The main characteristics of the new tax are then presented, and it is important to emphasize that the rates will still be defined in an ordinary law that should be discussed throughout the year 2025.

1. Introduction

Brazil's current tax system is characterized by a complex division of tax powers, excessive bureaucracy, a high number of types of taxes and high consumption taxation. Among other characteristics, this makes Brazil's tax system one of the most complicated in the world.

In order to improve the Brazilian tax system, a reform is being carried out with the following objectives: a) simplification – reducing the number of types of taxes and unifying taxes with the same tax base; b) Transparency – making the tax system clearer and easier to understand for the population; c) Stimulating the economy – a simpler and more efficient tax system should attract more investment and boost economic growth.

1 PhD in Tax Law from the University of São Paulo (USP) and Master in Tax Administration from UNED and the Instituto de Estudios Fiscales – IEF/SPAIN. Specialist in State Law from the School of the Attorney General's Office of the State of São Paulo. Specialist in Tax Law, Bachelor of Laws and Electrical Engineering from USP. Tax Auditor at the Tax Administration of the State of São Paulo – Brasil.

With the publication of the constitutional complementary law nº 132/23, the constitutional text changes in several aspects related to the tax field: the abolition of ISS, ICMS, PIS and COFINS[2] (Consumption taxation in Brazil) and the introduction of a tax on transactions in goods and services (IBS) and a new contribution on goods and services (CBS) are the most important changes.

The focus of the reform is on consumption taxes: at federal level, the federal social contributions (PIS and COFINS) are replaced by a new contribution (CBS – Contribuição sobre bens e serviços – Contribution on goods and services) applied to goods and services. The IPI (tax on industrial products) is maintained only for the benefit of the Manaus Free Trade Zone.

At the state level, the ICMS (which is levied on the movement of goods, interstate and interurban transport services and on telecommunications services) and at the municipal level, the ISS (tax on services in general) is replaced by the IBS (IBS – Imposto sobre bens e serviços – tax on goods and services).

The reform includes a new selective tax (IS) to be applied to the production, extraction, marketing or import of goods and services that are harmful to health or that are harmful to the environment.

The idea of the constitutional amendment was to create a model similar to the European Value Added Tax (VAT), but in a dual model, that is to say with shared competence between municipalities, states and the Federal District (with IBS) and the Union (with CBS and IS).

Although a large part of Constitutional Amendment No. 132 has already come into force, the complementary law that deals with the selective tax was approved by the National Congress in December 2024 and sanctioned by the President of the Republic on January 16, 2025. However, the rates that will be applied by the Selective Tax have yet to be published, so the law will not yet come into force at the moment.

OECD consider that consumption taxes such as VAT, sales taxes and excise duties are often categorised as indirect taxes. They are generally levied on transactions, products or events and collected from businesses in the production and distribution chain, before being passed on to final consumers as part of the purchase price of a good or service. They are not directly imposed on

---

2 ISS – Imposto Sobre Serviços – Municipal tax on the provision of services ICMS – Imposto sobre a Circulação de Mercadorias, sobre a prestação de serviços de Comunicação e sobre a prestação de serviços de transporte intermunicipal e interestadual – State tax levied on the provision of communication services, the provision of interstate and intermunicipal transport services and the circulation of goods PIS and COFINS – Contribuições Sociais Federais – Federal Social Contributions.

income or wealth but rather on the expenditure that income and wealth finance. VAT tax is a broad-based tax on final consumption by households collected – but not borne – by businesses through a staged process and Excise tax is levied on a limited range of defined goods assessed as a specific charge per unit based on characteristics of the product and imposed at a specific stage of production or distribution.[3]

2. Selective tax – main characteristics and possibility of state intervention in the economic domain and its justification

I consider the Brazilian selective tax a kind of excise tax. A number of general characteristics differentiate excise duties from value added taxes: a) They are levied on a limited range of products; b) They are not normally due until the goods enter free circulation, at a single stage in the supply chain; c) Excise charges are generally assessed by reference to the weight, volume, strength or quantity of the product (specific or *"ad quantum excise"*), combined in some cases, with its value (*ad valorem* excise); d) Consequently, and unlike VAT, the excise system is characterised by a small number of taxpayers at the manufacturing or wholesale stage (although, in some cases they can also be levied at the retail stage).

2.1 Use of tax as a vehicle to promote taxpayer behavior and stimulate economic development

I understand that most countries considered developed today have, at some point, used excise tax as inductive tax rules. We have the example of the taxation of oleomargarine in the United States. This product was developed during the time of Napoleon III to serve as food in times of war. Since the product was similar to butter, it became a competitor at a much lower price. The United States industry pressured the president to sanction the law that created a tax on oleomargarine and, in doing so, protect the local industry from competition.[4]

I understand that the most appropriate form of State intervention in the economy is through excise tax because it allows the jurisdictional entity an

3 OECD (2024), *Consumption Tax Trends 2024: VAT/GST and Excise, Core Design Features and Trends,* OECD Publishing, Paris, https://doi.org/10.1787/dcd4dd36-en.

4 SCHOUERI, Luis Eduardo. *Normas Tributárias Indutoras e Intervenção Econômica.* Rio de Janeiro: Forense, 2005, p. 118.

option, a choice of behavior to be followed. Therefore, when the State uses taxes as vehicles for inducing tax rules, it is seeking to implement, in a non-authoritarian manner, the objectives of a modern State, that is, the implementation of equality among its members through the promotion of economic development.

2.2 The economic domain

The economic domain refers to the market, that is, the sector of the economy in which economic agents operate. This sector is subject to State rules and regulations. Direct State action is permitted in exceptional cases. In these cases, it is necessary to ensure that there are no privileges for the State in order to preserve the principle of free initiative and free competition.[5]

The inductive function, an effective function that is not normally present in the text of the rule, is what characterizes what we call inductive tax rules. This function is the one that can induce a certain behavior of the taxpayer, through the granting of an advantage or through the imposition of a higher tax, based on certain behavioral choices of the same taxpayer.

The word option is important because it characterizes a non-imposition, characteristic of a modern State that seeks only to regulate the behavior of taxpayers and not to direct them compulsorily.

There is the option of the rule having the effect of inducing the taxpayer to adopt a behavior, such as, for example, the greater production of a certain product, in view of an exemption that allows a more attractive price for the consumer with the consequent increase in consumption. On the other hand, the rule may create obstacles to the consumption of a certain product, by means of a high tax, which would induce a reduction in consumption.

In terms of tax regulations, we have those that are justified by the financial needs of the State and their legitimacy is immediately recognized based on the State's financial needs. On the other hand, we have tax regulations that are justified by the State's intervention in the economic domain, the justification for which must be sought in each act of intervention carried out.

There are occasions when the opposite of what is expected happens, that is, the inducing effect is contrary to what the legislator intended. As an example, we have the case of the regulation that increased the ISS (Tax on Services, a Municipal Tax in Brazil) in the city of São Paulo. Instead of obtaining an

5 SCHOUERI, Luis Eduardo. *Normas Tributárias Indutoras e Intervenção Econômica.* Rio de Janeiro: Forense, 2005, p. 43.

increase in revenue, as desired by the legislator, this increase caused the headquarters of service providers to flee to cities around the capital of São Paulo, since they offered a lower ISS rate as an incentive. This led to a decrease in the collection of this tax in the city of São Paulo.

The inclusion of inductive tax rules as a measure of indirect State intervention in the economic domain requires verification that both the principles of economic law and the principles classically identified with tax rules are applied synergistically to limit State intervention and adapt the objective of the rule to its expected effect.[6]

Liberals in particular understand that the market would be a perfect model both for promoting economic efficiency and optimizing production factors and for regulating social relations.

We understand that every model is a theoretical abstraction of reality and works well in theory, since all the assumptions taken into account for developing the model are related and act exactly as expected. Markets, when presented in a model, are perfect. Their invisible hand would make all economic agents act in pursuit of their personal interests in such a way that they would end up indirectly benefiting the whole of society, which would benefit from an environment of perfect competition, stable prices, economic development on the edge of the production possibility frontier, accelerated growth in well-being and distribution of wealth.[7]

2.2.1 Imperfections of the market mechanism

However, we understand that the market mechanism model has imperfections that justify state intervention in the economic domain.

The first imperfection can be called **factor mobility,**[8] that is, in the capitalist system there is not always a balance between supply and demand, since producers and consumers do not act "rationally" as predicted by the system. There is a need for state intervention to correct possible supply deficits (in this case the state can act as a producer or importer of products) or demand deficits (in this case the state can act as a buyer) to reduce producers' losses and avoid long-term damage to a given sector of the economy.

---

6 SCHOUERI, Luis Eduardo. *Normas Tributárias Indutoras e Intervenção Econômica.* Rio de Janeiro: Forense, 2005, p. 37.

7 MASTRODI NETO, Josué. Pressupostos da intervenção do estado na economia. *Revista Tributária e de Finanças Públicas,* São Paulo, vol. 12, nº 54, p. 148–173, jan./fev, 2004.

8 SCHOUERI, Luis Eduardo. *Normas Tributárias Indutoras e Intervenção Econômica.* Rio de Janeiro: Forense, 2005, p. 74.

The second imperfection can be called **access to information.**[9] It is a prerequisite for the perfect functioning of the market that economic agents and consumers enjoy full access to information about products traded and their characteristics, including trading conditions.

When this does not occur, we have misinformation that can generate several distortions. This is why State intervention is justified, which usually takes place in the regulatory sphere, when it imposes on agents the obedience of certain rules (weights and measures, consumer protection, capital market legislation, etc.). Alternatively, the State can also induce the behavior of economic agents, for example, by making the granting of tax incentives conditional on companies adopting the form of corporations, thus subjecting themselves to requirements concerning the publication of their financial statements.

The third imperfection can be called **economic concentration.**[10] The market mechanism presupposes a large number of producers and consumers, so that the price, which is the result of the meeting of supply and demand curves, is set based on countless independent transactions.

However, in the search for survival, companies are also forced to become increasingly stronger, thus obeying a principle that says that one must grow, or one will be doomed to perish, that is, either the company will become dominant or it will end up being dominated.[11]

As a company grows, the likelihood increases that it will be able to influence price formation itself, giving rise to monopolies or oligopolies. The Federal Constitution seeks, in paragraph nº 4, of article 173, to repress arbitrary increases in profits and abuse of economic power aimed at dominating markets and eliminating competition. Antitrust rules also combat concentration in the economy.

It is also possible to use an inductive tax rule, such as, for example, the case of excluding the option for taxation based on presumed profit for companies whose revenue exceeds the limit imposed by law.

It is also worth remembering that our Constitution seeks to promote small and medium-sized companies, in order to protect them from the phenomenon of concentration. Brazil had the enactment of an inductive tax rule

---

9 SCHOUERI, Luis Eduardo. *Normas Tributárias Indutoras e Intervenção Econômica.* Rio de Janeiro: Forense, 2005, p. 74.

10 SCHOUERI, Luis Eduardo. *Normas Tributárias Indutoras e Intervenção Econômica.* Rio de Janeiro: Forense, 2005, p. 75.

11 SOUZA, Washington Peluso Albino de. *Direito Econômico.* 1.ed. São Paulo: Saraiva, 1980, p. 424.

called "Simples Nacional" that seeks to bring numerous small and medium-sized companies into legality.

The fourth imperfection is called **externalities.**[12] According to the normal rules of the market mechanism, the cost or profit of a private activity must be borne by the one who generates it. We have an externality when the cost or profit is borne by the community. The externality can be positive or negative. An example of a positive externality is when a company sets up in a certain region, attracting other businesses and, therefore, improving the general income level of the locality. An example of a negative externality is when we have a polluting company that causes environmental damage that is not borne by its perpetrators but rather by the entire community.

The argument of the so-called theory of externalities can be summarized in the fact that there are two types of costs in the production of consumer goods: a) private costs, those that are borne directly by the seller of a good and b) social costs, those that are borne by other agents in society. The natural tendency is for the seller of a good, through the selling price, to cover the private costs and the difference between the selling price and the private costs results in the private benefit of the operation (profit).

However, the consumption of certain goods entails costs that will be borne by other agents in society, for example, the consumption of a product that is harmful to the environment causes a worsening of people's quality of life and the deterioration of natural resources. The resulting damage is not only related to the seller's property, but also extends to broad social groups. This damage is considered to be social costs, which means that social costs and private costs must be treated differently.

Producers of goods must take into account not only private costs, but also social costs, because otherwise they will have an advantage over those producers who do not cause social costs, which implies unfair competition.

This argument has justified the establishment of the so-called sin tax (a type of excise tax) on the consumption of alcoholic beverages and tobacco. The cost of producing these goods takes into account the products used (raw materials, transport, machinery, labor, etc.), but does not take into account the social costs arising from the consumption of these goods: health costs, road accidents caused by excessive alcohol consumption, decreased productivity at work, social problems, etc.

The use of taxes on these goods would have the purpose of internalizing the social costs caused by the consumption of these goods so that producers would be charged for the losses caused.

---

12 SCHOUERI, Luis Eduardo. *Normas Tributárias Indutoras e Intervenção Econômica.* Rio de Janeiro: Forense, 2005, p. 76.

This form of fiscal solution to the problem of social costs, also called external costs or externalities, has its origin in the ideas formulated by Cecil Pigou in his book "The Economics of Welfare" (1920).[13] From this author's work it follows that through taxes (external costs) and subsidies (external benefits) these costs or benefits can be internalized by consumers.

The clearest example to illustrate these ideas is that of atmospheric pollution: in the fuel market, the immediate result will be that the price will be determined as the result of the negotiation between buyers and sellers of said fuels. The limits of this negotiation will be marked by the costs incurred in the extraction, transport and refining of raw materials, as well as by the utility derived by the consumers of said fuels, without any participation of third parties. However, there are also third parties who are forced to bear the external costs of said transaction, in the form of pollution. Through a Pigouvian tax, this external cost can be internalized, so that it is taken into account when setting the price of these fuels.

The fifth imperfection is called **collective goods,**[14] which means that goods are offered in a non-individualized way. An individual can enjoy a good without preventing others from enjoying the same good. The action of inductive tax rules can also be effective in this social context. We can exemplify this through tax incentives granted to cultural activities or the preservation of historical heritage. In most cases, the State itself offers these collective goods and uses tax rules with the primary purpose of collecting taxes to preserve these collective goods.

In addition to the problems of the imperfection of the market model, we could also justify State intervention in the economic domain through the implementation of the so-called positive objectives of the State. We believe that the current State is not the same as the one of the 19th century, which considered society divided into two groups: the weak and the strong. In this conception, the State should be concerned with the weakest. However, in a modern view, we can conceive of him as concerned with the economy, correcting distortions and also acting to conduct, coordinate and streamline the economy.[15]

---

13 PIGOU, Arthur Cecil. Available: https://edisciplinas.usp.br/pluginfile.php/4154221/mod_resource/content/0/Pigou-The_Economic_of_Welfare_1920.pdf.

14 SCHOUERI, Luis Eduardo. *Normas Tributárias Indutoras e Intervenção Econômica.* Rio de Janeiro: Forense, 2005, p. 78.

15 SCHOUERI, Luis Eduardo. *Normas Tributárias Indutoras e Intervenção Econômica.* Rio de Janeiro: Forense, 2005, p. 79.

2.2.2 Types of intervention

The State can intervene in the economic domain (in which case the intervention will be by absorption or participation) or on the economic domain (in which case the intervention will be by direction or by induction). Let us look at each case below.

2.2.2.1 Intervention by absorption or participation

We can call it State intervention in the economic domain when this intervention is made directly in the field of economic activity in the strict sense. In this case, the State acts as an economic agent. It can intervene by absorption or participation.[16] When it does so by absorption, the State assumes full control of the means of production and/or exchange in a given sector of economic activity in the strict sense; it acts under a monopoly regime. The 1988 Brazilian Federal Constitution establishes in its article 177 the cases of monopoly of State action. The monopoly should be restricted to cases in which the private sector has no interest or does not have available capital to carry out the economic activity or in which this sector is strategic for the development of the State. The latter case is becoming increasingly rare today. In the case of intervention by participation, the State assumes control of part of the means of production and/or exchange in a given sector of economic activity in the strict sense; it acts in competition with private companies that continue to carry out their activities in this same sector. In this case, it must submit to the same rules as competing companies so that there are no privileges and the principle of free competition is not harmed.

2.2.2.2 Intervention by direction

In this case, the State intervenes in the economic domain, that is, in the field of economic activity in the strict sense. We could say that it is an intense intervention, since the State exerts pressure on the economy, on the subjects of economic activity in the strict sense, establishing mechanisms and norms of behavior that do not allow choices for the economic agent subject to them.[17]

---

16 Grau, Eros Roberto, *A Ordem Econômica na Constituição de 1988:* (interpretação e crítica). 11.ed. São Paulo: Malheiros, 2006, p. 148.

17 Grau, Eros Roberto, *A Ordem Econômica na Constituição de 1988:* (interpretação e crítica). 11.ed. São Paulo: Malheiros, 2006, p. 148.

2.2.2.3 Intervention by induction

In this case, the State intervenes in the economic domain, that is, in the field of economic activity in the strict sense, but not as intensely as in other forms. It intervenes in a softer way, as it manipulates the instruments of intervention in accordance with and in compliance with the laws that govern the functioning of the markets. This mechanism is closer to the concept of a regulatory State that seeks, through regulatory agencies, to intervene in a less intrusive way in the economy.[18]

2.3 Compatibility of the use of extrataxation with the principle of tax capacity

Based on the premise that, in the case of intervention in the economic domain, in the form of induction, there would be a purpose legitimized by the legal system, in the form of internalization of social costs, in order to repair society for the damage caused by activities that are harmful to the environment, taxes with an extra-fiscal purpose would thus be justified.

However, there are scholars who are against the use of extrafiscal taxation because they believe that there is a violation of the principle of tax capacity. Bujanda[19] describes the problem as terrible because these interventions in the economic domain (usually exemptions) largely cause a radical change in the criteria for tax distribution. Taxes or tax exemptions are often intended to fulfill regulatory functions, and the consideration of the taxable capacity of individuals is subordinated, or at least coordinated, to the need to achieve certain specific purposes of public entities, to maintain the economic system in balance, and to ensure a certain pace of development. Due to exemptions for extrafiscal purposes, it may therefore occur that precisely those manifestations and signs of wealth that from the strict point of view of tax justice are exempted from taxation. In other words: it may happen that tax burdens are exempted from what, while it is fair to pay the tax, is considered useful not to pay it, on the understanding that the fraction of wealth that was not handed over to the tax authorities can provide a greater service to the community by ensuring that it has a different destination, which the legislator himself is responsible for establishing as a prerequisite for the exemption. When this is

---

18 Grau, Eros Roberto, *A Ordem Econômica na Constituição de 1988:* (interpretação e crítica). 11.ed. São Paulo: Malheiros, 2006, p. 149.

19 SAINZ DE BUJANDA, Fernando. *Hacienda y derecho:* introdución al derecho financiero de nuestro tiempo. 6v. 3º vol. Madrid: Instituto de Estúdios Políticos, 1973, p. 418.

based on an extrafiscal purpose, it causes, in short, a profound change in the system of political valuations that governs tax distribution.

We can see daily in the print and television media that the power over government bodies of certain influential minorities has grown, increasingly organized and seeking to obtain favoritism from the State for their interests.

That is why the development of complex political, social and economic plans requires, due to their complexity, that they end up being drawn up by a restricted group of high-ranking government authorities who are also subject to pressures, including electoral pressures, tending to favor with particular intensity the economic or ideological interests of the groups to which they belong.

From these considerations, we can conclude that Bujanda does not generally agree with the intervention of the State in the economic domain through extrafiscal tax rules. Along the same line of reasoning, we have Perfecto Yebra Martul-Ortega[20] when he says that the first function of every tax is to obtain an inflow of money in favor of the State. Most taxes were established for this purpose. Even if a tax (in an exceptional case) does not have as its main purpose the collection but rather the obtaining of economic-social results, it must comply with "*postulates of tax justice, because this is what must be a necessary condition of the tax. It will be possible to achieve other political-social goals of the State, but at the same time, it is necessary to take the tax into account: to be fair.*"

Klaus Tipke is of the opinion that the inducing tax rule should be subject to the principle of the social state and not to the principle of the capacity to contribute, since the issue of economic development is more related to tax incentives and extrataxation than to the principle of the capacity to contribute.

Tipke believes that "*subsidies are measured according to need or special merit. That is why we speak of the principle of need and the principle of merit. It is widely recognized that Tax Law should be guided by the principle of tax capacity. However, this does not apply to extrafiscal rules.*"[21] Tipke believes that tax capacity is not a fair parameter for extrafiscal taxes.[22]

---

20 YEBRA MARTUL-ORTEGA, Perfecto. *La justicia fiscal y el impuesto sobre la renta.* Santiago de Compostela (La Corunã): Universidad [Departmento de Economia Política, Hacienda Publica y Derecho Fiscal], 1973, p. 40.

21 TIPKE, Klaus; YAMASHITA, Douglas. *Justiça Fiscal e Princípio da Capacidade Contributiva.* 1.ed. São Paulo: Malheiros, 2002, p. 21.

22 TIPKE, Klaus, "*Sobre a Unidade da Ordem Jurídica Tributária*", *Direito Tributário, Estudos em Homenagem a Brandão Machado,* Luis Eduardo Schoueri e Fernando Aurélio Zilvetti (coord.). São Paulo: Dialética, 1998, p. 60–70.

Klaus Tipke classifies three groups of standards, based on the recognition of the principles that support tax laws, taking into account that the tax laws contained in the standards are of diverse motivation.[23]

A distinction must be made between rules for tax purposes, rules for social purposes and rules for simplification purposes. There is no talk of a dual or plural system. Rules for tax purposes and rules for social purposes do not actually belong to the same system. The rule of "unity of order in law" ("Einheit der Rechtsordnung") must also be observed when enacting rules for social purposes. Simplification rules do not constitute an independent subsystem, but merely have an auxiliary function within the subsystem of rules for tax purposes and the subsystem of rules for social purposes.

Within the scope of exemption orders, a distinction must also be made between exemptions for tax purposes, which are simply oriented towards the taxable capacity of the refined or limited taxable event, exemptions for social purposes and exemptions for simplification purposes; correspondingly, a distinction must be made between exemptions for tax purposes, exemptions for social purposes and exemptions for simplification purposes.

Fiscal norms (Fiskalzwecknormen).[24] Fiscal norms predominate in tax laws. They serve to satisfy the financial needs of the state by distributing the total amount of tax collected from the taxpayer. This is why the common good is financed.

Socially-oriented regulations (Sozialzwecknormen):[25] Tax laws are not widely disseminated by means of regulations with a socially-oriented objective in the broad sense. These are directive regulations (regulatory, interventionist, instrumentalist), economic policy (also agrarian policy, energy policy, development policy), social policy in the strict sense (especially redistributive), cultural policy, research policy, environmental policy, health policy, etc., which are not fiscally motivated. These can be called extrafiscal regulations.

Regulations with a socially-oriented objective may contain tax exemptions, but they may also contain higher tax burdens, compensation for losses and limits on deductions for losses or create autonomous taxes. Those who behave in accordance with the state directive will be exempted from taxes, while those who behave in a way that is contrary to that desired by the state directives will have their tax burden increased.

Simplifying rules (Vereinfachungszwecknormen):[26] for technical and economic reasons, they are intended to facilitate, simplify, make taxation

23 TIPKE, Klaus. *Die Steuerrechtsordnung.* 3 vols. Köln: Otto Schmidt, 1993, p. 121.

24 TIPKE, Klaus. *Die Steuerrechtsordnung.* 3 vols. Köln: Otto Schmidt, 1993, p. 122.

25 TIPKE, Klaus. *Die Steuerrechtsordnung.* 3 vols. Köln: Otto Schmidt, 1993, p. 122.

26 TIPKE, Klaus. *Die Steuerrechtsordnung.* 3 vols. Köln: Otto Schmidt, 1993, p. 124.

more practical and better managed. They are intended above all to avoid overcomplicating and difficult implementation of the law. Simplifying rules are also intended to simplify both tax and social rules by means of typicality, deductions, etc. Seen in this light, they are not a group of independent rules alongside social rules or tax rules.

Based on the premise that discrimination based on marital status, race, or nationality is not appropriate, according to Brazilian constitutional rules, we can consider that the taxable capacity is the fundamental criterion for distributing taxes. Therefore, the taxable capacity requires that the differentiating criteria be objective and are in the very essence of the thing to be discriminated.

The ability to contribute can be based on the theory of sacrifice, according to which those who have greater wealth and assets suffer a much smaller sacrifice than those who have less income or assets.[27]

The extrafiscal use of the tax must, however, observe certain limits, as explained by Moschetti:[28] a) the existence of an economic capacity is necessary; b) compliance of the fiscal intervention with the collective interest expressed in the constitutional norm; c) clarity of legislative purpose; d) respect for the constitutional principle of indirect interest (participant, involved), in particular, the relationship between tax payment and protection of property rights.

The use of taxes for social purposes cannot have their purpose distorted to the point of creating economic imbalance or violating legal principles. Naturally, the legislator does not have unlimited power to allow facilitation, advantage or disadvantage of formally equal economic capacity, in the name of the collective interest. On the contrary, the legislator needs to observe two requirements: economic capacity and collective demand.

These measures can only be taken in the presence of an effective economic capacity, which is always a necessary condition for the taxable capacity. However, it makes no sense to speak of the solidarity requirement when there is no economic capacity. The collective interest cannot be determined by the legislator's discretion, but is expressed in several constitutional norms of principle.

Moschetti cites several articles of the Italian Constitution that limit the discretion of the tax legislator, since these articles specify the collective inter-

---

27 GODOI, Marciano Seabra de. *Justiça, Igualdade e Direito Tributário.* São Paulo: Dialética, 1999, p. 190.

28 MOSCHETTI, Francesco. *Principio della capacita contributiva.* Padova: CEDAM, 1973, p. 217.

ests that the legislator must observe in order not to violate the principle of the taxable capacity.[29]

The tax exemption instrument can be used for development purposes with the intention of favoring a region, in order to free it from a situation of economic backwardness. It cannot be said that there is a situation of strong balance between developed areas, with low illiteracy rates, high average incomes, widespread public services, high levels of industrial production and employment on the one hand, and underdeveloped areas with exactly the opposite characteristics on the other.

Anticyclical fiscal measures aim to remove a serious economic obstacle that prevents the full development of the human person: inflation and/or depression, with the heavy social and moral consequences that they always bring with them. Fiscal measures aimed at development and economic stabilization, always in a way that favors employment, are justified as a necessary means of promoting the condition that makes the right to work effective.

Through them, exemption does not constitute the prevalence of another constitutional principle over the principle of tax capacity, but, on the contrary, the implementation of the latter; it cannot be said that there is tax capacity when there is formally economic capacity, but its taxation will not be suitable for implementing the collective interest; when the economic capacity is not qualifiable in the joint and several sense.

Whenever we use an inductive tax rule, we must ask ourselves whether the means are adequate for the end. In Brazil, the 1988 Constitution determines in its article 145, paragraph one, the graduation of taxes according to the economic capacity of the taxpayer. We believe that we could interpret, in this case, the economic capacity as being the taxpayer's tax capacity. Therefore, we understand that this constitutional guideline also limits the extrafiscal use of the tax.

In view of the above, we have demonstrated that there is no unanimous position in the doctrine on the conformity of the principle of tax capacity in relation to the application of inducing tax rules (excise tax). Inducing tax rules can be excellent and effective vehicles for State intervention in the economic domain. They must, however, be subject to the limitations on the power to tax like all tax rules and also conform to the principles of the Economic Constitution outlined in the Federal Constitution of 1988.

We understand that inducing tax rules do not lose their tax nature and therefore continue to be subject to tax canons, and it is therefore up to the jurist to study their compatibility with both tax law and economic law.

---

29 MOSCHETTI, Francesco. *Principio della capacita contributiva.* Padova: CEDAM, 1973, p. 250.

From the above, we argue that the analysis of the principle of equality for the tax rule in question must also be accompanied by the analysis of the tax capacity (which is a corollary of the principle of equality).

3. Main characteristics of the selective tax introduced by the recent Tax Reform

The environmental degradation that is currently present in the country does not allow human beings to fully enjoy the fundamental rights that are guaranteed by the constitution of the federative republic of Brazil in its article 225, which are an ecologically balanced environment and, consequently, a healthy quality of life. so that sustainability can be implemented, reconciling economic development and the preservation of natural resources for the present and future generations. In this sense, the introduction of the selective tax is welcome, which will help in the graduation of the tax burden in order to lead society to adopt environmental protection as a priority.

The Selective Tax, dealt with in section VIII of article 153 of the Federal Constitution, is levied on the production, extraction, marketing or import of goods and services that are harmful to health or the environment.

For the purposes of the incidence of the selective tax, the following goods are considered harmful to health or the environment:

Product	Rate
Vehicles (except trucks)	The rate will be defined according to: • energy efficiency • recyclability of materials • gas emissions zero rate for • vehicles intended for taxi drivers • vehicles intended for people with disabilities • sustainable light vehicles
Vessels and aircraft	rate set based on environmental sustainability criteria
cigarettes and smoking products	• staggered rates between 2029 and 2033 • progressive reduction of ICMS will be incorporated during this period
Alcoholic beverages	rate set according to the alcohol content
sugary drinks	rate will be defined according to specific regulations
lotteries, betting and fantasy sports games	rate will be set according to specific legislation
minerals (except for export)	maximum rate of 0.25 %

The inclusion of sugary drinks in the list of products subject to the selective tax is good news because these products often contain high levels of sugar in their composition, and the main problems associated with the consumption of these drinks are related to weight gain, which can lead to obesity and, consequently, chronic diseases such as diabetes.[30] It is important to highlight that, in addition to increasing the tax, it would be important to adopt measures such as, for example, front-of-package labeling, which indicates on a label on the front of the packaging which substances are present in excess in the goods, such as saturated fats, sugar and sodium, so that all consumers are aware of the nutritional quality of what they are purchasing.

I agree with the Consumer Protection Institute (IDEC)[31] in that ultra-processed foods should also be included in the list of products subject to selective taxation because these foods (stuffed cookies, snacks and instant noodles) cause chronic diseases due to their high levels of sodium, sugar and saturated fat. However, this has not happened. The resources collected through taxation should be invested in public policies that promote the health of the population, such as healthy eating programs and incentives for physical activity and improvements to the health system. However, unfortunately, the legislation approved does not guarantee that the resources will be used for these purposes.

Trucks were excluded from the selective tax because the National Congress understood that, if they were included, there would be a major impact on the prices of goods because freight would be increased and, considering that, unlike European countries that transport most goods by train, in Brazil trucks transport goods by highways, the economy would be greatly impacted as a whole.

Electric cars were included in the selective tax because the national congress understood that the impact of pollution from battery disposal will be high.

Fuels, unlike many countries, were excluded from the selective tax. I believe that Brazil missed a great opportunity to align itself with the most advanced policies regarding the promotion of alternatives for the use of renewable energy.

---

30 Study finds link between consumption of sugary drinks and increase in type 2 diabetes. For more information look at: https:// www.cfn.org.br/index.php/noticias/estudo-aponta-ligacao-entre-consumo-de-bebidas-adocadas-e-aumento-de-casos-de-diabetes-tipo-2/#:~:text=Um%20estudo%20publicado%20recentemente%20na,refrigerantes%2C%20sucos%20industrializados%20e%20energéticos.

31 For more information look at: https://idec.org.br/reforma-tributaria.

Representatives of companies responsible for the production of mineral goods argued that the consumption and production of mineral goods should not be discouraged, since the sector produces high income, jobs and attracts investment to the country. Therefore, burdening it with the selective tax would promote what is called "investor flight". The representatives also argued that the incidence of the new tax would make operations extremely expensive, which would have an impact on the entire production chain and would even affect the end consumer, since the extra cost would naturally be passed on. However, these arguments did not convince the National Congress, which decided to tax mineral assets because the extraction of these assets causes negative impacts on the environment.

The Selective Tax will be levied only once on the good or service, and any type of use of tax credits from previous transactions or generation of credits for subsequent transactions is prohibited. The Federal Tax Administration is responsible for administering and monitoring the Selective Tax.

The event giving rise to the Selective Tax is considered to have occurred at the time of:

I – the first supply of the good for any reason, including those arising from the legal transactions mentioned below:
  I – purchase and sale, exchange or barter, payment in kind and other types of alienation;
  II – lease;
  III – licensing, concession, assignment;
  IV – onerous loan;
  V – donation with consideration for the benefit of the donor;
  VI – onerous institution of real rights;
  VII – lease, including commercial lease;
  and VIII – provision of services.
II – the purchase at public auction;
III – the non-onerous transfer of the good produced;
IV – the incorporation of the good into the fixed assets by the manufacturer;
V – the extraction of a mineral good;
VI – the consumption of the good by the manufacturer;
VII – the supply or payment for the service, whichever occurs first;
VIII – the import of goods and services.

The Selective Tax does not apply to:

I – exports abroad of the following goods: coal, vehicles, vessels and aircraft, smoking products, alcoholic beverages, sugary beverages, mineral goods, prediction contests and fantasy sports.
II – transactions involving electric energy and telecommunications; and
III – goods and services whose rates are reduced in IBS/CBS, i.e.:
a) – education services;
b) – health services;
c) – medical devices;
d) – accessibility devices for people with disabilities;
e) – medicines;
f) – basic menstrual health care products;
g) – urban, semi-urban and metropolitan public transport services for road and subway passengers;
h) – food for human consumption;
i) – agricultural, aquaculture, fishing, forestry and extractive plant products *in natura;*
j) – agricultural and aquaculture inputs;
k) – national artistic, cultural, event, journalistic and audiovisual productions, sports activities and institutional communication;
l) – goods and services related to national sovereignty and security, information security and cybersecurity.

The calculation basis for the Selective Tax is:

I – the sales value in the commercialization;
II – the auction value in the auction;
III – the reference value in:
a) non-onerous transaction or consumption of the good;
b) extraction of minerals; or
c) sale of tobacco products;
IV – the accounting value of incorporation of the produced good into fixed assets.

In the sale of goods subject to the *ad valorem* tax rate, the calculation basis is the full amount charged in the transaction for any reason, including the amount corresponding to:

I – increases resulting from adjustments to the transaction value;
II – interest, fines, increases and charges;
III – discounts granted under conditions;

IV – transportation value charged as part of the transaction value, whether the transportation is carried out by the supplier itself or on its behalf and order;

V – taxes and public prices, including tariffs, levied on the transaction or borne by the supplier;

and VI – other amounts charged or received as part of the transaction value, including insurance and fees.

In the case of sales between related parties, in the event of incidence subject to the *ad valorem* rate and in the absence of the reference value, the calculation basis must not be lower than the market value of the goods, understood as the value charged in comparable transactions between unrelated parties.

Related parties are considered when at least one of them is subject to influence, exercised directly or indirectly by another party, which may lead to the establishment of terms and conditions in their transactions that differ from those that would be established between unrelated parties in comparable transactions.

The following are considered related parties:

I – the controlling company and its subsidiaries;

II – affiliates;

III – entities included in the consolidated financial statements or that would be included if the ultimate controlling company of the multinational group of which they are part prepared such statements if its capital were traded on the securities markets of its jurisdiction of residence;

IV – entities, when one of them has the right to receive, directly or indirectly, at least 25% (twenty-five percent) of the profits of the other or its assets in the event of liquidation;

V – entities that are, directly or indirectly, under common control or in which the same partner, shareholder or owner holds 20% (twenty percent) or more of the share capital of each;

VI – entities in which the same partners or shareholders, or their spouses, partners, relatives, by blood or by marriage, up to the third degree, hold at least 20% (twenty percent) of the share capital of each;

and VII – the entity and the individual who is the spouse, partner or relative, by blood or by marriage, up to the third degree, of a board member, director or controller of that entity.

The rates of the Selective Tax applicable to vehicles will be established by ordinary law. The rates on vehicles will be graduated in relation to each vehicle according to its classification in the following criteria, according to ordinary law:

I – vehicle power;
II – energy efficiency;
III – structural performance and assistive driving technologies;
IV – recyclability of materials;
V – carbon footprint;
VI – technological density;
VII – carbon dioxide emissions (energy-environmental efficiency), considering the well-to-wheel cycle;
VIII – vehicle recyclability;
IX – completion of manufacturing stages in the country;
and X – vehicle category.

The rates of the Selective Tax applicable to aircraft and vessels will be established by ordinary law and may be graduated according to environmental sustainability criteria under the terms of the ordinary law. The ordinary law may provide for a zero rate for vessels and aircraft with zero carbon dioxide emissions or with high energy-environmental efficiency.

The Selective Tax rates established in transactions involving extracted mineral goods shall respect the maximum percentage of 0.25% (twenty-five hundredths of a percent).

The taxpayer of the Selective Tax is:

I – the manufacturer, in the first commercialization, in the incorporation of the good into the fixed assets, in the transfer of the good in a non-onerous transaction or in the consumption of the good;
II – the importer in the entry of the good of foreign origin into the national territory;
III – the successful bidder in the auction;
IV – the extractive producer who carries out the extraction; or
V – the service provider, even if resident or domiciled abroad.

The following are required to pay the Selective Tax as responsible parties, without prejudice to other cases provided for by law and the application of the penalty of forfeiture:

I – the transporter, in relation to taxed products that he transports unaccompanied by tax documentation proving their origin;

II – the possessor or holder, in relation to taxed products that he possesses or keeps for the purpose of sale or industrialization, unaccompanied by tax documentation proving their origin;

III – the owner, possessor, transporter or any other holder of national products leaving the manufacturer with immunity for export, found in the country in a different situation, except when the products are in transit.

4. Conclusion

The initiative to tax goods that are harmful to the health of the population and goods that are harmful to the environment is very welcome. The selective tax will come into effect in 2027. By then, the rates to be used must be detailed.

The selective tax will play an important role in tax policy, not only as a source of revenue, but also as an instrument of social and economic regulation. In Brazil, the selective tax proposal aims to align the country with international taxation practices that seek to influence individual behavior in favor of public health and the environment. It is also important to note that Brazil will host COP 30 in Belém do Pará. This event will position the country as an important player in the global context on the issue of climate change, so that all measures aimed at achieving the goals that guarantee the sustainability of the planet should be applauded and supported.

Chapter 3
Players of the Green Deal: Private Enterprises and Policy Makers

von Ralf B. Schlemminger[1]

Nachhaltigkeitsmanagement und -reporting in der EU

Abstract

Sustainability management is increasingly developing into a "licence to operate". Socio-political framework conditions and expectations of customers and investors are responsible drivers. In addition to this there are the globally established standards for sustainability management, the increasing transparency of corporate sustainability practices and, in particular, the Corporate Sustainability Reporting Directive (CSRD) in the EU, which will come into effect from 2024. In future, up to 50,000 companies in the EU – compared to the current maximum of 12,000 companies – will be obliged to report in detail on their sustainability practices in their management report. However, if one follows the draft of the omnibus package for the de-bureaucratisation of sustainability reporting in the EU, the number of users is reduced to around 7,000. Nevertheless, this development marks a significant step towards the equalization of financial and sustainability reporting. Such reporting must not only be ensured, but also the structures of sustainability management and controlling and the value setting within companies must be developed further.

Keywords: definitions of sustainability, SDGs, triple bottom line, licence to operate, ESG ratings, NFRD, CSRD, ESRS, GRI, EFRAG, materiality analysis, five-stage model for a sustainable company

---

1 Prof. Dr. Ralf B. Schlemminger, Six Sigma Green Belt, lehrt Allgemeine Betriebswirtschaftslehre, insbesondere Controlling und Rechnungswesen an der Hochschule Bremen (seit 2015). Als gelernter Bankkaufmann und Diplom-Ökonom hat er zuvor über 20 Jahre in der Kreditwirtschaft gearbeitet und dort verschiedene (Führungs-)Funktionen innegehabt. Er ist Mitglied im Internationalen Controllerverein (ICV) und im Arbeitskreis der Controlling-Professuren an Hochschulen (AKC). Seine Forschungsschwerpunkte sind das strategische und das Nachhaltigkeitscontrolling, zu denen er regelmäßig Veröffentlichungen vornimmt. Kontakt: ralf.schlemminger@hs-bremen.de; HSB-Webseite: https://www.hs-bremen.de/person/rschlemminger/ .

A. Einleitung

Ein Nachhaltigkeitsmanagement entwickelt sich immer mehr zu einer „licence to operate“. Gesellschaftspolitische Rahmenbedingungen sowie Erwartungen von Kunden und Investoren sind verantwortliche Treiber. Anhand von sieben Fragen mit entsprechenden Antworten soll die Entwicklung des Nachhaltigkeitsmanagements und des -reportings in der EU aufgezeigt werden. Dabei wird der Bogen von einem Verständnis der Nachhaltigkeit und deren Entwicklung über die Darstellung der ab 2024 wirksam werdenden Corporate Sustainability Reporting Directive (CSRD) in der EU bis hin zur Implementierung bzw. Weiterentwicklung eines entsprechenden Sustainability Managements und Controllings gespannt.

B. Fragen und Antworten

1. Was ist unter Nachhaltigkeit bzw. nachhaltigem Management zu verstehen?

Es gibt verschiedene Ansätze, Nachhaltigkeit zu definieren. Einen grundlegenden Ansatz hat Hans Carl von Carlowitz (1645 – 1714), Oberberghauptmann aus Freiberg (Sachsen), in seinem Werk „Sylvicultura oeconomica“ geliefert. Er gilt als Schöpfer des forstwirtschaftlichen Nachhaltigkeitsprinzips:

> *Es sollte nur so viel Holz – damals der wichtigste Rohstoff – geschlagen werden, „wie durch planmäßige Aufforstung, durch Säen und Pflanzen nachwachsen konnte“ (O. V., 2015a).*

Der eigentliche Anstoß zur intensiven – auch wissenschaftlichen – Beschäftigung mit einer nachhaltigen Entwicklung ist in der Veröffentlichung des Buches „Grenzen des Wachstums“ von D. Meadows (und weiteren) im Jahre 1972 zu sehen; diese Ur-Studie zur Nachhaltigkeit wurde vom Club of Rome initiiert und gefördert (vgl. o. V., 2015b). Im Zuge der Befassung mit diesem Thema hat dann später die UN-(United-Nations-)Weltkommission für Umwelt und Entwicklung ihren sog. „Brundtland-Bericht“ im Jahre 1987 herausgegeben; die ehemalige norwegische Ministerpräsidentin Gro Harlem Brundtland hat diese Kommission geleitet. Dort wird Nachhaltigkeit auf die zentrale, allgemeingültige Formel gebracht:

> *„Eine nachhaltige Entwicklung ist eine Entwicklung, die die Bedürfnisse der heutigen Generation befriedigt, ohne die Fähigkeit künftiger Generationen zu gefährden, ihre eigenen Bedürfnisse zu befriedigen“* (United Nations, 1987).

Dieser allgemeine Definitionsansatz ist 2015 von der UN spezifiziert und in 17 weltweit gültige Nachhaltigkeitsziele überführt worden (s. Darst. 1).

Darst. 1: UN-Nachhaltigkeitsziele (Sustainable Development Goals, SDGs) (Die Bundesregierung, 2015)

Was ist vor dem Hintergrund dieses Nachhaltigkeitsverständnisses unter einem nachhaltigen Management, einer nachhaltigen Unternehmensführung, zu verstehen? – Eine Unternehmensführung wird dann als nachhaltig bezeichnet, wenn sie im Sinne des Triple-Bottom-Line-Ansatzes gleichermaßen ökonomische, soziale und ökologische Ziele verfolgt. Man spricht auch von einem Profit-People-Planet-(3-P-)Ansatz (s. Darst. 2). Hierzu gibt es allerdings auch eine modifizierte Variante mit der Vorrangstellung ökonomischer Zielkriterien vor den anderen beiden (vgl. Hornung, 2022).

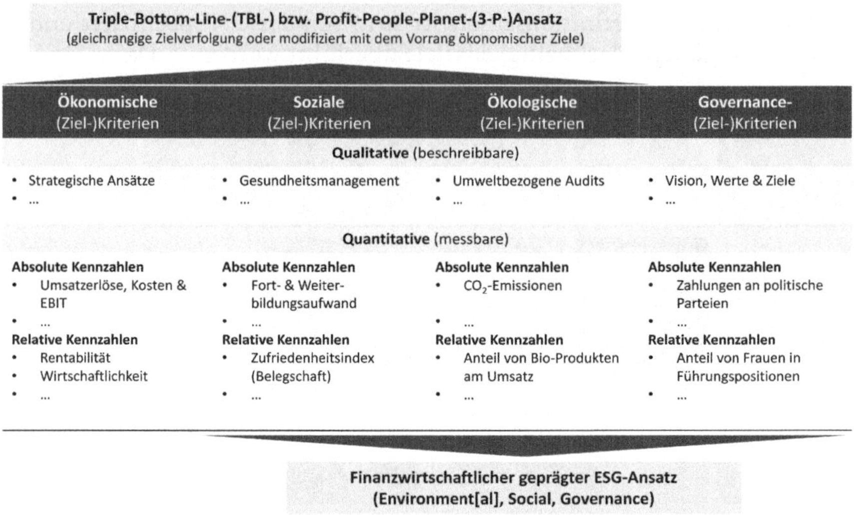

Darst. 2: Kriterien einer nachhaltigen Unternehmensführung (Biel, 2023, S. 79, in Anlehnung an Erchinger et al., 2022, S. 9, leicht modifiziert)

Neben diesem TBL- bzw. 3-P-Ansatz wird vielfach der sog. ESG-Ansatz zitiert, um eine nachhaltige Unternehmensführung zu kennzeichnen. Nach diesem finanzwirtschaftlich geprägten Ansatz liegt dann ein nachhaltiges Management vor, wenn Unternehmen ökologische (environment[al]), soziale (social) Zielkriterien sowie Kriterien einer „guten" Unternehmensführung (Governance) gerecht werden. Im strengen Sinne ist dies nicht ganz korrekt, da die ökonomische Dimension fehlt. Denn was haben Unternehmen und allgemein eine Gesellschaft davon, wenn in einem hohen Maße sozial- und umweltverträglich produziert wird, die Produkte des Unternehmens jedoch immer weniger gekauft werden und somit die Unternehmensexistenz bedroht ist?

2. Warum ist Nachhaltigkeit bedeutsam?

Warum nachhaltiges Wirtschaften gesamtgesellschaftlich bedeutsam ist, lässt sich anhand vieler Zustandsbeschreibungen des Planeten Erde beschreiben. Der sog. Erdüberlastungstag verdeutlicht sehr eindringlich, dass wir Menschen ökologisch auf Pump leben und mehr natürliche Ressourcen verbrauchen, als die Erde in einem Jahr zur Verfügung stellt (s. Darst. 3). 2023 lebten die Menschen so, „als stünden ihnen 1,7 Planeten zur Verfügung. Gehe der Ressourcenverbrauch so weiter, würden bereits 2030 zwei Erden verbraucht sein“ (Tagesschau, 2023).

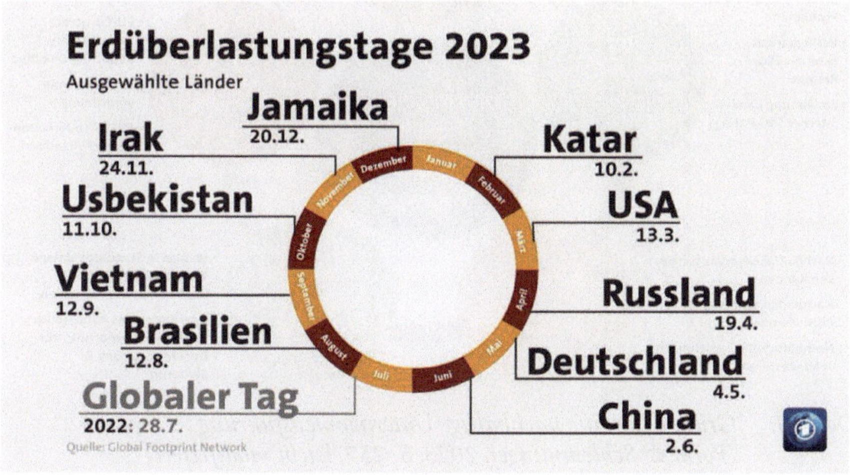

Darst. 3: Erdüberlastungstage (Steininger, 2023)

Weitere gesamtgesellschaftliche Gründe für nachhaltiges Handeln sind:

- der Klimawandel, sprich die Erderwärmung durch die Emission von Treibhausgasen (CO_2, Methan, Lachgas),
- die in diesem Zusammenhang stehenden Wetterextreme, d. h. sintflutartige Regenfälle, extreme Kälte- und Hitzeperioden sowie Stürme und Überflutungen,
- das Auftauen des Permafrosts bzw. die Arktiserwärmung, was zur Gefährdung von Küstendörfern führt, und
- die politischen Unruhen durch die Vergrößerung der Kluft zwischen Arm und Reich, die auf den klimabedingten Wegfall der Bewirtschaftungsmöglichkeiten ganzer Landstriche zurückzuführen ist.

Vor dem Hintergrund dieses negativen Zustands der Erde ist eine nachhaltige Führung von Unternehmen geboten. Mehr und mehr stellt ein solches Management eine „licence to operate“ dar. Im Detail lassen sich Gründe aus fünf Bereichen aufführen, wie sie in der Darst. 4 zum Ausdruck gebracht werden (vgl. Form & Schlemminger, 2023, S. 257 f.).

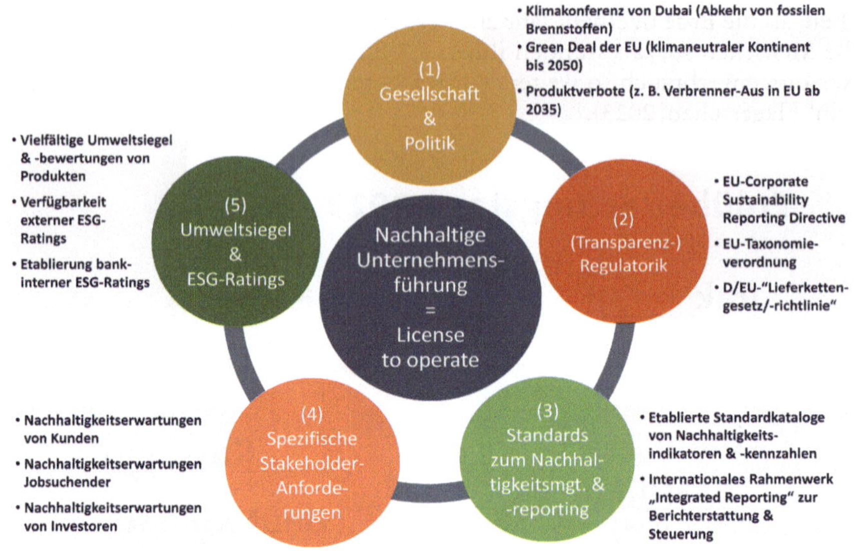

Darst. 4: Gründe für eine nachhaltige Unternehmensführung (Form & Schlemminger, 2023, S. 257, leicht modifiziert)

Gesellschaft und Politik (1) stellen immer mehr Nachhaltigkeitsanforderungen an unternehmerische Aktivitäten bzw. schaffen entsprechende Rahmenbedingungen. Ausdruck hierfür ist bspw. die weltweite Verständigung auf der Klimakonferenz in Dubai in 2023 über eine Abkehr von fossilen Brennstoffen, auch wenn es Kritikern nicht weit genug geht. Ein weiteres Beispiel ist die EU, die mit dem Green Deal einen klimaneutralen Kontinent bis 2050 anstrebt. In diesem Zusammenhang sind auch Produktverbote als Ausdruck des Nachhaltigkeitsanspruch einer Gesellschaft zu werten: Die EU beschloss in 2023 das faktische Aus des Verbrennungsmotors. Ab 2035 dürfen keine Pkw und Kleintransporter neu zugelassen werden, die $C0_2$ ausstoßen. Allerdings sind Verbrenner-Autos, die ausschließlich mit synthetisch erzeugten E-Fuels betankt werden, zulassungsfähig.

Die verschärfte (Transparenz-)Regulatorik (2) ist ein weiterer Grund, eine nachhaltige Unternehmensführung zu etablieren. Die Corporate Sustainability Reporting Directive (CSRD) in der EU, die EU-Taxonomieverordnung oder das deutsche „Lieferkettengesetz" bzw. die europäische „Lieferkettenrichtlinie" sind Beispiele einer solchen Regulierung (s. auch Frage 5).

Mittlerweile gibt es eine Reihe etablierter Standards zum Nachhaltigkeitsmanagement und –reporting (3). Hierzu gehören u.a. das internationale

Rahmenwerk „Integrated Reporting" oder Standardkataloge von Nachhaltigkeitsindikatoren und -kennzahlen auf globaler, europäischer oder deutscher Ebene (s. auch Frage 4).

Nicht zu vernachlässigen sind die spezifischen Stakeholderanforderungen (4) an die nachhaltige Ausrichtung von Unternehmen. Kunden erwarten nachhaltige Produkte bzw. Produktionsverfahren. Nach der GfK-Consumer-Life-Studie (30.000 Befragte aus 25 Ländern) ist Nachhaltigkeit bei den Deutschen ein zentrales Thema, wobei die Gruppe ökologisch orientierter Menschen unterschiedliche Ausprägungen aufweist, auf die das deutsche Marktforschungsinstitut GfK hinweist:

> *Die Konsumenten aus dem Segment Glamour Green mit einem Anteil von 30 Prozent „verzichten zwar auf wenig, bevorzugen beim Kauf aber Produkte mit nachhaltigen Aspekten. Das nachhaltige Produkt muss nach außen wirken und ist vor allem ein Statussymbol. Im Gegensatz dazu steht beispielsweise der mit 23 Prozent vertretene Typ ‚Green in Deed', für den nicht nur ein Teilaspekt, sondern das ganze Produkt sowie das Unternehmen selbst möglichst umweltschonend sein müssen"* (GfK, 2021).

Neben den Kunden scheint sich ebenfalls die Einstellung der Investoren geändert zu haben. Larry Fink, Chef des Vermögensverwalters Blackrock sagt einen fundamentalen Wandel der Finanzwelt voraus, was er in einem Brief an die Vorstandsvorsitzenden 2020 zum Ausdruck gebracht hat:

> *Der Klimawandel ist für die langfristigen Aussichten von Unternehmen zu einem entscheidenden Faktor geworden … ich bin überzeugt, dass wir vor einer fundamentalen Umgestaltung der Finanzwelt stehen … Künftig werden wir Nachhaltigkeit zu einem wesentlichen Bestandteil unserer Portfoliokonstruktion [machen] … uns von Anlagen trennen, die ein erhebliches Nachhaltigkeitsrisiko darstellen, wie zum Beispiel Wertpapiere von Kohleproduzenten"* (Blackrock, 2020).

Kunden und Investoren können sich in einem zunehmenden Maße über den Umweltbezug von Produkten oder ganzer Unternehmen informieren. Aufschluss hierüber sollen Umweltlabels und Nachhaltigkeits- oder ESG-Ratings geben (5). Zu den Umweltsiegeln bei Produkten muss man allerdings sagen, dass nicht immer „Öko" drin ist, wo „Öko" draufsteht. Die ESG-Ratings sind mittlerweile etablierte Praxis in der Finanzwirtschaft. Ratings anerkannter Nachhaltigkeits-Ratingagenturen stellen ihre Einstufungen der Öffentlichkeit über das Internet zur Verfügung. Auszüge aus dem Best-in-Class-Rating von dem deutschen Versicherungskonzern Allianz, vergeben von Morgan Stanley Capital International (MSCI), einem Research- und Servicedienstleister für die Investment Community, gehen aus der Darst. 5 hervor. Mittels Buchstaben wird die Nachhaltigkeitseinstufung zum Ausdruck gebracht.

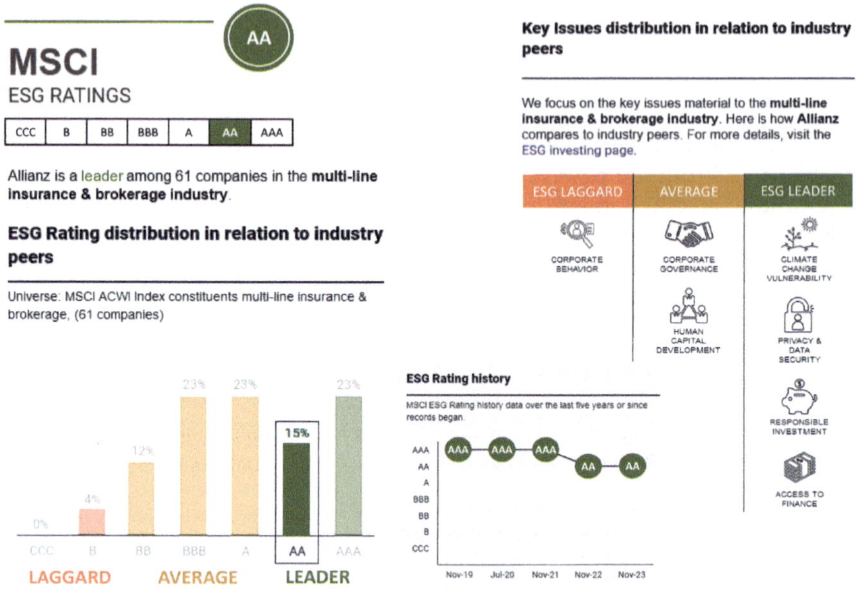

Darst. 5: MSCI-Best-in-Class-Rating der Allianz SE (MSCI, 2024, leicht modifiziert)

Kritiker dieser Art von Ratings bemängeln, dass der Beste immer noch unter Nachhaltigkeitsgesichtspunkten bedenklich wirtschaften kann. Eine Alternative stellen die Ratings von Sustainalytics dar, das zum Fondbewertungshaus Mornigstar gehört. Sie vergeben branchenübergreifende, absolute Bewertungen in Form von Risikopunkten. Wie dies bei der Allianz aussieht, verdeutlicht die Darst. 6.

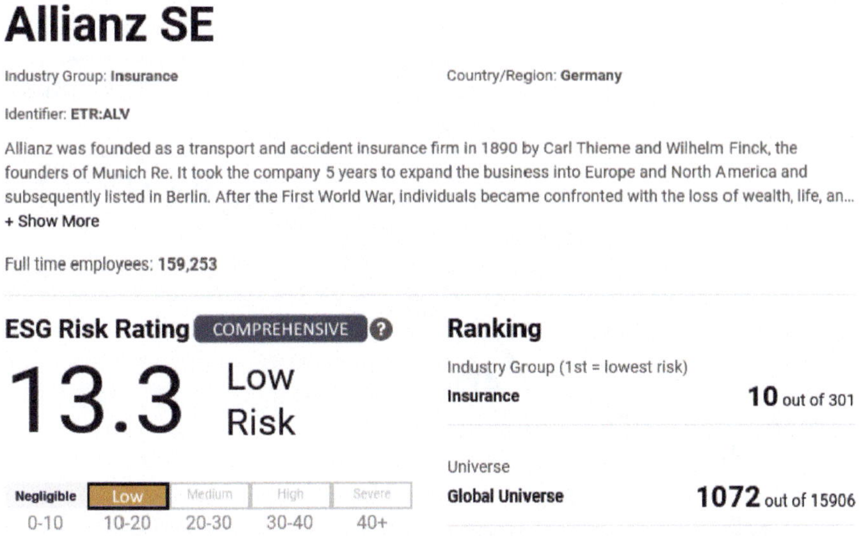

Darst. 6: Sustainalytics-Rating der Allianz SE (Sustainalytics, 2024, leicht modifiziert)

Auch hier gibt es Kritik: „Äpfel werden mit Birnen verglichen" – eine Zementfabrik kann gar nicht so umweltschonend produzieren, wie z. B. eine Wirtschaftsprüfungsgesellschaft in der Lage ist, ihre Prüfungs- und Beratungsdienstleistungen zu erbringen.

3. Welche Nachhaltigkeitsentwicklungen sind bei Unternehmen auszumachen?

Gemessen am Nachhaltigkeitsreporting ist Nachhaltigkeit bei den Unternehmen weltweit angekommen. Mittlerweile berichten 96 % der größten 250 Unternehmen über ihre ökonomische, soziale und ökologische Entwicklung. Vor rund 20 Jahren waren es lediglich 35 %, wie es aus einer Studie der Wirtschaftsprüfungs- und Beratungsgesellschaft KPMG (vgl. 2022a, S. 13) hervorgeht (s. Darst. 7).

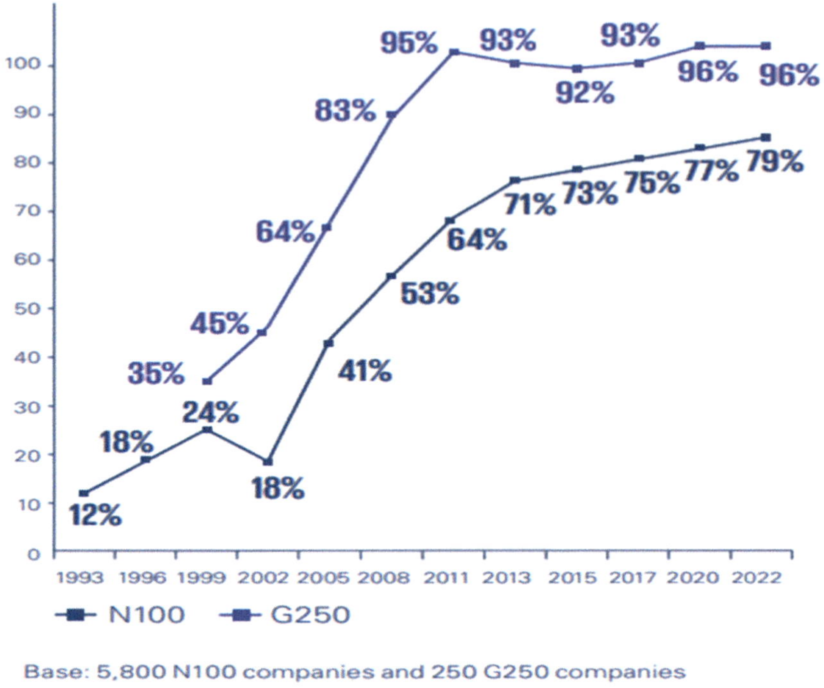

Darst. 7: Globale Entwicklung des Nachhaltigkeitsreportings (KPMG, 2022a, S. 13)

Eine deutliche Zunahme der Berichterstattung ist ebenfalls bei den 100 größten Unternehmen aus 52 Ländern zu verzeichnen; 79% konnten 2022 Nachhaltigkeitsberichte vorweisen. Allerdings: Es gibt Mängel im Hinblick auf Vollständigkeit, Vergleichbarkeit und Verlässlichkeit, da unterschiedliche Rechtsnormen und Kommunikationspolitiken vorliegen. Die Gefahr des Greenwashings besteht. Eine Studie der Wirtschaftsprüfungs- und Beratungsgesellschaft PwC bringt diese Problematik auf den Punkt:

> *„Rund acht von zehn Investor:innen vermuten ‚Greenwashing' in der ESG-Berichterstattung – das sollte Unternehmen und Regulatoren aufhorchen lassen. Das fehlende Vertrauen ist vor allem deshalb besorgniserregend, weil Nachhaltigkeitsinformationen immer häufiger die Entscheidungen von Anleger:innen und anderen Stakeholdern beeinflussen"* (PwC, 2022a).

Allerdings sind Harmonisierungs- und Standardisierungstrends beim Nachhaltigkeitsmangement und -reporting unverkennbar, wie dies der Wirtschaftswissenschaftler Klaus Schwab, Gründer des Weltwirtschaftsforums in Davos, betont:

> *"In den letzten Jahren haben Unternehmen einen verstärkten Fokus auf ökologische, soziale und andere nichtfinanzielle Faktoren gelegt, die für ihre langfristige Rentabilität und ihren Erfolg entscheidend sind. Verstärkt durch die zunehmende Nachfrage der Stakeholder nach konsistenten und vergleichbaren Daten gibt es nun eine Bewegung hin zu einer stärker harmonisierten nichtfinanziellen Berichterstattung auf der Grundlage gemeinsamer Metriken"* (KPMG, 2022a, S. 22).

4. Welche Standards haben sich bisher entwickelt?

Mittlerweile haben sich eine ganze Reihe von Rahmen- bzw. Regelwerken und Standards zum Nachhaltigkeitsmanagement und -reporting auf globaler und europäischer Ebene entwickelt. Europäische Unternehmen sollten nicht nur die europäischen Regelungen beachten, sondern ebenfalls die auf der globalen Ebene miterfassen. Denn diese fundieren vielfach europäische Standards. Zudem sind nationale Standards von Bedeutung. Eine Auswahl von globalen, europäischen und deutschen Nachhaltigkeitsrahmenwerken und -standards ist in der Darst. 8 wiedergeben.

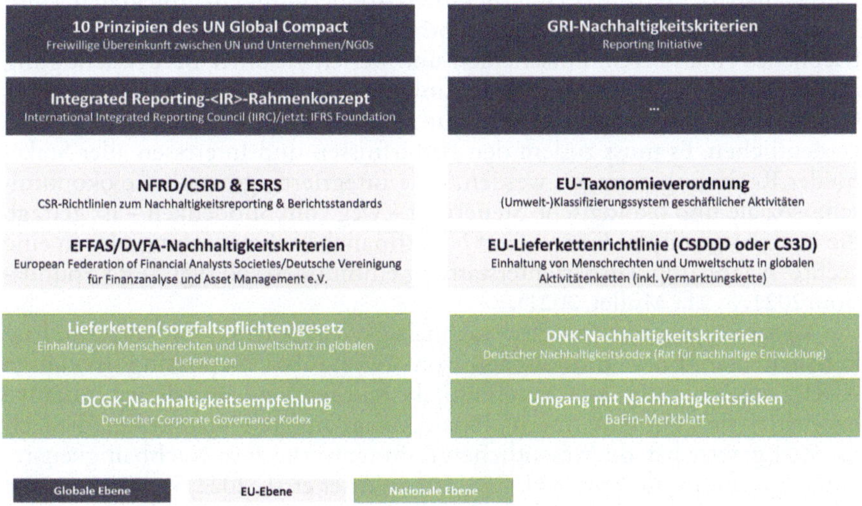

Darst. 8: Rahmenwerke und Standards zum Nachhaltigkeitsmanagement und -reporting

Auf **globaler Ebene** stellen die **zehn Prinzipien** zu Menschenrechten, Arbeitsnormen, Umweltschutz und Korruptionsbekämpfung des **UN Global Compact** einen Meilenstein in diesem Entwicklungsprozess dar; diese Initiative beruht auf den Vorschlag des UN-Generalsekretärs Kofi Annan im Januar 1999 auf dem Weltwirtschaftsforum in Davos. UN Global Compact gilt als die weltweit größte Initiative für verantwortungsvolle und nachhaltige Unternehmensführung, deren **Mission auch die 17 Nachhaltigkeitsziele der UN** umfasst. Diese Initiative stellt eine Kooperations-, Lern- und Dialogplattform dar, bestehend aus über 24.500 Mitgliedsunternehmen und -organisationen aus über 160 Ländern mit mehr als 60 lokalen Netzwerken (Stand: Februar 2024). Für Mitglieder besteht eine Verpflichtung zur jährlichen Berichterstattung (Communication on Progress, CoP) über ihren Fortschritt bei der Umsetzung der 10 Prinzipien und ihre Aktivitäten zur Förderung einer nachhaltigen Entwicklung (vgl. UN Gobal Compact, 2024; Engel et al., 2022, S. 100 ff.).

Ein weiteres bedeutsames Standardwerk ist das **Integrated-Reporting-<IR>-Rahmenkonzept** vom **International Integrated Reporting Council (IIRC)**, jetzt in der Verantwortung von der **IFRS Foundation.** Selbst wenn im Titel der Begriff Reporting steht, geht es bei diesem prinzipienbasierten Regelwerk nicht nur um eine Verzahnung von klassischen Finanz- mit Nachhaltigkeitsberichten eines Unternehmens, sondern um ein „Integrated Thinking". Wofür steht dieses Denkkonzept? Integrated Thinking steht für ein betriebliches Analysieren, Entscheiden und Berichten unter Berücksichtigung der Verbindungen und Wechselwirkungen wertschaffender Faktoren einer Organisation. Dabei sind Wertschaffung oder -vernichtung über die Zeit zu verdeutlichen. Es muss zudem den Bedürfnissen und Interessen aller Stakeholder Rechnung getragen werden. Eine integrierte, gesamthafte ökonomische, soziale und ökologische Steuerung – weg vom Silodenken – ist gefragt, die in eine verknüpfte Finanz- und Nichtfinanzberichterstattung, also in eine „echte" Nachhaltigkeitsberichterstattung einmünden soll (vgl. IFRS Foundation, 2021, S. 2 f.; Müller, 2021).

Weltweit prägend für das Nachhaltigkeitsreporting sind **Nachhaltigkeitskriterien bzw. -indikatoren** von der **Global Reporting Initiative (GRI)**, die erstmalig 2000 veröffentlicht worden sind. Bei dieser Initiative handelt es sich um eine internationale, unabhängige Organisation, die sich das Ziel gesetzt hat, die wesentlichen Rahmenwerke zum Nachhaltigkeitsreporting zu harmonisieren (vgl. GRI, 2024a; Auer et al., 2022, S. 129). Insofern gibt es laufende Anpassungen, wobei aktuell an branchenspezifischen Standards gearbeitet wird (s. Darst. 9). Diese Standards sind über das Internet frei verfügbar.

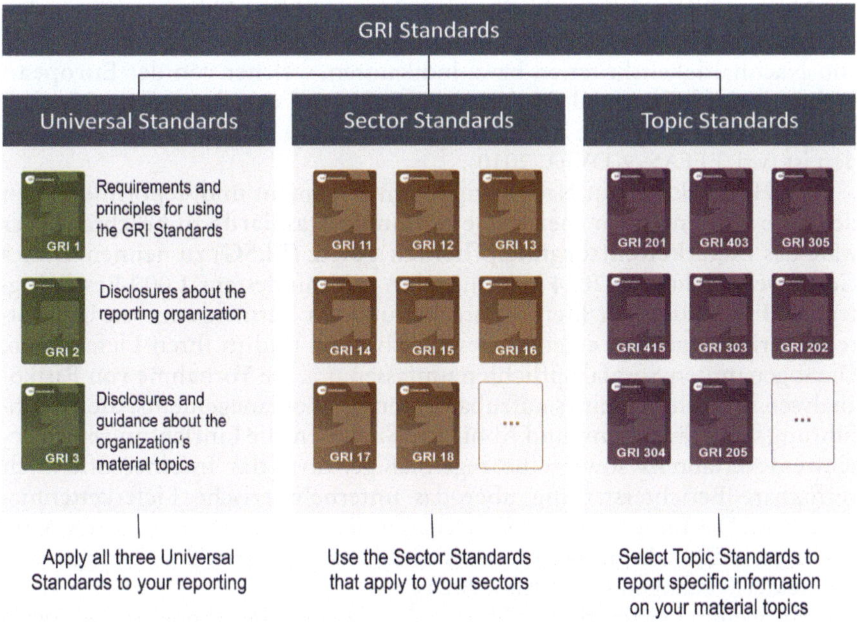

Darst. 9: GRI-Nachhaltigkeitskriterien bzw. -indikatoren (GRI, 2024b)

Die weltweite Anerkennung der GRI-Standards kann man daran festmachen, dass aus der Gruppe der 250 weltweit größten Unternehmen 78% der 240 mit einem Sustainability Reporting 2022 auf dieser Basis berichtet haben (vgl. KPMG, 2022a, S. 24).

Auf **europäischer Ebene** gibt es verbindlich anzuwendende Standards für ein Nachhaltigkeitsreporting. Hier ist die **Non-Financial Reporting Directive** (**NFRD**) zu nennen, die sog. CSR-Richtlinie 1.0, die mittlerweile durch die **Corporate Sustainability Reporting Directive** (**CSRD**) abgelöst worden ist. Da allerdings in Deutschland eine Umsetzung in Form einer HGB-Anpassung in 2024 nicht erfolgt ist, dürfen hiesige Unternehmen, die bislang zur Abgabe einer nichtfinanziellen Erklärung gemäß NFRD verpflichtet sind, weiterhin eine solche „einfache" Nachhaltigkeitsberichterstattung für das Geschäftsjahr 2024 vornehmen (vgl. Müller, 2025a). Ein weiteres Regelwerk ist die EU-**Taxonomieverordnung,** ein System zur Klassifizierung „grüner" Geschäftsaktivitäten. Dazu kommt die **EU-Lieferkettenrichtlinie** (**Corporate Sustainability Due Dilligence Directive, CSDDD oder CS3D**). Im Rahmen der Beantwortung der Frage 5 werden diese Standards näher beleuchtet.

Neben diesen Standards gibt es auf europäischer Ebene einen zu den GRI-Standards vergleichbaren, wenngleich etwa anders aufgebauten Katalog von Nachhaltigkeitskriterien bzw. -indikatoren, welcher von der **European Federation of Financial Societies** (**EFFAS**) und der **Deutschen Vereinigung für Finanzanalyse und Asset Management** (**DVFA**) aufgestellt worden ist (vgl. EFFAS & DVFA, 2010).

Im Hinblick auf ein Nachhaltigkeitsmanagement und -reporting haben deutsche Unternehmen spezifische **nationale Standards** zu beachten. Hier wäre das **Lieferketten(sorgfaltspflichten)gesetz** (**LkSG**) zu nennen. Dieses Gesetz verpflichtet ab 2024 Unternehmen mit mindestens 1.000 Beschäftigten zur Einhaltung der Menschenrechte und zur Vermeidung von Umweltrechtsverletzungen im eigenen Geschäftsbereich und in ihren Lieferketten. Die sogenannten Sorgfaltspflichten umfassen u.a. die Vornahme von Risikoanalysen im Rahmen eines aufzubauenden Risikomanagements, die Durchführung von Präventions- und Abhilfemaßnahmen, die Einrichtung eines Beschwerdeverfahrens sowie eine regelmäßige, über das Internet öffentlich verfügbare Berichterstattung über das unternehmerische Lieferkettenmanagement. Das Bundesamt für Wirtschaft und Ausfuhrkontrolle (BAFA) kontrolliert die Einhaltung des Gesetzes und kann bei Verstößen Zwangs- und Bußgelder verhängen (vgl. BAFA, 2024).

Ein weiterer bedeutsamer Standard auf nationaler Ebene ist der **Deutscher Corporate Governance Kodex** (**DCGK**). Es handelt sich hierbei um ein „Best-Practise"-Regelwerk über „gute" Leitung und Überwachung deutscher börsennotierter Gesellschaften mit Wiedergabe gesetzlicher Vorschriften, Empfehlungen („Soll-"Vorschriften) sowie Anregungen („Sollte-"Vorschriften). Die Kodex-Empfehlungen und -Anregungen sind zwar nicht verbindlich, es kommt jedoch gemäß § 161 AktG das Comply-or-Explain-Prinzip zum Tragen: Unternehmen müssen danach eine sog. Entsprechenserklärung abgeben und dabei Empfehlungs-Abweichungen samt Begründungen auflisten. Im DCGK ist mittlerweile eine nachhaltige Unternehmensführung in Form einer Empfehlung verankert:

> *„Der Vorstand soll die mit den Sozial- und Umweltfaktoren verbundenen Risiken und Chancen für das Unternehmen sowie die ökologischen und sozialen Auswirkungen der Unternehmenstätigkeit systematisch identifizieren und bewerten. In der Unternehmensstrategie sollen neben den langfristigen wirtschaftlichen Zielen auch ökologische und soziale Ziele angemessen berücksichtigt werden. Die Unternehmensplanung soll entsprechende finanzielle und nachhaltigkeitsbezogene Ziele umfassen"* (Regierungskommission Deutscher Corporate Governance Kodex, 2022).

Das **Merkblatt zum Umgang mit Nachhaltigkeitsrisiken der Bundesanstalt für Finanzdienstleistungsaufsicht** (**BaFin**) sollten deutsche Unternehmen ebenfalls beachten. Offiziell stellt dieses Merkblatt lediglich eine Orientierungshilfe zum Management dieser Risiken sowie ein Kompendium unverbindlicher Good-Practice-Ansätze im Umgang mit Nachhaltigkeitsrisiken für Kreditinstitute, Versicherungen und weitere Finanzinstitutionen dar (vgl. BaFin, 2020). Gleichwohl schlägt dieses Rahmenwerk auf deutsche Unternehmen durch, da sie im hohen Maße Fremdkapital und in gewissen Umfängen Versicherungsleistungen benötigen. Der Stellenwert einer Identifikation und Bewertung von Nachhaltigkeitsrisiken in den Kredit- und Versicherungsbewilligungsprozessen sollte daher weiter an Bedeutung gewinnen.

Analog zu den GRI-Standards auf globaler und den EFFAS/DVFA-KPIs auf europäischer Ebene gibt es auf nationaler Ebene einen Katalog von Nachhaltigkeitskriterien bzw. -indikatoren: den **Deutschen Nachhaltigkeitskodex** (**DNK**) vom **Rat für Nachhaltige Entwicklung** (**RNE**). Mit diesem Kodex werden deutschen Unternehmen unterstützt, Nachhaltigkeitsstrategien zu entwickeln und in die Nachhaltigkeitsberichterstattung einzusteigen. Auf der DNK-Webseite werden vielfältige Erklärungsdokumente zu europäischen Regelwerken bereitgestellt, Querverweise zu GRI- und EFFAS/DVFA-Indikatoren aufgezeigt sowie eine Datenbank über Nachhaltigkeitsberichte nach DNK-Standard von über 1.200 Unternehmen zur Verfügung gestellt (Stand: April 2024; vgl. RNE, 2024a).

5. Nachhaltigkeitsreporting: Welche EU-Anforderungen sind zu erfüllen?

In der EU ist 2014 mit der **Non-Financial Reporting Directive** (**NFRD**), der CSR-Richtlinie 1.0, ein verbindlicher Rahmen zur Nachhaltigkeitsberichterstattung geschaffen worden. Diese Richtlinie ist in Deutschland mit dem CSR-Richtlinien-Umsetzungsgesetz (CSR-RUG) in nationales Recht überführt worden. Unter dem Gesichtspunkt der Wesentlichkeit haben bestimmte Unternehmen neben einer kurzen Geschäftsmodell-Beschreibung eine sog. **nichtfinanzielle Erklärung** zu Umwelt-, Arbeitnehmer-, Sozial-, Menschenrechts- und Korruptions- bzw. Bestechungsbelangen abzugeben; diese ist im Lagebericht oder als gesonderter Bericht zu veröffentlichen (vgl. Müller & Stawinoga, 2022). Details zu Berichtsumfang und Anwenderkreis gehen aus der Darst. 10 hervor.

Darst. 10: NFRD und CSRD im Vergleich (Koch et al., 2024, S. 63, in Anlehnung an Aschfalk-Evertz, 2022, S. 1202ff.; RNE, 2024a; KPMG, 2022b; Müller & Stawinoga, 2022, leicht modifiziert)

Noch ein Hinweis zur **EU-Taxonomie-Verordnung:** Diese Verordnung umfasst ein System zur Klassifizierung ökologischer Aktivitäten sowie eine Pflicht zur Veröffentlichung nachhaltiger („grüner") Anteile an Umsatzerlösen, Investitions- (capital expenditures, CapEx) und Betriebsausgaben (operational expenditures, OpEx) im Rahmen der nichtfinanziellen Erklärung. Die Verordnung ist Teil des Aktionsplans zum nachhaltigen Wachstum und zielt auf eine Umlenkung der Kapitalflüsse in nachhaltige Wirtschaftsaktivitäten ab. Wie sind diese grünen Anteile zu ermitteln?

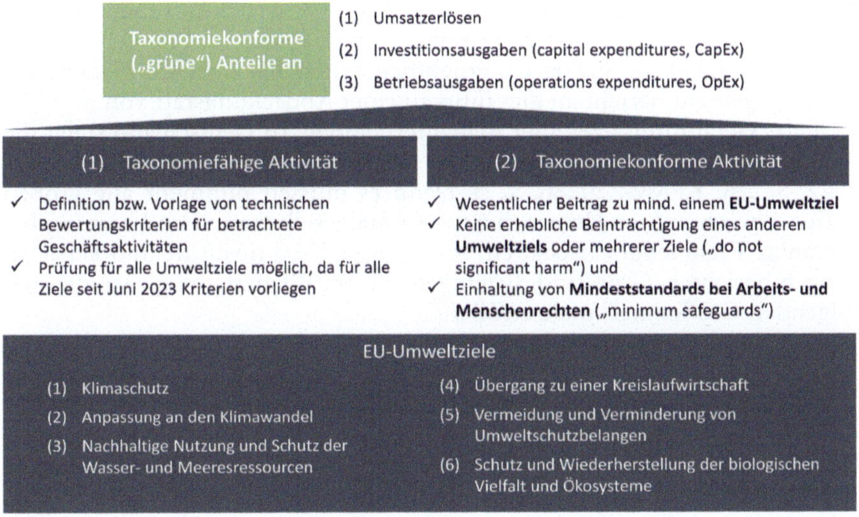

Darst. 11: EU-Taxonomie-Verordnung

Als erstes muss die Taxonomiefähigkeit einer Aktivität geprüft werden. Diese ist dann gegeben, wenn für sie technische Bewertungskriterien definiert worden sind. Zunächst lagen solche Kriterien lediglich für die ersten beiden Umweltziele vor, seit Juni 2023 auch für die restlichen vier (s. Darst. 11). Es ist dabei zu berücksichtigen, dass bspw. Betriebsausgaben lediglich bei einem Zusammenhang mit taxonomiefähigen Investitionen als taxonomiefähig eingestuft werden. Folglich wären Ausgaben für Solarpanels taxonomiefähig, die für den schlichten Bezug von Ökostrom dagegen nicht.

Danach erfolgt die Feststellung der Taxonomiekonformität. Hierfür muss eine Aktivität

- einen wesentlichen Beitrag zu mind. einem EU-Umweltziel leisten,
- zu keiner erheblichen Beeinträchtigung eines anderen Umweltziels oder mehrerer Ziele („do not significant harm") führen und
- nicht gegen Mindeststandards bei Arbeits- und Menschenrechten verstoßen („minimum safeguards").

Die Erfüllung der ersten beiden Anforderungen ist wiederum anhand der technischen Bewertungskriterien zu überprüfen (vgl. Aschfalk-Evertz, 2022, S. 1203; Möhrer et al., 2024, S. 17).

Mittlerweile ist die NFRD durch die **Corporate Sustainability Reporting Directive** (**CSRD**) weiterentwickelt worden, die eine umfangreichere

Nachhaltigkeitsberichterstattung sowie einen erweiterten Anwenderkreis zur Folge hat (s. Darst. 10). Schätzungsweise müssen anstatt ca. 11.600 bis 12.000 nunmehr 49.000 bis 50.000 Unternehmen in der EU über ihr Nachhaltigkeitsengagement berichten; dies führt zu einer Abdeckungsrate von mehr als 75% des Gesamtumsatzes aller EU-Unternehmen. In Deutschland steigt die Anzahl betroffener Unternehmen von ca. 550 auf 15.000 (vgl. Borcherding, 2022, S. 226; KPMG, 2022b, S. 2). Denn es müssen nunmehr alle großen haftungsbeschränkten Unternehmen (Kapitalgesellschaften und haftungsbeschränkte Personengesellschaften) sowie große Kreditinstitute und Versicherungen berichten. Groß sind diejenigen, die am Bilanzstichtag zwei der drei folgenden Größenmerkmale erfüllen:

- Bilanzsumme: mehr als 25 Mio. €,
- Umsatzerlöse: mehr als 50 Mio. €,
- Beschäftigte: mehr als 250 (im Geschäftsjahresdurchschnitt).

Dazu kommen kapitalmarktorientierte kleinere und mittlere Unternehmen (KMU), ausgenommen Kleinstunternehmen) sowie Nicht-EU-Unternehmen mit mindestens einem Tochterunternehmen bzw. einer Niederlassung in der EU bei einem Nettoumsatz von über 150 Mio. € in der Gemeinschaft. Es müssen jedoch nicht alle Unternehmen sofort berichten. Es gibt ein sog. Phase-in mit Start der Unternehmen, die bereits der NFRD unterliegen; sie müssen 2025 über das Geschäftsjahr 2024 berichten. Danach erfolgt eine sukzessive Ausweitung des Anwenderkreises (vgl. RNE, 2024b).

Der Bericht wird verpflichtender Bestandteil des Lageberichts und muss inhaltlich von externen Prüfern wie etwa vom Abschlussprüfer geprüft werden, was bei der nichtfinanziellen Erklärung gemäß NFRD nicht der Fall gewesen ist (lediglich Prüfung der Vorlage und Veröffentlichung der Erklärung). Dabei wird das Prüfungsniveau nach und nach von begrenzter Sicherheit (limited assurance) auf hinreichende Sicherheit (reasonable assurance) angehoben; dieses höhere Niveau bedeutet, dass z.B. Kontrollen im Rahmen des Reportingprozesses im Hinblick auf ihre Wirksamkeit nunmehr geprüft werden oder stichprobenartige Erhebungen zunehmen (vgl. KPMG, 2024). **Die Veröffentlichung im Lagebericht und die Verpflichtung zur inhaltlichen Prüfung markieren einen signifikanten Schritt hin zur Gleichstellung von Finanz- und Nachhaltigkeitsberichterstattung.**

Bei der CSRD ist besonders die Bestimmung hervorzuheben, dass die Nachhaltigkeitsberichterstattung nach einem einheitlichen EU-Berichtsstandard, dem European Sustainability Reporting Standard (ESRS), zu erfolgen hat. Der Aufbau dieses Standards folgt einer „Würfel-Logik" mit den drei Kanten „Reportingbereiche", „ESG-Themengebiete" sowie „Bezugsebenen", wie dies in der Darst. 12 zum Ausdruck gebracht wird (vgl. KPMG, 2023, S. 10).

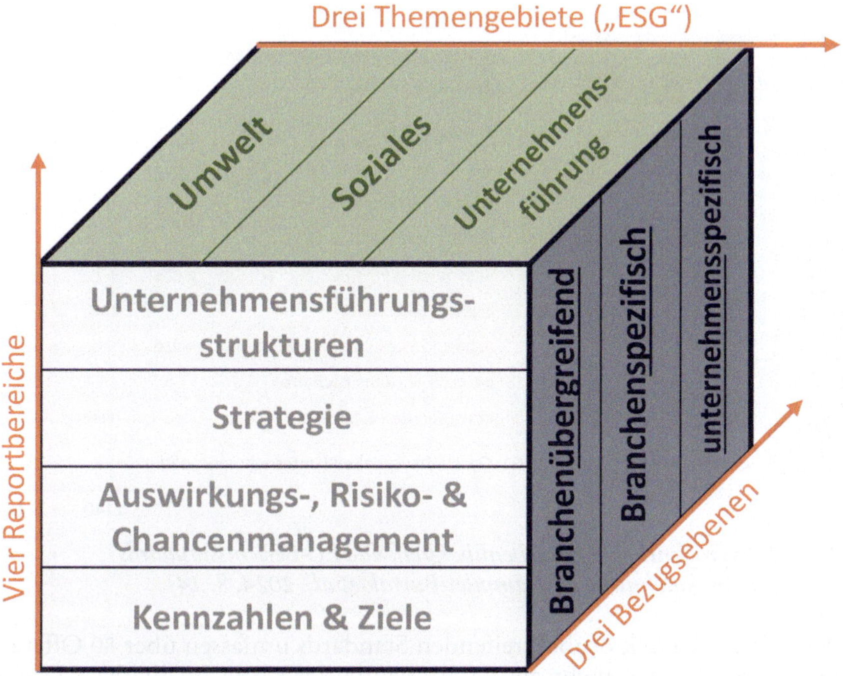

Darst. 12: Aufbau der ESRS (in Anlehnung an KPMG, 2023, S. 10)

Bislang sind erst zwölf branchenübergreifende Standards von der EU-Kommission als delegierte Verordnung verabschiedet worden: zwei Querschnittsstandards sowie zehn themenspezifische Standards (s. Darst. 13). Sie sind übrigens unmittelbar anwendbares Recht, die CSRD bedarf dagegen einer Überführung in nationales Recht der Mitgliedsstaaten.

			Datenpunkte gesamt	Datenpunkte freiwillig
Übergreifend		ESRS 1: Allgemeine Anforderungen	0	0
		ESRS 2: Allgemeine Angaben	146	12
Themenbezogen	Environment (E)	ESRS E1: Klimawandel	217	15
		ESRS E2: Umweltverschmutzung	72	20
		ESRS E3: Wasser- & Meeresressourcen	51	18
		ESRS E4: Biodiversität & Ökosysteme	125	65
		ESRS E5: Ressourcenverbrauch & Kreislaufwirtschaft	67	19
	Social (S)	ESRS S1: Eigene Belegschaft	198	57
		ESRS S2: Arbeitskräfte in der Wertschöpfungskette	71	18
		ESRS S3: Betroffene Gemeinschaften	69	18
		ESRS S4: Konsumenten & Endverbraucher	69	19
	Governance (G)	ESRS G1: Geschäftsverhalten (Unternehmenspolitik)	55	10
			1140	271

Darst. 13: Veröffentlichte branchenübergreifende EU-Berichtsstandards (in Anlehnung an Kämmler-Burrak et al., 2024, S. 14)

Diese branchen-/sektorübergreifenden Standards umfassen über 80 Offenlegungsstandards mit mehr als 1.100 quantitativen bzw. qualitativen Datenpunkten, wobei davon rd. 270 freiwillig sind. ESRS 2 „Allgemeine Standards" sind verpflichtend zu veröffentlichen, ansonsten kommt die doppelte Wesentlichkeit (s. Frage 6) zum Tragen mit Ausnahme von „ESRS E1: Klimawandel". Bei diesem Standard wäre die mangelnde Wesentlichkeit zu begründen (vgl. EFRAG, 2024; Kämmler-Burrak et al., 2024, S. 13 f.).

Bei der Umsetzung gibt es Erleichterungen in den ersten Berichtsjahren (Phase-in). Aktuell arbeitet die European Financial Reporting Advisory Group (EFRAG), eine private Vereinigung, die die EU-Kommission bei der (Weiter-)Entwicklung des Finanz- und Nachhaltigkeitsreportings unterstützt, an Vorschlägen zu branchenspezifischen Berichtsstandards. Laut dem Aktionsplan der EU-Kommission sollen diese nicht wie ursprünglich vorgesehen Ende Juni 2024 verabschiedet werden, sondern erst zwei Jahre später Mitte 2026 (vgl. RNE, 2024b).

Im Hinblick auf den Schutz von Menschenrechten und Umwelt in globalen Liefer- und Wertschöpfungsketten ist mittlerweile auf **europäischer Ebene** das Pendant zum deutschen LkSG verabschiedet worden: die **EU-Lieferkettenrichtlinie (Corporate Sustainability Due Dilligence Directive,**

CSDDD oder CS3D). Die Länder haben diese bis Mitte 2026 in nationales Recht umzusetzen. Betroffen sind EU-Unternehmen mit durchschnittlich mehr als 1.000 Beschäftigte und einem Nettoumsatz von mehr als 450 Mio. € sowie bestimmte Nicht-EU-Unternehmen; eine stufenweise Anwendungspflicht ist vorgesehen. Diese Richtlinie baut auf dem LkSG auf, wobei einige, mitunter strengere Regelungen zu beachten sind. Im Hinblick auf den Schutz der Umwelt werden bspw. Pflichten aus internationalen Umweltabkommen oder der Schutz der biologischen Vielfalt betont. Zudem wird ein Plan zur Minderung des unternehmerischen Einflusses auf den Klimawandel verlangt (Climate Transition Plan). Eine nachhaltige Wirtschaft sowie die Begrenzung der Erderwärmung gemäß dem Pariser Klimaabkommen soll so gewährleistet werden. Weitere Unterschiede gibt es bei: der Reichweite der Pflichten (anstatt Bezug „nur" auf die Lieferkette, nunmehr auf die Aktivitätenkette auch mit mittelbaren Lieferanten sowie der Produktvermarktungskette), der Vorgabe einer zivilrechtlichen Haftung sowie der Ausnahme von der jährlichen Berichterstattung über die Sorgfaltspflichten für die Unternehmen, die der CSRD unterliegen (vgl. BMUV, 2025; Würz, 2024; Wartecker, 2024, S. 172 f.).

6. Wesentlichkeitsanalyse: Warum ist sie wichtig und wie ist sie zu erstellen?

Wie es bei den Ausführungen zur NFRD und CSRD schon deutlich geworden ist, ist für ein Nachhaltigkeitsreporting die Durchführung einer Wesentlichkeitsanalyse – auch Materialitätsanalyse genannt – unerlässlich. Denn mit ihre können Vielfalt und Komplexität ökonomischer, ökologischer und sozialer Herausforderungen einer nachhaltigen Unternehmensführung reduziert werden und die relevanten Handlungsfelder selektiert und priorisiert werden. Nach dem Wesentlichkeitsprinzip zu handeln, ist in der Rechnungslegung keine Unbekannte; in der angloamerikanischen und internationalen ist ein solches Prinzip verankert.

Eine Wesentlichkeitsanalyse schafft die Grundlage für die (Neu-)Festlegung von Nachhaltigkeitszielen, -strategien und -vorhaben, so dass sie zu Recht als das strategische Schlüsselinstrument im Nachhaltigkeitsmanagement bezeichnet werden kann (vgl. Form & Schlemminger, 2023, S. 258).

Welche Anforderungen an eine Wesentlichkeitsanalyse sind zu beachten? Nach der CSRD ist die doppelte Wesentlichkeit gefragt, d. h., die Analyse muss sowohl die Finanzauswirkungen durch die Umwelt, speziell durch Nachhaltigkeits-/ESG-Faktoren, auf das Unternehmen (Outside-in-Perspektive) als auch die Auswirkungen der Geschäftsaktivitäten auf Menschen,

Gesellschaft und Umwelt zum Ausdruck bringen (Inside-out-Perspektive). In der Darst. 14 sind verschiedene Beispiele dieser Perspektiven aufgeführt.

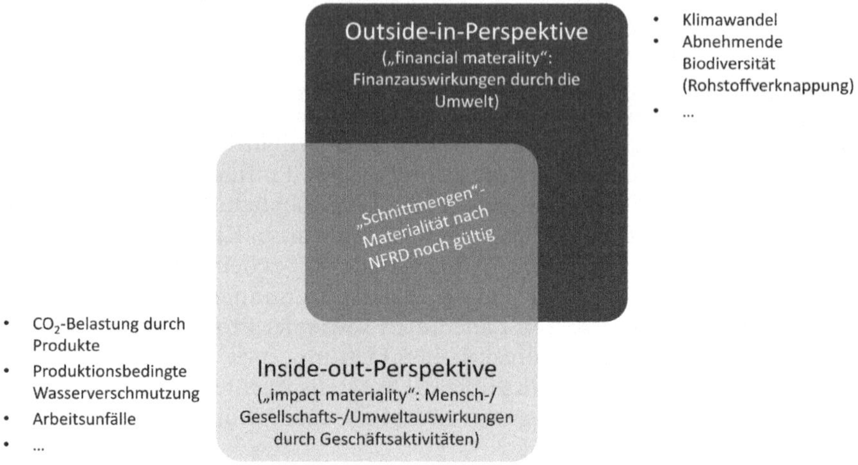

Darst. 14: Prinzip der doppelten Wesentlichkeit

Die Komplexität einer Analyse hat insofern zugenommen, als dass nach der NFRD lediglich die „Schnittmengen“-Materialität gefragt gewesen ist. Danach sind nur die Themen herauszuarbeiten gewesen, die aus beiden Perspektiven gleichzeitig bedeutsam sind. Nach der CSRD ist nunmehr jede Perspektive für sich allein relevant, also aus der „Und“- ist eine „Oder“-Bedingung geworden, was eine Ausweitung der als wesentlich einzustufenden und dann zu berichtenden Themen zur Folge haben wird (vgl. Onischka & Kämmler-Burrak, 2023, S. 63f.; PwC, 2022b). Hierzu ein Beispiel aus der Praxis:

> *„Wurde über die Anzahl der Arbeitsunfälle in einem Unternehmen bisher nicht berichtet, da der Sachverhalt lediglich auswirkungsrelevant war, aber nicht geschäftsrelevant, so wäre zukünftig zwingend darüber zu berichten“* (Borcherding, 2022, S. 231).

Wie ist eine Wesentlichkeitsanalyse prinzipiell aufgebaut? Sie ist eine Synthese der Stakeholder- und der Unternehmens/Geschäftsperspektive auf Nachhaltigkeitsthemen bzw. nachhaltigkeitsbezogenen Handlungsfeldern. Die Relevanzeinschätzungen aus diesen Perspektiven werden üblicherweise in einer Wesentlichkeitsmatrix zusammengeführt, wobei vielfach die Geschäftsrelevanz auf der Abzisse (X-Achse) und die Stakeholderrelevanz auf der Ordinate (Y-Achse) dargestellt werden. Die Darst. 15 verdeutlicht eine solche „klassische“ Matrix von Schaeffler, einem börsennotierten deutschen Zulieferer der Automobil- und Maschinenbauindustrie. Faktisch weist diese Matrix drei Dimensionen auf, da die Themen noch in vier Gruppen eingeteilt worden sind, was an der Farbgebung zu erkennen ist.

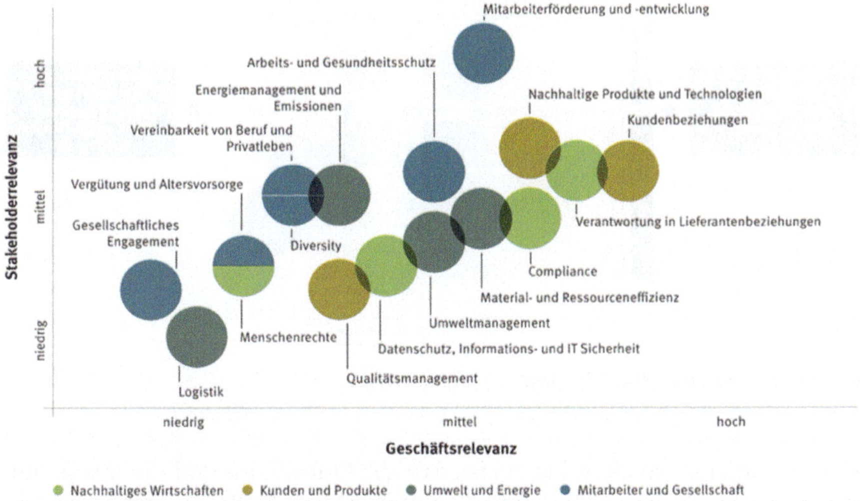

Darst. 15: Wesentlichkeitsmatrix von Schaeffler (Schaeffler, 2018)

Da sowohl die Outside-in als auch die Inside-out-Perspektive darzustellen und zudem die Auswirkungen bzw. Chancen- und Risikopotenziale von Nachhaltigkeitsthemen zu verdeutlichen sind, ist nicht dieses klassische Variante, sondern eine Zielscheibenmatrix zu empfehlen (s. Darst. 16).

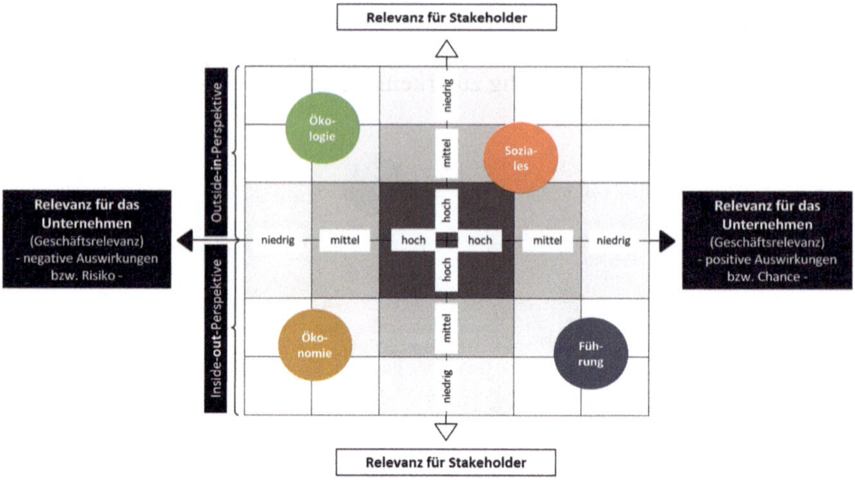

Darst. 16: „Zielscheiben"-Wesentlichkeitsmatrix (Form & Schlemminger, 2023, S. 261, leicht modifiziert)

Der Vorteil einer solchen Matrix ist, dass die Outside-in- und die Inside-out-Perspektiven durch die obere und die untere Matrix-Hälfte separat dargestellt werden können und die negativen und positiven Geschäftsauswirkungen (bzw. Geschäftsrisiken und -chancen) durch die linke und die rechte Hälfte. Da die Relevanzeinstufungen „umgekehrt" zum Ausdruck gebracht werden, stehen wie bei einer Zielscheibe die hochbedeutsamen Themen im Zentrum dieser Matrix. Somit wird differenziert, aber dennoch Übersichlich der Handlungsbedarf deutlich. Durch eine ergänzende Kategorisierung der Themen nach den ESG-Nachhaltigkeitsdimensionen zuzüglich Ökonomie kann die Aussagekraft noch erhöht werden (vgl. Form & Schlemminger, 2023, S. 261).

Wie sollte nun eine Wesentlichkeitsanalyse durchgeführt werden? – Hierzu gibt es verschiedene Vorgehensmodelle, aus denen sich eine Vorgehensweise mit sieben Schritten ableiten lässt, wie in der Darst. 17 verdeutlicht (vgl. Form & Schlemminger, 2023, S. 260 ff.).

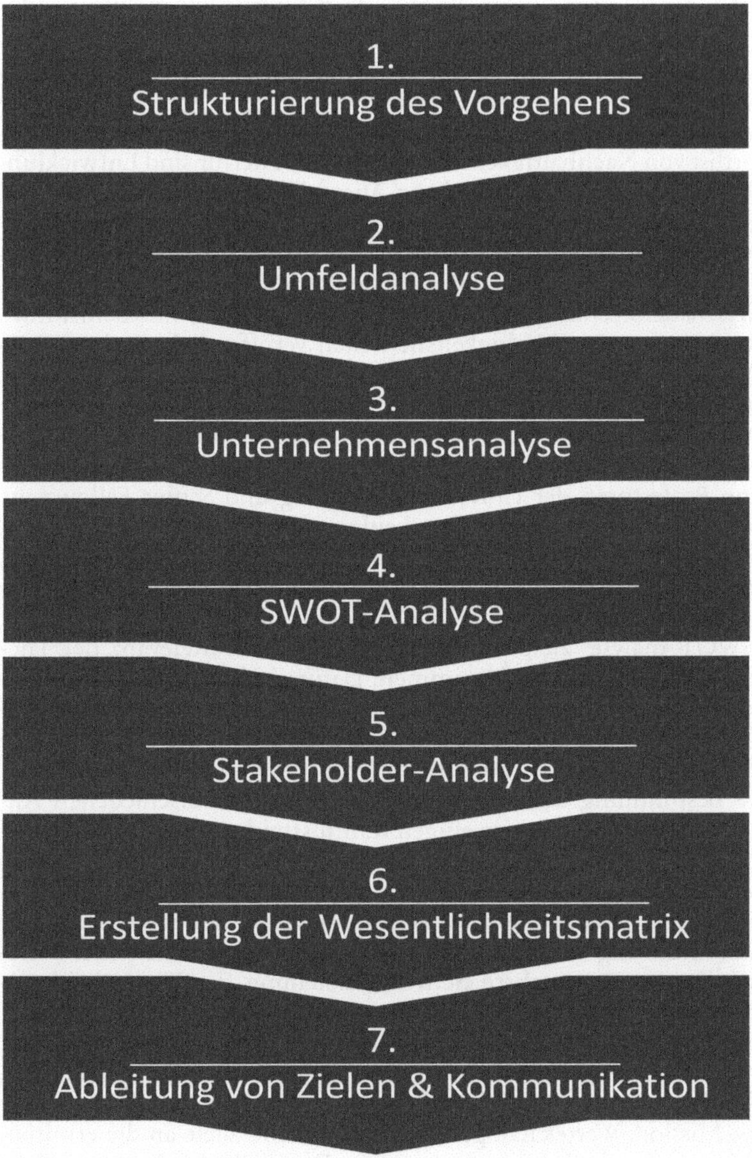

Darst. 17: Durchführungs-/Anwendungsschritte der Wesentlichkeitsanalyse (Form & Schlemminger, 2023, S. 260, leicht modifiziert)

Der **erste Schritt** „Strukturierung des Vorgehens“ umfasst die Festlegung der Matrixvariante, die Auswahl von Tools zur Analyse von Umfeld und Unternehmen, die Integration der Analyse in den (strategischen) Managementprozess sowie die Einbindung betroffener Funktionsträger (Abteilungen). Der **zweite Schritt** „Umfeldanalyse“ läuft auf die Erstellung einer Long- und später Shortlist von Nachhaltigkeitsthemen hinaus. Hierfür sind Entwicklungen und Trends zu analysieren und deren Auswirkungen bzw. Chancen- und Risikopotenziale einzuschätzen. Hier können Veröffentlichungen von Wettbewerbern, insbesonder wenn sie „gute“ Nachhaltigkeitsberichte erstellt haben, sehr hilfreich sein. Informationen hierzu könnte das Institut für ökologische Wirtschaftsforschung (IÖW) liefern, das zusammen mit dem future e.V. ein Ranking von Nachhaltigkeitsberichten veröffentlicht (vgl. IÖW & future e. V., 2021). Ein anderer Anhaltspunkt ist der „Building Public Trust Award“ für die besten Nachhaltigkeitsberichterstattungen. Dieser Preis wird von der Sustainable Finance Research Group (SFRG) – unterstützt von PwC – in verschiedenen Kategorien vergeben; die SFRG setzt sich aus einer Gruppe von Professoren der Universität Hamburg und Senior Fellows aus dem Finanzsektor zusammen. Die Entscheidung über die Preise fällt eine unabhängige Fachjury aus Experten aus Wissenchaft und Praxis (vgl. SFRG, 2023). Gegenstand des **dritten Schrittes** „Unternehmensanalyse“ ist die Ermittlung der Stärken und Schwächen eines Unternehmens. Der **vierte Schritt** „SWOT-Analyse“ zielt darauf ab, die (Geschäfts-)Relevanz der Themen für das Unternehmen zu bestimmen. Dafür sind die (Shortlist-)Nachhaltigkeitsthemen aus der Umfeldanalyse mit den ermittelten Stärken-Schwächen-Positionen des Unternehmens in Beziehung zu setzen. Der **fünfte Schritt** „Stakeholder-Analyse“ umfasst die Ermittlung der relevanten Stakeholder, die Bestimmung der jeweiligen Bedeutung der verschiedenen Anspruchsgruppen anhand der jeweiligen Einflussstärke und Einflusswahrscheinlichkeit (Beziehungsintensität) und schlussendlich die Einschätzung der Relevanz durch die zuvor bestimmten bedeutsamsten Gruppen. Für eine solche Relevanzeeinschätzung kann die Einrichtung eines Stakeholder-Beirats, die Durchführung von Stakeholder-Workshops oder Stakeholder-Befragung sinnvoll sein. Der **sechste Schritt** „Erstellung der Wesentlichkeitsmatrix“ beinhaltet die Verortung der Nachhaltigkeitsthemen nach den Relevanzeinstufungen, wie sie sich aus der SWOT- und Stakeholderanalyse gemäß den vorangegangen Schritten ergeben haben. Im Rahmen des **siebten, abschließenden Schrittes** „Ableitung von Zielen & Kommunikation“ sind Vision bzw. Mission, Wertekataloge sowie strategische Ziele an die ermittelten Nachhaltigkeitserfordernisse anzupassen. Die Ziele wiederum sind in Nachhaltigkeitsstrategien und entsprechende -vorhaben zur überführen. Im Rahmen der gesetzlichen Grundlagen hat die Geschäftsleitung ihre Kommunikationspolitik festzulegen, zu der auch die Gestaltung des Nachhaltigkeitsreportings gehört.

7. Was ist zu tun, um ein „robustes" Nachhaltigkeitsmanagement und -reporting zu etablieren?

Um ein „robustes" Nachhaltigkeitsmanagement und -reporting zu etablieren, ist eine Umsetzung von drei verbundenen Projekten zu empfehlen:

(1) Zunächst haben **CSRD-pflichtige** Unternehmen für ein „compliancegerechtes" Nachhaltigkeitesreporting zu sorgen, was durch ein **CSRD-Umsetzungsprojekt** zu realisieren wäre. Dies ist eine unabdingbare Pflichtübung, um berichtsfähig zu werden.
(2) Zudem wäre im Rahmen eines **Aufbauprojektes** ein **leistungsstarkes Nachhaltigkeitsmanagements & -controllings** zu schaffen. Proaktiv sollten die Nutzenpotenziale eines Nachhaltigkeitsmanagement – wie etwa Stärkung der Wettbewerbsfähigkeit durch nachhaltigere Produkte, Reduzierung des Ressourcenverbrauchs, höhere Kundenzufriedenheit und -bindung sowie verbesserte Finanzierungsfähigkeit – eingeschätzt und ausgeschöpft werden können.
(3) Schließlich muss für eine **unternehmensweite Verankerung der Nachhaltigkeit** gesorgt werden, was nach den ersten beiden Projekten noch nicht der Fall sein muss. Hierfür wäre ein **Projekt über Nachhaltigkeitsnormen und -werte** zu implementieren. Denn „Integrated Thinking" sollte auf allen Ebenen in den Köpfen der Mitarbeitenden sein. Nach einer Studie der Personalberatung Odjers Berndtson scheint hier noch eine größere Baustelle vorzuliegen:

> *„Drei Viertel der befragten Vorstände und Geschäftsführer haben Nachhaltigkeitskriterien im Purpose ihres Unternehmens verankert. Klare ESG- und Nachhaltigkeitsthemen zu etablieren, wird als Chefsache gesehen. Die schlechte Nachricht: Der von der Führungsspitze entgegengebrachte Elan ebbt bereits in den darunterliegenden Managementebenen stark ab"* (Odgers Berndtson, 2021).

(1) CSRD-Umsetzungsprojekt

Ein CSRD-Umsetzungsprojekt zur Realisierung eines compliancegerechten Nachhaltigkeitsreportings umfasst verschiedene Aufgabenfelder (bzw. Teilprojekte). Nach einem 5-Phasen-Modell, wie in der Darst. 18 aufgeführt, wären nachfolgende Aufgaben wahrzunehmen (vgl. Kämmler-Burrak et al., 2024, S. 11 ff.).

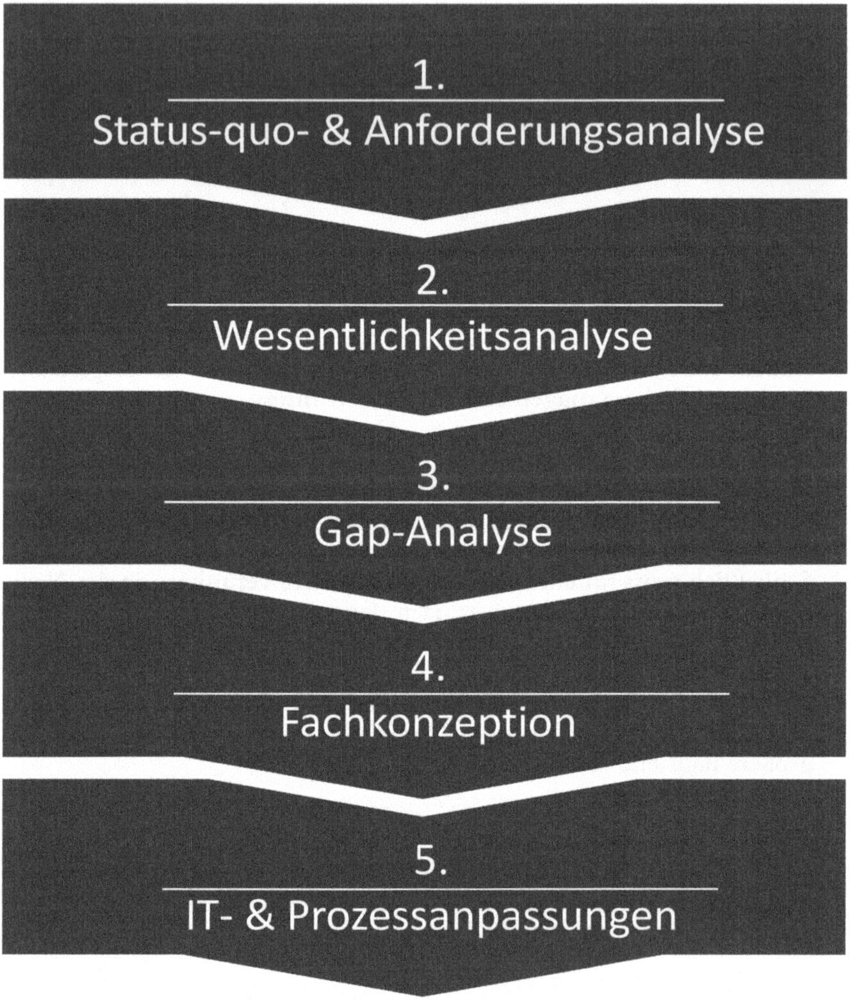

Darst. 18: CSRD-Umsetzungsprojekt
(in Anlehnung an Kämmler-Burrak et al., 2024, S. 13)

Gegenstand der **ersten Phase** „Status-quo- & Aufgabenanalyse" ist die Projektbasis mit Fachexperten zu legen. Neben Controlling und Rechnungwesen wären bspw. Vertreter aus den Einheiten Nachhaltigkeit, Public/Investor Relations, Personal oder Organisation & IT einzubinden, um eine inhaltliche Anforderungs- und unternehmensbereichsspezifische Betroffenheitsanalyse vorzunehmen. Die **zweite Phase** „Wesentlichkeitsanalyse" zielt darauf ab, die Nachhaltigkeitsthemen zu identifizieren und damit die zu erhebenden Datenpunkte zu reduzieren. Wie schon dargestellt (s. Frage 5), umfassen die verabschiedeten Berichtsstandards über 1.100 Datenpunkte. Mittels einer „Gap-Analyse" in der **dritten Phase** ist die Lücke zwischen vorhandenen und zu berichtenden Informationen auf Geschäftsfeld- bzw. -bereichsebene zu identifizieren, die letztendlich Daten-, Schnittstellen- und Prozess-Gaps darstellen. Im Rahmen der **vierten Phase** „Fachkonzeption" sind fachliche Anforderungen und Fachkonzepte zu definieren bzw. zu erstellen sowie IT- und Prozessmodelle zu konzipieren. Zu dieser Modellierungsarbeit gehören zahlreiche Prozesse von der (Daten-)Erhebung bzw. Beschaffung bis hin zum Reporting. Angesichts der inhaltlichen Prüfung des CSRD-Nachhaltigkeitsbericht im Lagebericht ist hierbei die Etablierung von Qualitätssicherungsprozessen unabdingbar. Die Fachkonzepte sollten insgesamt mit der Konzeption von Managementsystemen verknüpft werden (wie etwa der Konzeption des generellen Planungs- und Kontrollsystems, des Performance-Management-Systems oder des Risikomanagementsystems). In der **fünften Phase** „IT- & Prozessanpassungen" werden bestehende IT-Systeme erweitert bzw. neue (Standard-)Lösungen integriert sowie Schnittstellen im Rahmen von Data-Warehouse-(DW-)/Data-Lake-(DL-)Strukturen angepasst. Zudem werden die neuen bzw. veränderten Prozesse verankert, so dass schlussendlich die CSRD-Berichtsfähigkeit vorliegt.

(2) Aufbauprojekt Nachhaltigkeitsmanagement und -controlling

Ein Aufbauprojekt über ein leistungsstarkes Nachhaltigkeitsmanagement und -controlling umfasst drei Aufgabenfelder bzw. Teilprojekte (s. Darst. 19).

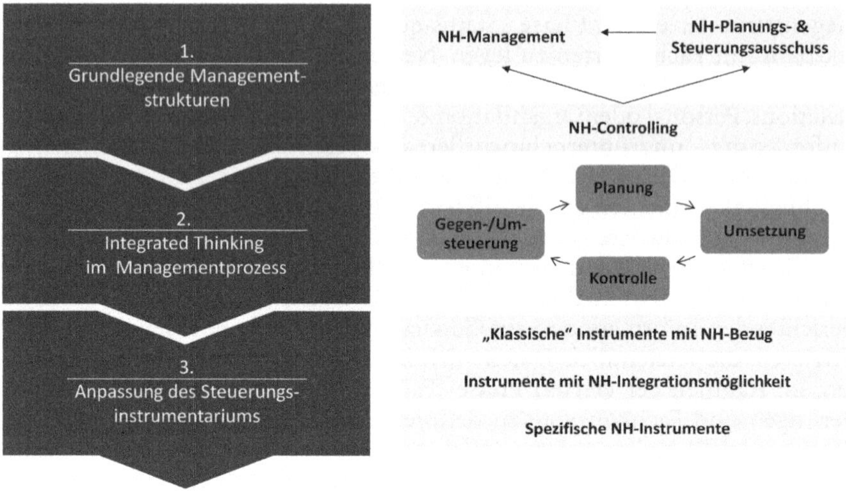

Darst. 19: Aufbauprojekt Nachhaltigkeitsmanagement und -controlling

Im Rahmen des **ersten Teilprojektes** „Grundlegende Managementstrukturen“ geht es um die Weiterentwicklung und das Zusammenspiel von **Management** (**a**), **Controlling** (**b**) und eventuell vorhandener **Planungs- und Steuerungsausschüsse** (**c**).

Damit sich eine **Management** (**a**) zu einem **Nachhaltigkeitsmanagement** weiterentwickeln kann, braucht es eine entsprechende Führungsunterstützung. Insofern sollte sich das „Frühungsunterstützungssystem“ **Controlling** (**b**) zu einem **Nachhaltigkeitscontrolling** weiterentwickeln. Ein solches Controlling hätte die Zielsetzung (bzw. Gesamtaufgabe), das Management bei der Planung, Kontrolle und Steuerung des Unternehmens nicht nur aus der ökonomische, sondern ebenfalls dazu aus der sozialen und ökologischen Perspektive zu unterstützen (vgl. Friedag, 2022). Ein Nachhaltigkeitscontrolling zeichnet sich insofern durch die Ausrichtung auf den Profit-People-Plant-Ansatz aus, wobei die Vernetzung dieser drei Perspektiven gemäß der Integrated-Thinking-Philosophie zu beachten ist.

Vielfach wird das Nachhaltigkeitscontrolling als **Green Controlling** bezeichnet, obwohl es mehr ist als ein „reines“ Umwelt- oder Ökocontrolling (vgl. Schaltegger, 2022). Ganz praktisch gedacht, würde dieses Nachhaltigkeitscontrolling als Navigator, Pfadfinder oder Business Partner das Management unterstützen, die fünf Stufen hin zum nachhaltigen Unternehmen hinaufzusteigen. Die Darst. 20 verdeutlicht dieses Fünf-Stufen-Modell.

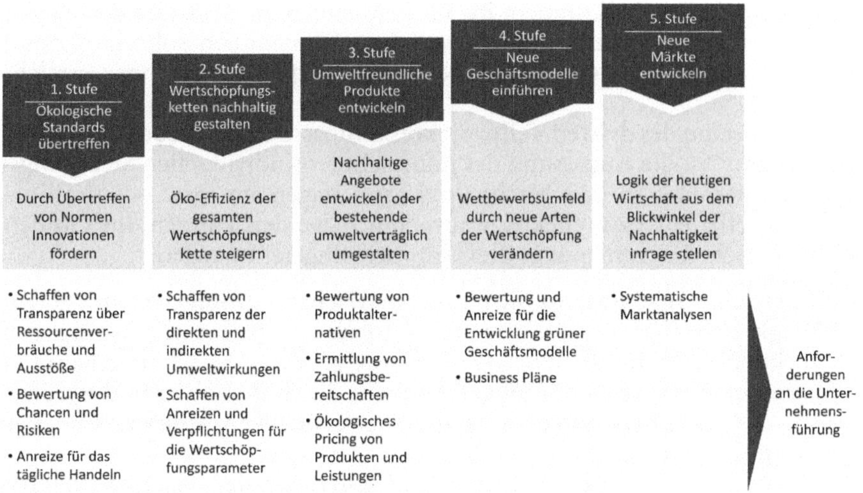

Darst. 20: Fünf-Stufen-Modell zum nachhaltigen Unternehmen nach Nidumolu, Prahalad & Rangaswami (ICV, 2011, S. 4, in Anlehnung an Nidumolu et al., 2009, S. 6)

Durch ein derart ausgerichtetes Führungsunterstützungssystem wird das Management mehr und mehr in die Lage versetzt, sich zu einem nachhaltigen Management zu entwickeln. Ähnliches gilt für sog. **Planungs- und Steuerungsausschüsse** (c), die sich aus Vertretern verschiedener Einheiten wie etwa Controlling, Rechnungswesen, Organisation & IT oder Personal zusammensetzen. Solche Ausschüsse werden gerade in größeren Unternehmen zusätzlich zur Primärorganisation eingerichtet, um die Geschäftsführung insbesondere bei der strategischen Steuerung ganzheitlich zu unterstützen (vgl. Schlemminger, 2022, S. 95 f. und 534). Unter der Leitung eines Nachhaltigkeitscontrollings – das Controlling ist traditionell für die Koordination der Führungsteilsysteme verantwortlich – würde sich ein solches Gremium zu einem **nachhaltigen Planungs- und Steuerungsausschuss** entwickeln können.

Das **zweite Teilprojekt** „Integrated Thinking im Managementprozess" bezieht sich auf die Managementprozesse. Klassischerweise unteilt man diese in einen strategischen und einen operativen Prozessablauf, die wiederum in die Teilprozesse (bzw. Prozessphasen) „Planung", „Umsetzung", „Kontrolle" und „Gegen- bzw. Umsteuerung" untergliedert werden können. Im Rahmen seiner Steuerungs(unterstützungs-) und Koordinationsfunktion hätte ein Nachhaltigkeitscontrolling darauf zu achten, dass ökonomische, soziale und ökologische Zielkriterien in allen Abläufen und Phasen durchgängig und integriert berücksichtigt werden. Schlussendlich soll eine konsequente Ausrichtung des Unternehmen auf diese drei Dimensionen erreicht werden.

Gegenstand des **dritten Teilprojektes** „Anpassung des Steuerungsinstrumentariums" ist die Anpassung des unternehmensindividuellen Steuerungsinstrumentariums, so dass Nachhaltigkeitsmanagement- bzw. –controllingaufgaben effizient bzw. effektiv wahrnehmen werden können. Im Groben können solche Instrumente in drei Gruppen eingeteilt werden:

- **„Klassische" Instrumente mit „automatischem" (integriertem) Nachhaltigkeitsbezug:** Bei solchen Tools werden soziale oder ökologische Aspekte üblicherweise einbezogen. Hierzu gehören die schon genannten Instrumente wie etwa die **SWOT-Analyse,** die **Stakeholderanalyse,** aber auch die **PESTEL-Analyse** oder die sog. **Früherkennungssysteme der dritten Generation.**
- **„Klassische" Instrumente mit der Möglichkeit der Nachhaltigkeitsintegration bzw. -ausrichtung:** Solche Tools erlauben, soziale oder ökologische Aspekte aufzunehmen oder herauszustellen. Beispiele für diese Instrumentengruppe sind **Portfolioanalysen** mit Adressierung von Kombinationen aus Bioprodukten und entsprechenden Märkten als eigenständige Geschäftsfelder, die **Balanced Scorecard (BSC)** mit der Weiterentwicklung zur Sustainability BSC oder das **Rechnungswesen** mit dem Umweltkostenrechnungsansatz, ökologische und soziale Kosten explizit zu erfassen und zu verrechnen (wie etwa Kosten eine Kläranlage).
- **Spezifische („traditionelle") Nachhaltigkeitsinstrumente:** Hier wären die **Wesentlichkeitsanalyse** mit Abdeckung grds. aller Nachhaltigkeitsaspekte oder **Instrumente** mit **sozialer oder ökologischer Fokussierung** zu nennen. Diese Instrumentengruppe umfasst bspw. die zahlreichen **„Öko-Tools"** (Ökobilanz, ökologische Gewinn- und Verlustrechnung, ökologischer Fußabdruck, Ökoeffizienzanalyse), das **Carbon Accounting** oder **Sozial- und Umweltindikatoren.**

(3) Projekt über Nachhaltigkeitsnormen und -werte

Damit Nachhaltigkeit auf allen Ebenen in einem Unternehmen gelebt wird, sprich ein „Integrated Thinking" in den Köpfen ist, ist ein Projekt zu empfehlen, in dem **Vision (a)** und **Wertekatalog (b)** unter Nachhaltigkeitsgesichtspunkten überarbeitet und schlussendlich **Leitsätze (c)** zur Kommunikation nach innen und außen entwickelt werden.

Unter der **Vision** (**a**) versteht man ein Zukunftsbild eines Unternehmens, das eine Antwort auf die Frage liefert „Wo sehen wir uns langfristig?“ bzw. eine „generelle unternehmerische Leitidee .., die zwar szenarische, aber dennoch realistische und glaubwürdige Aussagen einer anzustrebenden und im Prinzip auch erreichbaren Zukunft formuliert“ (Vahs & Schäfer-Kunz, 2012, S. 25).

Der **Wertekatalog** (**b**) beinhaltet die Normen und Werte, auf deren Grundlage gehandelt wird und die somit Identität eines Unternehmens bestimmen.

Die **Leitsätze** (**c**) fassen Vision, Wertekatalog und sowie die strategische Ausrichtung in kurzen Sätzen zusammen. Sie dienen dazu, einerseits nach innen Verhalten und Entscheidungsfindung und andererseits nach außen das Verständnis vom Unternehmen zu prägen.

In einem solchen Projekt sollten die Mitarbeiterinnen und Mitarbeiter hierarchie- und bereichsübergreifend eingebunden werden. Auch wenn die Leitblanken für ein Projekt von der Geschäftsführung vorgegeben werden, ist es identitätsstiftend, wenn sich die Beschäftigten einbringen können. Zudem wird ein größerer Ideenpool genutzt, es ist von einer höheren Akzeptanz auszugehen, zumal Mitwirkende Multiplikatoren darstellen. Die praktische Arbeit könnte in Workshops durchgeführt werden, moderiert von fachspezifischen Externen. Warum Externe? Für Unternehmensberatungen oder Coaches spricht nicht nur deren fachliche und methodische Kompetenz auf dem Gebiet der Normen- und Werteentwicklung, sondern ebenfalls die neutrale Stellung im Projekt, um bei Bedarf die Wogen in hitzigen Diskussionen glätten zu können.

C. Ausblick

Für die Implementierung eines robusten, regelkonformen Nachhaltigkeitsmanagement und -reportings ist ein konsequentes **Monitoring der rechtlichen Rahmenbedingungen** (1), **die Anwendung von Leitfäden und Orientierungshilfen** (2) sowie ein **Scannen des Marktes von DV-Systemen** (3) zu empfehlen.

Im Rahmen der **Monitoringaufgabe** (**1**) haben gerade deutsche Unternehmen, die potenziell von der CSRD-betroffen sind, einerseits den Fortgang der deutschen Gesetzgebung zur CSRD-Umsetzung zu verfolgen, aber auch die auf EU-Ebene angestoßene Omnibusverordnung. Ziel dieser Verordnung ist die Bündelung von Nachhaltigkeitsberichtpflichten nach CSRD, CSDDD, Taxonomieverordnung und eventuell weiteren Regelungen. Gemäß der Budapester Erklärung zur Wettbewerbsfähigkeit Europas der EU-Staats- und

Regierungschefs sollen die Berichtspflichten um mindestens 25 Prozent reduziert werden. Die EU-Kommission hat dazu bereits im ersten Halbjahr 2025 konkrete Vorschläge zu unterbreiten. Diese Forderung nach Vereinfachung ist nicht unumstritten, denn bei einem Schnellschuss könnten Menschenrechte und Umwelt auf der Strecke bleiben oder sogar generell die Glaubwürdigkeit der EU-weiten Nachhaltigkeitsbemühungen. Auf jeden Fall nimmt die Unsicherheit bei den Unternehmen zu (vgl. Herzog, 2025). Optimisten halten allerdings dagegen, das „eine Entlastung beim Reporting Raum für wirksame Nachhaltigkeitsstrategien [schaffe]“ (Grabmeier, 2025).

Die nachfolgende Darst. 21 verdeutlicht die Erleichterungsvorschläge gemäß der Omnibus-Initiative bezogen auf die CSRD-Nachhaltigkeitsberichterstattung; den „Stop-the-Clock“-Vorschlag haben EU-Parlament und -Rat bereits zugestimmt. Die Zahl der Anwender in der EU wird sich auf ca. 7000 Unternehmen reduzieren; inwieweit dies jedoch so eintritt, ist vom weiteren Verlauf des Gesetzgebungsverfahren abhängig.

Inhalt	• EU-Berichtsstandard: Reduzierung der Datenpunkte sowie Fokus auf quantitative anstatt qualitative Angaben, keine Einführung der vorgesehenen sektorspezifischen ESRS • Verhinderung Trickle-Down-Effekt in der Wertschöpfungskette: Einbeziehung von Informationen nur von CSRD-pflichtigen Unternehmen • Keine automatische Anwendung der EU-Taxonomie-Verordnung (diese zukünftig verpflichtend für Unternehmen: Beschäftigte > 1.000 <u>und</u> Umsatz > 450 Mio. €) • Prüfung: ausschließlich mit „begrenzter“ Sicherheit, das später vorgesehene „hinreichende“ Sicherheitsniveau entfällt
Anwender	Haftungsbeschränkte Unternehmen: • Beschäftigte > 1.000 <u>und</u> • Umsatz > 50 Mio. € Umsatz oder Bilanzsumme > 25 Mio. € (= Grenzen für große Kapitalgesellschaften) Keine Anwendung mehr von: • nach § 267 HGB großen Kapital- und denen gleichgestellten Personenhandelsgesellschaften • börsennotierten KMU.
Zeit	• „Stop the Clock“: Verschiebung der geplanten Erstanwendung für Wave 2 (GJ 2025: urspr. große Unternehmen) und 3 (GJ 2026: urspr. kapitalmarktorientierte KMU) um 2 Jahre

Darst. 21: Erleichterung bei CSRD-Berichtspflicht gemäß Omnibus-Initiative (vgl. Müller, 2025b)

Bei der **Anwendung von Leitfäden und Orientierungshilfen** (2) sind gerade die Leitfäden sowie die Diskussionspapiere der European Financial Reporting Advisory Group (EFRAG), welche die EU-Kommission bei der Entwicklung des Finanz- und Nachhaltigkeitsreporting unterstützt, zu berücksichtigen (mitunter gemeinsam mit GRI bzw. IFRS Foundation veröffentlicht). Beispiele sind die EFRAG-Umsetzungshilfe für die strategierelevante Wesentlichkeitsanalyse, das GRI-/EFRAG-Mappingtools zur Verdeutlichung der Interoperabilität von GRI-Kriterien und ESRS oder der EFRAG-/IFRS Foundation-Leitfaden über das Zusammspiel von ESRS und IFRS Sustainability Disclosure Standards, um gerade die Reportingarbeit zu vereinfachen (vgl. EFRAG, 2024; GRI/EFRAG, 2023; EFRAG/IFRS Foundation, 2024).

Es liegt auf der Hand, dass eine integrierte Steuerung die Fortentwicklung von DV-Systemen erforderlich macht. Skalierbare Data-Warehouse- und Data-Lake-Strukturen zur Verarbeitung, Speicherung, Auswertung einer Vielzahl von strukturieren und unstrukturierten Daten sind ins Auge zu fassen. Im Hinblick auf eine verständliche Aufbereitung für Entscheidungsträger sind Dashboard-Ansätze zu empfehlen, die ein Selfcontrolling ermöglichen. Hierfür sollte der **Markt von DV-Systemen laufend gescannt werden (3)**; eine Vielzahl von ESG-Softwareprodukten zum ESG-Daten-, -Performance- und -Disclosure-Management wird mittleweile angeboten (vgl. Neubauer, 2024, S. 183). Eine Anwendung von Scoring-Modellen zur Auswahl geeigneter DW-/DL-Systeme bzw. einzelner DV-Komponenten ist zu empfehlen, damit eine zielgerichte, auf die jeweiligen Unternehmensverhältnisse zugeschnittene und damit systematische DV-Fortentwicklung gelingt.

Literaturverzeichnis

Aschfalk-Evertz, A. (2022). EU-Taxonomie-Verordnung. WISU - Das Wirtschaftsstudium, 51(11), S. 1200 - 1205.

Auer, C., Borcherding, N., & Möller, V. (2022). C Nachhaltigkeitsberichterstattung: § 8 Frameworks, Standards, Guidance. In: Freiberg, J., & Bruckner, A. (Hrsg.), Corporate Sustainability. Kompass für die Nachhaltigkeitsberichterstattung. Freiburg: Haufe-Lexware, S. 115 - 205.

BAFA (2024). Lieferketten. Von URL: https://www.bafa.de/DE/Lieferketten/Ueberblick/ueberblick_node.html#doc1469782bodyText2 (Abruf: 26.02.2024).

BaFin (2020). Merkblatt zum Umgang mit Nachhaltigkeitsrisiken, Stand: 13.01.2020. Von URL: https://www.bafin.de/SharedDocs/Downloads/DE/Merkblatt/dl_mb_Nachhaltigkeitsrisiken.pdf;jsessionid=10932C8B39B2D7A2F282E3C66BDCD1BD.internet982?__blob=publicationFile&v=2 (Abruf: 26.02.2024).

Biel, A. (2023). ESG-Kriterien: ökonomischer und ökologischer Hebel? Messen und Steuern der ESG-Kriterien im Management und Controlling. Alfred Biel im Interview mit Rebekka Erchinger, Prof. Dr. Rosemarie Koch und Prof. Dr. Ralf Schlemminger. In: Controller Magazin, 49(6), S. 78 - 85.

Blackrock (2020). Eine grundlegende Umgestaltung der Finanzwelt. Brief von Larry Fink an Vorstandsvorsitzende. Von URL: https://www.blackrock.com/ch/privatanleger/de/larry-fink-ceo-letter (Abruf: 20.02.2024).

BMUV (2025). Europäische Lieferkettenrichtlinie (CSDDD). Von URL: https://www.bmuv.de/themen/nachhaltigkeit/wirtschaft/lieferketten/europaeische-lieferkettenrichtlinie-csddd (Abruf: 14.02.2025).

Borcherding, N. (2022). C Nachhaltigkeitsberichterstattung: § 9 Handelsrechtliche Nachhaltigkeitsberichterstattung. In: Freiberg, J., & Bruckner, A., (Hrsg.), Corporate Sustainability. Kompass für die Nachhaltigkeitsberichterstattung. Freiburg: Haufe-Lexware, S. 207 - 234.

Die Bundesregierung (2015). Die 17 globalen Nachhaltigkeitsziele verständlich erklärt. Von URL: https://www.bundesregierung.de/breg-de/themen/nachhaltigkeitspolitik/nachhaltig keitsziele-erklaert-232174 (Abruf: 01.03.2024).

EFFAS, & DVFA (2010). KPIs for ESG. A Guideline for Integration of ESG into Financial Analysis and Corporation Valuation. Version 3.0. Von URL: https://effas.com/wp-content/uploads/2021/09/KPIs_for_ESG_3_0_Final.pdf (Abruf: 21.02.2024).

EFRAG (2024). Materiality Assessment. Implementation Guidance. Von URL: https://www.efrag.org/sites/default/files/sites/webpublishing/SiteAssets/IG%201%20Materiality%20Assessme nt_final.pdf (Abruf: 17.02.2025).

EFRAG & IFRS Foundation (2024). ESRS-ISSB Standards. Interoperability Guidance. Von URL: https://www.efrag.org/sites/default/files/sites/webpublishing/SiteAssets/ESRS-ISSB%20Sta ndards%20Interoperability%20Guidance.pdf (Abruf: 17.02.2025).

Engel, M., van den Berg, C., & Herzberg, L. (2022). Der UN Global Compact und das Deutsche Global Compact Netzwerk – eine Initiative für verantwortungsvolle und nachhaltige Unternehmensführung. In: Schwager, B. (Hrsg.), CSR und Nachhaltigkeitsstandards: Normung und Standards im Nachhaltigkeitskontext. Berlin: Springer Gabler, S. 99 - 115.

Erchinger, R., Koch, R., & Schlemminger, R. B. (2022). ESG(E)-Kriterien - die Schlüssel zum Aufbau einer nachhaltigen Unternehmensführung. Eine Eignungsanalyse ausgewählter Standardkriterien. Wiesbaden: Springer Gabler.

Form, S., & Schlemminger, R. B. (2023). Nachhaltigkeitsmanagement und -controlling: Die Wesentlichkeitsanalyse. In: WISU - Das Wirtschaftsstudium, 52(3), S. 257 - 268.

Friedag, H. R. (2022). Green Controlling. In: ICV, ControllingWiki. Von URL: https://www.con trolling-wiki.com/de/index.php/Green_Controlling (Abruf: 29.02.2024).

GfK (2021). Earth Day: "Glamour Green" oder "Green in Deed"? Von URL: https://www.gfk.com /de/presse/earth-day-2021 (Abruf: 20.02.2024).

Grabmeier, S. (2025). On or off the Omnibus. Von URL: https://www.haufe.de/sustainability/debatte/rethinking-sustainability-chancen-der-omnibus-vo_575768_640794.html?ecmId=4 4576&ecmUid=6883059&chorid=&em_src=nl&em_cmp=news%2FPortal-Newsletter%2F Sustainability%2F478%2F%2F2025-01-29%2 (Abruf: 18.02.2025).

GRI (2024a). The global leader for impact reporting. Von URL: https://www.globalreporting.org/ (Abruf: 21.02.2024).

GRI (2024b). GRI Standards. Von URL: https://www.globalreporting.org/media/s4cp0oth/gri-gristandards-visuals-fig1_family-2021-print-v19-01.png (Abruf: 01.03.2024).

GRI & EFRAG (2023). GRI-ESRS Interoperability Index [Draft]. Von URL: https://www.global reporting.org/media/z2vmxbks/gri-standards-and-esrs-draft-interoperability-index_202311 30-final.pdf (Abruf: 17.02.2024).

Herzog, C. (2025). „Omnibus"-Verordnung: EU will Berichtspflichten konsolidieren. Von URL: https://www.haufe.de/sustainability/strategie/eu-kommission-will-berichtspflichten-konsolidieren_575772_636968.html (Abruf: 14.02.2025).

Hornung, M. (2022). Triple Bottom Line. In: ICV, ControllingWiki. Von URL: https://www.controlling-wiki.com/de/index.php/Triple_Bottom_Line (Abruf: 20.02.2024).

ICV (2011). Green Controlling - eine (neue) Herausforderung? Relevanz und Herausforderungen der Integration ökologischer Aspekte in das Controlling aus Sicht der Controllingpraxis. Ergebnisse einer ICV-Studie. Von URL: https://www.icv-controlling.com/fileadmin/Assets/Content/AK/Green%20Controlling/ICV11_Studienbericht_Green_Controlling_final.pdf (Abruf: 29.02.2024).

IFRS Foundation (2021). International <IR> Framework. Von URL: https://integratedreporting.ifrs.org/wp-content/uploads/2021/01/InternationalIntegratedReportingFramework.pdf (Abruf: 21.02.2024).

IÖW & future e. V. (2021). CSR-Reporting in Deutschland 2021. Von URL: https://www.ranking-nachhaltigkeitsberichte.de/fileadmin/ranking/user_upload/2021/Ranking_Nachhaltigkeitsberichte_2021_Ergebnisbericht_1.pdf (Abruf: 28.02.2024).

Kämmler-Burrak, A., Schulze, M., & Sommer, K.-S. (2024). CSRD - Eine neue Ära der Nachhaltigkeitsberichterstattung. Überblick zur neuen EU Coporate Sustainability Reporting Directive und den Implikationen für Unternehmen. In: Controller Magazin, 49(1), S. 10 - 15.

Koch, R., Schlemminger, R. B., & Schöner, L. (2024). Offenlegung von ESG-KPIs im DAX 40 in den Jahren 2019 - 2021. Eine empirische Untersuchung anhand der EFFAS/DVFA-Richtlinie im Zeitverlauf. In: Controlling - Zeitschrift für erfolgsorientierte Unternehmenssteuerung, 36(1), S. 61 - 69.

KPMG (2022a). Big shifts, small steps. Survey of Sustainability Reporting 2022. Von URL: https://assets.kpmg.com/content/dam/kpmg/xx/pdf/2023/04/big-shifts-small-steps.pdf (Abruf: 20.02.2024).

KPMG (2022b). Richtlinie zu Nachhaltigkeitsberichterstattung (CSRD). Von URL: https://assets.kpmg.com/content/dam/kpmg/de/pdf/Themen/2023/09/csrd-richtlinien-zur-nachhaltigkeitsberichterstattung-2023-KPMG.pdf (Abruf: 28.02.2024).

KPMG (2023). Get ready for European Sustainability Reporting Standards. Understandig the first set of ESRSs. November 2023. Von URL: https://assets.kpmg.com/content/dam/kpmg/xx/pdf/2022/07/talkbook-get-ready-for-esrs.pdf (Abruf: 01.03.2024).

KPMG (2024). Prüfungspflichten bei der Nachhaltigkeitsberichterstattung. EU-Richtlinie für Corporate Sustainability Reporting (CSRD). Von URL: https://kpmg.com/at/de/home/insights/2021/08/pruefungspflichten-bei-der-nachhaltigkeitesberichterstattung.html (Abruf: 26.02.2024).

Möhrer, M., Kämmler-Burrak, A., & Harms, S. (2024). Wesentlichkeit im Rahmen der EU-Taxonomie-Berichterstattung. In: Controller Magazin, 49(1), S. 16 - 21.

MSCI (2024). ESG Ratings & Climate Search Tool: Allianz SE. Von URL: https://www.msci.com/our-solutions/esg-investing/esg-ratings-climate-search-tool/issuer/allianz-se/IID000000002156841 (Abruf: 01.03.2024).

Müller, S. (2021). Integrated Reporting. In: ICV, ControllingWiki. Von URL: https://www.controlling-wiki.com/de/index.php/Integrated_Reporting (Abruf: 20.02.2024).

Müller, S. (2025a). Konsequenzen einer verspäteten Umsetzung der CSRD ins HGB. Von URL: https://www.haufe.de/finance/jahresabschluss-bilanzierung/konsequenzen-einer-verspaeteten-umsetzung-der-csrd_188_636544.html (Abruf: 14.02.2025).

Müller, S. (2025b). Omnibus-Initiative: Entwurf mit weitreichenden Änderungen veröffentlicht. Von URL: https://www.haufe.de/finance/jahresabschluss-bilanzierung/omnibus-verordnung-nachhaltigkeit_188_643014.html (Abruf: 27.05.2025).

Müller, S., & Stawinoga, M. (2022). Nichtfinanzielle Erklärung. In: ICV, ControllingWiki. Von URL: https://www.controlling-wiki.com/de/index.php/Nichtfinanzielle_Erklärung (Abruf: 26.02.2024).

Neubauer, C. (2024). ESG-Reporting und Software im Fokus. In: CFO aktuell. Zeitschrift für Finance & Controlling, 18(5), S. 181 - 183.

Nidumolu, R., Prahalad, C. K., & Rangaswami, M. R. (2009). In fünf Schritten zum nachhaltigen Unternehmen. In: Harvard Business Manager, k. A.(12), S. 1 - 11.

O. V. (2015a). Hans Carl von Carlowitz, 1713. In: Aachener Stiftung Kathy Beys, Lexikon der Nachhaltigkeit. Von URL: https://www.nachhaltigkeit.info/artikel/hans_carl_von_carlowitz_1713_1393.htm (Abruf: 20.02.2024).

O. V. (2015b). Nachhaltige Entwicklung. In: Aachener Stiftung Kathy Beys, Lexikon der Nachhaltigkeit. Von URL: https://www.nachhaltigkeit.info/artikel/forum_nachhaltige_entwicklung_627.htm (Abruf: 05.02.2024).

Odgers Berndtson (2021). Sustainability & Leadership Studie - Die Ergebnisse. Von URL: https://www.odgersberndtson.com/de-de/insights/sustainability-leadership-studie-die-ergebnisse/ (Abruf: 29.02.2024).

Onischka, M., & Kämmler-Burrak, A. (2023). Richtig vorbereiten auf die CSRD. 4-Punkte-Plan zur Umsetzung der neuen Reporting-Anforderungen bei MVV-Energie. In: Controller Magazin, 48(3), S. 60 - 66.

PwC (2022a). Global Investor Survey 2022 – Ergebnisse für Deutschland. PwC Studie: Investor:innen bemängeln ESG-Reporting. Von URL: https://www.pwc.de/de/nachhaltigkeit/global-investor-survey-2022-ergebnisse-fuer-deutschland.html (Abruf: 20.02.2024).

PwC (2022b). Doppelte Materialität – Mehr als eine regulatorische Pflichtaufgabe. Von URL: https://blogs.pwc.de/de/sustainability/article/232878/doppelte-materialitaet-mehr-als-eine-regulatorische-pflichtaufgabe/ (Abruf: 07.03.2024).

Regierungskommission Deutscher Corporate Governance Kodex (2022). Deutsche Corporate Governance Kodex. Von URL: https://dcgk.de/de/kodex.html (Abruf: 26.02.2024).

RNE (2024a). Deutscher Nachhaltigkeitskodex (DNK). Von URL: https://www.deutscher-nachhaltigkeitskodex.de/ (Abruf: 26.02.2024).

RNE (2024b). EU erzielt Einigung zur Weiterentwicklung der Richtlinie für die nicht-finanzielle Berichterstattung. Von URL: https://www.deutscher-nachhaltigkeitskodex.de/media/qzsbxjqz/dnk-factsheet-zur-csrd_oktober-2023.pdf (Abruf: 26.02.2024).

Schaeffler (2018). Nachhaltigkeitsbericht 2018: Strategie und Nachhaltigkeitsmanagement/Wesentlichkeit und Stakeholdermanagement. Von URL: https://www.schaeffler-nachhaltigkeit

sbericht.de/2018/strategie-und-nachhaltigkeitsmanagement/wesentlichkeit-und-stakeholdermanagement.html (Abruf: 29.02.2024).

Schaltegger, S. (2022). Nachhaltigkeitscontrolling. In: ICV, ControllingWiki. Von URL: https://www.controlling-wiki.com/de/index.php/Nachhaltigkeitscontrolling (Abruf: 29.02.2024).

Schlemminger, R. (2022). Strategisches Controlling. Von der Zielsetzung bis zur Implementierung. Stuttgart: W. Kohlhammer.

SFRG (2023). Building Public Trust Award. Von URL: https://www.sfrg.org/bpta (Abruf: 29.02.2024).

Steininger, A. (2023). Was bedeutet der Erdüberlastungtag. In: Tagesschau. Von URL: https://www.tagesschau.de/wissen/klima/erdueberlastungstag-122.html (Abruf: 01.03.2024).

Sustainalytics (2024). Company ESG Risk Ratings: Allianz SE. Von URL: https://www.sustainalytics.com/esg-rating/allianz-se/1008477053 (Abruf: 01.03.2024).

Tagesschau (2023). Weltbevölkerung hat Ressourcen für 2023 verbraucht. Von URL: https://www.tagesschau.de/inland/erdueberlastungstag-ressourcen-102.html (Abruf: 20.02.2024).

UN Gobal Compact (2024). Von URL: https://unglobalcompact.org/ (Abruf: 21.02.2024).

United Nations (1987). Report of the World Commission on Environment and Development: Our Common Future (Brundtland-Report). Von URL: https://sustainabledevelopment.un.org/content/documents/5987our-common-future.pdf (Abruf: 20.02.2024).

Vahs, D., & Schäfer-Kunz, J. (2012). Einführung in die Betriebswirtschaftslehre (6. Ausg.). Stuttgart: Schäffer-Poeschel.

Wartecker, G. (2024). EU Green Deal: Die unternehmerische Sorgfaltspflicht in Bezug auf Menschenrechte und Umweltschutz wird zur Pflicht. In: CFO aktuell. Zeitschrift für Finance & Controlling, 18(5), S. 172 - 173.

Würz, K. (2024). EU-Lieferketten-Richtlinie verabschiedet! Von URL: https://www.haufe.de/sustainability/soziales/ein-ueberblick-die-eu-lieferketten-richtlinie-csddd_575770_625620.html (Abruf: 14.02.2025).

Beate Zimpelmann[1]

The Green Deal in multi-level policy: the example of the Bremen Climate Enquiry Commission and the implementation of its findings

Global oil consumption has already exceeded the historic mark of 100,000,000 barrels of oil – per day – in 2019 and is increasing. Global CO_2 emissions continue to rise. The agreed climate target of 1.5 degrees of warming was exceeded for a whole year for the first time in 2024 and can no longer be met. This puts the partial decarbonisation in Germany into perspective. Although emissions here fell by 46 per cent between 1990 and 2023, some climate-damaging production was relocated abroad. In the transport sector, greenhouse gas emissions have risen anyway, which is why the Federal Environment Agency is quite rightly calling on politicians to make improvements to "drastically" reduce emissions (see Brand, Brunnengräber 2025).

Global climate policy

When we look at global climate policy, we should remember the following:

Climate research assumes that the political 2 degree target may not be enough to safely prevent irreversible feedbacks caused by tipping elements in the Earth system.

This is why the UN Climate Change Conference in Paris in December 2015 decided to limit global warming to "well below" two degrees Celsius compared to pre-industrial times and to make efforts to limit it to 1.5 degrees in order to minimise these risks as far as possible.

In concrete terms, the agreement in 2015 meant meeting the two-degree target with a probability of more than 66% and at the same time maintaining a 50% chance of achieving the 1.5°C limit. This results in a fixed CO_2 budget, i.e. an upper limit for emissions that may be released until 2100.

Of great importance for this approach was that strong climate protection measures should be implemented quickly, that global greenhouse gas emis-

1 Prof. Dr. Beate Zimpelmann, City University of Applied Sciences Bremen.

sions should peak by 2020 at the latest and then be halved every decade, and that these targets can only actually be achieved if we remove CO_2 that has already been released into the atmosphere – so-called negative emissions.

As we all know, this interim target has not been achieved.

Stefan Rahmstorf, one of Germany's leading climate researchers, outlined a reduction pathway in 2017. The figure for 2017 is estimated at a maximum of 600 billion worldwide tonnes of carbon dioxide assumed for a 50% chance of achieving the climate target. From the perspective of 2017, however, compliance with this target requires a global emissions turnaround by 2020 at the latest.

The longer effective climate protection measures are postponed, the faster the remaining budget will be exhausted and the more emissions will have to be reduced in the future. And at some point, of course, this results in reduction paths that are completely unrealistic. Conversely, rapid emission reductions in the present allow the point at which zero emissions must be achieved to be pushed further into the future.

According to more recent calculations from 2020, this residual budget now amounts to around 500 billion tonnes of carbon dioxide. Current data also show that global CO_2 emissions are not declining, but have continued to rise in 2021, 2022 and 2023 compared to pre-coronavirus pandemic levels.

In recent years, climate research has seen us on the path to a global temperature increase of 3 degrees Celsius in terms of actual emissions and climate policies.

The Green Deal

Against this backdrop, we look at the **EU's Green Deal.**

The EU has set clear climate targets for its member states, which Germany has not achieved by 2024.

The EU wants to reduce its emissions of climate-damaging greenhouse gases by 55 per cent by 2030 compared to 1990 and become climate-neutral by the middle of the century, i.e. not emit more greenhouse gases than are saved.

Member states and the EU Parliament have adopted important plans that are likely to drastically change Europe's way of life and economy. For example, the EU will ban new cars with combustion engines from 2035, focus on more renewable energies and expand emissions trading. The number of emission credits will be reduced more quickly and the allocation of free certificates will be gradually abolished.

But: According to the EU Environment Agency (EEA), the European Union is only partially on track with its climate, environmental and sustainability targets.

Despite steady progress, more decisive action is needed, the agency said – including in boosting a circular economy, combating species extinction and reducing the ecological footprint of consumption.

In the wake of the war, the Community is adapting its climate legislation. This is a good thing, says CDU MEP Peter Liese: "The Russian aggression in Ukraine has of course dominated the year, and we have to be flexible here in the short term. That is why we are giving citizens and industry time to breathe. Emissions trading will be tightened, but the effect will not be felt until 2027"(Mayr 2023).

From this date, emissions trading will also cover CO_2 emissions from road transport and buildings; for private individuals, it will only apply – if at all – from 2029.

The European Union has set the right priorities in its decisions following the outbreak of war, says Christoph Bals, Political Director of the think tank Germanwatch: find new energy suppliers, save energy, switch to renewables quickly. However: "In terms of concrete measures, the purchase of LNG gas has so far been the main focus. Case study Germany: In the transport sector in particular, but also in the building sector, not even the previous climate targets have been achieved. But we need to get out of oil and gas faster"(Mayr 2023).

In a landmark achievement, the European Union reported an 8% reduction in net greenhouse gas emissions in 2023, according to the latest "Trends and Projections" report from the European Environment Agency (EEA). This significant reduction marks a milestone on the EU's path to climate neutrality, a goal to be achieved by 2050 under the EU Climate Law. The latest report emphasises that the reduction has been achieved through a decrease in coal use, a significant increase in renewable energy sources and improved energy efficiency in the EU Member States (see Müller 2024).

Preliminary forecasts indicate that the current measures would reduce net emissions by 43% by 2030. Additional planned measures could increase this reduction to 49%. However, this shows that a gap remains, emphasising the need for Member States to further improve and implement their National Energy and Climate Plans (NECPs) (Müller 2024).

The transition to renewable energy sources has proven to be crucial for reducing emissions in the EU. According to EEA estimates, renewable energy now accounts for 24% of total energy consumption in the EU – a significant increase compared to just 10% in 2005.

At the same time, energy consumption across the EU continues to fall: primary energy consumption has fallen by 19% and final energy consumption by 11% since 2005.

The transition from fossil fuels to renewable energies has had an enormous impact, particularly in the energy sector, where emissions have been halved since 2005.

The industrial sector has also achieved a 30% reduction in emissions during this period, mainly through improved energy efficiency and optimised processes. This progress is largely due to the EU Emissions Trading System (ETS), which has created a regulatory environment that encourages emission reductions in sectors with high greenhouse gas emissions (see Müller 2024).

Although significant progress has been made in the energy and industrial sectors, developments in other areas covered by the Effort Sharing Regulation (ESR) are mixed.

For example, the buildings sector has seen a remarkable 30% reduction in emissions since 2005, thanks to energy-efficient refurbishments and sustainable heating and insulation methods.

The transport and agriculture sectors, on the other hand, faced greater challenges in achieving comparable reductions.

The EEA emphasises that achieving the proposed 2040 target of a 90% reduction in emissions, as envisaged by the European Commission, requires both predictable and flexible policy frameworks that take into account the scale and speed of the necessary changes.

According to the EEA's analysis, the projected emission levels for 2040 and 2050 remain above the targets, even if many Member States introduce new measures (see EEA Report 2024).

Regional climate policy

With this in mind, let's take a look at Bremen.

Bremen's climate policy already has a long tradition and can boast activities in all relevant areas. It is consistently rated very highly in various comparisons of municipal approaches. In some areas, it even stands out in particular – for example in car sharing. Overall, it has long been very differentiated and Bremen has been a pioneer in climate policy at local level nationwide.

And yet: in the 30 years between 1990 and 2020, Bremen's emissions were only reduced by just under 6% – instead of the 40% that Bremen's climate policy aimed for. This very sobering situation is the starting point for the parliamentary commission of enquiry that worked in 2020 and 2021.

Let's first take a quick look at the data to understand the situation a little better:

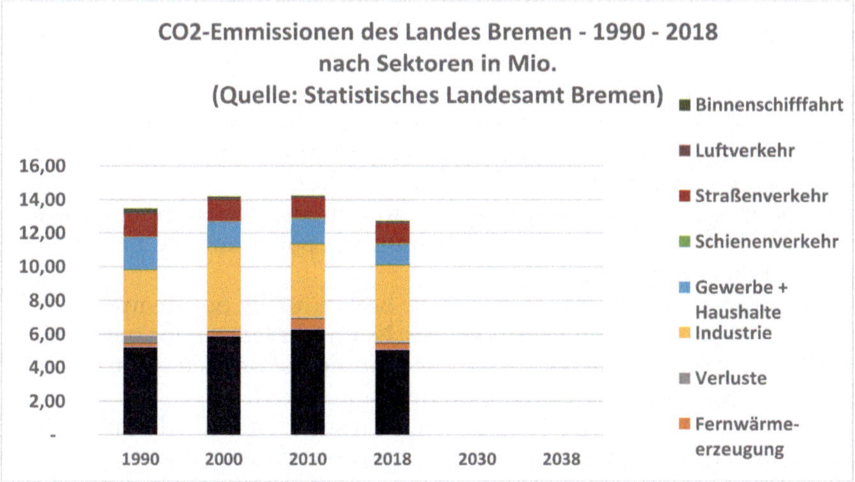

The graph shows Bremen's emissions by sector over time – and we can see that 4 sectors are particularly significant: electricity generation (black), which fluctuates at a high level, industry (yellow), whose emissions have actually increased, buildings (blue), whose emissions have fallen by around 1/3 (which is certainly not easy to see here), and road transport (red), which has slightly lower emissions.

Let's take a look at the most important influencing factors in the individual sectors:

In the electricity sector, the decisive factor is the delayed energy transition and the continuation of coal-fired power generation prior to the decision to phase out coal. This is controlled at federal level. It is also important that the energy producers are privatised, i. e. companies make the decisions here. Bremen has hardly any influence here.

In industry, emissions are dominated by the steel industry. Bremen is home to a basic materials industry. Emissions here are determined by economic trends and global market-driven corporate strategies. Transformative approaches have long been unimaginable.

In the buildings sector the falling emissions are a result of improved standards in new construction + refurbishment of existing buildings – both are directly attributable to federal building legislation and the accompanying measures at local level (energy advice and local funding programmes, for example).

In the transport sector, we are seeing slightly lower emissions – this is due to significantly more efficient vehicles. At the same time, however, there is a very significant increase in traffic – both for cars and goods vehicles. This reflects the approaches of transport policy, both nationally and regionally, which are primarily focussed on the car.

It is important here once again to address Bremen's limited scope for action and the decisive role of the federal government and the EU – both in terms of legislative powers and financial resources.

The areas in which Bremen has the most important options of its own in the multi-level state system are clearly transport policy and the area of buildings and their heating supply.

In all areas, it is clear that there have been virtually no attempts to make truly transformative changes for decades. Neither at federal nor state level.

This was the starting point for the redefinition of Bremen's climate policy in 2020 – the goal of the Enquete Commission's work.

The Enquete Climate Commission, an institution of the Bremen parliament, was a novum, the first one in Germany on communal level.

All parties (9 representatives) were represented plus experts (9) and permanent guests (environmental and business associations, labour unions, members of the state administration). Work began in May 2020 and the final report is available since December 2020.

It had described its goals as follows:

- Development of a comprehensive orientation of all areas of action towards the goal of climate neutrality,
- Convergence with EU and national policy with limited options for local authorities,
- Managed transformation for all sectors.

In my view, the challenge is most clearly expressed in this statement by Patrick Graichen, who participated in the Enquete as an external expert. "We have to pull all the levers to the limit".

The Enquete's approach is explicitly to orientate itself on the Paris goals – and to do for all areas what climate policy has not yet done consistently at either federal or local level, namely to think about a comprehensive, controlled transformation.

Due to the repeatedly emphasised central importance of federal and EU policy, the role of the different policy levels was also explicitly considered here.

The emissions pathway developed by the Enquete is based on the Paris targets and an emissions budget broken down to Bremen.

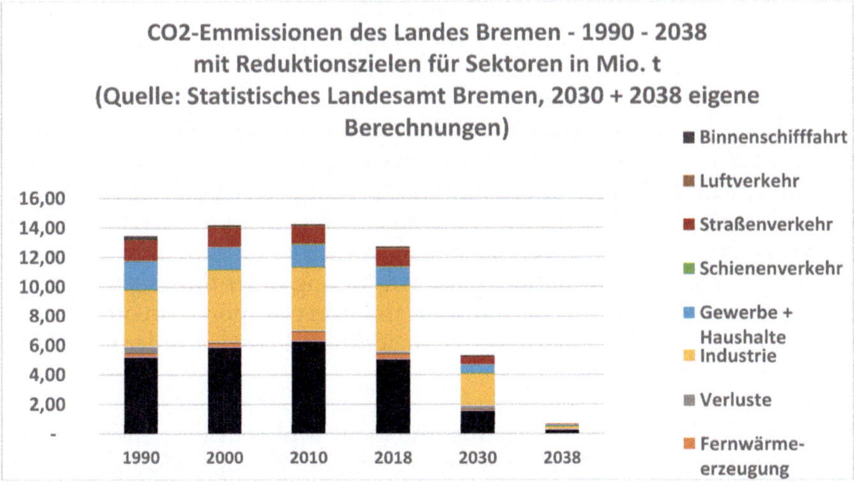

Specific reduction quotas are derived for the different sectors.

Let's take a look at the key measures in the most important sectors:

In energy generation, the expansion of renewable energies, i.e. wind and solar energy, is crucial. This is largely controlled at federal level – in Bremen, the focus is primarily on the expansion of PV systems on public and private roofs. We are actually at the very beginning here.

In the transformation of the steel industry, we are dependent on the strategy of a multinational company, i.e. Arcelor Mittal, and the actual expansion of the hydrogen infrastructure. It is important to note that there are very clear time windows for necessary replacement investments in such plants, which mean that there are very precise and tight time windows for change that must be utilised in order to achieve change – and which mean that additional acceleration of a transformation is not possible. For Bremen, this path is a decisive factor in securing the location. This is crucial for Bremen as a business location, even though Arcelor Mittal is responsible for almost half of Bremen's emissions.

Specifically, the plant is planning to retain the site and is making concrete preparations to enter into hydrogen technology, the subsidies from Brussels are also in place and Bremen has promised co-financing. However, it remains to be seen what concrete steps will be taken in view of the tense global market situation for the German steel industry.

Transport policy is about the conversion to e-mobility, but not only. For example, the Enquete's assumptions are also based on the fact that the number of passenger cars will be reduced by 66% by 2038. The number of cars per 1000 inhabitants is expected to fall from 428 to 150. That is a very important point. Transport performance, i.e. the total number of kilometres driven, is also set to fall – by 30% in the car sector by 2030. However, there were special votes from individual parties.

One key instrument is the massive expansion of local and regional public transport. For example, we absolutely need services for regional commuter transport, which is much more important from a climate perspective than inner-city transport. And here we have no concrete plans to date. In the coming years, politicians will have to make statements on how they intend to finance the expansion of public transport. Among other things, the Enquete also proposed the principle of "transport finances transport" – in other words, that car traffic should be burdened with additional costs in order to support local public transport.

In the area of buildings and heating, the focus is of course on the standards for new buildings and the refurbishment rate for existing buildings. The Enquete Commission determined that the measure with the greatest CO_2-saving effect here would be a separate, very expensive state funding programme for building refurbishment. The second most effective measure is a state heating law and this would also involve very ambitious Bremen targets for the conversion of the heating supply. Gas consumption is to be reduced by 56% by 2030 – how exactly do politicians intend to achieve this?

Another challenge is the conversion of district heating and new local heating networks to truly climate-neutral renewable energies. Here we only have very vague ideas for district heating, and it is now clear from the current plans of the local energy supplier that its expansion cannot take place quickly enough. For local heating, we need clear statements on which options should be supported here: how do we view urban geothermal initiatives that want to organise themselves as cooperatives? Should there be a municipal infrastructure? Politicians are already lagging behind the time targets set out in the Enquete report. However, local heating networks in particular offer an opportunity to supply climate-friendly energy to those neighbourhoods that cannot be connected to district heating networks and also to create cost-effective and participatory solutions.

The financial framework conditions are crucial: the realisation of this climate policy is only possible with a huge investment. This involves investments, operating costs, but clearly also additional personnel. The Enquete Commission assumed that the public sector will need around 6–7 billion euros in one-off investment costs and around 200–380 million euros per year in long-term operating costs. Of course, similar costs are incurred everywhere in Germany, as various studies show for individual sectors and for Germany as a whole. It is quite clear that these burdens can only be met through additional debt, either at local level, for example in Bremen, or through support from the federal government and then through debt there. The judgement of the Federal Constitutional Court of November 2023 sets limits to this.

In February 2023 Bremen's parliament approved 2.5 billion euros for climate protection, enshrining certain reporting obligations for greenhouse gas emissions. A preliminary balance sheet is due by the end of March 2025 for the first reporting year 2023. However, the State Statistical Office will not be able to provide this. This is a very time-consuming process and the necessary positions are not available – not least due to necessary budget cuts as a result of the debt brake. The 2.5 billion approved for climate protection measures could also not be realised due to the debt brake.

This means that although the Enquete Commission in Bremen is an excellent example of cross-party, expert-led political decision-making, it is unlikely, that the measures can be implemented in the form that was intended.

It remains to be seen which measures can still take effect despite reduced financial ressources and where the municipality will utilise its room for manoeuvre, particularly in municipal heat planning. The current discussion is focussing on issues such as the conversion of district heating and new local heating networks to truly climate-neutral renewable energies and citizen participation. There are promising approaches from local initiatives here and their promotion could be a great opportunity.

Especially when it comes to issues such as the transport transition, doubts are justified as to whether the state government is prepared to boldly move forward and decide on far-reaching changes to strengthen the environmental network and significantly reduce the number of cars in the city.

It remains to be seen which measures can still take effect and where the municipality will utilise its room for manoeuvre.

But it is doubtable if a climate-neutral Bremen by 2038 is even possible.

The devil is in the concrete implementation.

Literature:

Agora Energiewende, Wuppertal Institut (2019): Klimaneutrale Industrie: Schlüsseltechnologien und Politikoptionen für Stahl, Chemie und Zement. Berlin, November 2019.

Brand, Brunnengräber: Kein Klimaschutz ohne soziale Kämpfe, Blätter für deutsche und internationale Politik, 2/2025.

Bremische Bürgerschaft 2021: Abschlussbericht der Enquetekommission „Klimaschutzstrategie für das Land Bremen“, Bremen.

EEA Report: Trends and Projections in Europe; Luxembourg 2024.

Friedlingstein, P., O'Sullivan, M., Jones, M. W., Andrew, R. M., Gregor, L., Hauck, J., ... & Zheng, B. (2022). Global carbon budget 2022. Earth System Science Data, 14(11), 4811–4900. https://essd.copernicus.org/articles/14/4811/2022/#executive_summary, (retrieved on 26.2. 2025)

EEA 2021: Benchmarks Städte und Gemeinden. Bundesgeschäftsstelle European Energy Award, Berlin. https://www.european-energy-award.de/fileadmin/Downloads/Oeffentliche_Downloads/Benchmarks/Benchmarks_Staedte_und_Gemeinden/Benchmarks_4.Quartal_2021_SuG.pdf

IPCC, 2018: Zusammenfassung für politische Entscheidungsträger. Deutsche IPCC-Koordinierungsstelle, ProClim, Österreichisches Umweltbundesamt, Bonn/Bern/Wien, November 2018.

Irmisch, Janne; Haupt, Wolfgang; Eckersley, Peter; Kern, Kristine; Müller, Hannah (2022): Klimapolitische Entwicklungspfade deutscher Groß- und Mittelstädte. IRS Dialog Forschungsberichte, Erkner.

Kemmerzell, Jörg; Anne Hofmeister (2019): Innovationen in der Klimaschutzpolitik deutscher Großstädte, in: Politische Vierteljahresschrift, Jg. 60, Nr. 1, 95–126.

Mayr, Jakob (2023) Der Krieg und das Klima Verschiebt die EU ihr Jahrhundertprojekt? https://www.tagesschau.de/ausland/europa/eu-klima-ziele-101.html (abgerufen am 26.2. 2025)

Müller, Renée: Energiewende treibt erhebliche CO_2-Reduktion in der gesamten EU voran, November 2024, https://tibo.energy/de/news/eea-report-2024 (abgerufen am 25.2.2025).

Otto, A.; Kern, K.; Haupt, W.; Eckersley, P.; Thieken, A. H. (2021): Ranking local climate policy: assessing the mitigation and adaptation activities of 104 German cities. In: Climatic Change 167, 1–2. doi: 10.1007/s10584-021–03142-9

Rahmstorf, Stefan (2017): Können wir die globale Erwärmung rechtzeitig stoppen? https://scilogs.spektrum.de/klimalounge/koennen-wir-die-globale-erwaermung-rechtzeitig-stoppen/ (abgerufen am 26.2.2025)

Rahmstorf, Stefan (2020): Berechnung zum Emissionsbudget. Wie gut ist das neue Klimaziel der EU-Kommission? In: Spiegel Online, 4. Oktober 2020. https://www.spiegel.de/wissenschaft/mensch/eu-kommission-was-taugt-das-neue-klimaziel-a-f9578265-ac73-4993-abc0-748d4051b510 (abgerufen am 265.2.2025)

SRU (2022): Wie viel CO2 darf Deutschland maximal noch ausstoßen? Fragen und Antworten zum CO2-Budget. Stellungnahme des Sachverständigen Rates für Umweltfrage (SRU), Berlin.

Statistisches Landesamt Bremen: CO_2-Emissionen aus dem Endenergieverbrauch (Verursacherbilanz) seit 1990 nach Emittentensektoren – Land Bremen. Download von: https://www.statistik.bremen.de/themen/energiestatistik-energiebilanzierung-und-co2-emissionen-1914 (abgerufen am 26.2.2025)

UNEP (2017). The Emissions Gap Report 2017. United Nations Environment Programme (UNEP), Nairobi

Wieland, Joachim (2022): Rechtliche Rahmenbedingungen zur Deckung des Finanzbedarfs für die nötigen Investitionen in Klimaneutralität im Land Bremen. Rechtsgutachten für die Bremische Bürgerschaft.

Chapter 4
Resources

Rainer Lisowski[1]

Biodiversity and the question of political power

An attempt to assess political power in the implementation of EU biodiversity targets at the lower end of the legal cascade using standard political science theories

Summary: The essay examines the concept of political power and is part of a larger research project. The essay develops a specific operationalization of political power intended for an empirical study on the EU's biodiversity goals within the framework of the Green Deal. The developed concept of power aims to clarify how and what kind of power is used at the municipal level, and whether powerful actors dilute or reinforce the EU's goals before their local implementation. Various concepts of power, including coercion, mediation, and collective mobilization, are analyzed in connection with EU directives, such as expanding protected areas and promoting biodiversity-friendly agriculture. Theories from Machiavelli, Weber, and contemporary thinkers like Han and Naím provide the theoretical foundation. The study introduces a power matrix to evaluate actors and means of power in local contexts. Lastly, initial findings from an exploratory interview are briefly cited, suggesting that local administrations may not be aware of the EU's biodiversity goals but act in their spirit, often relying on negotiation rather than coercion.

Keywords: Political power, biodiversity, EU Green Deal, municipal implementation, power concepts, legal cascade, empirical political research

1 Rainer Lisowski is Professor for Public Management at the School of International Business, University of Applied Sciences Bremen, Germany. He has studied Political Science and Economics. Before being appointed as Professor in Bremen he worked in various functions in Public Management, public and private companies. He travels to Africa and Asia on a regular base for research and lecturing purposes. His research is mainly empirically driven, often following qualitative research paradigm. He has published several books on various political issues. Contact: rainer.lisowski@hs-bremen.de.

A. Preliminary considerations[2]

Each academic discipline has its characteristic terminology. In law, the focus lies on legality and legitimacy or the question of legal certainty. In economics, terms such as efficiency, revenue, or profit are central. In political science, key concepts include conflict, consensus, interests—and most importantly, power.[3] Political science, more than any other discipline, places a central emphasis on the study of power.[4]

For the subject of biodiversity examined here, the concept of power is crucial for two reasons:

(1) On one hand, the EU formulates goals and directives in its Green Deal packages aimed at fostering biodiversity within member states. Such goals cannot be achieved without power. Legal scholars might argue that the legal cascade ensures the EU's vision is implemented from the top down. However, from a political science perspective, one must critically ask: Is this truly the case? Or does the anticipated cascade get diluted or intensified through the influence of powerful actors?

(2) On the other hand, power always necessitates certain instruments. Power is not a mythical force nor an electric current; it only manifests through specific means. Investigating these means is particularly valuable in the context of assessing whether the goals for increased biodiversity are diluted or intensified.

---

2 Disclosure: the AI "ChatGPT" was used to translate this chapter from German to English, due to efficient time-management. Quotations that were originally in German have been translated into English, using the same AI.

3 Hiltrud Naßmacher identifies these seven terms: interest, conflict, consensus, power, opposition, legitimacy, and legality, cf. Naßmacher (1997, pp. 5–12). Nitschke also includes "power" in his list of key terms, cf. Nitschke (2020, p. 12).

4 What is political? To answer this question, one would need to look for typically political categories. Such categories, which structure a specific field of inquiry, are often outlined based on a polarity. In morality, the polarity is between good and evil. In aesthetics, it is between beauty and ugliness. In economics, between profitable and unprofitable. Against this backdrop, Schmidt proposes the polarization between friend and enemy for defining the political. It is important to note that the enemy does not have to be morally evil. It is by no means about a psychological or individual difference in the sense of a personal enemy. Instead, it concerns the struggle between groups in the public sphere. Politics, therefore, inherently has a polemical character. For a conflict to unleash political power, it must be strong enough to shape people into a friend-enemy framework. At the same time, the unity of the state mitigates excessively extreme political hostility. Cf. Schmitt (2002, 26–31, 37).

The aim of this study is to extract key dimensions of political power from the literature. These will then be used in a planned, future research project to empirically investigate whether and how the EU's Green Deal objectives for biodiversity are altered—diluted or intensified—as they cascade down from the EU level to the municipal level. In this regard, this study serves as a preliminary investigation for an ongoing research project.[5]

B. Levels of Theory

It is first necessary to briefly clarify which theoretical level we are addressing. Broadly speaking, four levels of theoretical analysis can be distinguished (see Table 1).

Table 1: Levels of social sciences theory

Theoretical Approach/Level	Description
Epistemological Level and Meta-Theory	How is knowledge generated in the social sciences? What can we know at all?
Intellectual History Level	(Historical) theories of political ideas, terms, concepts, and configurations.
Social Theory	Fundamental statements and concepts about politics and society (e.g., Marxist social theory).
Empirical Political Research	Empirically grounded analysis of political phenomena.
Practical Politics	*The level of political reality.*

The highest, *epistemological level* fundamentally deals with the question of human cognitive abilities, delving deeply into philosophy and extending beyond the scope of this study's interest. Examples of such meta-theories include Karl Popper's epistemological philosophy ("critical rationalism").[6]

The *intellectual history level* examines political ideas or terms from their historical or philosophical foundations. Here, it would be worthwhile to ana-

5 Interdisciplinary research project "BioDivStrat" to examine municipal biodiversity strategies within the research cluster "Dynamics, Tensions, and eXtreme Events" (DTX) at Bremen University of Applied Sciences. The project aims to investigate, using the example of several lower nature conservation authorities (UNBs) located within districts and independent cities, how and whether the EU's objectives are being pursued and implemented.

6 Cf. Popper (1994) and Popper (1997). Critical rationalism was not chosen by chance; the author sees Karl R. Popper's approach as the most successful attempt to meet the primary quality criteria of research in the social sciences.

lyze the evolution or shifts in the ideas and concepts of power and identify which dimensions are relevant for this investigation. While Machiavelli,[7] for instance, describes techniques and strategies of power—viewing power as coercion, fueled by a mix of violence potential (rulers need armed forces), resources (rulers require means to build and maintain this potential), and skills (rulers must be cunning, manipulative, and adept at deploying resources and force)—Thomas Hobbes focuses more on power resources: "The power of a man, generally speaking, is his present means to obtain some future apparent good (…)."[8] In this understanding, Hobbes's concept of power closely resembles Max Weber's famous definition of power as the ability to impose one's will despite resistance.[9] This level, therefore, holds relevance for the present investigation and will be briefly addressed in the following section.

On the *social theory level,* the concept of power within grand social theories warrants examination. For Marx, power lies in the ability of the capitalist class to appropriate the surplus value created by workers, relying on the state as a means to sustain their economic dominance.[10] For Bourdieu, power encompasses the idea of symbolic power, which can already be seen in his "Distinction", where he discusses cultural capital as a tool for asserting cultural norms and symbols.[11] Since power analysis in grand social theories often represents only one of many elements, this level will not be explored further here.

Situated close to political practice and the general subject of political science is *empirical political research.* The term here is used more broadly, encompassing not only quantitative studies but also the observation and analysis of political processes with the goal of identifying theoretical patterns. Numerous fruitful approaches can be found at this level, such as Nye's well-known distinction between "hard power" and "soft power"[12] or Naím's typology of four different forms of power.[13]

---

7 Cf. Machiavelli (1978).

8 Hobbes (1984, p. 66) German Original: „Die Macht eines Menschen besteht, allgemein genommen, in seinen gegenwärtigen Mitteln zur Erlangung eines zukünftigen anscheinenden Guts (…)."

9 Cf. Weber (2000, p. 62)

10 Cf. Marx (2004).

11 For the "structuring of social space," see especially Chapter 2. Bourdieu engages more extensively with the various forms of capital starting on page 195. Much later, he writes that classification systems are less instruments of knowledge and more instruments of power. Cf. Bourdieu (1987, 195ff., 744.).

12 Joseph Nye describes "soft power" as a mix of cultural attractiveness, political values, and foreign policy aligned with legitimate moral authority. Cf. Nye (2015, 59ff.).

13 Cf. Naim (2014, pp. 23–25).

C. Theories of Political Power

C.1. Power as Coercion and Effective Mediation

Empirical investigations require a clear theoretical framework that remains manageable. Thus, it is legitimate to limit the depth of intellectual history analyses in order to focus on the concrete examination of power effects in practice. This aligns with established methods in empirical political science. Despite this methodological focus on a clear and manageable framework, a brief review of intellectual history is valuable to trace the development of key power concepts. The following overview demonstrates how various understandings of power—from its foundation in coercion to subtler forms of mediation—have shaped the analysis of political processes.

Viewed from the intellectual history of the concept of power, it undoubtedly played a role in ancient political theory. However, there was no comprehensive political idea of power as conceptualized by the Greeks or Romans. Why would there be? The idea of pursuing power for its own sake would have been highly alien, if not outright reprehensible, to philosophers like Plato, whose political views were heavily intertwined with ethical questions.[14] It was not until the early modern period that a genuine interest in power and its acquisition as a social technique emerged. The name Machiavelli is particularly prominent in this context, especially for his treatise Il Principe. However, Machiavelli is more concerned with the acquisition and security of power than with a nuanced understanding of what power is. For him, power is primarily coercion. Asked how the strength of a ruler can be assessed, Machiavelli's answer is straightforward: Is the ruler able to defend themselves and maintain authority? Here, he identifies the military, financial resources, fortified positions, and—interestingly—the acceptance of citizens as decisive aspects.[15] This fundamental idea of power as coercion persisted for a long time. Approximately four centuries later, Carl Schmitt articulated a similar thought in relation to state power: state sovereignty endures as long as no one rises to challenge it in civil war. This echoes Hobbes: the sovereignty of law, for Schmitt, simply means the sovereignty of the entity that enacts the law.[16] Across these varying perspectives, a common thread emerges—a conception of power characterized by its *force*-fulness, its coercion, as abstractly described by Max Weber in his famous formulation: the ability to impose one's will against the resistance of others.

14 Cf. for concise presentation to: Schwarz et al. (2017, 119f.).
15 Cf. Machiavelli (1978, pp. 45–48).
16 Cf. Schmitt (2002, 43, 66).

In modern times, however, this aspect of power that focuses solely on coercion has become too simplistic. One reason is straightforward: there is often a lack of self-determination in Western democracies. Power, according to the German-Korean philosopher Byung-Chul Han, always requires a commitment to oneself. Modern states, however, (rightfully) distribute and dilute power. In Han's words, they create "side spaces" of power, thereby preventing closure.[17] Thus, solely relying on coercion may no longer be sufficient to address the question of power today.[18] For Han, power is therefore a continuum that emanates from a self (whether a person or institution) and extends outward toward others, radiating influence. Han adds that if a power-wielding individual or institution successfully presents itself in a way that leads others to perceive their own goals and desires as aligned with those of the powerful, the greater the power exerted. In this scenario, the other party ultimately complies willingly. The less mediation succeeds, the more coercion must be employed—a suboptimal scenario, as coercion undermines the power of the institution or individual, provoking resistance.[19]

Thus, power operates most effectively when it engenders internalized behavior—when the subjects of power act as desired from the outset. Ideally, the subjects not only act but also think in the manner desired by the source of power. This could be summarized as follows: "The sphere of power expands the more the possibility of enforcement inherently shapes the behavior of the subjects."[20]

In examining evidence of power exertion within the legal cascade of the EU's biodiversity plans, two aspects must be investigated: the possibilities and instruments of coercion on one hand, and the means and possibilities of mediation on the other. Empirical political research can help elaborate on this distinction further.

C.2. Concepts of Power in Empirical Political Science

What Han explores on a fundamental philosophical level is addressed in a significantly more concrete manner by Mosés Naím, a politically and practi-

17 Cf. Han (2015, 96ff.).

18 In eine ähnliche Richtung argumentiert Rosanvallon, der die Macht der repräsentativen Demokratie, Entscheidungen zu treffen und durchzusetzen, stark geschwächt sieht. Cf. Rosanvallon (2018).

19 Cf. for this idea in general: Han (2015, 11, 15, 30).

20 Cf. Weiß (1995, p. 307) German original: „Der Raum der Macht ist um so größer, je mehr die Möglichkeit der Durchsetzung von vorn-herein das Handeln der Adressaten bestimmt."

cally experienced thinker, former Venezuelan minister, former director of the World Bank, and former editor-in-chief of *Foreign Policy.* According to Naím, power can take four distinct forms. In essence, this reflects, in a somewhat more differentiated way, the dichotomy of *coercion* and *mediation* introduced in section C.1.[21] He defines four specific manifestations that power can assume in order to assert itself:[22]

1. *Muscles* – asserting power through the use of force, if necessary;
2. *Codes* – relying on symbols, codes, or rules to establish accepted authority;
3. *Persuasion* – successfully convincing others to see things the way power wants them to;
4. *Rewards* – using financial incentives to prompt desired behavior.

This set of four elements can be aptly understood as instruments of power, as metaphors like *muscles* or *rewards* clearly suggest. However, instruments do not deploy themselves; they require human agency to wield them. For this reason, turning our attention to the United States proves insightful. Rieger and Schultze highlight that, particularly in the U.S., empirical power analyses are predominantly shaped by a more behaviorist approach. In line with a "decision-making approach",[23] the focus lies on actors and their behavior rather than on normative or structural questions.

One of the most foundational contributions to the empirical concept of power comes from Robert A. Dahl. Unlike the aforementioned, more philosophical works, Dahl measures the concept of power—not only through the instruments or *means* of power, but additionally also identifies—by addressing the following issues:[24] *base,* the *amount* and the *scope* of power.

(a) Base of power

Weber famously distinguishes the "crystalline" concept of authority (Herrschaft) from the "amorphous" (Weber) concept of power (Macht).[25] From a social perspective, power can indeed take on almost any form, which is why

21 Naim speaks of coercion and authority, as well as influence and persuasion. Cf. Naim (2014, p. 16).

22 Cf. Naim (2014, pp. 23–25).

23 Vgl. Rieger and Schultze (1994, p. 245). This led, among other things, to mathematical ideas for formally representing power. While this can be intellectually interesting, it doesn't really move us forward in applied research, especially if we assume that power has become "fuzzy" today.

24 Cf. Dahl (1957, p. 203).

25 Cf. Weber (2000, p. 62).

Weber refers to it as amorphous. In the political context, however, the basis of power might be defined somewhat more narrowly, even though Weiß considers Thomas Hobbes' notion of political power similarly unspecific. Political power can, in fact, be purely fictitious: those who are preceded by a reputation for power already possess power by virtue of that reputation.[26]

If one defines it more narrowly, power can be derived from political sources, such as the regulatory power of (democratic) institutions or the mobilizing power of large followings. Power can also have an economic basis, such as the financial power of corporations or the lobbying power of interest groups. There are communicative sources of power, including the reach and influence of media and media creators. Additionally, power can be of a political-theological nature, recognizing the potency of ideologies, convictions, and belief systems.

(b) Amount of power

Intensive power possesses a high degree of penetrative and enforcement capability, a characteristic not shared by extensive power. Symmetrical power relations are marked by approximately equal influence among actors, whereas asymmetrical power relations reveal a clear hierarchy. Centralized power is monopolistic or concentrated in the hands of a few actors or institutions, while decentralized power is often distributed within networks or collaborative decision-making mechanisms. Latent power is invisible, revealing itself only in specific situations, whereas manifest power is directly observable, such as in decisions or conflicts. Empirically, latent power can be examined through the analysis of agenda-setting or tacit consent, while manifest power is captured through concrete decision-making processes and their enforcement.

(c) Scope of power

Broad power relations encompass a wide range of actors, whereas narrow power is limited to specific thematic areas. The spatial scope of power addresses the geographical reach it can encompass. The temporal reach of power varies significantly between state power and societal power relations: state power, in the form of laws, is designed for long-term stability and generally lacks an "expiration date." In contrast, societal power relations are more dy-

---

26 Cf. Weiß (1995, p. 307).

namic and subject to constant change. Power structures that dominate today may be challenged and shifted tomorrow by new actors, values, or technologies.

The preceding discussion will be summarized in a matrix. However, it is worthwhile to first introduce another dimension that has not yet been sufficiently addressed.

C.3. Collective Mobilization Power in Transformation Processes

The preceding discussion of power primarily focuses on "classical" power constellations within parliamentary democracies. However, new social movements, activism, and social media—along with the attempts they fuel to achieve societal transformation without direct parliamentary representation—may necessitate a third expansion of the concept of power.

In this context, some ideas proposed by Flor Avelino in the *Journal of Power* could prove particularly fruitful. Avelino presents a meta-theoretical framework for examining power in processes of social change and innovation.[27] An important complementary aspect that can be drawn from Avelino's essay is the concept of collective mobilization. Collective mobilization can take the form of a muscle (mobilized followers) without being a muscle itself; it can enforce codes (in the sense of altered norms) without being a code itself; it can operate through persuasion and reward (e.g., social recognition, "likes") without being confined to these mechanisms.

By integrating the contents of sections C.1 to C.3, the following construct of power emerges:

Table 2: Matrix of the Developed Concept of Power

	Instrumentes of power (means)				
	Coercion		**Mediation**		**Collective Mobilization**
	Muscles	**Codes**	**Persuasion**	**Rewards**	
Base of power	Physical Strength, Use of Force	Accepted Rules, Symbols, Institutional Authority	Discourse Control, Communicative Skills, Media Power	Financial Resources, Economic Power	Networks, Shared Values, Identity, Disruptive Ideas, Ability to Challenge Existing Structures

27 Cf. Avelino (2021).

	Instrumentes of power (means)				
	Coercion		Mediation		Collective Mobilization
	Muscles	Codes	Persuasion	Rewards	
Amount of power	Spatially Limited, Potentially Intensive, Directly Related to Conflicts	Moderate Intensity, Broad and Temporally Stable Rules (e.g., Laws)	Variable, Theme-Specific, Flexible	Extent Highly Dependent on Resources (Power Base)	Variable, Dependent on the Degree of Mobilization and the Compatibility of Value Systems
Scope of power	Spatially Limited, Directly Related to Conflicts, Typically Short-Term	Broad, Temporally Stable Rules (e.g., Laws and Norms)	Theme-Specific, Flexibly Applicable	Usually Limited to Specific Groups or Contexts	Potentially Global, with Possibly Far-Reaching Impact on Social, Political, and Economic Systems

Having now elaborated on the concept of power in greater theoretical detail, enabling its operationalization, the next step will address how this concept of power applies to the planned case study.

D. The Political Overarching Goals of the EU Green Deal in the Field of Biodiversity

D.1. The Key Objectives of the EU

Biodiversity is a central component of the EU Green Deal. Healthy ecosystems are essential for providing vital resources such as water, soil, and air. They contribute to combating climate change, for instance, by enabling forests and peatlands to store carbon. The EU Green Deal aims, among other goals, to halt the decline of biodiversity and ensure the sustainable use of natural resources.

Particularly relevant in this context are the following three key documents from the European Commission:

Year	Document	Comment
2020	EU Biodiversity Strategy for 2030 (COM(2020) 380final)	Strategic Paper on Biodiversity Conservation: Direct Link to the EU Green Deal
2020	EU Strategy „From Farm to Fork“	Strategic Paper on the Ecological Transformation of Agriculture, One of the Main Influencing Factors on Biodiversity.

Year	Document	Comment
2023	Regulation on Nature Restoration (2022/0195 (COD))	Draft of a Binding Regulation. Status: Now in Force (August 2024).

The first key document is the *EU Biodiversity Strategy for 2030* from 2020. This strategy integrates and reinforces central aspects of the *Farm to Fork* paper from the same year. It provides the substantive foundation for the *Regulation on Nature Restoration,* which, at the time of the presentation, had not yet been adopted. The general direction of the Commission's biodiversity protection initiatives becomes clear from the headings of document COM(2020)380. These initiatives primarily aim to:

1. Expand areas of land, defined by the Member States, for less intensive use, stricter protection, and better connectivity;
2. Halt the encroachment of natural areas by development, restore greenery where possible, or even reverse land use;
3. Reduce emissions into the environment overall.

In detail, the Commission outlines numerous measures, such as improving protected areas (expansion, coherence, corridors), increasing forest and green cover (tree planting, urban greening, forest information systems), and managing invasive species (preventing introduction, population management).[28] Empirical evaluation of these partly general objectives becomes particularly feasible when they are quantified. Let us focus on the question of protected areas. The Commission states that at least 30% of the EU's land area should be designated as protected, which represents an increase of at least 4 percentage points compared to 2020, when approximately 26% was protected. Particular emphasis is placed on improving strict protection, with the EU aiming to achieve a target of 10% by 2030, compared to the current 3% under strict protection. Member States are expected to demonstrate "significant progress in the legal designation of new protected areas and the integration of ecological corridors" (European Commission) by the end of 2023. The responsibility for implementation lies with the Member States, either through Natura 2000 or national protection programs.[29]

Turning to the agricultural sector, the Commission identifies farmers as the "custodians of our soil" (European Commission) and emphasizes the im-

28 Cf. (EU Biodiversitätsstrategie für 2030. Mehr Raum für die Natur in unserem Leben, 2020).

29 Compare for this paragraph: (EU Biodiversitätsstrategie für 2030. Mehr Raum für die Natur in unserem Leben, 2020, pp. 4–6). The Commission announced guidelines for implementation.

portance of safe, sustainable, and affordable food. It expresses the goal of supporting the "transition to fully sustainable practices" (European Commission). The Commission references both the Common Agricultural Policy (CAP) and the EU Farm to Fork strategy, adopting two key objectives from the latter:

(a) reducing the use of chemical pesticides by 50% by 2030,[30] and
(b) ensuring that at least 10% of agricultural land features diverse landscape elements to enhance biodiversity, such as buffer strips, fallow land, hedgerows, dry stone walls, or ponds.

Member States are explicitly called upon to translate the mentioned 10% target into their respective national territories. Furthermore, 25% of agricultural land is to be managed organically or biologically by 2030.[31]

In addition to numerous specific objectives (and many exemptions), the *Regulation on Nature Restoration* establishes three distinct, quantitatively measurable targets: Member States are required to take measures to restore certain habitat types to improve their condition, provided they are currently not in a favorable state. By 2030, at least 30% of these habitat types must be restored; by 2040, the target increases to at least 60%; and by 2050, at least 90%.

D.2. Integration of the Power Matrix and Objectives

This paper aims to prepare for an empirical investigation. To analyze the implementation of EU biodiversity goals at the local level, the developed power matrix will be used, applied to municipal actors and processes. The reason for this is that while the German federal government can create a national plan to achieve the EU's stated land area goals, it ultimately requires the approval and action of the municipal level. This is because municipalities have territorial authority and cannot be compelled to provide land. Local authorities, farmers, NGOs, and citizens' initiatives are thus considered key stakeholders, and their approach to the EU target objectives will be examined. The focus is on whether and how the quantitative targets set out in the three EU papers, such as the expansion of protected areas or the reduction of chemical pesticides, are being implemented locally.

---

30 This goal is not included in the selection of objectives to be investigated, as it is more of a state-level rather than a municipal task.

31 For all this cf. (EU Biodiversitätsstrategie für 2030. Mehr Raum für die Natur in unserem Leben, 2020, 8f.).

The subsequent study will rely methodologically on document analysis, interviews, field studies, and quantitative surveys. Local development plans, environmental reports, and land data will be analyzed to capture changes in protected areas and biodiversity-promoting measures. Interviews with local actors will provide qualitative insights into their perceptions and influence on the implementation of the goals. Field studies and on-site visits will assess whether the intended measures have actually been implemented.

When combining the power matrix with the EU goals, the following sets of questions emerge for the intended further investigation:

1) Do the local administrations under investigation possess sufficient **amount of power** – measured by the (centralized? asymmetric?) **power base** of expertise, human resources, political majorities, and financial means – to implement the EU-quantified goals using coercive **power means** such as regulations, statutes, and land acquisitions? Furthermore, are the municipalities well-connected with higher levels (e.g., state government) in such a way that they can receive additional support for implementation? Is the **scope of their power** substantively comprehensive, or is it so limited by numerous exceptions that it must be considered constrained?
2) What **power means** of collective mobilization – such as promoting relevant values (e.g., protection and improvement of biodiversity), criticizing existing structures, and building transformation alliances – do the declared changemakers of the status quo (e.g., environmental protection organizations) possess locally to enforce the EU's quantified goals? Is their **power base,** in the form of societal support, and their **power amount,** in the form of societal pressure groups and communicative power, sufficient, or do they prove inadequate due to asymmetry with other actors and decentralization? Does their power base and **scope** increase through cooperation and alliances? Can their reach be amplified through the targeted use of social media? Are they successful in establishing a new value framework locally and using societal codes as a power tool to promote the desired transformation? Can noticeable shifts in public opinion be identified in the process?
3) What **power means** of collective mobilization – such as spreading relevant values (e.g., food security, job losses, loss of property), criticizing the planned change, and building prevention alliances – do the supporters of the status quo (e.g., agriculture) possess locally to prevent or soften the EU's quantified goals? Is their **power base,** in the form of political networking and societal support, and their **power amount,** in the form of mobilizable societal pressure, sufficient for purpose, or do they prove in-

adequate? Are they able to protect the existing value framework locally and ultimately use societal codes as a **power means** to avoid the desired transformation and prevent or mitigate the quantified goals?

The following three quantified EU goals are established for the upcoming investigation:
- Expansion of Protected Areas: At least 30% of land areas should be placed under protection by 2030, with 10% under strict protection. Any percentage not achieved in Municipality A will require compensatory action in Municipality B.
- Biodiversity-sensitive Agriculture: At least 10% of agricultural land should be enhanced with biodiversity-rich landscape elements such as fallow land, hedges, or buffer strips by 2030.
- Restoration of Damaged Habitats: By 2030, at least 30% of damaged habitat types should be restored to a good condition. This goal increases to 60% by 2040 and 90% by 2050.

E. Outlook

As part of the preliminary investigation, which includes this paper, an initial exploratory interview was conducted. It took place on January 4, 2024, lasted two hours, and was held with an employee from the Lower Nature Conservation Authority of an independent city in Lower Saxony. The employee holds a university degree, has worked in the authority for decades, and is primarily responsible for biodiversity-related issues in the field of practical environmental protection. After the interview, the employee provided non-public documents related to the planned tightening of regulations in a protected area. Specifically, these documents were a draft regulation for the stricter protection rules for wet meadows in a 347-hectare IUCN Category IV area located on the outskirts of the city.

In light of the research objective outlined here, the employee seemed unimpressed by the EU's goals. On the one hand, he pointed out that these goals were, in his opinion, rather unknown at the municipal level. On the other hand, he expressed the view that the EU's goals were generally too complicated to be implemented in the local political reality. While it might not matter from the EU's perspective whether these goals are associated with the EU or not, it is important to note that the objectives of the local authority do align with the direction desired by the Commission.

What was even more interesting, however, were the comments on the strategy of the administration and how they intended to achieve their goals.

Although the measure took the form of a forceful means – a regulation, a legal obligation – the approach was, in effect, a negotiation. What the authority was preparing was an inofficial pre-negotiation with landowners *before* the actual negotiation. The latter refers to the legally required involvement of public interest groups, such as agricultural associations. Since the authority viewed these groups as opponents in this case but considered the actual landowners to be open to compromise, they did not attempt to use coercion or force. Instead, they preferred collaboration and hoped to better achieve their codes (a compromise between agriculture and environmental protection) through this approach. This behavior suggests that the administration ultimately assessed its own power base, its capacity, and its reach as insufficient to enforce its goals if necessary. However, further research is needed, and the developed power matrix along with the formulated sets of questions could play a useful role in this.

References

Avelino, F. (2021). Theories of power and social change. Power contestations and their implications for research on social change and innovation. *Journal of Political Power, 14*(3), 425–448. https://doi.org/10.1080/2158379X.2021.1875307

Bourdieu, P. (1987). *Die feinen Unterschiede: Kritik der gesellschaftlichen Urteilskraft* (1st ed.). *Suhrkamp Taschenbuch Wissenschaft: Vol. 658.* Suhrkamp.

Dahl, R. (1957). The Concept of Power. *Behavioural Science*(2), 201–215.

EU Biodiversitätsstrategie für 2030. Mehr Raum für die Natur in unserem Leben, MITTEILUNG DER KOMMISSION AN DAS EUROPÄISCHE PARLAMENT, DEN (2020).

Han, B.-C. (2015). *Was ist Macht?* [Nachdr.]. *Reclams Universal-Bibliothek: Nr. 18356.* Reclam.

Hobbes, T. (1984). *Suhrkamp-Taschenbuch Wissenschaft: Vol. 462. Leviathan oder Stoff, Form und Gewalt eines kirchlichen und bürgerlichen Staates* (W. Euchner, Trans.) (I. Fetscher, Ed.). Suhrkamp.

Machiavelli, N. (1978). *Der Fürst* (6. Aufl.). *Kröners Taschenausgabe: Bd. 235.* Kröner.

Marx, K. (2004). *Das Kapital: Kritik der politischen Ökonomie; der Produktionsprozess des Kapitals* (5. Aufl.). Parkland-Verl.

Naim, M. (2014). *The End of Power: From Boardrooms to Battlefields and Churches to States, Why Being in Charge isn't What it Used to be.* The Perseus Books Group.

Naßmacher, H. (1997). *Politikwissenschaft* (2., unwesentl. veränd. Aufl. [Paperback-Ausg.]. Oldenbourg.

Nitschke, P. (2020). *Einführung in die Politikwissenschaft* (2. erweiterte und aktualisierte Auflage). *Studium kompakt.*

Nye, J. S. (2015). *Is the American century over? Global futures series.* Polity Press.

Popper, K. R. (1994). *Vermutungen und Widerlegungen. Die Einheit der Gesellschaftswissenschaften: Band 86.* Mohr.

Popper, K. R. (1997). *Vermutungen und Widerlegungen. Die Einheit der Gesellschaftswissenschaften: Vol. 97.* Mohr.

Rieger, G., & Schultze, R.-O. (1994). Machttheoretische Ansätze. In J. Kriz, D. Nohlen, & R.-O. Schultze (Eds.), *Lexikon der Politik/hrsg. von Dieter Nohlen: Bd. 2. Politikwissenschaftliche Methoden* (pp. 243–254). Beck.

Rosanvallon, P. (2018). *Die Gegen-Demokratie: Politik im Zeitalter des Misstrauens* (M. Halfbrodt, Trans.) (Sonderausgabe für die Bundeszentrale für Politische Bildung). *Schriftenreihe/Bundeszentrale für Politische Bildung: Band 10188.* Bundeszentrale für Politische Bildung.

Schmitt, C. (2002). *Der Begriff des Politischen: Text von 1932 mit einem Vorwort und drei Corollarien* (7. Aufl. (5. Nachdr. der Ausg. von 1963)). Duncker und Humblot.

Schwarz, M., Breier, K.-H., & Nitschke, P. (2017). *Grundbegriffe der Politik: 33 zentrale Politikbegriffe zum Einstieg* (2., aktualisierte und erweiterte Auflage). *Studienkurs Politikwissenschaft.* Nomos.

Weber, M. (2000). *Wirtschaft und Gesellschaft. Hauptwerke der Großen Denker.* Voltmedia.

Weiß, U. (1995). Macht. In D. Nohlen & R.-O. Schultze (Eds.), *Lexikon der Politik/hrsg. von Dieter Nohlen: Bd. 1. Politische Theorien* (pp. 305–315). Beck.

Chapter 5
Smart Specialisation, Green Growth and the Workforce

Sergejs Stacenko,[1] *Tatjana Muravska*[2]

Driving Green Growth and Innovation: EU Cultural and Creative Industries Ecosystem as a Catalyst for Sustainable Development

Summary: EU Industrial Strategy serves as a vital engine for innovation, economic competitiveness and societal advancement, generating employment opportunities and creating value. The Cultural and Creative Industries (CCIs) have a unique role in promoting green growth and sustainable competitiveness thereby enhancing their contribution to economic development and addressing pressing environmental challenges. CCIs face several obstacles in the 21st century such as digital disruption, audience fragmentation, and a lack of necessary knowledge and skills. The creative sector holds potential for business development and innovation, stimulated by increasing demand for creative content and technological progress.

The article emphasises the importance of ensuring synergy between the CCIs ecosystem and competitiveness of the EU, along with green strategy economic and business interests. The authors focus on EU and national government policies and frameworks that promote collaboration between industrial and creative sectors, thereby enhancing competitiveness and driving innovation. The study underlines the potential for future research on the evaluation of the CCIs contribution to business development trends and societal well-being. The authors conclude that the EU policy framework for the CCIs ecosystem development should be integrated into Member States' national programmes with a focus on promoting green growth and sustainable practices. The CCIs can maintain their role as engines of innovation and competitive-

---

1 Sergejs Stacenko, Dr in Public Administration, a Sworn Advocate. Visiting professor and a researcher at universities in Latvia, Germany, Georgia, Kazakhstan and India. His research and publications cover EU legal environment, employment policies, legal issues related to labour disputes, innovation digitalisation and educational policies. Contact: sergejs.stacenko@inbox.lv.

2 Tatjana Muravska, Dr., Professor in Regional Economy and European Integration at the Riga Stradins University, Latvia and Jean Monnet Professor, expert at the University of Latvia. Her research and publications have covered social and economic issues in the EU. Currently she works on innovative economy matters and educational policies. Contacts: tatjana.muravska@lu.lv; tatjana.muravska@rsu.lv.

ness and contribute to the wider goals of environmental sustainability and social responsibility.

Keywords: Cultural and Creative Industry, EU Competitiveness, EU Industrial Strategy, Knowledge Economy, Skills

A. Introduction

The EU Single Market supports the development of policies and funding mechanisms that can help Cultural and Creative Industries overcome challenges, such as market barriers and different regulations such as national laws regarding copyright, intellectual property, labour and taxation. The differences in standards and regulation can complicate distribution and sharing the creative content. Additionally, market fragmentation related to creative products, for instance, films and music often refer to localisation and requirements, which can make impediments to their competitiveness on a broader scale. Furthermore, EU Member States have specific cultural policies that promote local content, which can act as a barrier to entry for foreign CCIs. Barriers include quotas for local content on streaming platforms and public funding mechanisms that support national arts. Moreover, the digital divide between the EU regions can affect the ability of CCIs to reach their audience effectively. The removal of the abovementioned barriers contributes to the economic and cultural strength and competitiveness of the EU.

Additionally, the EU Industrial Strategy can provide frameworks and support for CCIs by recognising their potential to drive economic growth and enhance competitiveness of the EU and its Member States. CCIs open up new possibilities in times of scientific breakthrough, for example visualisation of techniques, for example, to turn big data into information for such sectors as healthcare, smart retail, optimisation of urban planning, increasing citizens' awareness and change their behaviour for energy-efficient living. The EU ought to focus on promoting new products and technologies within the creative industries among other sectors. In addition, digitisation protects and valorises cultural heritage such as transforming archives and collections from museums into a digital information system that creates common resources and has an important cultural, economic and societal impact. Creative industries foster innovation while supporting the development of unique artistic expressions and contributing to sustainable economic growth in a rapidly evolving digital landscape.

CCI sectors are characterised by close links with other sectors, they create economical spillover effects. The enhancement of competitiveness needs to be linked with the development of high added value activities. Moreover, establishing adequate preconditions for cultural infrastructure is essential for fostering smart, sustainable, and inclusive growth.

Cultural heritage, along with CCI, serves as a fundamental pillar for sustainable growth, social unity, and competitiveness within the EU. They are essential for building more resilient and inclusive societies across Europe. The rich cultural heritage of Europe inspires creativity, promotes overall well-being, drives economic prosperity, and nurtures a sense of community. While Member States mainly oversee policy in this domain, the EU is dedicated to protecting and improving cultural heritage, as well as reinforcing the European cultural and creative sectors.

The article put emphasises on the importance to ensure a new balance between CCIs and EU competitiveness, along with strategic economic interests. The authors will assess the impact of government policies and frameworks that encourage industrial and creative industries to collaborate and as a result to foster competitiveness and promote innovation. The article aims to contribute to discussions about EU competitiveness and CCIs related to economic development, decisive innovation, as well as future-proofing skills and digital content creation.

CCIs are integral of the EU Industrial Strategy, which provides the framework for CCIs that contribute to the innovation, economic and technological advancement. CCIs also promote cultural diversity and social cohesion through collaborative efforts. The EU supports the development of creative industries by encouraging initiatives focused on sustainability, competitiveness and digital technology integration. This ensures adequate resources, government and business initiatives to meet evolving market demands and contribute significantly to the EU's economic growth. CCIs ecosystem can generate economic wealth as being knowledge-intensive and based on individual creativity and talent. More importantly, CCIs are critical to a shared sense of European identity, culture and values. In economic terms, these industries show economic growth above average and create jobs, particularly for young people, while strengthening social cohesion.[3]

The article examines the case of Latvia as one of the EU Member States. The country's creative industries are currently evolving and growing with the government and relevant institutions focusing on enhancing the competitiveness of CCIs and promoting research in this field. The contribution of culture to societal well-being is undeniable. The economic impact of cultural sector and creative industries in Latvia remains insufficiently studied, which

3 European Commission. The importance of cultural and creative sectors. https://culture.ec.europa.eu/cultural-and-creative-sectors/cultural-and-creative-sectors.

hampers the development of effective policy actions and further green competitiveness and innovation.

B. EU Competitiveness and Industrial Strategy Framework for Creative Industries

EU competitiveness[4] of industries is boosted by the EU Industrial Strategy[5] and New Industrial Policy[6] framework that should become integrated in the national green industrial policies and regulate economic, technological and environmental developments as well as to encourage innovation.[7] The EU Council adopted conclusions on the future of Industrial Policy[8] that require coordinated actions in innovative technologies, regulation, and standardisation, which help to avoid fragmentation in the Single Market and to develop a solid regulatory framework focused on ensuring competition and access to the Single Market, with common or mutually recognised standards in green innovation and digitalisation. The EU has already implemented various legislative, policy, and funding measures. Moreover, the EU's European Green Deal[9] and the Digital Decade Policy Programme[10] that followed the EU Digital Strategy[11] support modernisation of the legal framework and adaption of EU funding for the audiovisual sector as to align with evolving market

4 The Dragi Report: A Competitiveness Strategy for Europe (Part A), 2024. European Commission.

5 Updating the 2020 New Industrial Strategy:Building a stronger Single Market for Europe's recovery. Brussels, 5.5.2021. COM(2021) 350 final.

6 'A New Industrial Strategy for Europe', Communication from the Commission to the European Parliament, the European Council, the Council, the European Economic and Social Committee and the Committee of the Regions, COM(2020) 102 final.

7 Johnson, E. How Policy Framworks Shaoe the Future of European Industries: A Focuse on Regulatory Impacts and Sustainable Development. Global Economic Review: Journal of Economics, Policy, and Business Development. Volume 01, Issue 01, January 2025.

8 A competitive European industry driving our green, digital and resilient future, Brussels, 24 May 2024. 10127/24.

9 The European Green Deal. Communication from the Commission to the European Parliament, the European Council, the Council, the European Economic and Social Committee and the Committee of the Regions COM(2019) 640 final.

10 Decision (EU) 2022/2481 of the European Parliament and of the Council of 14 December 2022 establishing the Digital Decade Policy Programme 2030. *OJL 323/4, 19.12.2022, p. 4–26.*

11 The EU Digital Strategy 2022, Brussels, 30.6.2022. C(2022) 4388 final, pp.7–14. Proposal for a Regulation of the European Parliament and of the Council establishing the Creative Europe programme (2021 to 2027) and repealing Regulation (EU) No 1295/2013 COM/2018/366 final – 2018/0190 (COD).

trends, business activities and consumer behaviours in the time of the technological and digital revolution.[12] These legal framework and standards help to enhance the competitiveness and cultural diversity of the EU's audiovisual industry. The audiovisual sector is a cornerstone of cultural industries, contributing significantly to cultural expression, economic vitality, and social dynamics in an increasingly interconnected world. Its adaptability to technological advances and changing market landscapes also underlines its importance in the broader cultural economy.

The cultural and creative sectors face significant challenges.[13] They contend with increased competition from global players like search engines and social platforms, demanding new business models and digital technology consumption. The digital shift is changing the way how cultural goods are created, produced and consumed, resulting in intensified global competition on a global scale.

Europe's cultural and linguistic diversity results in a fragmented market lacking critical mass, limiting the transnational circulation of works. There is a growing concern over market concentration, with a few major players dominating sales in some cultural fields. While the audiovisual industry is recognised internationally, it struggles for competitiveness within the Digital Single Market, as co-productions outperform national films.

Additionally, disinformation poses a threat to democratic discourse, highlighting the importance of diverse media in offering varying perspectives. These transnational challenges call for a coordinated European strategy to harness the potential of the sectors for jobs and social inclusion.

The new Creative Europe programme[14] aims to build on previous successes by promoting innovative cross-border initiatives and enhancing international collaboration. It will foster new business models, support artists and professionals, and encourage wider participation in culture, thereby contributing to a more inclusive European society.

CCIs are in a strategically important position to promote smart, sustainable and inclusive growth in all EU Member States, and thus contribute fully to the achievement of the objectives of the Europe 2020 Strategy, which is the EU's growth strategy.[15] CCIs are by nature inter-disciplinary; they combine

---

12 Proposal for a Regulation of the European Parliament and of the Council establishing the Creative Europe programme (2021 to 2027) and repealing Regulation (EU) No 1295/2013COM/2018/366 final - 2018/0190 (COD).

13 Creative Europe Programme 2021–2027. Brussels, 30.5.2018, COM(2018) 366 final.

14 Ibid.

15 EUROPE 2020. A strategy for smart, sustainable and inclusive growth. Brussels, 3.3.2010 COM(2010) 2020 final.

culture on one hand and economy on the other. Arts and culture are often described as the core in a system where the cultural and creative industries come together. Together the core cultural and artistic expressions and the cultural and creative industries provide a great potential for local, regional and national development and spill-over effects on the wider economy.

The policy instrument implementation shall be improved to promote the introduction and development of new creative industries' services and products by SMEs as well as the extension of export capacity of SMEs by integrating good practices and experiences identified in other European countries and regions. In addition, the implementation of this policy instrument shall enhance capacities of public servants and promote CCIs among workers and the public at large by aligning other policy instruments.

C. Decisive Innovation and Governmental Strategies

The EU features robust and dynamic CCIs that are vital for preserving Europe's cultural diversity, enhancing social unity, and boosting the continent's international interest. These industries rank among the most vibrant sectors in Europe. As per Eurostat data, CCIs provided employment for 7.8 million individuals in the EU in 2023, accounting for 3.8% of the total workforce and encompassing 1.2 million enterprises[16] Emerging literature increasingly highlights the innovation capacity of CCIs, particularly their ability to interconnect the innovation processes of other manufacturing and services sectors with innovative and creative outputs. This innovation potential positions CCIs as key players in fostering interdisciplinary collaboration and enhancing overall competitiveness. However, EU policymakers should take advantage of CCIs for the delivery of a *Smart Europe*– as part of the Europe 2020 agenda.[17] Currently, there appears a lack of support for the CCIs and a deficiency in establishing a cohesive agenda at the EU and Member States levels. Furthermore, as creative industries represent a unique group of cultural subsectors driven by individual or collective creative activities, these industries produce high-value-added products and services. The output of CCIs is based on individual or collective creative activity which creates products and services with high added value, using intellectual property, characterized by functionality, innovation and potential for creating new jobs and social well-

16 Cultural employment 2023. Eurostat, 2024.

17 EUROPE 2020. A strategy for smart, sustainable and inclusive growth, Brussels, 3.3.2010, COM(2010) 2020 final.

being.[18] To strengthen this framework, it is essential to implement supportive measures such as tailored vocational training programs, funding opportunities for startups in the CCIs sector, and initiatives that promote cross-border collaboration. Additionally, fostering partnerships between educational institutions and industry players can enhance the skills and creativity of the workforce, ensuring that Europe maintains its competitive edge in the global market while nurturing its rich cultural heritage. Ultimately, an integrated and proactive policy approach that elevates the role of CCIs can drive sustainability, inclusivity, and innovative growth across the EU, creating a vibrant cultural landscape that is economically beneficial and socially enriching.

D. The Cultural and Creative Industries Ecosystem in Latvia: Scale and Scope

1. A concept of Cultural and Creative Industry in Latvia

A concept of CCIs in Latvia is relatively new,[19] it has significantly developed during the last 10 years – it is important for the economic sector and as a source of employment. The development of the industries is linked to issues of national identity, culture and language, and influence unique export offerings as well as the potential for marketing Latvia abroad.[20] The CCIs ecosystem is supported by the EU, for example, implementation of 'design thinking' approaches in developing government policy and programmes. Promotion of design as a part business strategy and innovation element such as awareness raising strategy and campaign in the state institutions. There is also funding by the Latvian government given to researchers on culture and creative industries in educational institutions.[21] These studies can serve as an example, based on individual and collective creativity, skills and talents, which by way of generating and utilizing intellectual property, are able to increase welfare

18 The Guidelines for Cultural Policy 2022–2027 "Country of Culture. The Cabinet of Ministers Nr. 143 Riga 2022. gada 1.03. (Nr. 12 26). https://www.vestnesis.lv/op/2022/45.9.

19 Vanags, Alf, Miķelsone, Anda, Gubins, Sergejs (2007) Creative industries in Latvia. BICEPS, Riga. https://culturelablv.files.wordpress.com/2009/04/ri-apskats2007.pdf.

20 Cultural Policy Guidelines 2014–2020. "Creative Latvia", Cabinet Order No. 401, 29 July 2014.

21 *Cultural and creative ecosystem of Latvia as a resource of resilience and sustainability.* Project VPP-MM-LKRVA-2023/1–0001 funded by the LR Ministry of Culture of the Republic of Latvia, the State Research Programme "Latvian Culture – a Resource for National Development" 2023–2026.

and create jobs.[22] Creative industries generate, develop, produce, utilise, display, disseminate, and preserve products of economic, cultural and/or recreational value. Creative industries encompass the following sectors: architecture design, cinematography, performing arts, visual arts, music, publishing, television, radio and interactive media, advertising, computer games and interactive software, cultural heritage, cultural education, recreation, entertainment and other cultural activities. CCIs play a pivotal role in arts-based education in Latvia, significantly influencing both educational practices and the broader cultural landscape.

Cultural and creative industries are one of the developing sectors of the economy and a notable source of employment opportunities in Latvia. The sector encompassing culture, entertainment and sport accounted for 1.8% of the national economy in 2023. Notably, the growth rates of culture and creative industries have not demonstrated significant progress. From 2011 to 2019 the growth rate was 4.6%. In contrast, during 2020 and 2021, it dropped to just 0.3%. According to the Ministry of Economy's forecast, the growth rate is projected to be 4.0% from 2022 to 2030 and 3.4% from 2031–2040.[23]

Employment in cultural and creative industries is expected to be 2,900 by 2024–2030, but for 2031–2040, the demand is anticipated to decline by 0.4 thousand.[24] These trends may be attributed to demographic tendences resulting in a negative population growth. The contribution of the creative industries to overcoming the effects of the crisis caused by the Covid-19. The main issues to be addressed in the implementation of this priority are related to the cultural infrastructure and material and technical base, opportunities to work professionally in the field of culture, receiving equal and competitive remuneration for equivalent work.[25] The availability of tools for specific cultural sub-sectors, types of cultural organisations, in particular professional arts institutions, non-governmental organizations and self-employed creators, is crucial; at the same time, the international recognition and competitiveness of Latvia's cultural and creative industries must be strengthened.

---

22 *Policies for cultural Creative industries: the HUB for innovative regional development* (CRE:HUB). Interreg Europe, European Regional Development Fund 2016–2020.

23 LR Ministry of Economy. Labour Market forecast 2024. https://www.lmsp.lv/documents/view-ext/780965ae22ea6aee11935f3fb73da841/EM%20Informatīvais%20ziņojums%20Par%20darda%20tirgus%20prognozēm%202024%20augusts.pdf.

24 Ibid.

25 The Guidelines for Cultural Policy 2022–2027 "Country of Culture". The Cabinet of Ministers Nr. 143 Riga 2022. gada 1.03. (Nr. 12 26).

2. The Government approach to Cultural and Creative Industries

In Latvia, the economic potential of cultural and creative industries was first updated at the national level in the late 1990s, when one of the first assessments of the economic importance of the cultural sector emphasised that it could be a profitable sector.[26] For example, in the study "Creative Industries in Latvia" of the Baltic International Centre for Economic and Political Studies (BICEPS), it was calculated that in 2007, 4.8 % of the total number of employees in Latvia were employed in creative industries, and 7 % of Latvian companies operated in them.[27] For the first time, creative industries were recorded in the State Cultural Policy Guidelines for 2006–2015.[28] This is referred to as the transfer of creative industries effect. The first strategic document for the development of cultural and creative industries at the national level is the "Guidelines for Cultural Policy 2014–2020 "Creative Latvia",[29] in which two of the four main directions for achieving the priorities and policy goals of cultural policy are directly related to the creative industries – development of the competitiveness of cultural and creative industries, as well as promotion of the availability of creative territories and cultural services. The positive impact characteristic of cultural and creative industries can help foster more creative governance, modern teaching methods and lifelong learning, new quality social services, quality tourism, sustainable territorial development, a more innovative economy, environmental sustainability, and a competitive identity – a creative country for creative and cohesive people. Globally, creative industries are positioned as a driving force for stimulating innovation and economic competitiveness not only within the sector itself but also in the economy at large, indirectly promoting the development of other economic sectors (spillover effects). Regional issues of creative industries were focused on the research project "Creative industries in small cities: potential and contribution to sustainability" funded by the Latvian Science Council in 2020, which was implemented in the programme of Fundamental

---

26 LR Ministry of Culture(1998). Assessment of the economic significance of the cultural sector. https://www. km. gov.lv/sites/km/files/kult_sekt_nozimig_19981.pdf.

27 Vanags, Alf, Miķelsone, Anda, Gubins, Sergejs (2007) Creative industries in Latvia. BICEPS, Riga. https://culturelablv.files.wordpress.com/2009/04/ri-apskats2007.pdf.

28 Council conclusions on the transfer effect of cultural and creative industries. Promoting Innovation, Economic Sustainability, and Social Inclusion. Official Journal of the EU 2015/C 172/04.

29 Cultural Policy Guidelines 2014–2020. "Creative Latvia", Cabinet Order No. 401, 29 July 2014.

and Applied Studies.[30] Another project funded by the Latvian government is funded by the Ministry of Culture of the Republic of Latvia in the framework of the State Research Programme "Latvian Culture – a Resource for National Development (2023–2026)".[31]

A further document the "Guidelines for Cultural Policy 2022–2027 "Country of Culture" can be considered as a step in solving these problems. They entered into force on 1 March 2022.[32] Experts in Latvia contributed to the research about the role of creative industries and digital transformation underlined a prerequisite for their further development. The research confirms[33] that qualified labour is on demand. In this respect education of children and young people in its formal and informal forms is badly needed on the country.

This long-standing, comprehensive document identifies the sustainable development of the cultural and creative industries as one of the key strategic priorities (along with the cultural offer available to the public, active public participation in cultural processes, preservation and creative use of cultural heritage, as well as the generation of talent and the professional development of cultural workers).[34]

The most important directions of action for the development of creative industries and digital transformation are defined in the strategic document "Guidelines for Cultural Policy 2022–2027 "Country of Culture". Those are:

1. Support for innovation (technological and non-technological innovation).
2. Strengthening competitiveness and supporting exports.
3. Stimulating the crossover-effects of the cultural and creative industries and closer sectoral cooperation with a view to creating innovative solutions.
4. Developing a culture of experimentation.
5. Support mechanisms for ecosystem actors in the creative industries.
6. Availability of information and networking opportunities.

---

30 Creative industries in small cities: potential and contribution to sustainability. No. VPP-MM-LKRVA-2023/1–0001, funded by the Ministry of Culture of the Republic of Latvia in the framework of the State Research Programme "Latvian Culture – a Resource for National Development" (2023–2026).

31 Ibid.

32 The Guidelines for Cultural Policy 2022–2027 "Country of Culture". The Cabinet of Ministers Nr. 143 Riga 2022. gada 1.03. (Nr. 12 26).

33 Cane, Renate, Steinbergs, Kaspars (2022). The Role of Digital Transformation in Creative Industries Companies in Regions. DOI: 10.22616/ESRD.2022.56.042.

34 Council Conclusions on Culture as a Catalyst for Creativity and Innovation. Brussels, 12 May 2009. https://cultureactioneurope.org/wp-content/uploads/2015/02/2009-creativyandinnovation.pdf.

3. Are Cultural and Creative Industries in Latvia a remedy to increase technological improvements and economic advances?

Digital transformation is an integral part of policy planning documents, which is vividly confirmed by the Digital Transformation Guidelines for 2021–2027 of Latvia.[35] The vision defined in the document emphasises the importance of technology for the development of society and the competitiveness of the business and for the development of creativity. It describes the relatively low level of digital transformation in small and medium-sized enterprises in Latvia, which is very typical as well for creative industries. Funding for these lines of action is provided from the state budget and EU funds, such as the European Regional Development Fund, as well as part of the funding for regional development activities in the field of creative industries and digital transformation is provided in local government budgets. Similarly, during the programming period of the EU funds 2021–2027, the previous successful support for the business incubator of creative industries continues. In its turn, the plan of the Latvian Recovery Fund submitted to the European Recovery Fund envisages 20% (365.2 million euros) for digital transformation and 20% or 370 million euros for the reduction of inequality.[36] Part of these funds will also be trained for the development of creative industries[37] and their digital transformation, including in the regions of Latvia.

These efforts are aimed at creation of new knowledge based on an interdisciplinary research approach towards the resilience of the CCIs in the current processes, especially by shedding light on the dynamics of the cultural offer and accessibility in the face-to-face and digital environment, as well as the employment and education processes of the sector.

The interplay between creative industries and arts-based education in Latvia not only enriches the educational experience but also contributes to the growth of the country's economy. This synergy prepares students to tackle future challenges in a rapidly changing world, equipping them with valuable skills and fostering a lifelong appreciation for the arts.

---

35 Jakobsone, M. (2021) Latvia – Digital transformation Guidelines 2021–2027. https://digital-skills-jobs.europa.eu/en/actions/national-initiatives/national-strategies/latvia-digital-transformation-guidelines-2021–2027.

36 The Latvian Recovery and Resilience Plan. https://commission.europa.eu/business-economy-euro/economic-recovery/recovery-and-resilience-facility/country-pages/latvias-recovery-and-resilience-plan_en.

37 Cultural and creative industries definition. LR Ministry of Culture. https://www.km.gov.lv/lv/kulturas-un-radoso-industriju-definicija.

4. Knowledge and future-proofing skills

The CCIs often apply new forms of employment such as ICT-based mobile work, portfolio work, crowd employment or collaborative employment (co-working). Many creative workers engage in irregular (often low paid) part-time or temporary forms of employment as well as hybrid models, for example combining freelancing with other professions to provide the financial stability to maintain their creative activities. As CCIs require a work force with a unique mix of skills (including business knowledge, creative entrepreneurship, e-skills, technical as well as traditional skills), some sectors face a general shortage of talent. Creating stronger partnerships between CCIs, social partners as well as education and training providers is seen as one way of improving the provision of the right "cross-disciplinary curricula" needed in the creative sectors.

Creative industries inspire the development of innovative learning environments and pedagogical approaches already in schools. For instance, design thinking principles may be applied to problem-solving, encouraging critical thinking and collaboration among students. Moreover, creative industries in Latvia provide opportunities for local artists to engage with educational institutions. Collaborations between educational institutions and artists can enhance curriculum delivery and provide students with firsthand experience of professional practices. Latvia has a rich cultural heritage that serves as a foundation for arts education. Educational programmes at all levels often include traditional arts and crafts, folklore, and music, promoting students' understanding of their own cultural identity while instilling respect for cultural diversity. Arts-based education often extends beyond the classroom, engaging communities through public art projects, performances, and exhibitions. This engagement fosters a sense of belonging and encourages students to contribute to their local environments creatively.

The skills cultivated through arts-based education—such as creativity, critical thinking, and collaboration—are increasingly recognized as essential for the workforce. Creative industries help shape educational programmes that prepare students for various careers in arts and culture, design, media, and technology.

The Latvian government, as discussed above, recognises the significance of the creative sector, aligning cultural and educational policies to support the growth of creative industries. This includes funding arts programmes in schools and promoting creative methodologies in education. The inherently interdisciplinary nature of the CCIs combines culture and economy, providing significant potential for regional and national development. To fully realise this potential, the implementation of policy instruments facilitates the introduction and development of new services and products by SMEs.

E. Conclusion and Potential for Future Research

The EU's emphasis lies on enhancing the sustainable and green competitiveness and cultural diversity, particularly in the CCIs. Moreover, the ongoing digital shift requires the adaptation of business models within CCIs to remain competitive and inclusive. Integration of the EU Industrial Strategy within national frameworks support a cohesive approach in addressing green innovative technologies, regulations, and standards. This is essential for preventing fragmentation in the Single Market and ensuring competitiveness of the EU.

EU policy frameworks must remain adaptable, responding to emerging challenges and ensuring that industries can leverage new technologies and business models for continued growth and success. Ultimately, CCIs hold a strategically important position for promoting smart, sustainable, and inclusive growth across EU Member States. CCIs play a critical role in maintaining Europe's cultural diversity, promoting social unity, and enhancing the continent's international interest. Additionally, these industries are increasingly recognised for their innovation capacity, notably their ability to link creative processes with other sectors. This interconnection fosters interdisciplinary collaboration but also enhances overall competitiveness of the EU economy.

Despite the importance of the CCIs, there is a noticeable lack of support and cohesive policy initiatives for CCIs at both the EU and national levels. This gap indicates an opportunity for policymakers to leverage the potential of CCIs in alignment with the objectives of the EU economic competitiveness strategies. Building partnerships between educational institutions and industry can play a vital role in nurturing talent and ensuring that the workforce is equipped with relevant skills, thus reinforcing Europe's competitive advantage in the creative sector. To improve conditions for knowledge development though comparative analysis of best practicies and innovative strategies for CCIs across EU Member States and regions helps to incorporate a concept of sustainability onto CCIs to ensure responsible growth and competitiveness. Governments could set up a continuous monitoring to adapt strategies to emerging trends in CCIs. An integrated and proactive policy framework is crucial for elevating the role of CCIs, promoting sustainability, inclusivity, and progressive growth in the EU. This approach can cultivate a dynamic cultural landscape that simultaneously drives economic benefits and social well-being.

The concept of CCIs in Latvia is relatively new but has evolved significantly over the past decade. These industries are crucial to the country's national identity. In economic terms, CCIs contribute to the reviald competitive advantages of the economy as a source of employment, unique export opportunities, representing a vital sector in the overall national economy.

Latvia's government has recognised the economic potential of CCIs through various policy documents and strategic guidelines and emphasise the importance of innovation, sustainable competitiveness, and cross-sector cooperation to enhance the creative industries.

Digital transformation is a fundamental element of Latvia's policy planning. Despite acknowledging its importance, the level of digital integration in CCIs remains low. Funding from both state and EU sources aims to bolster digital initiatives and improve the resilience of creative industries.

The creative sector requires a diverse and innovative skill set that includes business knowledge and technical proficiency. However, there is a shortage of talent in certain areas. Strengthening partnerships between CCIs, their ecosystem that includes educational institutions, and social partners, is crucial for addressing this gap and developing relevant cross-disciplinary curricula.

The integration of creative industries into broader sustainable and competitive economic and social policies is essential for further development and increase in competitiveness.

List of References

European Commission. The importance of cultural and creative sectors. https://culture.ec.europa.eu/cultural-and-creative-sectors/cultural-and-creative-sectors

Cane, R., Steinbergs, K. (2022). The Role of Digital Transformation in Creative Industries Companies in Regions. DOI: 10.22616/ESRD.2022.56.042

A competitive European industry driving our green, digital and resilient future, Brussels, 24 May 2024. 10127/24.

Council Conclusions on Culture as a Catalyst for Creativity and Innovation. Brussels, 12 May 2009. https://cultureactioneurope.org/wp-content/uploads/2015/02/2009-creativyandinnovation.pdf

Creative Europe Programme 2021–2027. Brussels, 30.5.2018, COM(2018) 366 final.

Creative industries in small cities: potential and contribution to sustainability. No. VPP-MM-LKRVA-2023/1–0001, funded by the Ministry of Culture of the Republic of Latvia in the framework of the State Research Programme "Latvian Culture – a Resource for National Development" (2023–2026).

Cultural employment 2023. Eurostat, 2024.

Cultural Policy Guidelines 2014–2020. "Creative Latvia", Cabinet Order No. 401, 29 July 2014.

Cultural and creative ecosystem of Latvia as a resource of resilience and sustainability. Project VPP-MM-LKRVA-2023/1–0001 funded by the LR Ministry of Culture of the Republic of Latvia, the State Research Programme "Latvian Culture – a Resource for National Development" 2023–2026.

Decision (EU) 2022/2481 of the European Parliament and of the Council of 14 December 2022 establishing the Digital Decade Policy Programme 2030. OJL 323/4, 19.12.2022, p. 4–26.

The Dragi Report: A Competitiveness Strategy for Europe (Part A), 2024. European Commission.

The EU Digital Strategy 2022, Brussels, 30.6.2022. C(2022) 4388 final, pp.7–14.

The European Green Deal, Communication from the Commission to the European Parliament, the European Council, the Council, the European Economic and Social Committee and the Committee of the Regions COM(2019) 640 final.

EUROPE 2020. A strategy for smart, sustainable and inclusive growth. Brussels, 3.3.2010

COM(2010) 2020 final.

The Guidelines for Cultural Policy 2022–2027 "Country of Culture. The Cabinet of Ministers Nr. 143 Riga 2022. gada 1.03. (Nr. 12 26). https://www.vestnesis.lv/op/2022/45.9

Jakobsone, M. (2021) Latvia – Digital transformation Guidelines 2021–2027 https://digital-skills-jobs.europa.eu/en/actions/national-initiatives/national-strategies/latvia-digital-transformati on-guidelines-2021–2027

Johnson, E. How Policy Framworks Shaoe the Future of European Industries: A Focuse on Regulatory Impacts and Sustainable Development. Global Economic Review: Journal of Economics, Policy, and Business Developemnt. Volume 01, Issue 01, January 2025.

The Latvian Recovery and Resilience Plan. https://commission.europa.eu/business-economy-euro/economic-recovery/recovery-and-resilience-facility/country-pages/latvias-recovery-and-resilience-plan_en

LR Ministry of Culture (1998). Assessment of the economic significance of the cultural sector. https://www. km. gov.lv/sites/km/files/kult_sekt_nozimig_19981.pdf

LR Ministry of Economy. Labour Market forecast 2024. https://www.lmsp.lv/documents/view-ext/780965ae22ea6aee11935f3fb73da841/EM%20Informatīvais%20ziņojums%20Par%20da rda%20tirgus%20prognozēm%202024%20augusts.pdf

A New Industrial Strategy for Europe', Communication from the Commission to the European Parliament, the European Council, the Council, the European Economic and Social Committee and the Committee of the Regions, COM(2020) 102. Final.

Updating the 2020 New Industrial Strategy:Building a stronger Single Market for Europe's recovery.

Brussels, 5.5.2021. COM(2021) 350 final.

Proposal for a Regulation of the European Parliament and of the Council establishing the Creative Europe programme (2021 to 2027) and repealing Regulation (EU) No 1295/2013 COM/2018/366 final – 2018/0190 (COD).

Policies for cultural Creative industries: the HUB for innovative regional development (CRE:HUB).Interreg Europe, European Regional Development Fund 2016–2020.

Vanags, A., Miķelsone, A., Gubins, S. (2007) Creative industries in Latvia. BICEPS, Riga. https://culturelablv.files.wordpress.com/2009/04/ri-apskats2007.pdf

Acknowledgement

The research has been supported by the EC-funded project Jean Monnet Actions in the field of Higher Education: Modules. No101127202 "Green Business and Entrepreneurship in the European Single Market"

Girts Jirgensons,[1] *Tatjana Muravska*[2]

The Green Deal in Healthcare: EU Labour Mobility and the Outflow of Medical Practitioners from Latvia

Summary: The Green Deal emphasises sustainability and encourage medical practitioners to adopt sustainable practices that result in a healthier environment, leading to better overall public health. Free movement of labour is one of the pillars in the EU Single Market. EU legislation on the recognition of professional qualifications suggests the framework within which medical doctors can migrate freely between EU Member States to practise their profession. In recent years, the emigration of medical practitioners from Latvia has been one of the most pressing problems in the health sector with consequences for the population related to availability of health services. Migration is a complex socio-economic phenomenon influenced by numerous factors. In many cases migration trends relate to the decisions taken by the state and healthcare management. The authors aimed at understanding the dynamics and reasons of the outflow of healthcare practitioners and medical doctors specifically as well as the role of the state in preventing this tendency. Special emphasis is placed on the training of residential doctors as a promising strategy to retain healthcare professionals in the country. The legal framework for reclaiming public funding allocated that the residency programmes has been evaluated. The article concludes that the emigration of healthcare practitioners from Latvia poses a significant threat to the effective healthcare system. The state should implement proactive policies towards creating a stimulating working environment to prevent the outflow of medical doctors and encourage their influx.

Keywords: EU Single Market, Outflow, Healthcare Practitioners and Medical Doctors, Resident Doctors, Health Policy

---

1 Girts Jirgensons, PhD candidate in Economics and Business Studies at the Riga Stradins University, Latvia. His research and publications cover legal environment in the EU and Latvia, employment policies, legal issues related to labour disputes, residency programmes for young medical doctors. Contact: girts.jirgensons@vm.gov.lv.

2 Tatjana Muravska, Professor in Regional Economy and European Integration at the Riga Stradins University, Latvia and Jean Monnet Professor. Her research and publications have covered social and economic issues in the EU. Contact: tatjana.muravska@rsu.lv.

A. Introduction

The free movement of workers is a fundamental principle of the European Union. Indeed, EU citizens are entitled to look for a job in another EU country, and the objectives that are set out in EU policy on the healthcare sector are proved to be correct. The conclusion of the 1992 Maastricht Treaty marked a significant change, as the European Union Citizenship Institute was established. From that point on, the freedom of movement was extended to citizens of the European Union, as well as to their family members who are not EU citizens.[3] It is believed that without the freedom of movement for workers, the labour market of the European Union could not achieve stability. Regions with high unemployment rates and low wages could emerge, leading to a surplus of labour supply in those areas, while other regions might experience labour shortages where wages would consequently be significantly higher. As a result, countries with higher labour costs would produce more expensive goods and services that could not compete effectively with those from countries with cheaper labour. Furthermore, any EU Member State would have problems achieving and implementing these objectives in a situation with insufficient human resources.

2004's enlargement influenced on the labour market in Latvia leading to an outflow of labour in general and medical practitioners in particular. Ensuring that healthcare is accessible and of high quality is a key aspect of both the Green Deal and the free movement of practitioners.[4] By supporting mobility, countries can address shortages in areas where a number of local practitioners is insufficient, promoting health equity and ensuring that all groups of population benefit from sustainable healthcare practices.

Although the shortage of healthcare practitioners in Latvia was not immediately apparent after this enlargement, it is now clear that patients in the country face harsh consequences in their healthcare service experiences on a daily basis. In 2013, the EU has passed the legislation[5] on the recognition of professional qualifications, which poses new opportunities and challenges for doctors wanting to live and work in a European country other than the one in which they originally qualified.

3 Treaty on the Functioning of the European Union (2012) Official Journal C 326/47, p. 76.

4 The European Green Deal. Brussels, 11.12.2019, COM(2019) 640 final.

5 Directive 2005/55/EC of the European Parliament and of the Council of 20 November 2013 amending Directive 2005/36/EC on the recognition of professional qualifications and Regulation (EU) No 1024/2012 on administrative co-operation through the Internal Market information System ('the IMI Regulation').

Furthermore, a healthcare models are different in the EU Member States, which affect the accessibility, quality, and efficiency of healthcare services available to their populations. These variations can lead to disparities in health systems' outcomes, as some countries may have better resources and infrastructure, while others struggle with funding and workforce shortages. Additionally, differences in healthcare policies and regulation can influence availability of healthcare services to population and the overall management of public health system. In the authors' opinion, the task of the system includes (1) improvement of health for individuals, families, and society, (2) protection of the population from health hazards, (3) insuring people against financial risks caused by ill health, (4) offering equal access to healthcare, (5) enabling people to participate in decision-making that affects their health and the overall health system. Nevertheless, the efficiency of the health services depends on the healthcare model, it is important to distinguish what type of the model exist in the country.

The authors' observation shows that the healthcare system in Latvia represents the Beveridge model, considering historical experience, cultural characteristics, available resources, and expertise. The most characteristic features of this system include (1) coverage of the entire population, (2) financing from the general revenues of the state budget. Since the Beverage model relies on state funding for its services, the system struggles with inadequate resources and inefficient resource allocation. Economic constrains can affect salaries and job satisfaction for healthcare professionals. It funding for healthcare is limited medical professionals, particularly medical doctors, may seek employment in countries where the healthcare system is more efficient. The National Health Service in Latvia[6] has universal population coverage, general tax-financed health care provision and a purchaser-provider split. The Ministry of Health is responsible for defining national health policies and regulations. It also regulates public health, while the Centre for Disease Prevention and Control coordinates and implements public health activities.[7]

Discussions in Latvia keep focus on management of the healthcare system. One of the central issues is the division of funds between the state and medical establishments as service providers. The separation of the money holder from the service provider is not complete; however, the money holder operates autonomously, and services can also be purchased from other healthcare providers.[8] In the authors' opinion, there are questions about

6 Cabinet of Ministers of the Republic of Latvia No. 359 26, May 2022.

7 The Regulations of the Cabinet of Ministers 13 April 2004, No. 286.

8 Slokenberga, S. et al., 2015, pages 47–49.

whether the Beveridge model is truly functioning in the country based on the assumption that availability of health services is not entirely ensured by the state. Another urgent matter that complicates the fully implement the Beveridge model is the outflow of medical professionals from the country in recent years which negatively affects the supply of health services in contrarily to their demand for them. This issue is widely discussed and reflected in the media, and people experience its consequences in their everyday lives when receiving healthcare services.[9]

There is no completely accurate data on the number of healthcare practitioners who have left Latvia, however, according to information by the Latvian Association of Doctors, about 100 to 150 healthcare professionals prepare documentation each year for the recognition of their qualifications in foreign countries through this association. Currently, a shortage is about 300 doctors and 8000 nurses in Latvia.[10]

Assuming that a healthy society should be one of the country's priorities, this must be supported by an adequate number of medical doctors, as ensured by state health policy and sound decisions made by state authorities.

B. Management of Human Resources in the Health Sector

Health care is extremely labour-intensive. This is one of the most significant sectors of the economy on the EU, providing employment for 9,7% of the EU workforce.[11] At the same time, health systems in Europe are facing increasingly complex challenges that demand innovative solutions and could, in turn, impact the demand for healthcare practitioners.

The restructuring of healthcare in the EU and Latvia, along with technological and economic changes, affect the desires of healthcare workers as well as the nature and scope of their work. Furthermore, public health and healthcare are increasingly recognised as productive factors contribute to the economic progress and well-being of people.

Latvia has a national health system with strong government management, but which remains severely underfunded. Even though health expenditure per capita has increased by 75% since 2010, the level remains the fourth lowest in the EU. Only 61% of health expenditure is publicly funded, and the

9 Diena, Latvian daily newspaper, 2023.

10 Latvian Association of Doctors, 2024.

11 Eurostat, 2023.

share of out-of-pocket spending is the second highest in the EU.[12] Despite significant gains over the past two decades, the life expectancy of the Latvian population remains one of the lowest in the EU. The gender gap in life expectancy is over nine years, which is the second highest in the EU. Additionally, life expectancy of in the country shows considerable variation based on educational attainment.

Health workforce shortage is an important problem in Latvia. The number of practising medical doctors was 3.3 per 1 000 population in 2019 – significantly below the average for the EU 3.9 per 1 000, while the number of nurses was only about half the EU average and one of the lowest in the EU.[13] In addition, healthcare practitioners are predominantly concentrated in urban areas, which creates equity and accessibility challenges for population in rural areas. This urban-rural divide is aggravated by a notable aging workforce and substantial disparities in the distribution of healthcare professionals across different regions in the country. Additionally, environmental factors play a crucial role in shaping public health outcomes. Encouraging the mobility of healthcare professionals can enhance the dissemination of knowledge and expertise in environmental health, ultimately leading to improved health outcomes nationwide. Practitioners from regions with successful green initiatives can share best practicies in managing health risks related to pollution and climate change.

There is also a lack of doctors in some specialities, while in the regions there is a shortage of doctors in almost all specialities. A statement of the World Health Organisation in 2023, reflected, and emphasised the challenges outlined above: "There is a shortage of specialists of all kinds, including surgeons, anaesthetists, internists, narcologists, and psychiatrists. The most challenging issue for regional hospitals is to provide specialists on duty for emergency care in regions of the country."[14]

Many doctors will retire in the coming decades. The average age of general practitioners is 54 years. More than a quarter of general practitioners are at least 60 years old. To tackle the lack of the workforce, the medical training capacity has been increased and medical graduated reached 454 in 2020. In 2022 15.5 medical doctors graduating in the EU for every 100 000 inhabitants. The highest ratios were recorded in Latvia in 2022- 27.7 per 100 000 inhabi-

---

12 OECD/European Observatory on Health Systems and Policies (2021), Latvia: Country Health Profile 2021, State of Health in the EU, OECD Publishing, Paris/European Observatory on Health Systems and Policies, Brussels.

13 Ibid.

14 WHO, 2023.

tants.[15] In the number of students in academic year 2024/25, the second most popular programmes in the country are health and welfare 19.3 percent making up 14.5 thousand of total number of students. Over the past decade the largest rise – in health and welfare programmes – 3.8 thousand students.[16]

To assessment of the human resources and the efficiency of the state management in the health care sector shows[17] the following problems: 92% of doctors graduating from residencies start working in the health sector, while the benchmark is not met for other professions – only 52% of nurses and 54% of midwives start working in Latvia after completing their studies. Overall, only 65% of young professionals who have obtained the qualification remain in the Latvian labour market after receiving their diplomas.

It is generally assumed, that the main reasons why the Ministry of Health has not been able to effectively manage its human resources development policy is due to insufficient funding for remuneration. The Ministry has not been able to achieve the increase in the average salary of healthcare practitioners to 2.5 times the average in the national economy wages by 2021.[18] Furthermore, the long-standing historical neglect of the underpayment of those employed in healthcare[19] has led to a shortage of healthcare practitioners and has also had a negative impact on the prestige of the profession, therefore, addressing the human resources challenges in the health sector must be a long-term priority for the Ministry of Health in order to ensure accessible health care for the population.

C. The Reasons for Emigration of the Medical Doctors

1. The Survey's results

In 2023 and 2024, the authors conducted a Survey among medical doctors' regarding the reasons for emigration. The Survey was conducted with more than 300 medical respondents from one of the largest hospitals in the country Pauls Stradins Clinical University Hospital.

---

15 Eurostat (2024) Which countries have the most doctor and dentist graduates?

16 The Central Statistical Bureau of Latia, 2024.

17 OECD/European Observatory on Health Systems and Policies (2021), Latvia: Country Health Profile 2021, State of Health in the EU, OECD Publishing, Paris/European Observatory on Health Systems and Policies, Brussels.

18 Ibid.

19 The State Audit Office of the Republic of Latvia (2019) Human Resources in Health Care. Audit report.

As can be seen form the Figure1 below, the absolute majority of respondents indicates that the main reason for emigration is remuneration of 68 percent. But there are other reasons such as remuneration and working conditions of 22 percent, working conditions only of 4 percent and other reasons of 6 percent.

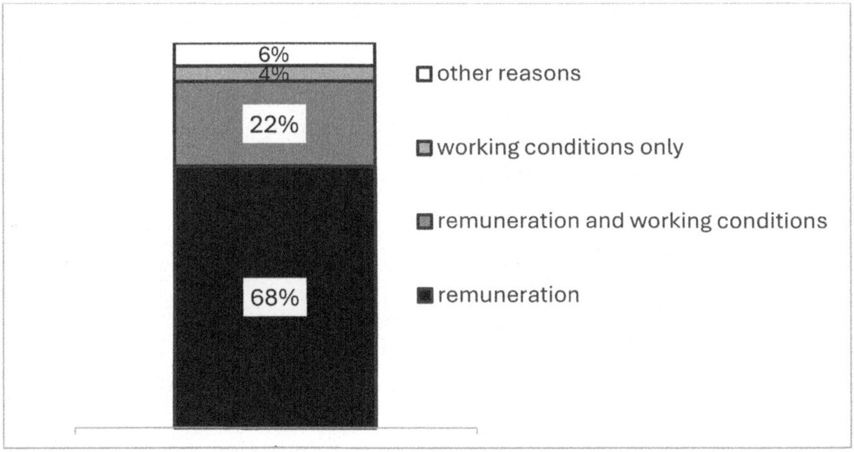

Figure 1: Reasons for out-migration of medical personal

The remuneration and working conditions together represent a significant part of motivations, while the quality of working conditions alone also influences decisions to emigrate. Furthermore, factors such as personal safety, family reunification pay an essential role in shaping individuals' choices to seek employment abroad. This multifaceted approach to understanding emigration highlights the complexity of personal and economic factors at play.

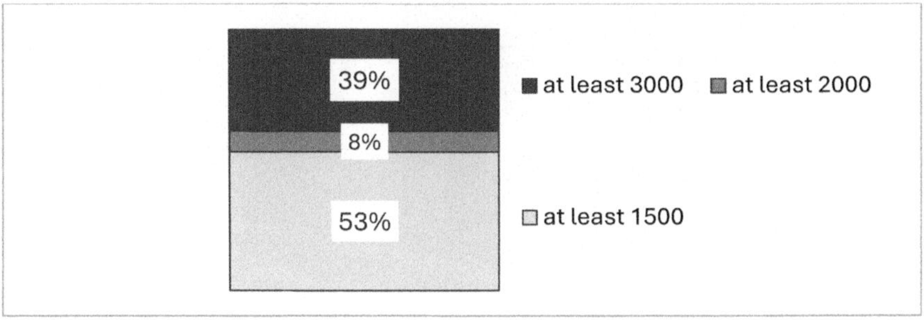

Figure 2: Desired remuneration of young doctors (net salary in euros)

Most of the respondents indicated that they would like to receive at least 3000 euros net after the graduation of residency, Figure 2. This expectation reflects their desire for competitive compensation that acknowledges their extensive training and the demanding nature of the profession. Additionally, many of young doctors expressed concerns about the rising cost of living and the need to secure financial stability as they began their careers, emphasising that adequate remuneration is crucial for attracting and retaining talent in the healthcare sector.

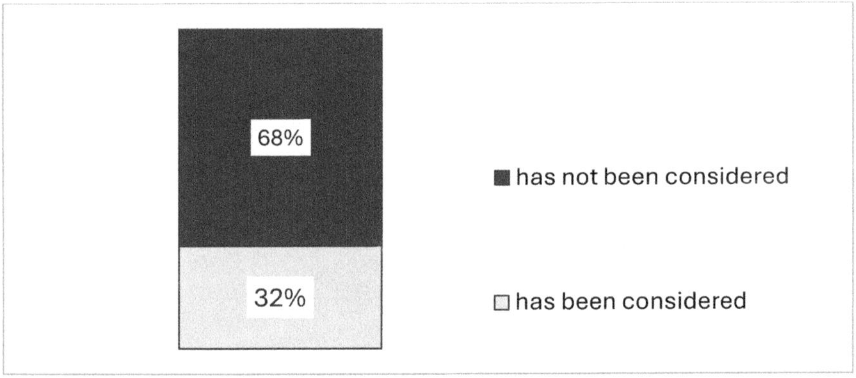

Figure3: Has the emigration been considered?

Emigration has been considered by 32 percent of respondents, indicating a significant level of interest in leaving the country, Figure 3. Moreover, among those contemplating emigration, many expressed concerns about their current working conditions, social stability, and future prospects in their home country, suggesting that a range of motivation drives this intent to explore opportunities abroad.

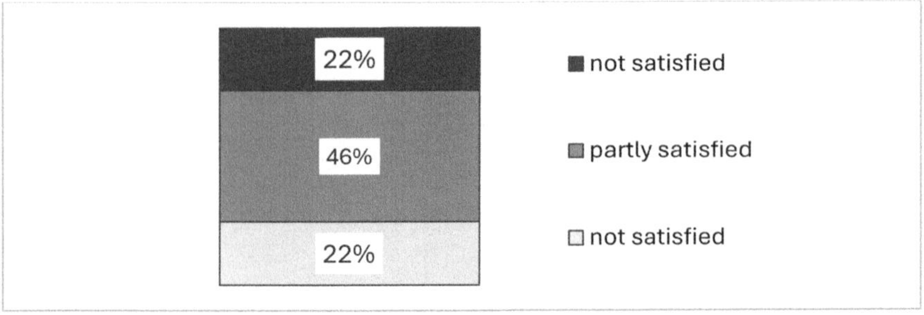

Figure4: How satisfied are you with your working conditions?

From the answers given, it can be assumed that most of the respondents are to some extent dissatisfied with the working conditions. 46 percent are partially satisfied but 22 percent are not satisfied at all. This indicates a pressing need for improvements in the workplace, as many expressed concerns about factors such as inadequate resources, long hours, and lack of support from management. Addressing these issues could significantly enhance overall job satisfaction and retention of staff, ultimately leading to better patient care and a more stable healthcare system.

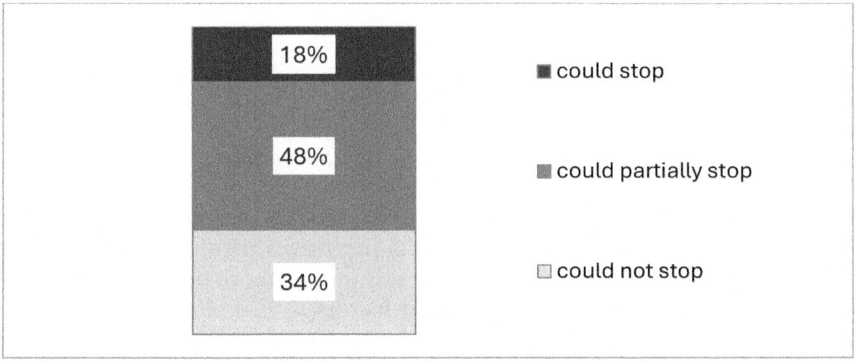

Figure 5: Can raising remuneration help to stop out-migration?

It can be concluded that not only remuneration is the factor that the state should work on in order to motivate medical doctors to stay in Latvia. Other critical aspects include improving working conditions, providing ongoing professional development opportunities, ensuring job security, and enhancing the overall healthcare infrastructure, Additionally, addressing issues such as workload, access to resources can significantly influence doctors' decisions to remain in the country, fostering a more attractive and supportive environment for healthcare professionals.

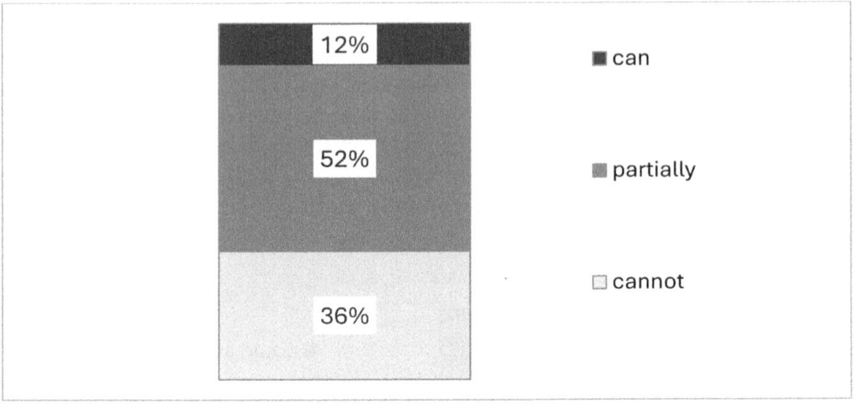

Figure 6: Can raising remuneration stimulate doctors to return?

Raising remuneration is an important reason in stimulating medical doctors to return to the home country, as financial incentives are often a key factor in their decision-making process. However, it is important to note that increased remuneration is a crucial element. Other factors, as it is seen from the above assessment of the answers to the Survey's questions, such as working conditions, professional development opportunities, working conditions, work-life balance, and the overall healthcare environment, also significantly impact medical doctors' decisions to come back. Therefore, a comprehensive approach that includes both better remuneration and improvements of other factors important for doctors to stay in the home country is likely to be more effective in encouraging doctors not to leave or to return.

Another example of motivation to leave is the following: among those who have left the country are medical practitioners who took out loans they could not repay and have ended up under the scrutiny of debt collectors and bailiff as a result of the economic crisis of 2008–2009. Besides, it is still a common situation in Latvia that medical practitioners have to be engaged in several job positions to be able to provide themselves with decent living.[20]

A reason for emigration is professional development and social security. It is tempting to work in a top-end clinic abroad, and just in one job rather than several. Doctors abroad not only have economic security but also social security, with various relocation allowances and social benefits. The above processes have a strong impact: national losses followed outflow, such as, for example, macroeconomic situation as the inflow of remittances from emi-

20 Portal Doctus, 2024.

grants to Latvia contributes to inflation, which in turn limits the international competitiveness of Latvian businesses.

An additional loss related to the returns on the state investments in the education system. Most of the emigration is of young people who have relatively recently completed their education in Latvia. It can be estimated that the cost of training of one medical doctor resident in a residency programme can range from euro 20 thousand to euro 40 thousand depending on the duration of studies and the speciality.[21] A loss in tax payments to the state is observed, which is considered as the unearned income that the emigrant could have given to the national economy. This mainly means the unearned tax revenues to state and local budgets.

It can be confidentially stated that the primary motivating factor for doctors to leave the country is financial remuneration alongside various other factors. For example, young doctors choose to go abroad due to the higher quality of residency training and working conditions.[22] Additionally, board-certified doctors to train and supervise young professionals is limited.

A severe shortage of doctors is observed in public hospitals, where young doctors have to be trained and acquire the speciality. However, staff shortages often force young doctors to fulfil their working hours with too many on-calls and other 'system' maintenance tasks, thus reducing time for learning the speciality subjects and having quality conversations with a supervisor. This not only hinders their professional development but also impacts their overall job satisfaction and mental well-being, potentially leading to burnout and a decreased commitment to their chosen field. As a result, addressing these issues is crucial for fostering a more supportive environment that enables young doctors to thrive both academically and professionally.

2. Training and attracting young resident doctors

It is essential for the country to train young resident doctors who are enrolled in an accredited residency programme to gain a medical speciality. These doctors have an employment relationship with the medical institution offering the training, where they provide healthcare services under the supervision of a certified doctor registered in the Register of Healthcare Practitioners. The medical professional residency programmes are provided by specialised universities in cooperation with medical institutions and the Ministry of Health.

21 Cabinet of Ministers, regulations No.685, 2011.
22 Ibid.

Residency is the education of a medical doctor in an employment relationship with a medical institution providing an educational programme, to acquire a speciality in accordance with an accredited professional residency training programme in medicine. It is an essential part of medical education and a prerequisite for obtaining a medical certificate, which entitles a doctor to practice independently and fully in their speciality. The minimum duration of a residency training programme for a person who has already acquired the profession of 'doctor' to be eligible for authorisation to practice medicine independently, in accordance with their chosen competence, after completing a full-time medical study programme, is set separately for each basic speciality of the medical profession. The scope of the resident doctor's independent professional work[23] shall be determined by the head of the medical institution based on an assessment of the theoretical knowledge and professional skills acquired by the resident doctor by a certified and trained specialist in the relevant speciality.[24]

The procedure for financing the residency and the procedure for recovering funds shall be determined by LR Ministry Cabinet Regulation No. 685 of 30 August 2011 Procedure for Admission, Distribution, and Funding of the Residency. The Paragraph 3 of the Regulation No. 685[25] states the following: The LR Ministry of Health shall calculate the number of residency places to be financed from the State budget based on the following data: (1)information provided by medical institutions on the number of doctors needed, (2) the number of doctors not working in their main job, (3) the number of unemployed doctors, (4) the number of doctors expected to reach retirement age within the next five years, (5) mutual analysis of statistics data on the provision of doctors in the European Union member states, (6) demographic situation and development projections, (7) projections of the number of healthcare practitioners for full-time workloads.

The mechanism that prepares young doctors in Latvia is good enough; however, many young doctors do not end up in the public sector after their residence or in the private sector. Young Doctors' Association underlines the above regulatory framework as a reason for emigration, which stipulates the condition to work for 3 years in the public sector after completing the residency. Procedure for Admission, Distribution, and Funding of the Residency. In this regard, the Young Doctors' Association has said: 'This violates the free movement of labour and severely restricts a young doctor's choice of future workplace. For example, if a young doctor decides to go for an internship or

23 Young Doctors' Association.2019.

24 Slokenberga, S. et al., 2015, pp.277.

25 Cabinet of Ministers Regulation No. 685, 2011.

further research abroad after their residency, they will have to reimburse their residency expenses. Latvian Young Doctors' Association believes[26] that such attempts to forcibly keep young specialists in the country only encourage and will encourage the emigration of residents and promote the shortage of doctors in Latvia. These Cabinet Regulations have been in force for several years, and reality has shown that such coercive restrictions do not work in the long term and will not retain young professionals in the country.

However, when young professionals faced with a situation of refund the state budget those investments spent in their education or to work for a certain period, the residents believe that their right to freedom of choice of occupation is being violated and could in fact even be considered as forced labour. According to the Article 106 of the Constitution of Latvia: "Everyone has the right to freely choose the occupation and workplace that suit their abilities and qualifications. Forced labour shall be prohibited. Involvement in the elimination of disasters and their consequences and employment in accordance with a court ruling shall not be considered forced labour."[27] The Constitutional Court concluded that the regulatory framework established by the Cabinet of Ministers complies with the Constitution,[28] that is seen in the Box 1.

Box 1: The Constitutional Court judgment of 3 May 2012 in Case No. 2011-14-03 (The Constitutional Court's judgment, 2012

The Concluding statement: "First, according to Regulation No. 120 and Regulation No. 972, a person could choose the means for funding their studies in the residency. The Constitutional Court emphasises that the regulatory enactments do not impose an obligation on a person, but only the right to conclude a contract governed by public law on the payment of the individual's training in residency from the State budget funds. An individual can also pay themselves for their residency training or use the resources of other natural or legal persons, without being obliged to work for a specific medical institution for three years after completing the residency or to reimburse the state budget for the funds spent on their training. Secondly, if an individual has chosen to study in a residency at public expense, they are given the opportunity to choose which of several medical institutions to work in for the next three years. Thirdly, if an individual wishes to work in another medical institution in Latvia or leave Latvia, they can reimburse the state budget funds spent on the residency training. In addition, these funds shall be repaid over five years, in monthly instalments and without a penalty, instead of being repaid in full immediately. Persons enrolled in a residency who freely choose to enter a training contract for the payment of training from the State budget funds, at the

26 Young Doctors' Association, 2019.

27 The Constitution of the Republic of Latvia. Adopted by the Constitutional Assembly of Latvia on 15 February 1922.

28 The Constitutional Court's judgment of 3 May 2012 in Case No. 2011- 14-03.

same time assume certain obligations towards the State. This contract governed by public law is a win-win situation: on the one hand, the State commits to pay for the individual's training during the residency, and on the other, the individual commits to work in the public health system for three years after completing the residency. Thus, the term 'Harm to the rights of the individual' should only be used conditionally in this case. The State has the right to require a person to fulfil the obligations they have undertaken. However, the benefit of this restriction on the right of an individual for the whole society is the possibility to receive healthcare services guaranteed under Article 111 of the Constitution *(Satversme)* or to recover the State budget funds for the investment in the training of the individual. Consequently, the benefit to society outweighs the fundamental right of the individual contained in the contested regulation".

Despite the judgment of the Constitutional Court, there is an opinion that, in any event, the obligation to work in the public sector for 3 years after completing the residency, as stipulated in the Regulation No. 685, contradicts EU law.[29] Specifically, EU law promotes the free movement of labour within the EU, suggesting that individuals should have the right to choose their employment without being bound by such obligations. This perspective emphasises the need to align national regulations with EU principles to ensure that healthcare professionals can exercise their rights to work freely across the EU. However, in a situation where the State has funded education of an individual, to oblige the individual to work for a certain period in the public sector as a medical practitioner and to provide healthcare services to the population.[30]

Article 111 of the Constitution postulates that the State shall protect human health and guarantee a minimum level of medical assistance to everyone.[31] The framework established by Regulation No. 685 is one of the mechanisms by which the State seeks to ensure the existence and accessibility of medical practitioners and the services they provide to the population. In the authors' view, the 3-year compulsory employment period should not be regarded as disproportionately long.

29 Cabinet of Ministers Regulation No. 685, 2011.

30 Jirgensons, G. (2024) EU Helath Policy and the Healthcare Labour Market in Latvia: The Out-Migration of Healthcare Practitioners. *Studia Europejskie – Studies in European Affairs*, 1/2024 pp.149–163, pp. 149–163. DOI:10.33067/SE.1.2024.8.

31 The Constitution of the Republic of Latvia. Adopted by the Constitutional Assembly of Latvia on 15 February 1922.Article 111.

3. Possible solutions for solving human resource problems

In recent years, the Latvian healthcare system has faced significant challenges, primarily the availability of publicly funded healthcare services and workforce issues. A major reason for doctors leaving the country is salary; therefore, the government must secure funding to increase healthcare personnel remuneration. However, it's important to note that the significance of salary as a reason for emigration has diminished over time. Based on the Survey's result it could be said that the decision to emigrate may influence such factors as social security benefits, state guarantees, better access to childcare, improved healthcare quality, mortgage loan availability for families, professional development opportunities, and access to advanced technologies. Addressing these challenges is essential for retaining young professionals. However, to find solutions to the above listed issues requires time.

As it was already underlined, there is a shortage of medical doctors, especially general medical specialists in rural areas. Expanding the use of telemedicine could help alleviate this problem. Telemedicine uses telecommunications technology to deliver medical services remotely, encompassing phone calls, video chats, emails, and text messages. It is also known as telehealth, digital medicine, e-health, or m-health.

Telemedicine offers several advantages, such as: accessibility (provides remote care to patients in remoted regions), cost- reduction (lowers remote care to patients in remoted regions, lower healthcare costs for patients and providers), experience sharing facilitates the exchange of knowledge among health professionals). Moreover, telemedicine promotes green and sustainable services to population.

However, there are also disadvantages, for example, increased risk of errors (remote consultations may lead misunderstandings), telemedicine cannot replace physical examinations (important diagnostic elements may be missed), regulatory changes needed (current laws may need to adapt to reflect telemedicine operation), time-consuming for doctors (managing remote consultations can be challenging for healthcare providers).

Another potential solution to the workforce problem is to consider shortening residency programmes in certain specialties. However, this proposal should be thoroughly evaluated by the Ministry of Health in collaboration with medical associations.

Finally, many students from Eastern countries are studying medicine in Latvia, but most leave to pursue residency positions in Western Europe after graduation. The Ministry of Health should explore strategies to retain these graduates, such as increasing residency salaries, enhancing the quality of training, and possibly providing housing assistance for these young professionals.

D. Conclusions

The EU's fundamental principles ensure the free movement of labour and recognition of professional qualifications in various of professions, which are crucial factors for the migration of EU citizens within the Single Market. As a result, countries and regions with low average wages in EU could supply labour to those areas, where wages are considerably higher.

The authors observe that the healthcare system in Latvia adheres to the Beveridge model, considering historical experience, cultural characteristics, available resources, and expertise. This model has led to a largely centralised healthcare system, where the National Health Service in Latvia provides universal population coverage, general tax-financed healthcare provision and a purchaser–provider split. The Ministry of Health is responsible for defining national health policies and regulations. It also regulates public health, while the Centre for Disease Prevention and Control coordinates and implements public health activities. The Ministry of Health aims to ensure that Latvia's healthcare system has sufficient qualified human resources. This includes effective human resources planning, improving remuneration and social guarantees, and aligning education with healthcare labour market demands. Despite these objectives the number of healthcare practitioners is declining, medical staff is aging, and there are significant regional disparities in healthcare distribution. The authors conclude that responsible government institutions should implement proactive policies aimed at improving of the health system and preventive measures to reduce the outflow of medical practitioners from the country. Developing policies that facilitate the movement of healthcare professionals while ensuring that they are trained in and advocate for sustainable practices can create a workforce that is aligned with the goals of the Green Deal.

The authors examined the reasons for the outflow of medical professionals, specifically medical doctors, from Latvia to other EU countries. Many issues in the healthcare system appeared from inadequate public funding. Authors conclude that a substantial increase of funding in public sector is essential to address these matters. The analysis reveals that financial remuneration is the primary reason for emigration, alongside better career opportunities, access to advanced technologies, social security, and improved working conditions. The need for improved management to address the unavailability of health practitioners is urgent. However, in case of existing partnerships, The Green Deal can promote the exchange of medical professionals who are trained in sustainable healthcare practices. This can enhance the capacity of healthcare systems to respond to challenges posed by environmental factors, thus fostering resilience.

The system of residency for young doctors should be improved. Currently, the regulatory framework mandates three years of public sector work post-residency, has not effectively reduced emigration rates. Many young doctors choose to leave after completing their residency. The authors suggest amending regulations to exempt individuals from repaying study costs if they abandon their studies for uncontrollable reasons. Furthermore, reimbursement should not apply to those who serve in critical shortage areas, such as emergency medicine and surgery. It's also important to consider that current regulations may conflict with EU laws on labour mobility. The authors recommend that the Ministry of Justice assess and improve the regulatory framework to ensure compliance with EU standards.

The state must leverage available human resources to provide necessary healthcare services; otherwise, the ongoing outflow of practitioners may compromise the sustainability of Latvia's healthcare system.

List of References

Treaty on the Functioning of the European Union (2012) Official Journal C 326/47, p. 76. Available at:https://eurlex.europa.eu/LexUriServ/LexUriServ.do?uri=CELEX:12012E/TXT:en:PDF

The European Green Deal. Brussels, 11.12.2019, COM(2019) 640 final.

Directive 2005/55/EC of the European Parliament and of the Council of 20 November 2013 amending

Directive 2005/36/EC on the recognition of professional qualifications and Regulation (EU) No 1024/2012 on administrative co-operation through the Internal Market information System ('the IMI Regulation')

The Constitution of the Republic of Latvia. Adopted by the Constitutional Assembly of Latvia on 15 February 1922. Available at: https://www. saeima.lv/en/legislative-process/constitution

The Constitutional Court's judgment of 3 May 2012 in Case No. 2011- 14-03. Available at: https://www.satv.tiesa.gov.lv/wp-content/uploads/2016/02/2011-14-03_Spriedums.pdf

The Regulations of the Cabinet of Ministers 13 April 2004, No. 286 "By-laws of the Ministry of Health", Available at: https://likumi.lv/ta/id/87141-veselibas-ministrijas-nolikums

The Regulations of the Cabinet of Ministers 1 November 2011, No. 286, "Regulations of the National Health Service", Available at: https://likumi.lv/ta/id/239184-nacionala-veselibas-dienesta-nolikums

The Regulations of the Cabinet of Ministers of 30 August 2011, No. 685 "Procedures for the admission, distribution and financing of residency of residents", Available at: https://likumi.lv/ta/id/235421-rezidentu-uznemsanas-sadales-un-rezidenturas-finansesanas-kartiba

Amendments to the Regulations of the Cabinet of Ministers of 30 August 2011, No. 685 "Procedures for the admission, distribution and financing of residency of residents" No. 53.

18.01.2022. Latvijas Vestnesis, No.2022/14.19. Available at: https://www.vestnesis.lv/op/2022/14.19

Cabinet of Ministers of the Republic of Latvia No. 359 26, May 2022. Public Health Guidelines 2021–2027. Available at: https://likumi.lv/ta/id/332751-sabiedribas-veselibas-pamatnostad nes-2021–2027-gadam

The Central Statistical Bureau of Latia, 2024.Available at: https://stat.gov.lv/en/statistics-themes/education/higher-education/press-releases/22128-topicalities-higher-education?themeCode=IG

Diena. Latvian daily newspaper (2023) Currently, there is a shortage of 300 doctors and 8000 nurses in Latvia. Available at: https://www.diena.lv/raksts/latvija/zinas/lab-patlaban-latvija-trukst-300-arstu-un-8000- masu-14295960

Eurostat (2024) Which countries have the most doctor and dentist graduates? Available at: https://ec.europa.eu/eurostat/web/products-eurostat-news/w/ddn-20240805-1

Eurostat (2023) Employment. Annual Statistics. Available at: https://ec.europaeu/eurostat/statistics-explained/index.php?title=Employment_-_ annual_statistics

Jirgensons, G. (2024) EU Helath Policy and the Healthcare Labour Market in Latvia: The Out-Migration of Healthcare Practitioners. *Studia Europejskie – Studies in European Affairs*, 1/2024 pp.149–163, pp. 149–163. DOI:10.33067/SE.1.2024.8.

OECD/European Observatory on Health Systems and Policies (2021), Latvia: Country Health Profile 2021, State of Health in the EU, OECD Publishing, Paris/European Observatory on Health Systems and Policies, Brussels.

Portal Doctus (2024) "In search of the Happy Land. Global migration of medical practitioners". Available at: https://www.doctus.lv

The State Audit Office of the Republic of Latvia (2019) Human Resources in Health Care. Audit report. Available at: https://www.lrvk.gov.lv/lv/revizijas/revizijas/noslegtas-revizijas/cilvekresursi-veselibas-aprupe

Slokenberga, S. et al. (2015) Medical Law 2015. Riga: Courthouse Agency

World Health Organisation (2023) Small countries face challenges in human resources for health. Available at: https://www.who.int/latvia/news/item/21-04-2023-small-countries-face-challenges-in-humanresources-for-health--says-working-group

Young Doctors Association (2019) "The main reasons for the shortage of doctors are pay and working conditions". Available at: https://www. ekonomika.lv/jauno-arstu-asociacija-arstu-trukuma-galvenie-iemesliatalgojums-un-darba-apstakli/

Radu-Ioan Popa[1]

Workforce and migration – vulnerabilities in a climate change context

Summary: The theoretical and practical debates have sparked an increased attention in the last years over the topic of climate change context and its impact on people strategies to adapt, cope and integrate in host communities, investigating public perception on mobility and numerous reactions to change. The "classical" work migration due to economic reasons has been reinforced by a new response in mobility, due to gradual or extreme environment transformation, which forces people to look for work opportunities elsewhere, to adapt to new work settings and communities, in their effort to retrieve a sense of place, balance, security, normality and well-being. So far, the growing concerns over grim statistical projections on human displacement due to environment change have outlined a collection of challenges and vulnerabilities both for the migrant population and the receiving communities. In this sense, public perception over migration, the in-group out-group interactions, work integration view solicit more research and analysis, reaffirming social sciences stance to approach, explore, test, explain, implement and contribute to today's reality dilemmas solutions.

Keywords: workforce, climate change, work integration, work migration, socio-psychological features.

A. General perspectives

I. Workforce migration and climate conditions

Today's societies face multiple challenges and crises that seem to act continuously, sometimes in an overlapping manner, giving no pause for adaptation

---

1 Assoc. Prof. Dr. Radu-Ioan Popa is part of the Department of Social Work, Journalism, Public Relations and Sociology team, at "Lucian Blaga" University of Sibiu, Romania. His main research interests and publications focus on the human resources management, vulnerable groups, human-artificial intelligence interactions. He is also an Honorary Fellow at Munich University of Applied Sciences, Germany. Contact: radu.popa@ulbsibiu.ro.

and a smooth management of change. From climate change to economic crises, from wars to various factors of instability, people have been forced to adapt or look for diverse strategies, coping with lack of resources, the need for security, seeking better life conditions and the promise of well-being. In the last years there have been plenty of debates, analysis, research and projections over the coming developments and configurations of socio-economic settings, impact on daily life as we know it, means of adaptation and strategies to be adopted, in the context of climate change and its main effect – migration. Climate change may be perceived as one of the major sources for migration and work mobility, apart from conflicts, economic uncertainty, social security and other life stability threating factors.

The statistical projections are somehow grim, in terms of no action and given the current status of rapid climate change climate rapid change and evolutions, data showing for example that an expected increase by 2050 sits somewhere between 200 million to 1 billion migrants, given the fact that just in 2019, the observed raise in number of migrants was 3.5% (272 million) from 2.8% in 2000, an increase of 100 million people (Laczko & Aghazarm, 2009; Sironi, Bauloz & Emmanuel, 2019; United Nations, 2019; Adlam, 2020).

The two concepts of climate change and climate migration are interlinked, the first one being seen often as a threat, while the second as a direct effect, which has the potential to bring uncertainty in both positive or negative ways (Adlam, 2020). From another perspective, migration can be seen as an adaptation to the social and economic risks created by the climate change outcomes (Faist, 2016), either to references like extreme weather events (Shultz & Rechkemmer, 2022) or simply due to a constant shifting of the environment conditions, downgrading the settings for a normal work and life (Adamo, 2023). Even if the term "climate refugee" expresses the vulnerable group of people that are forced to relocate internally or externally, from their home countries, temporarily or permanently, due to sudden or gradual environment changes which impact negatively their lives and conditions for living (Sironi, Bauloz & Emmanuel, 2019), there are still ongoing debates and research over the term acceptance, case inclusion, complexity clarification and category representation. In one study, Moawad (2024) indicated that climate shock mobility may be either temporary or permanent, internal or international, voluntary or forced.

Aside from the cause of mobility, in this case climate change, the urge to protect people migrating becomes a frontrunner obligation and providing the opportunity to adapt, integrate, educate, work and live in the new settings. One particular interest of the present chapter resides in the workforce aspects, in the case of people who relocated due to environment crises. In general terms, the exodus of workforce from one region to another, from one country to another, has been an ongoing event with a long history. People have always migrated for work, for better conditions and economic reasons. In Europe, the work mobility has been a natural means of trade exchanges, cultural intersections and community living, historically speaking. Nowadays, for example, there is a collection of standardized factors that favor work force mobility inside the European Union (e.g. from work legislation and work mobility regulations, free work mobility principles, work rights, work access, work equality etc.).

On the other hand, the challenges with an aging population, low birth rates, combined with a growing demand for personnel in various sectors, decreased or lack of work force in some specific areas (e.g. industry, services, health, education etc.), add to the need of better understanding workforce migration and its integration in the new settings. Moreover, workforce migration due to climate change brings extra specific requirements and comprehension.

People who are displaced due to the environment impact are forced to migrate not only because there is a temporary or permanent threat to their life safety but also due to the fact that their means of living, including work and work outcomes are affected (e.g. losing jobs, losing places of work, losing resources to fulfill work tasks etc.). In this case, their social safety is related to their work safety, including the need to provide for their families, support themselves and others financially, afford to live under normal circumstances and so on. In this view, migration due to climate change forces a search for work on terms of surviving first, and not on economic reasons, which drive a standard work migration in normal situations more likely.

Regarding a climate crisis, displaced people can benefit from social protection, both formal in terms of state policy, regulations, relief strategies (e.g. financial aid, relocation services, food assistance, social work services, psychological assistance, access to education and health, work access and integration on the host country labor market etc.) and informal, given the host community active participation and involvement, support networks, informal stakeholders (e.g. providing shelter, access to information, employment opportunities, solidarity etc.), this ensuring an adequate adaptation to the labor market as well (Portes & Rumbaut, 2006; Levitt et al., 2016; Schwerdtle et al., 2020; Hodges et al., 2024).

On the opposite, if the legislation is unclear in the reception country, regulations are missing or not properly applied, if there are limited or no relief strategies and resources, and if the informal social protection agents are missing or dysfunctional, the migrant integration on the workforce market can face work abuse, inequalities, work exploitation and mistreatment, denial of work access and opportunities (Menjivar, 2000; Del Real, 2019; Hodges et al., 2024).

In an interesting study, Hodges et al. (2024) found that people challenged with displacement due to environment crisis, rely heavily on the informal social protection, like personal support networks, that can open the path for accessing formal social protection services or even replace them, in a situation that raises concerns about the capacity of formal assistance to reach those in need and the equity principle for all. In other words, climate victims are more likely to solicit support through their informal networks, using whatever resources these connections and systems may provide, shadowing the formal structure and sources of support, diminishing their efficiency and presence.

Even if at first glance, the process might seem to work, risks are always involved, as presented previously, with regard to imbalanced access to information and formal support, conflict, community rejections and divisions, work exploitation and work right denial etc. So even if transnational ties can act as a source for social protection in the case of climate refugees, looking for a host country, looking for work and resettlement, there is a growing concern about the formal outreach and relief programs availability, accessing options, personalized content and service to those in need.

In another study, Koirala and Bashyal (2025) underlined, in a systematic review, the implications of transnational migration on income diversification, livelihood enhancement, food security and ecological restoration which impact policy making, decision making and long-term macro-economic objectives. The authors illustrated several effects of workforce reduction in the home country, under the substitution frame, from increased workload, workforce shortage, high labor wage, to rural gentrification and a growing work pressure on those who remain (Koirala & Bashyal, 2025).

As seen in other migration studies on the workforce subject, the effects of displacement can be radical on the origin country, where the work force exodus creates imbalances in the country's economy, affecting the welfare state, disrupting the normal flow of personnel in key positions and the natural replacement of work force with newer generations (Bayrak et al., 2023; Moawad, 2024; Madondo & Dhobha, 2025). The shortage of workforce, the constant flow of skilled workers, all the way to entire resettlements of people in certain areas due to climate conditions, increase the severe depopulation rate and relocation of those remaining soon after, making resilience more difficult or impossible once the displacement reaches this point. From this perspective, climate change or climate disasters trigger not only immediate transformations on the affected areas but also long-term impact processes that engage further vulnerabilities both for the people and the areas they live in. In the case of work force migration, at a certain point and rate, it will determine more people moving out of the home area towards other locations.

Bayrak et al. (2023) found that emigration status had no mitigating influence on climate-change effects nor to the strategies adopted by workers, yet the results indicated some impact of climate change on income status, households management, dependency on remittances and coping strategy, describing specific challenges to small production businesses, differences between income and their unbalanced impact, aging and out migration phenomenon, concluding that climate stressors trigger uneven effects on the communities and individuals.

Overall, people migration due to environment causes and threats imply seeking a certain social security in host areas, which solicits at the same time a work integration for adaptation and survival. At the same time workforce migration due to a climate crisis included in a more generalized migration model, involves a double effect, one on the origin area, confronted with workforce shortages and the other one on the host location, region or country, challenged with the integration mechanism of the new comers. If life-threatening extreme weather events and dramatic changes in climate will continue to develop and thrive, migration will become the new normal, on the long run, encompassing the work and economic mobility in a mobility for survival and tomorrow's security.

II. Social features of work integration in host communities

At a first look, the scholarly literature focuses on key causes, process and effects of climate migration, analyzing policies, impacts, individual and community responses to change, personal discourse over the migration itinerary or simply patterns of migration and main drivers. However, the question of exploring social and psychological traits of climate migration including the workforce relocation due to the environment is somehow secondary and not gaining full attention and momentum.

Apart from climate, economic and political factors that can trigger migration, resettling determines a series of social and psychological challenges when it comes to a new location adaptation, community and work integration. Strictly referring to work opportunities in the new setting, the climate refugee or migrant is liable to encounter a collection of barriers until securing a job in the host community. From a social point of view, the public perception on climate change as well as on the reception of climate migrants is widely divided between acceptance or rejection, the host population sometimes tending to react in an opposite manner to the climate discourse (Singh

& Swanson, 2017; Gillis et al., 2023; Raimi et al., 2024). There is no consensus whether climate migrants are perceived as economic or political ones (Spilker et al., 2020; Arias & Blair, 2022; Raimi et al., 2024), the concepts overlapping in this sense, as indicated before. Migration due to environment crisis includes also a strong economic motive, people resettling to areas where they can farm, produce, work and gain, ensuring their daily needs and normal living.

Another social variable, besides the public perception, refers to the community inclusion practices in the work sector, including here various reactions and attitudes towards migrants and the climate topic. The major models on social groups underline here the "classical" clash between the ingroup and outgroup when it comes to new comers' adaptation and integration in the host community. Trop and Liberman (2012) indicated there is a risk of generating an ingroup mentality in the receiving communities when climate migration is addressed from a local stance and close-up position. At the same time, whether local or international, migration has the potential to trigger ingroup attitudes and reactions in the host communities when it comes to receiving incoming new members. As the scholar works have presented so far, the fear towards outgroup participants lead to "protection" behaviors, which are quick to be on display (e.g. rejection, avoidance, risk perception, negative attitudes, threat perception and fears etc.) when the members of the ingroup local community are challenged with the reality of receiving members of an outgroup inside their structures (Everett, Faber & Crockett, 2015; O'Donnell et al., 2019; Raimi et al., 2024). In other studies, research has observed that if domestic migrants or even international ones are perceived as part of the ingroup, on the basis that the local community projects similar possible situations for relocating due to environment conditions, then the reception becomes more open, adaptation and integration being supported by the locals (Lujala et al., 2020; Kim, Kay & Schuldt, 2021; Raimi et al., 2024).

Besides overall public perception and group functioning, the perception on work integration itself of migrants raises various questions. From the migrant point of view, work adaptation may provide security overall, a mean to accommodate and retake a daily normal functioning. On the other hand, the host community may perceive work adaptation as a will to integrate and participate. Other scholar studies argue that in contrast migration presence may lead to higher competition and conflict on the labor market, over employment opportunities (Turhan & Armiero, 2019; Spilker et al., 2020; Lujala et al., 2020; Tubi & Kapinga, 2024). Even if these effects are difficult to analyze, confirm and generalize, various authors draw attention over the usual narratives that might influence potential disruptions, both ethnic, cultural and social between those incoming in search for a job and local residents (Gaikwad & Nellis, 2017; Spilker et al., 2020, Tubi & Kapinga, 2024). Moreover, the sociocultural dimensions of migration, with regard to employment status, work perception and attitudes, income expectation and projection, community participation, affect the integration process from both migrants and receiving communities point of view, underlying the importance of psychological predictors as well (e.g. having a positive mindset, objective life expectations, empowering personal beliefs, cognitive judgements), on supporting an optimal transition and adaptation or biasing them (Duque et al., 2025).

Social perception on work integration of migrants relies heavily on public perception, existing community narratives on the subject, groups behavior, global discourse and political views, host communities being under numerous pressure points in their reception of newcomers which are directly impacted nevertheless.

B. Psychological features of work integration in a climate change context

The social perspective on work challenges due to environment conditions brings also to attention the numerous psychological variables, which shape the mobility process of climate migrants, from root causes to projections, search experiences and potential outcomes. The scholarly literature is also scarce, results being disparate and too few on the matter. Studies focus more on immediate public views, climate justice, social transformations rather than on the overall individual perceptions, experiences and behaviors, critical, social and psychological approaches to climate crisis (Fernandes-Jesus et al., 2024). Following a focus group analysis, Fritz et al. (2024), observed that the main drivers for climate management and adaptation reside in individual behavior change, top-down industry centered reconsideration as well as technology-centered dynamics, while major barriers are represented by the economic systems and interests, lack of awareness and international coordination or cooperation. In another view, the lack of proper communication and support policies will result in tensions, in the case of migrant mobility and job searching within the local communities that are recipient, diminishing the public support and cohesion, sometimes disfranchising the climate migrant, part of a risk outgroup (Mols & Jetten, 2016; Stanley, Leviston & Tseung-Wong, 2023). Living with a constant assault on social identity and job security, climate migrants are challenged with the risk of inadequate work access and opportunities, inequal rights and restrictions. The burden of feeling "not welcomed" or "not invited" can be translated in fewer to no options to work, to get familiar with, to adapt and to integrate in a functional labor market, which leads to negative psychological outcomes of being rejected and isolated. The perception of threat at work imports two sides of understanding, one in which the migrant experiences the denial of acceptance and integration, and the other in which the community "fears" job losing, impact on work style and unknown or unwanted interferences in their organizational culture, climate, views, objectives and functioning.

Detaining a sense of place or belonging refers to people's attachment, both cognitive and emotional, for their familiar environment which in turn shapes a specific balance, stability and fluency of life, with deep impact on personal identity, experience and behaviors (Brown & Perkins, 1992; Rubin, Garfin & Wong-Parodi, 2024). Naturally the place of origin contains also the person's habitual work environment and activities which are familiar. In climate migration, people lose contact with their initial home, with their job and work context and need to develop a new attachment to the reception environment in all aspects, following a dynamic natural transaction due to constant context and conditions changes. From this perspective the migrant worker needs to find connections with the new workplace, to fit in and to feel involved and included. Work integration in a climate change context will always require an identity and work process retake, reallocating personal resources in an effort to build a sense of place after losing it, a sense of community (Fernandes-Jesus et al., 2024), or growing "roots" again (Blackwell, Aranda & Rosa, 2023). Rubin, Garfin and Wong-Parodi (2024) stated that further research is needed in exploring and understanding place attachment and detachment, personal experience, fears and emotions with regard to climate migration. Work integration in a host environment may trigger fears and stress of potential inclusion rejection, adding up to the detachment state from the previous context. By exploring these negative states in association with climate change, distress, perceptions or awareness, new insights can be depicted on human behavior patterns and perspectives (Weiß, Gutzeit & Hein, 2024; Cipriani, Gemignani & Menicucci, 2024). Social cohesion, detaining skills and expertise, certain positive beliefs can ease the adaptation process (Al Maamari, 2024). On the opposite, Stanley, Leviston and Tseung-Wong (2023) found that ideological attitudes and threat perceptions have the potential to act as barriers in migrant adequate integration in the recipient society, more attention being needed in implementing support programs, inclusion and people well-being.

New frontiers in research will have to undergo in-depth analysis of climate migration and the challenges of workforce demands and stances. In this light of things, Table 1 contains several future directions proposals for research, regarding workforce migration in a climate change condition.

Table 1: *Future research directions and themes for workforce migration*

Direction	Topics
Concepts	– Construct validation – Work impact self-evaluation on host community – Environment and work displacement process – Community acceptance and work adaptation – Work integration barriers and facilitators – Cultural variations – Stereotypes on climate migration – Socio-psychological variables and climate migration – Formal and informal support – Public perception, social representations and awareness
Methodologies	– Longitudinal approaches on workforce mobility and adaptation due to climate change – Existing evaluation instruments validation – New methods and instruments for data collection exploration – Experimental design approach on work migration due to climate conditions – Qualitative data analysis – Research participants specific segmentation – Context and causal relations testing
Results	– External validity target – Thematic representativeness on climate and work migration outcomes – Nuances of climate migration and work implications – Prediction models testing
Implications	– Policy crafting and actions on migration, work, integration and climate – Vulnerabilities prevention and management through regulatory mechanisms and guidelines – Participation and decision-making of migrants and reception communities – Coping strategies and support interventions for migrants – Education programs development

Despite recent research and works, there is a long path for social sciences and theory to explore the dynamics of climate migration, its impact on the workforce and adaptation. Given the sense of urgency and constant crisis, the challenge resides in keeping track with the momentum while providing solution-oriented research and insight.

C. Conclusion

After following the systematic itinerary through the challenges brought by environment changes on the labor market and work integration, the discourse underlines the necessity to invest more in researching climate mobility, work solicitations and demands. As observed previously, studies are still scarce on the matter, with heterogenous data. Going beyond climate justice, policies, drivers and public perception, an increasing interest arises in exploring and explaining social and psychological factors of climate migration. Understanding socio-psychological mechanisms of place detachment and attachment, work attitudes and relocation impact, as well as context-related experiences towards work integration and host community narratives, may bring the society approach closer to respond adequately to work and climate crisis.

Overall, support strategies for sustainability and efficiency in adapting the labor market to climate change will rely heavily on the nexus comprehension, between rapid transformation, the unique human response to adaptation and the never ending search for welfare and well-being.

List of References

Adamo, S.B., Future trends: The challenges of climate displacement, in: Integrative social work practice with refugees, asylum seekers, and other forcibly displaced persons, eds. Murakami, N.J. & Akilova, M., 2023, p. 123–149, Cham: Springer

Adlam, J., No room at the inn? Re-imagining social inclusion at the intersections between climate change, globalisation, homelessness, and human migration, Journal of Social Work Practice, 2020, 34(4), p. 379–392, https://doi.org/10.1080/02650533.2020.1781802

Al Maamari, R.H.H., Enhancing resilience to climate events: A multi-capital approach in social work, International Journal of Disaster Risk Reduction, 2024, 113, 104883, https://doi.org/10.1016/j.ijdrr.2024.104883

Arias, S.B./Blair, C.W., Changing tides: Public attitudes on climate migration, The Journal of Politics, 2022, 84(1), p. 560–567, https://doi.org/10.1086/715163

Bayrak, M.M./Van Hieu, T./Tran, T.A./Hsu, Y.Y./Nien, T./Quynh, D.T.T., Climate change adaptation responses and human mobility in the Mekong Delta: local perspectives from rural households in An Giang Province, Vietnam, Humanities and Social Sciences Communications, 2023, 10(1), p. 1–14, https://doi.org/10.1057/s41599-023-01817-5

Blackwell, R./Aranda, E./Rosa, A., "We always remember the Island": Puerto Rican climate migrants' emotional meanings of home, Emotion, Space and Society, 2023, 49(1), 100974, 10.1016/j.emospa.2023.100974

Brown, B.B./Perkins, D.D., Disruptions in place attachment, in: Place Attachment. Human Behavior and Environment, vol. 12, eds. Altman, I. & Low, S.M., 1992, p. 279–304, Boston: Springer

Cipriani, E./Gemignani, A./Menicucci, D., Awareness of everyday effects of climate change: The climate change perceptual awareness scale (CCPAS), Heliyon, 2024, 10(19), e38461, https://doi.org/10.1016/j.heliyon.2024.e38461

Del Real, D., Toxic ties: The reproduction of legal violence within mixed-status intimate partners, relatives, and friends, International Migration Review, 2019, 53(2), p. 548–570. https://doi.org/10.1177/0197918318769313

Duque, M./Vo, D.H./Montero-Zamora, P./Cobb, C.L./Sahbaz, S./Ertanir, B./Bautista, T./Watkins, L.G./Acaf, Y./Macias, M.A./Alpysbekova, A./Garcia, M.F./Rodriguez, J./Bates, M.M./Calderon, I.A./Maldonado-Molina, M.M./Bartholomew, J.B./Pinedo, M./Lee, T.K./Salas-Wright, C.P./Schwartz, S.J., Longitudinal determinants of thriving in Puerto Rican climate crisis migrants on the U.S. mainland: A structural equation model, Social Science & Medicine, 2025, 366, 117615, https://doi.org/10.1016/j.socscimed.2024.117615

Everett, J.A.C./Faber, N.S./Crockett, M., Preferences and beliefs in ingroup favoritism. Frontiers in Behavioral Neuroscience, 2015, 9(15), p. 1–21. https://doi.org/10.3389/fnbeh.2015.00015

Faist, T., Transnational social protection in Europe: A social inequality perspective, Oxford Development Studies, 2016, 45, p. 20–32. https://doi.org/10.1080/13600818.2016.1193128

Fernandes-Jesus, M./Cecconi, A./Esposito, F./Vargas-Moniz, M./Albanesi, C., Socio-psychological perspectives on climate-related migration: A systematic review and research agenda, Community Psychology in Global Perspective, 2024, 10(2), p. 156–190, https://doi.org/10.1285/i24212113v10i2-2p156

Fritz, L./Baum, C.M./Brutschin, E./Low, S./Sovacool, B.K., Climate beliefs, climate technologies and transformation pathways: Contextualizing public perceptions in 22 countries, Global Environmental Change, 2024, 87, e102880, 10.1016/j.gloenvcha.2024.102880

Gaikwad, N./Nellis, G., The majority-minority divide in attitudes toward internal migration: Evidence from Mumbai, American Journal of Political Science, 2017, 61(2), p. 456–472. https://doi.org/10.1111/ajps.12276

Gillis, A./Geiger, N./Raimi, K./Cunningham, J.L./Sarge, M.A., Climate change–induced immigration to the United States has mixed influences on public support for climate change and migrants, Climatic Change, 2023, 176(5), p. 1–30, https://doi.org/10.1007/s10584-023–03519-y

Hodges, J.C./García, M.F./Schwartz, S.J./Vaughn, M.G./Maldonado-Molina, M.M./Bates, M./Calderón, I./Brown, E.C./Rodríguez, J./Salas-Wright, C.P., Social protections and climate migration: Service navigation among Puerto Ricans displaced by hurricane Maria, Social Work, 2024, 69(4), p. 347–355. https://doi.org/10.1093/sw/swae036

Kim, B./Kay, D.L./Schuldt, J.P., Will I have to move because of climate change? Perceived likelihood of weather- or climate-related relocation among the US public, Climatic Change, 2021, 165(9), p. 1–8. https://doi.org/10.1007/s10584-021–03026-y

Koirala, S./Bashyal, S., The land left behind: a systematic review of transnational migration-induced change and its implication for rural sustainability in Nepal, Humanities and Social Sciences Communications, 2025, 12(1), p. 1–12, https://doi.org/10.1057/s41599-024–04180-1

Laczko, F./Aghazarm, C. (eds.), Migration, environment and climate change: Assessing the evidence, International Organization for Migration (IOM), 2009, Geneva, https://publications.iom.int/books/migration-environment-and-climate-change-assessing-evidence

Levitt, P./Viterna, J./Mueller, A./Lloyd, C., Transnational social protection: Setting the agenda, Oxford Development Studies, 2016, 45, p. 2–19. https://doi.org/10.1080/13600818.2016.1239702

Lujala, P./Bezu, S./Kolstad, I./Mahmud, M./Wiig, A., How do host–migrant proximities shape attitudes toward internal climate migrants?, Global Environmental Change, 2020, 65, 102156, https://doi.org/10.1016/j.gloenvcha.2020.102156

Madondo, E./Dhobha, H., Harnessing migration for sustainable development in Africa: challenges and opportunities, International Journal of Research in Business and Social Science, 2025, 14(1), p. 80–88, https://doi.org/10.20525/ijrbs.v14i1.3770

Menjivar, C., Fragmented ties: Salvadoran immigrant networks in America, 2000, London: University of California Press

Moawad, D., Does environmental change affect migration especially into the EU? Social Sciences, 2024, 13(3), 160, https://doi.org/10.3390/socsci13030160

Mols, F./Jetten, J., Explaining the appeal of populist right-wing parties in times of economic prosperity, Political Psychology, 2016, 37(2), p. 275–292, doi:10.1111/pops.12258

O'Donnell, A.W./Neumann, D.L./Duffy, A.L./Paolini, S., Learning to fear outgroups: An associative learning explanation for the development and reduction of intergroup anxiety, Social and Personality Psychology Compass, 2019, 13(3), p. 1–15, https://doi.org/10.1111/spc3.12442

Portes, A./Rumbaut, R.G., Immigrant America: A portrait (revised, expanded, and updated), 3rd edition, 2006, London: University of California Press

Raimi, K.T./Sarge, M.A./Geiger, N./Gillis, A./Cunningham, J.L., Effects of communicating the rise of climate migration on public perceptions of climate change and migration, Journal of Environmental Psychology, 2024, 93(1), p. 1–17, https://doi.org/10.1016/j.jenvp.2023.102210

Rubin, N./Garfin, D./Wong-Parodi, G., Exploring antecedents to climate migration: sense of place, fear and worry, and experience, Environmental Research Letters, 2024, 19(10), p. 1–14, 10.1088/1748–9326/ad6fb9

Schwerdtle, P.N./McMichael, C./Mank, I./Sauerborn, R./Danquah, I./Bowen, K.J., Health and migration in the context of a changing climate: A systematic literature assessment, Environmental Research Letters, 2020, 15(10), 103006, https://doi.org/10.1088/1748–9326/ab9ece

Shultz, J.M./Rechkemmer, A., Climate change, migration, & population health, in: Migration and health, eds. Galea, S., Ettman, C.K., & Zaman, M.H., 2022, p. 63–77, London: University of Chicago Press

Singh, S.P./Swanson, M., How issue frames shape beliefs about the importance of climate change policy across ideological and partisan groups, PLoS One, 2017, 12(7), e0181401, https://doi.org/10.1371/journal.pone.0181401

Sironi, A./Bauloz, C./Emmanuel, M. (eds.), Glossary on migration, International Migration Law No. 34, International Organization for Migration (IOM), 2019, Geneva, https://publications.iom.int/books/international-migration-law-ndeg34-glossary-migration

Spilker, G./Nguyen, Q./Koubi, V./Bohmelt, T., Attitudes of urban residents towards environmental migration in Kenya and Vietnam, Nature Climate Change, 2020, 10(7), p. 622–627, https://doi.org/10.1038/s41558-020–0805-1

Stanley, S.K./Leviston, Z./Ng Tseung-Wong, C.N., Support for climate-driven migration in Australia: Testing an ideology-based threat model, Current Research in Ecological and Social Psychology, 2023, 4, 100119, https://doi.org/10.1016/j.cresp.2023.100119

Trope, Y./Liberman, N., Construal level theory, in: Handbook of Theories of Social Psychology, vol. 1, eds. Van Lange, P. A. M., Kruglanski, A.W., & Higgins, E.T., 2012, p. 118–134, London: Sage Publications Ltd

Tubi, A./Kapinga, A.G., Rural migrants in urban centers: Sources of vulnerability or agents of adaptive capacity, Habitat International, 2024, 152(1), 103173, https://doi.org/10.1016/j.habitatint.2024.103173

Turhan, E./Armiero, M., Of (not) being neighbors: Cities, citizens and climate change in an age of migrations, Mobilities, 2019, 14(3), p. 363–374, https://doi.org/10.1080/17450101.2019.1600913

United Nations, Migration stock wallchart, UN Department of Economic and Social Affairs Population Division, 2019, https://doi.org/10.18356/c36d3e0d-en

Weiß, M./Gutzeit, J./Hein, G., Development and validation of the Domain-specific Climate Change Distress Scale, Journal of Environmental Psychology, 2024, 98, 102392, 10.1016/j.jenvp.2024.102392

Chapter 6
Green Deal Implementation and Competitiveness: Hydrogen

Nils Schuckenberg[1]

Der Markthochlauf von erneuerbarem Wasserstoff im Spannungsfeld zwischen Klimaschutz und Wettbewerb: Eine wettbewerbsrechtliche Bewertung der Förderung infolge von Auktionsverfahren der Europäischen Wasserstoffbank

Abkürzungsverzeichnis

°C	Grad Celsius
%	Prozent
&	und
ABl.	Amtsblatt
Abs.	Absatz; Absätze
Abschn.	Abschnitt(e)
ACER	Agentur für die Zusammenarbeit der Energieregulierungsbehörden
AEL	Alkalische Elektrolyse
AEMEL	Anionenaustauschmembran-Elektrolyse
AEUV	Konsolidierte Fassung des Vertrags über die Arbeitsweise der Europäischen Union (ABl. (EU) C 202/1 v. 7.6.2016, S. 47 ff.)
Alt.	Alternative(n)
Anhang zum Finanzierungsbeschluss 2023	Annex to the Commission Decision on the financing of actions under the Innovation Fund, serving as the financing decision for 2023 and as a decision launching calls for proposals, C(2023) 7827 final

1 Nils Schuckenberg, Alumnus der Hochschule Bremen aus dem Studiengang Europäische Wirtschaft und Verwaltung.

Anhang zum Finanzierungsbeschluss 2024	Annex to the Commission Decision on the financing of actions under the Innovation Fund, serving as a financing decision for 2024–2030 and a decision launching calls for proposals in 2024, C(2024) 8011 final
Art.	Artikel
Aufl.	Auflage
BDEW	Bundesverband der Energie- und Wasserwirtschaft e. V.
bspw.	beispielsweise
Buchst.	Buchstabe(n)
bzw.	beziehungsweise
ca.	circa
Call	Aufforderung zur Einreichung von Vorschlägen (engl.: Call for Proposal)
Call 2023	Innovation Fund auction call for proposals – Innovation Fund auction call for RFNBO Hydrogen (INNOVFUND-2023-AUC-RFNBO-Hydrogen) [Version 1.1 v. 20.12.2023]. https://ec.europa.eu/info/funding-tenders/opportunities/docs/2021– 2027/innovfund/wp-call/2023/call-fiche_innovfund-2023-auc-rfnbo-hydrogen_en.pdf
Call 2024	Innovation Fund auction call for proposals – Innovation Fund fixed premium auction call 2024 for RFNBO Hydrogen (INNOV-FUND-2024- AUC-RFNBO-Hydrogen) [Version 1.0 v. 3.12.2024]. https://ec.europa.eu/info/funding-tenders/opportunities/docs/2021– 2027/innovfund/wp-call/2024/call-fiche_innovfund-2024-auc-rfnbo- hydrogen_en.pdf
CCD	CO_2-Differenzvertrag
CCS	Carbon Capture and Storage
CD	Differenzvertrag
CHJU	Clean Hydrogen Partnership (rechtl.: Clean Hydrogen Joint Undertaking)
CINEA	Europäische Exekutivagentur für Klima, Infrastruktur und Umwelt
CO_2	Kohlenstoffdioxid
deleg.	delegierte(n)

deleg. Innovationsfondsverordnung	Deleg. Verordnung (EU) 2019/856 der Kommission v. 26.2.2019 zur Ergänzung der Richtlinie 2003/87/EG des Europäischen Parlaments und des Rates in Bezug auf die Funktionsweise des Innovationsfonds (ABl. (EU) L 140 v. 28.5.2019, S. 6 ff.); zuletzt geändert durch: Deleg. Verordnung (EU) 2023/2537 der Kommission v. 15.9.2023 zur Änderung der Deleg. Verordnung (EU) 2019/856 zur Ergänzung der Richtlinie 2003/87/EG des Europäischen Parlaments und des Rates in Bezug auf die Funktionsweise des Innovationsfonds (ABl. (EU) L v. 20.11.2023)
deleg. Verordnung über Treibhausgaseinsparungen	Deleg. Verordnung (EU) 2023/1184 der Kommission v. 10.2.2023 zur Ergänzung der Richtlinie (EU) 2018/2001 des Europäischen Parlaments und des Rates durch die Festlegung einer Unionsmethode mit detaillierten Vorschriften für die Erzeugung flüssiger oder gasförmiger erneuerbarer Kraftstoffe nicht biogenen Ursprungs für den Verkehr (ABl. (EU) L 157/11 v. 20.6.2023, S. 11 ff.); zuletzt geändert durch: Deleg. Verordnung (EU) 2024/1408 der Kommission v. 14.3.2024 zur Änderung der Deleg. Verordnung (EU) 2023/1184 der Kommission im Hinblick auf die Anpassung eines Fachbegriffs an die Richtlinie (EU) 2018/2001 des Europäischen Parlaments und des Rates (ABl. (EU) L v. 21.5.2024)
deleg. Verordnung zur RFNBO-Produktion	Deleg. Verordnung (EU) 2023/1185 der Kommission v. 10.2.2023 zur Ergänzung der Richtlinie (EU) 2018/2001 des Europäischen Parlaments und des Rates durch Festlegung eines Mindestschwellenwertes für die Treibhausgaseinsparungen durch wiederverwertete kohlenstoffhaltige Kraftstoffe und einer Methode zur Ermittlung der Treibhausgaseinsparungen durch flüssige oder gasförmige erneuerbare Kraftstoffe nicht biogenen Ursprungs für den Verkehr sowie durch wiederverwertete kohlenstoffhaltige Kraftstoffe (ABl. (EU) L 157/20 v. 20.6.2023, S. 20 ff.)
d. h.	das heißt
Doppelbuchst.	Doppelbuchstabe(n)
Durchführungsbeschluss	Durchführungsbeschluss (EU) 2021/173 der Kommission v. 12.2.2021 zur Einrichtung der Europäischen Exekutivagentur für

	Klima, Infrastruktur und Umwelt, der Europäischen Exekutivagentur für Gesundheit und Digitales, der Europäischen Exekutivagentur für die Forschung, der Europäischen Exekutivagentur für den Innovationsrat und für KMU, der Exekutivagentur des Europäischen Forschungsrats sowie der Europäischen Exekutivagentur für Bildung und Kultur und zur Aufhebung der Durchführungsbeschlüsse 2013/801/EU, 2013/771/EU, 2013/778/EU, 2013/779/EU, 2013/776/EU und 2013/770/EU (ABl. (EU) L 50/9 v. 15.2.2021, S. 9 ff.)
EFTA	Europäische Freihandelsassoziation
EG	Europäische Gemeinschaft
EG-Fusionskontrollverordnung	Verordnung (EG) 139/2004 des Rates v. 20.1.2004 über die Kontrolle von Unternehmenszusammenschlüssen (ABl. (EU) L 24 v. 29.1.2004, S. 1 ff.)
EGV	Konsolidierte Fassung des Vertrags über die Gründung der Europäischen Gemeinschaft (ABl. (EG) C 340 v. 10.11.1997, S. 173 ff.); zuletzt geändert durch: Vertrag über den Beitritt der Republik Bulgarien und Rumäniens zur Europäischen Union (ABl. (EU) L 157/11 v. 21.6.2005, S. 11 ff.)
EHO	European Hydrogen Observatory
Einl.	Einleitung
EL	Ergänzungslieferung
Emissionshandelsrichtlinie	Richtlinie 2003/87/EG des Europäischen Parlaments und des Rates v. 13.10.2003 über ein System für den Handel mit Treibhausgasemissionszertifikaten in der Gemeinschaft und zur Änderung der Richtlinie 96/61/EG des Rates (ABl. (EU) L 275/32 v. 25.10.2003, S. 32 ff.); zuletzt geändert durch: Verordnung (EU) 2024/795 des Europäischen Parlaments und des Rates v. 29.2.2024 zur Einrichtung der Plattform „Strategische Technologien für Europa" (STEP) und zur Änderung der Richtlinie 2003/87/EG und der Verordnungen (EU) 2021/1058, (EU) 2021/1056, (EU) 2021/1057, (EU) 1303/2013, (EU) 223/2014, (EU) 2021/1060, (EU) 2021/523, (EU) 2021/695, (EU) 2021/697 und (EU) 2021/241 (ABl. (EU) L v. 29.2.2024)
engl.	englisch
ENNOH	Europäisches Netzwerk der Wasserstoffnetzbetreiber (engl.: European Network of Network Operators for Hydrogen)

ErwG	Erwägungsgrund; Erwägungsgründe
et al.	und andere (lat.: et alia)
etc.	und so weiter (lat.: et cetera)
EU	Europäische Union
EuG	Gericht der Europäischen Union
EuGH	Gerichtshof der Europäischen Union
EUR	Euro
EUV	Konsolidierte Fassung des Vertrags über die Europäische Union (ABl. (EU) C 202/1 v. 7.6.2016, S. 13 ff.)
e. V.	eingetragener Verein
EWR	Europäischer Wirtschaftsraum
EWR-Abk	Abkommen über den Europäischen Wirtschaftsraum (ABl. (EG) L 1 v. 3.1.1994, S. 3 ff.); zuletzt geändert durch: Beschluss des Gemeinsamen EWR-Ausschusses 228/2024 v. 23.9.2024 zur Änderung von Protokoll 47 (Beseitigung technischer Handelshemmnisse für Wein) zum EWR- Abkommen [2024/3032] (ABl. (EU) L v. 19.12.2024)
f.	folgende
ff.	fortfolgende
Finanzierungsbeschluss 2023	Commission Decision of 22.11.2023 on the financing of actions under the Innovation Fund, serving as the financing decision for 2023 and as a decision launching calls for proposals, C(2023) 7827 final
Finanzierungsbeschluss 2024	Commission Decision of 25.11.2024 on the financing of actions under the Innovation Fund, serving as a financing decision for 2024–2030 and a decision launching calls for proposals in 2024, C(2024) 8011 final
Fraunh. ISE	Fraunhofer-Institut für Solare Energiesysteme
FuelEU-Verordnung für den Seeverkehr	Verordnung (EU) 2023/1805 des Europäischen Parlaments und des Rates v. 13.9.2023 über die Nutzung erneuerbarer und kohlenstoffarmer Kraftstoffe im Seeverkehr und zur Änderung der Richtlinie 2009/16/EG (ABl. (EU) L 234/48 v. 22.9.2023, S. 48 ff.)

Gas- und Wasserstoffrichtlinie	Richtlinie (EU) 2024/1788 des Europäischen Parlaments und des Rates v. 13.6.2024 über gemeinsame Vorschriften für die Binnenmärkte für erneuerbares Gas, Erdgas und Wasserstoff, zur Änderung der Richtlinie (EU) 2023/1791 und zur Aufhebung der Richtlinie 2009/73/EG (ABl. (EU) L v. 15.7.2024)
Gas- und Wasserstoffverordnung	Verordnung (EU) 2024/1789 des Europäischen Parlaments und des Rates v. 13.6.2024 über die Binnenmärkte für erneuerbares Gas, Erdgas sowie Wasserstoff, zur Änderung der Verordnungen (EU) 1227/2011, (EU) 2017/1938, (EU) 2019/942 und (EU) 2022/869 sowie des Beschlusses (EU) 2017/684 und zur Aufhebung der Verordnung (EG) 715/2009 (ABl. (EU) L v. 15.7.2024)
GD	Generaldirektion
gem.	gemäß
Genehmigungsbeschluss zur Anwendung von Beiträgen pro Einheit	Decision of 27.10.2023 authorising the use of unit contributions for auction actions under the Innovation Fund (Ares(2023)7322991)
GW	Gigawatt
Haushaltsordnung 2018	Verordnung (EU, Euratom) 2018/1046 des Europäischen Parlaments und des Rates v. 18.7.2018 über die Haushaltsordnung für den Gesamthaushaltsplan der Union, zur Änderung der Verordnungen (EU) 1296/2013, (EU) 1301/2013, (EU) 1303/2013, (EU) 1304/2013, (EU) 1309/2013, (EU) 1316/2013, (EU) 223/2014, (EU) 283/2014 und des Beschlusses 541/2014/EU sowie zur Aufhebung der Verordnung (EU, Euratom) 966/2012 (ABl. (EU) L 193/1 v. 30.7.2018, S. 1 ff.); zuletzt geändert durch: Verordnung (EU, Euratom) 2022/2434 des Europäischen Parlaments und des Rates v. 6.12.2022 zur Änderung der Verordnung (EU, Euratom) 2018/1046 im Hinblick auf die Festlegung einer diversifizierten Finanzierungsstrategie als allgemeine Methode für die Mittelaufnahme (ABl. (EU) L 319/1 v. 13.12.2022, S. 1 ff.)
Haushaltsordnung 2024	Verordnung (EU, Euratom) 2024/2509 des Europäischen Parlaments und des Rates v. 23.9.2024 über die Haushaltsordnung für den Gesamthaushaltsplan der Union (ABl. (EU) L v. 26.9.2024)

Hrsg.	Herausgebende
IEA	Internationale Energieagentur
Industrieemissionsrichtlinie	Richtlinie 2010/75/EU des Europäischen Parlaments und des Rates v. 24.11.2010 über Industrieemissionen (integrierte Vermeidung und Verminderung der Umweltverschmutzung) (ABl. (EU) L 334/17 v. 17.12.2010, S. 17 ff.); zuletzt geändert durch: Richtlinie (EU) 2024/1785 des Europäischen Parlaments und des Rates v. 24.4.2024 zur Änderung der Richtlinie 2010/75/EU des Europäischen Parlaments und des Rates über Industrieemissionen (integrierte Vermeidung und Verminderung der Umweltverschmutzung) und der Richtlinie 1999/31/EG des Rates über Abfalldeponien (ABl. (EU) L v. 15.7.2024)
inkl.	inklusive
IPCC	Zwischenstaatlicher Ausschuss für Klimaänderungen
IPCEI	Wichtige Vorhaben von gemeinsamem europäischem Interesse (engl.: Important Projects of Common European Interest)
iVm	in Verbindung mit
Kap.	Kapitel
kg	Kilogramm
kt	Kilotonne(n)
KUEBLL	Leitlinien für staatliche Klima-, Umweltschutz- und Energiebeihilfen 2022 (ABl. (EU) C 80/1 v. 18.2.2022)
kWh	Kilowattstunde(n)
lat.	lateinisch
MGA 2023	Innovation Fund Model Grant Agreement Unit Grants (INNOV-FUND UNIT MGA – Multi & Mono) [Version 1.1 v. 1.10.2023]. https://ec.europa.eu/info/funding-tenders/opportunities/docs/2021–2027/innovfund/agr-contr/unit-mga_innovfund_v1.1-01102023_en.pdf
Mio.	Millionen
Mrd.	Milliarde(n)
Mt	Megatonne(n)
MW	Megawatt
Nr.	Nummer(n)
o. D.	ohne Datum

PEMEL	Protonenaustauschmembran-Elektrolyse
Proposal	Antrag zwecks Teilnahme am Auktionsverfahren
Protokoll (Nr. 27) über den Binnenmarkt und den Wettbewerb	Protokoll (Nr. 27) über den Binnenmarkt und den Wettbewerb (ABl. (EU) C 202/308 v. 7.6.2016)
rechtl.	rechtlich
RED II	Richtlinie (EU) 2018/2001 des Europäischen Parlaments und des Rates v. 11.12.2018 zur Förderung der Nutzung von Energie aus erneuerbaren Quellen (ABl. (EU) L 328/82 v. 21.12.2018, S. 82 ff.)
RED III	Richtlinie (EU) 2018/2001 des Europäischen Parlaments und des Rates v. 11. Dezember 2018 zur Förderung der Nutzung von Energie aus erneuerbaren Quellen (ABl. (EU) L 328/82 v. 21.12.2018, S. 82 ff.); zuletzt geändert durch: Richtlinie (EU) 2024/1711 des Europäischen Parlaments und des Rates v. 13.6.2024 zur Änderung der Richtlinien (EU) 2018/2001 und (EU) 2019/944 in Bezug auf die Verbesserung des Elektrizitätsmarktdesigns in der Union (ABl. (EU) L v. 26.6.2024)
ReFuelEU-Verordnung für den Luftverkehr	Verordnung (EU) 2023/2405 des Europäischen Parlaments und des Rates v. 18.10.2023 zur Gewährleistung gleicher Wettbewerbsbedingungen für einen nachhaltigen Luftverkehr (ABl. (EU) L v. 31.10.2023); zuletzt berichtigt durch: Berichtigung der Verordnung (EU) 2023/2405 des Europäischen Parlaments und des Rates vom 18.10.2023 zur Gewährleistung gleicher Wettbewerbsbedingungen für einen nachhaltigen Luftverkehr (ABl. (EU) L v. 26.2.2024)
RFNBO	erneuerbare Kraftstoffe nicht biogenen Ursprungs (engl.: renewable fuels of non-biological origin)
Rn.	Randnummer(n)
S.	Seite(n)
SOEC	Hochtemperatur-Elektrolyse (engl.: Solid Oxide Electrolyzer Cell)
t	Tonne(n)
Terms and Conditions 2023	Innovation Fund Auction Terms and Conditions [Version 0.1]. https://climate.ec.europa.eu/system/files/2023-08/ innovationfund _pilotauction_termsandconditions_en.pdf

Terms and Conditions 2024	Innovation Fund IF24 Auction Terms and Conditions [Version 0.2]. https://climate.ec.europa.eu/document/download/b996825e-cd36-44c1-8 95d-a780062f626d_en?filename=2024%2009%2025%20Final%20TC_ 2nd%20Round%20RFNBO%20H2_IF_TCforPublication_Clean.pdf
u.	und
u. a.	unter anderem
Übereink von Paris	Übereinkommen von Paris (ABl. (EU) L 282/4 vom 19.10.2016, S. 4ff.)
Unterabs.	Unterabsatz; Unterabsätze
Unterabschn.	Unterabschnitt(e)
v.	vom; von
vgl.	vergleiche
z. B.	zum Beispiel

1. Einleitung

1.1 Thema

Im Zuge der Vision von Klimaneutralität bis 2050 identifizierte der europäische Green Deal die Dekarbonisierung des Energiesektors als entscheidend zur Erreichung der Klimaziele, da die Erzeugung und der Verbrauch von Energie insgesamt 75% der EU-Treibhausgasemissionen verursachen.[2] Die EU-Wasserstoffstrategie weist dabei dem Wasserstoff als Energieträger eine maßgebliche Rolle zu, insbesondere bezüglich der Dekarbonisierung von energieintensiven Industrieverfahren, bei denen eine Reduzierung der Treibhausgasemissionen anderweitig nur schwer zu erreichen ist.[3] Hierfür ist die Förderung des Markthochlaufs von erneuerbarem Wasserstoff entscheidend. Dieser wurde zwar aufgrund der Kosten gegenüber fossilem Wasserstoff als aktuell noch nicht wettbewerbsfähig eingeschätzt,[4] aber zugleich als die Option identifiziert, welche langfristig am besten mit den EU-Klimazielen ver-

2 Vgl. Europäische Kommission (2019), S. 6f.
3 Vgl. Europäische Kommission (2020d), S. 1.
4 Vgl. Europäische Kommission (2020d), S. 3.

einbar ist.[5] Daher wurden bezüglich der heimischen Produktion von erneuerbarem Wasserstoff ambitionierte Ziele gesetzt: Bis 2030 sollen in der EU Elektrolyseure mit einer Leistung von mindestens 40 Gigawatt (GW) installiert werden, um jährlich bis zu 10 Megatonnen (Mt) erneuerbaren Wasserstoff zu produzieren.[6] Als Reaktion auf den russischen Angriffskrieg wurde im REPowerEU-Plan die Bedeutung von erneuerbarem Wasserstoff unterstrichen und das Produktionsziel von 10 Mt bekräftigt sowie um weitere 10 Mt durch Importe erweitert.[7]

Allerdings zeigt ein von der Agentur für die Zusammenarbeit der Energieregulierungsbehörden (ACER) veröffentlichter Marktbeobachtungsbericht, dass die heimische Produktion von erneuerbarem Wasserstoff Stand 2023 nur 0,02 Mt betrug.[8] Dies ist mit einer weiten Lücke zwischen Ambitionen und tatsächlicher Implementierung in Verbindung zu setzen, welche eine Anfang 2025 veröffentlichte Studie identifizierte.[9] So wurden Stand 2022 nur 2% der angekündigten Kapazitäten dem Zeitplan entsprechend realisiert, sodass enorme Subventionen notwendig wären, um die festgelegten Ziele bis 2030 zu erreichen.[10]

Im Sinne dieses Förderbedarfs könnten neue wettbewerbsorientierte Förderinstrumente wie Ausschreibungsmechanismen (z. B. Auktionen) zur Zielerreichung beitragen. Dabei ergibt sich angesichts dieser potenziellen Markteingriffe ein Konflikt mit dem europäischen Wettbewerbsgedanken, welcher sich insbesondere im Grundsatz des unverfälschten Wettbewerbs[11] ausdrückt. Die rechtliche Grundlage für die zuvor erwähnten Förderinstrumente wurde in der im Zuge des „Fit für 55"-Pakets[12] überarbeiteten Emissionshandelsrichtlinie geschaffen: Diese sieht im Rahmen von Ausschreibungsmechanismen die Vergabe von Differenzverträgen (CDs), CO_2-Differenzverträgen (CCDs) und Verträgen über feste Prämien vor.[13] Bei den hier untersuchten Auktionen finden bisher Verträge über feste Prämien Anwendung.[14] Die dafür benötigten Mittel stammen aus dem Innovationsfonds[15] und damit aus

---

5 Vgl. Europäische Kommission (2020d), S. 6.
6 Vgl. Europäische Kommission (2020d), S. 7.
7 Vgl. Europäische Kommission (2022), S. 8f.
8 Vgl. ACER (2024), S. 4.
9 Vgl. Odenweller & Ueckerdt (2025), S. 110. Im Rahmen der Studie wurden 137 Projekte über den Verlauf von drei Jahren beobachtet.
10 Vgl. Odenweller & Ueckerdt (2025), S. 117.
11 Nach Protokoll (Nr. 27) über den Binnenmarkt und den Wettbewerb.
12 Vgl. Europäische Kommission (2021), S. 4.
13 Nach Art. 3 Doppelbuchst. ab-ad der Emissionshandelsrichtlinie.
14 Nach Kap. 2 Abschn. 2.1 Nr. 1.5 Terms and Conditions 2024.
15 Nach Art. 10a Abs. 8 Unterabs. 11 der Emissionshandelsrichtlinie.

den Einnahmen[16] des EU-Emissionshandels. Auktionen sollen somit im Zuge der neu etablierten Europäischen Wasserstoffbank eine zentrale Rolle bei der Schaffung eines heimischen Marktes für erneuerbaren Wasserstoff einnehmen.[17] Im Oktober 2024 unterzeichneten die final ausgewählten Begünstigten einer ersten Pilotauktion ihre jeweiligen Fördervereinbarungen[18] und am 03. Dezember 2024 wurde ein zweites Auktionsverfahren[19] gestartet.

Auch der zuletzt verkündete „Clean Industrial Deal" bestätigte die zentrale Rolle des Wasserstoffs bei der Dekarbonisierung des Energiesektors; ein für das erste Quartal 2025 vorgesehener delegierter Rechtsakt bezieht sich allerdings nur auf die Produktion von kohlenstoffarmem Wasserstoff, aber zugleich ist für das dritte Quartal der Aufruf für das nächste Auktionsverfahren der Europäischen Wasserstoffbank vorgesehen.[20]

1.2 Forschungsfrage

In den obigen Ausführungen wird deutlich, dass der Markthochlauf von erneuerbarem Wasserstoff politisch gewollt ist und dabei zugleich wettbewerbsrechtliche Prinzipien zu berücksichtigen sind. So ergibt sich ein Spannungsfeld zwischen den politischen Klima- und Dekarbonisierungszielen der EU auf der einen Seite und dem europäischen Wettbewerbsgedanken auf der anderen Seite. Dabei stellt sich folgende zentrale Frage:

Wie ist die Förderung der heimischen Produktion von erneuerbarem Wasserstoff innerhalb des Europäischen Wirtschaftsraums durch infolge von Auktionsverfahren der Europäischen Wasserstoffbank vergebene feste Prämien im Lichte des europäischen Wettbewerbsgedankens zu bewerten?

1.3 Aufbau der Arbeit

Im Sinne der Forschungsfrage ist zunächst in Kapitel 2 anhand von Fachliteratur und politischer Dokumente ein grundlegendes Verständnis des europäischen Wasserstoffmarktes zu etablieren. Dazu liefert Abschnitt 2.1 einen kurzen historischen Abriss über die menschliche Energienutzung und deren Folgen, woraus sich die Notwendigkeit der Wasserstofferzeugung herleiten

---

16 Nach Art. 10a Abs. 8 Unterabs. 1 der Emissionshandelsrichtlinie.
17 Vgl. Europäische Kommission (2023a), S. 7.
18 Vgl. GD Klimapolitik (2024b), Abs. 2.
19 Vgl. Europäische Kommission (2024b), Abs. 1.
20 Vgl. Europäische Kommission (2025), S. 8 f.

lässt. In dem Zuge werden die relevanten Eigenschaften von Wasserstoff sowie verschiedene Möglichkeiten der Gewinnung dargestellt. Daran anschließend beschreibt Abschnitt 2.2 anhand von Angebot und Nachfrage die Ökonomie des europäischen Wasserstoffmarktes und soll insbesondere die aktuell fehlende Wirtschaftlichkeit erneuerbaren Wasserstoffs verdeutlichen. Dagegen wird in Abschnitt 2.3 anhand des wasserstoffpolitischen Rahmens erläutert, warum auf europäischer Ebene ein politischer Wille zur Förderung des Markthochlaufs von erneuerbarem Wasserstoff besteht und wie sich dieser konkret in Strategien und Zielvorgaben manifestiert. Diese bilden wiederum die politische Grundlage für die Regulierung des Wasserstoffmarktes, welche im anschließenden Kapitel thematisiert wird.

In Kapitel 3 wird in dem Sinne zunächst kurz die Funktionsweise des europäischen Mehrebenensystems und dessen Bedeutung für den Europäischen Wirtschaftsraum (EWR) dargestellt. Daran anschließend erfolgt anhand relevanter Rechtsakte eine Analyse der Marktregulierung, wobei sich die Gliederung an der Wertschöpfungskette orientiert. Bezüglich erneuerbaren Wasserstoffs ist dabei insbesondere die Zertifizierung von großer Bedeutung. Eine zentrale Rolle nimmt außerdem die Regulierung der Wasserstoffinfrastruktur ein, welche Angebot und Nachfrage überhaupt erst verknüpft und eine Teilnahme am Marktgeschehen ermöglicht. Dieser Abschnitt soll zudem verdeutlichen, wie regulatorische Maßnahmen zur Gewährleistung gleicher Wettbewerbsbedingungen beitragen. Insgesamt werden in diesem Kapitel auch der Regulierungsumfang und der Harmonisierungsgrad dieser Regelungen betrachtet.

Kapitel 4 widmet sich dann konkret der angebotsseitigen Förderung des Markthochlaufs von erneuerbarem Wasserstoff. Dafür ist zunächst kurz die grundlegende Funktionsweise der Europäischen Wasserstoffbank darzustellen, bevor Zielsetzung, rechtlicher Rahmen und Mittelherkunft der hier untersuchten Auktionsverfahren thematisiert werden. Daran anschließend wird überwiegend anhand der Pilotauktion, aber auch unter Berücksichtigung des zweiten Auktionsverfahrens das Design dieses Fördermechanismus erläutert, welcher zur Beantwortung der formulierten Forschungsfrage bewertet werden soll. Zuvor ist allerdings noch die vertragliche Ausgestaltung der Förderung zu betrachten.

Anschließend wird in Kapitel 5 zunächst die primärrechtliche Bedeutung des Wettbewerbsbegriffs analysiert, um dann unter Berücksichtigung von relevanter Rechtsprechung und Fachliteratur einen Bewertungsmaßstab im Sinne dieses Wettbewerbsverständnisses zu bilden. Anhand dessen ist im Folgenden der Eingriffscharakter der Förderung zu bewerten, wobei insbesondere auch die wettbewerbliche Ausgestaltung des Auktionsdesigns zu berücksichtigen ist. Außerdem stellt sich die Frage, inwiefern eine mögliche

Einschränkung des Wettbewerbs aus anderen primärrechtlich verankerten Gründen zu rechtfertigen wäre.

Zuletzt werden im Fazit die zentralen Erkenntnisse dieser Arbeit aufgeführt. Außerdem soll ein Ausblick gegeben werden, welche Aspekte im Rahmen zukünftiger Forschung näher zu untersuchen sind.

2. Grundlagen des europäischen Wasserstoffmarktes

In den folgenden Abschnitten sind die naturwissenschaftlichen, ökonomischen und politischen Grundlagen dargestellt, welche zum Verständnis des europäischen Wasserstoffmarktes nötig sind. Dieses Verständnis bildet den Ausgangspunkt, um die anschließende Analyse der Marktregulierung durch europäische Gesetzgebung nachzuvollziehen. Aufbauend auf dieser Analyse wird dann die Förderung des Markthochlaufs von erneuerbarem Wasserstoff im Rahmen von Auktionsverfahren der Europäischen Wasserstoffbank betrachtet und angesichts der primärrechtlichen Bedeutung des Wettbewerbsbegriffs bewertet.

2.1 Naturwissenschaftliche Grundlagen

2.1.1 Menschliche Nutzung von Energiequellen und ihre Auswirkungen

Im Allgemeinen wird die in Energieträgern enthaltene Energie nicht direkt genutzt, sondern diese zunächst in nutzbare Energie umgewandelt, weswegen folgende Begriffe zu unterscheiden sind:[21] Primärenergie bezeichnet Energie in ihrem natürlichen Zustand, welche dann infolge von Umwandlungsprozessen nach den Gesetzen der Thermodynamik den Endabnehmenden als Endenergie zugeführt wird. Bei der Nutzung wird diese wiederum in die letztendliche Nutzenergie umgewandelt. Dabei gibt der Nutzungsgrad als Verhältnis des Nutzens zur eingesetzten Energie jeweils Aufschluss über die Effizienz einer Energieumwandlung.

Smil beschreibt aufschlussreich, wie eine Reihe von Entwicklungen im Laufe der Industrialisierung die menschliche Energienutzung prägte:[22] Beginnend mit der Dampfmaschine verbreiteten sich neue Technologien zur Nutzung fossiler Brennstoffe und zeitgleich neue Verfahren zur Aufbereitung der Rohbrennstoffe wie die Raffination von Rohöl. Entscheidend war

21 Vgl. Wesselak et al. (2017), S. 3 f. u. 40.
22 Vgl. Smil (2017), S. 226.

zudem die Etablierung von Elektrizität als völlig neue Form kommerzieller Energie. Dabei wurde sich der bei der Verbrennung verschiedenster fossiler Brennstoffe entstehende Dampf zu Nutze gemacht, um Generatoren zur Stromerzeugung anzutreiben. Allerdings gab es bereits zu diesem Zeitpunkt erste Formen der Primärelektrizität, welche nicht auf fossilen Brennstoffen, sondern der Nutzung von Wasserkraft beruhten.

Die Auswirkungen der Nutzung fossiler Energieträger und der damit verbundenen CO_2-Emissionen zeigen sich im anthropogenen Treibhauseffekt, welcher verstärkend zu dem natürlichen hinzutritt.[23] Der Zwischenstaatliche Ausschuss für Klimaänderungen (IPCC) wertet in diesem Zusammenhang den menschlichen Einfluss auf die Erderwärmung als eindeutig gegeben[24] und die globale Erdtemperatur sei seit 1970 mit hoher Sicherheit stärker gestiegen[25] als in jedem Vergleichszeitraum der vergangenen 2.000 Jahre. Die Einführung einer globalen Erdtemperatur dient in dem Sinne nicht nur der Bewertung der Erderwärmung, sondern zugleich als Bezugsgröße zur Beurteilung der Klimaveränderungen.[26] Um den anthropogenen Treibhauseffekt und seine Folgen zu begrenzen, sei laut dem IPCC aus naturwissenschaftlicher Perspektive neben der Verringerung anderer Treibhausgasemissionen eine Reduktion der CO_2-Emissionen auf mindestens Netto-Null erforderlich.[27]

Außerdem sind fossile Energieträger endlich, was ebenso für die Kernenergieträger gilt.[28] Kernenergie kann mittels entsprechender Kraftwerke ohne Treibhausgasemissionen in elektrische Energie umgewandelt werden.[29] Allerdings erscheint dies aufgrund anhaltender Diskussionen bezüglich der hohen Kosten und Verzögerungen bei der Errichtung von Kernkraftwerken, der Sicherheitsbedenken und der nicht final geklärten Frage nach der Entsorgung nuklearen Abfalls immer weniger als eine zukunftstaugliche Alternative.[30]

Dagegen besteht eine weitere Möglichkeit in der Nutzung erneuerbarer Primärenergieträger, welche sich innerhalb des menschlichen Zeithorizonts von selbst erneuern.[31] Die erneuerbaren Energien bieten verschiedene Mög-

---

23 Vgl. Lillich (2024), S. 15.
24 Vgl. IPCC (2021), S. 3.
25 Vgl. IPCC (2021), S. 7.
26 Vgl. Lillich (2024), S. 19.
27 Vgl. IPCC (2021), S. 30.
28 Vgl. Wesselak et al. (2017), S. 7.
29 Vgl. Smil (2017), S. 282.
30 Vgl. Smil (2017), S. 284.
31 Vgl. Wesselak et al. (2017), S. 111.

lichkeiten der emissionsfreien Strom- und Wärmeerzeugung:[32] Bspw. werden die kinetischen Energien der Wind- und Wasserströme sowie der Gezeiten und die Strahlungsenergie der Sonne genutzt, um diese vor allem in elektrische, aber auch thermische Energie umzuwandeln. Daneben bietet die Nutzung von Biomasse und geothermischer Energiequellen zusätzliches Potenzial.

Die erneuerbaren Energien hatten 2024 bereits einen Anteil von 46,1 % an der öffentlichen Nettostromerzeugung in der EU, wobei die Windkraft (18,9 %) und die Solarkraft (9,6 %) am relevantesten waren.[33] Allerdings bedeutet die zunehmende Nutzung erneuerbarer Primärenergiequellen eine steigende Fluktuation im Energieangebot, sodass Versorgungssicherheit nur durch die Integration von Speichersystemen gewährleistet werden kann, welche sowohl Schwankungen zwischen lastschwachen und -starken Zeiten als auch eine fluktuierende Nachfrage (z. B. Schichtbetrieb in der Industrie) ausgleichen können.[34] Für diesen Zweck gewinnt Wasserstoff als Speichermedium zunehmend an Bedeutung, da er im Vergleich zu Alternativen eine hohe Speicherkapazität sowie lange Speicherdauer aufweist und flexibel einsetzbar ist.[35] Außerdem kann Wasserstoff bspw. bei entsprechender Umstellung der Stahlwerke potenziell als Rohstoff zur Stahlherstellung im Direktreduktionsverfahren eingesetzt werden; andere Einsatzmöglichkeiten bestehen u. a. in der chemischen Industrie und dem Verkehrssektor.[36] Im folgenden Unterabschnitt werden diese grundlegenden Eigenschaften von Wasserstoff sowie unterschiedliche Möglichkeiten der Wasserstoffgewinnung näher beleuchtet.

2.1.2 Eigenschaften von Wasserstoff und seine Gewinnung

Elementarer Wasserstoff tritt als H_2-Molekül auf, ist ein farb- sowie geruchsloses Gas, schmilzt bei -259 °C und siedet bei -253 °C.[37] Er ist sehr energiereich und weist im Vergleich zu Dieselkraftstoff einen dreifach höheren Heizwert auf, weswegen er außerordentlich gut zur Bereitstellung thermischer

---

32 Vgl. Lodhi et al. (2024), S. 109 f.

33 Nach Daten des Fraunh. ISE (2025). Die Anteile der Wind- und Solarkraft sind ebenfalls bezüglich der gesamten Nettostromerzeugung angegeben.

34 Vgl. Hilgedieck et al. (2020), S. 1097 f.

35 Vgl. Yue et al. (2021), S. 9.

36 Vgl. Jahn et al. (2022), S. 86, 99 f. u. 124. Siehe Unterabschn. 2.2.3 für einen Überblick bezüglich aktueller und potenzieller Einsatzfelder von Wasserstoff.

37 Vgl. Binnewies et al. (2016), S. 379.

oder elektrischer Energie durch Energiewandlung geeignet ist.[38] Dabei ist allerdings zwischen der gravimetrischen und der volumetrischen Energiedichte zu unterscheiden:[39] Bezogen auf eine bestimmte Masse speichert Wasserstoff so viel Energie wie kein anderer Stoff. Dagegen ist die Energiedichte bezogen auf das Volumen unter Umgebungsbedingungen aufgrund des gasförmigen Aggregatzustandes deutlich niedriger als die konventioneller Energieträger. Aus diesem Grund sind spezielle Verfahren zur Erhöhung der Speicherdichte notwendig, was zugleich die Komplexität bei der Speicherung und dem Transport von Wasserstoff erhöht.

Ebenso komplex ist die Frage nach der Gewinnung von Wasserstoff. Dieser macht zwar ca. 75 % der Materie im Universum aus, jedoch bestand lange wissenschaftlicher Konsens, dass elementarer Wasserstoff auf der Erde nur in geringen Mengen zu finden ist und ansonsten gebunden vorliegt.[40] Der natürlich vorliegende Wasserstoff, auch als weißer Wasserstoff bezeichnet, tritt in untertägigen Formationen auf, wobei die Wirtschaftlichkeit sowie Umweltverträglichkeit einer potenziellen Förderung noch zu klären ist.[41] *Zwaan et al.* demonstrieren allerdings anhand eines neu entwickelten Modells, dass unter bestimmten Gebirgseinheiten potenziell weitaus größere natürliche Wasserstoffvorkommen vorliegen könnten als bisher angenommen.[42] Da dies nur einen ersten Schritt auf dem Weg zu einer möglichen industriellen Gewinnung natürlichen Wasserstoffs darstellt, werden im Folgenden verschiedene Verfahren zur Erzeugung elementaren Wasserstoffs betrachtet, welche den europäischen Wasserstoffmarkt in unterschiedlichem Ausmaß prägen.

In der Literatur und Praxis finden sich dabei diverse uneinheitliche Farbbezeichnungen zur Kategorisierung von Wasserstoff.[43] Dabei ist zu beachten, dass diese nicht die Eigenschaften des Wasserstoffs betreffen, sondern die Art und Weise, wie er gewonnen wurde. Es handelt sich hierbei allerdings um keine rechtssicheren Definitionen. Daher wurde durch das Inkrafttreten zweier delegierter Verordnungen[44] von den bisherigen Farbschemata abgewichen, indem die drei Kategorien „erneuerbar", „kohlenstoffarm" und „fossil" etabliert wurden.[45] Die Ausgestaltung dieser Kategorien wird bei der Darstel-

38 Vgl. Bockelmann et al. (2024), S. 29.
39 Vgl. Geißelbrecht et al. (2024), S. 52 f.
40 Vgl. Ludwig (2024), S. 12.
41 Vgl. Bockelmann et al. (2024), S. 31.
42 Vgl. Zwaan et al. (2025), S. 7 f.
43 Vgl. u. a. Bockelmann et al. (2024), S. 30; Nationaler Wasserstoffrat (2022), S. 2; Hydrogen Europe (o. D.).
44 Dies sind die deleg. Verordnung zur RFNBO-Produktion und die deleg. Verordnung über Treibhausgaseinsparungen.
45 Vgl. Erbach & Svensson (2023), S. 3.

lung des rechtlichen Rahmens näher erläutert.[46] An dieser Stelle soll lediglich ein grundlegender technischer Überblick relevanter Verfahren zur Wasserstoffproduktion gegeben werden, wobei die Kategorisierung bisher mittels Farbbezeichnungen erfolgt. *Ocenic & Tanțău* stellen allerdings in ihrer komparativen Analyse überzeugend dar, dass diese Farbkategorisierungen aufgrund der Vielzahl an Akteur:innen aus u.a. Industrie und Politik sowie des Fehlens einer wissenschaftlichen Basis eine einheitliche Logik vermissen lassen und dadurch bei manchen Verfahren die entstehenden Treibhausgasemissionen verschleiert würden.[47]

Aus diesem Grund stehen die genutzten Energiequellen und Rohstoffe sowie das Entstehen von Treibhausgasemissionen im Fokus des folgenden Überblicks. Dieser ist nicht abschließend, sondern soll ein grundlegendes Verständnis vermitteln, und orientiert sich an der übersichtlichen Darstellung von *Bockelmann et al.*:[48] Stand 2024 wird die Wasserstoffproduktion von der Nutzung fossiler Rohstoffe dominiert.[49] Bevorzugtes Verfahren ist dabei die Dampfreformierung von Erdgas bzw. des enthaltenen Methans, wobei letztendlich CO_2 emittiert wird. Noch verstärkt werden diese Emissionen durch die zusätzliche Verbrennung von Erdgas zwecks Energiezufuhr. Alternativ wird in vergleichbaren Verfahren Kohle als Rohstoff verwendet, was eine noch höhere Menge an Treibhausgasemissionen bedeutet. Daher werden derzeit Verfahren entwickelt und bereits genutzt, welche diese Emissionen bei der Nutzung fossiler Rohstoffe vermeiden sollen. Dabei handelt es sich zum einen um Verfahren zur Abscheidung sowie Speicherung des bei der Dampfreformierung entstehenden CO_2 (engl.: Carbon Capture and Storage – CCS) und zum anderen um die Methanpyrolyse, bei der neben dem Wasserstoff fester Kohlenstoff erzeugt wird. Außerdem entsteht Wasserstoff als Koppelprodukt bei manchen industriellen Prozessen wie der Chlor-Akali-Elektrolyse, wobei diese Mengen angesichts des zukünftigen Bedarfs als lediglich gering erscheinen. Die meiste Bedeutung für eine nachhaltige Zukunft wird daher der Wasserelektrolyse beigemessen. Da für diesen energieaufwendigen Prozess aktuell die Zufuhr elektrischer Energie notwendig ist, bestimmt die Herkunft dieser den Beitrag zur Dekarbonisierung. Zur Erzeugung von erneuerbarem Wasserstoff muss die elektrische Energie daher aus der Nutzung erneuerbarer Primärenergiequellen stammen. Alternativ wird die Nutzung von mittels Kernenergie bereitgestelltem Strom stark diskutiert.

46 Siehe Abschn. 3.2.
47 Vgl. Ocenic & Tanţău (2023), S. 119.
48 Vgl. Bockelmann et al. (2024), S. 30.
49 Siehe dazu auch Unterabschn. 2.2.2.

Bei der Wasserelektrolyse wird üblicherweise Wasser in einem Elektrolyseur, im Wesentlichen bestehend aus einem Elektrolyt, einer Kathode und einer Anode, unter Zufuhr elektrischer Energie gespalten, wobei an der Kathode Wasserstoff und an der Anode Sauerstoff entsteht.[50] Zur Hochskalierung in der industriellen Anwendung werden Elektrolysezellen in großer Anzahl zu einem sogenannten Stack zusammengeschaltet.[51] Bezüglich der Umsetzung dieses Grundprinzips haben sich verschiedene Verfahren etabliert, welche *Wetterau* aus praxisnaher Perspektive grundlegend darstellt und anhand ihrer Vorteilhaftigkeit bewertet:[52] Als das am stärksten verbreitete, aber zugleich weniger effiziente Verfahren gilt die alkalische Elektrolyse (AEL). Insbesondere in großen Anlagen mit konstanter Stromversorgung werden hierbei basische Lösungen als Elektrolyte genutzt und Wasserstoff mit hohem Reinheitsgrad erzeugt. Eine höhere Effizienz weist die Protonenaustauschmembran-Elektrolyse (PEMEL) auf, welche zudem für den Betrieb bei schwankender Stromzufuhr besser geeignet ist. Nachteilig ist die Verwendung des seltenen Rohstoffs Iridium bei der Herstellung der Elektroden. Das neue Verfahren der Anionenaustauschmembran-Elektrolyse (AEMEL) kombiniert den basischen Elektrolyt einer AEL mit der Membran einer PEMEL. Dadurch sollen sich die Vorteile einer PEMEL unter Verwendung der kostengünstigeren Komponenten einer AEL ergeben. Zuletzt können bei der Hochtemperatur-Elektrolyse (engl.: Solid Oxide Electrolyzer Cell – SOEC) die Potenziale von Solarenergie oder Geothermie ausgeschöpft werden, um unter Nutzung eines keramischen Festoxid-Elektrolyten bei Temperaturen bis zu 900 °C Wasserstoff zu erzeugen.

2.2 Ökonomie des europäischen Wasserstoffmarktes

Wie bereits einleitend erwähnt, wird im Rahmen dieser Arbeit die Regulierung des europäischen Wasserstoffmarktes analysiert, um anschließend die Förderung des Markthochlaufs von erneuerbarem Wasserstoff zu betrachten und aus wettbewerbsrechtlicher Perspektive zu bewerten. Dafür ist zunächst ein grundlegendes ökonomisches Verständnis des europäischen Wasserstoffmarktes nötig, bevor im nachfolgenden Abschnitt das politische Einwirken auf die Marktentwicklung verdeutlicht wird.

---

50 Vgl. Chatenet et al. (2022), S. 4587.
51 Vgl. Farchmin (2017), S. 233.
52 Vgl. Wetterau (2024), S. 59 f.

2.2.1 Abgrenzung des Marktes und Datenlage

Grundsätzlich ist ein Markt als die Gesamtheit aller Austauschprozesse zu verstehen, die auf dem Zusammentreffen von Anbietenden und Nachfragenden basieren.[53] Eng verbunden mit der Idee eines funktionierenden Marktes ist der Wettbewerbsbegriff, dessen Bedeutung im Primärrecht innerhalb dieser Arbeit näher untersucht wird.[54] An dieser Stelle genügt das Verständnis von Wettbewerb als das Zusammenwirken der Kräfte des Marktes (Angebot und Nachfrage) zur Preisbildung,[55] um ein grundlegendes Verständnis der Marktsituation zu gewinnen. In diesem Sinne werden hier Angebot und Nachfrage gegenübergestellt, um ein möglichst aktuelles ökonomisches Bild des europäischen Wasserstoffmarktes zu vermitteln. Außerdem werden die Herstellungskosten für Wasserstoff als maßgeblicher Kostenfaktor dargestellt. Insgesamt stehen insbesondere die Wasserelektrolyse und die Frage nach der Wettbewerbsfähigkeit erneuerbaren Wasserstoffs im Fokus dieses Abschnitts.

Bei der Betrachtung eines Marktes stellt sich zunächst die Frage, wie dieser Markt zu definieren und abzugrenzen ist. Dies spielt zudem eine bedeutende Rolle im europäischen Wettbewerbsrecht. So ist zur Anwendung des zentralen Art. 102 AEUV hinsichtlich einer möglicherweise missbräuchlichen Ausnutzung einer marktbeherrschenden Stellung im ersten Schritt der relevante Markt zu bestimmen. Dabei sind insbesondere der sachlich relevante Markt und der räumlich relevante Markt festzulegen.[56] An dieser Stelle ist zu beachten, dass sich dieses wettbewerbsrechtliche Verständnis eines Marktes von der Verwendung des Begriffes im geschäftlichen Kontext unterscheidet,[57] was im Folgenden verdeutlicht wird.

Entscheidendes Kriterium bei der Bestimmung des sachlich relevanten Marktes ist die Austauschbarkeit der Produkte oder Dienstleistungen.[58] Wie bereits dargestellt, ist Wasserstoff flexibel einsetzbar, sodass sowohl der Handel mit dem Wasserstoff an sich als auch mit Wasserstoffträgern wie z. B. Ammoniak oder Methanol infrage kommt.[59] So könnten sich je nach Anwendungsbereich unterschiedliche Wertschöpfungsketten bilden, in denen die

---

53 Vgl. Fritsch (2018), S. 6.

54 Siehe Abschn. 5.1.

55 Vgl. Fritsch (2018), S. 7.

56 Vgl. Urteil des EuGH v. 14.2.1978, United Brands/Kommission, C-27/76, ECLI:EU:C:1978:22, Rn. 10 f.

57 Vgl. Europäische Kommission (2024c), Rn. 19.

58 Vgl. Urteil des EuGH v. 30.1.2020, Generics (UK) und andere, C-307/18, ECLI:EU:C:2020:52, Rn. 129; Urteil des EuGH v. 13.2.1979, Hoffmann-La Roche/Kommission, C-85/76, ECLI:EU:C:1979:36, Rn. 51.

59 Siehe Unterabschn. 2.1.2.

Produkte nicht austauschbar wären. Folglich wären auch die Märkte voneinander abzugrenzen. Allerdings sind zu diesem Zeitpunkt der Marktentwicklung viele Fragen diesbezüglich noch ungeklärt und die verfügbaren Daten zur Marktsituation stellen allgemein das Angebot und die Nachfrage bezüglich Wasserstoff dar, was die folgenden Ausführungen dieses Abschnitts verdeutlichen.[60] Wie einzelfallabhängig eine wettbewerbsrechtliche Abgrenzung des sachlich relevanten Marktes, auch hinsichtlich der Unterscheidung zwischen erneuerbarem, kohlenstoffarmem und fossilem Wasserstoff, vorzunehmen wäre, wird die Rechtsprechung zeigen und wäre im Rahmen zukünftiger Forschung zu untersuchen.

Gleiches gilt für die Festlegung des räumlich relevanten Marktes. Als räumlich relevant gilt ein Markt, soweit in seinem Gebiet die Wettbewerbsbedingungen hinreichend homogen sind und sich von den Wettbewerbsbedingungen benachbarter Gebiete spürbar unterscheiden.[61] Im Sinne der Fragestellung dieser Arbeit wird der betrachtete Markt räumlich vom EWR ausgehend abgegrenzt,[62] da nur Projekte innerhalb des EWR zu den Auktionsverfahren der Europäischen Wasserstoffbank zugelassen sind.[63] Mitglieder des EWR sind die 27 EU-Mitgliedsstaaten sowie Island, Liechtenstein und Norwegen als Mitgliedsstaaten der Europäischen Freihandelsassoziation (EFTA).[64] Der Handel mit Staaten außerhalb des EWR, insbesondere durch Importe, wird ebenfalls kurz betrachtet, ist aufgrund der geringen Intensität allerdings aktuell noch zu vernachlässigen.[65]

Den folgenden Ausführungen zur Marktlage liegen die vom European Hydrogen Observatory (EHO) bereitgestellten Daten zugrunde. Das EHO ist eine öffentlich zugängliche Plattform und liefert als Initiative der Clean Hydrogen Partnership (rechtl.: Clean Hydrogen Joint Undertaking – CHJU) umfangreiche Daten über den europäischen Wasserstoffsektor.[66] Die CHJU bildet als öffentlich-private Partnerschaft ein Bindeglied zwischen der Europäischen Kommission und den Interessensvertretungen Hydrogen Europe

60 Siehe insbesondere Unterabschn. 2.2.2 u. 2.2.3.

61 Vgl. Urteil des EuG v. 30.9.2003, Cableuropa und andere/Kommission, T-346/02 u. T-347/02, ECLI:EU:T:2003:256, Rn. 115; Urteil des EuG v. 7.5.2009, NVV und andere/Kommission, T-151/05, ECLI:EU:T:2009:144, Rn. 52; Urteil des EuGH v. 14.2.1978, United Brands/Kommission, C-27/76, ECLI:EU:C:1978:22, Rn. 11.

62 Die im Folgenden verwendeten Quellen inkludieren weitere europäische Staaten wie Großbritannien und die Schweiz. Soweit eine Bereinigung der Daten nicht möglich war, ist dies entsprechend vermerkt.

63 Nach Kap. 6 Abs. 5 Call 2023; Kap. 6 Abs. 4 Call 2024.

64 Vgl. EUR-Lex (o. D.).

65 Siehe Unterabschn. 2.2.2.

66 Vgl. EHO (o. D.-a).

sowie Hydrogen Europe Research, wodurch die Integration der Interessen und Kapazitäten von Politik, Industrie und Wissenschaft zur Förderung sauberer Wasserstofftechnologien gelingen soll.[67] Diese Interessensvielfalt spiegelt sich auch in den am EHO beteiligten Organisationen wider.[68] Ein hohes Maß an Ausgewogenheit und Qualität der veröffentlichten Daten ist somit anzunehmen. Außerdem berufen sich weitere relevante Akteur:innen in ihren Veröffentlichungen auf die Daten des EHO, so auch die ACER in ihrem Marktbeobachtungsbericht 2024. Diesem liegen zudem die Wasserstoff-Projektdatenbank der Internationalen Energieagentur (IEA) sowie die S&P Global Commodity Insights zugrunde, wobei sich nach Auswertung durch die ACER eine generelle Konsistenz der Datenbanken ergeben habe und Abweichungen lediglich aufgrund der Verwendung unterschiedlicher Maße und Umrechnungsfaktoren bestünden.[69] Die IEA ist zudem eine Mitwirkende des EHO, was die Konsistenz der Daten stützt.[70] Da hier der europäische Wasserstoffmarkt betrachtet wird, liefert das EHO somit die umfassendsten Daten, bei denen von einer hohen Glaubwürdigkeit auszugehen ist. Der zuletzt veröffentlichte und damit möglichst aktuelle Stand ist überwiegend der vom Ende des Jahres 2023, welcher nun im Folgenden dargestellt wird.

2.2.2 *Wasserstoffangebot*

Zunächst ist das Wasserstoffangebot zu betrachten. Dafür werden insbesondere die heimischen Produktionskapazitäten, aber auch der noch geringe Einfluss von Wasserstoffimporten dargestellt. Soweit nicht anderweitig gekennzeichnet, basieren die folgenden Angaben auf der interaktiven Karte des EHO.[71]

Die vorhandene Produktionskapazität betrug 2023 knapp 10,58 Mt, wobei ca. 7,44 Mt tatsächlich hergestellt wurden. Also wurden die Kapazitäten zu ungefähr 70 % ausgeschöpft. Von der Gesamtmenge wurden über 44 % in den drei führenden Staaten Deutschland, den Niederlanden und Polen produziert. Lediglich knapp 0,4% der Gesamtmenge wurden mittels Wasserelektrolyse hergestellt und 0,6% durch Dampfreformierung unter Anwendung von CCS. Die klassischen Dampfreformierungsverfahren wiesen einen

67 Vgl. CHJU (o. D.).
68 Vgl. EHO (o. D.-f).
69 Vgl. ACER (2024), S. 31.
70 Vgl. EHO (o. D.-f).
71 Siehe EHO (o. D.-e).

dominierenden Anteil von über 91 % auf, während der Rest auf industrielle Prozesse entfiel, bei denen Wasserstoff als Koppelprodukt entsteht.

Wie bereits dargestellt, wird der Wasserelektrolyse das größte Zukunftspotenzial zugeschrieben.[72] Daher ist die Entwicklung der Kapazitäten und potenziellen Produktionsmengen anhand eines aktualisierten Datensatzes aus dem Dezember 2024 genauer zu betrachten. Dieser stellt alle Projekte dar, die bereits in Betrieb genommen wurden oder sich derzeit in Bau befinden.[73] In der Regel werden die Kapazitäten der Elektrolyseure dabei in Megawatt (MW) angegeben, weswegen eine Umrechnung notwendig ist. Dabei wurden die vom EHO getroffenen Annahmen angewendet.[74] Bei planmäßiger Fertigstellung aller Projekte ergäbe sich somit im Jahr 2027 eine jährliche Produktionsmenge von knapp 0,35 Mt bei einer Kapazität von ca. 0,51 Mt.

Bei der Wasserstofferzeugung wird zudem unterschieden zwischen dem Wasserstoff für den Eigenbedarf (engl.: captive hydrogen), welcher in einer Anlage vor Ort verbraucht wird, und dem Wasserstoff für den Handel (engl.: merchant hydrogen), welcher für den externen Vertrieb und Verkauf bestimmt ist.[75] Ersterer machte einen dominierenden Anteil von 88 % der Produktionskapazitäten (inkl. Großbritannien und der Schweiz) aus.[76] Im Bereich der Wasserelektrolyse stellten sogar nur zwei von insgesamt 141 Produktionseinheiten Wasserstoff für den Handel her.[77] Außerdem spielten Wasserstoffimporte nur eine Rolle im Rahmen des innereuropäischen Handels:[78] Lediglich knapp 156 Tonnen (t) Wasserstoff wurden von außerhalb importiert, während die Niederlande allein über 19 Kilotonnen (kt) aus Belgien importierte. Dies machte ca. 66 % des in Europa (inkl. Großbritannien und der Schweiz) gehandelten Wasserstoffs (merchant hydrogen) aus.

2.2.3 Wasserstoffnachfrage

Wie bereits erwähnt, ist die Flexibilität von Wasserstoff eine seiner herausragenden Eigenschaften, weswegen eine Vielzahl möglicher Anwendungsfelder besteht, insbesondere in der Industrie und im Energie- sowie Mobilitätssek-

72 Siehe Unterabschn. 2.1.2.
73 Siehe EHO (2024b).
74 Nach EHO (o. D.-e) werden zur Berechnung der Produktionsmenge folgende Annahmen getroffen: Die Effizienz der Elektrolyseure beträgt 49 Kilowattstunden pro Kilogramm (kWh/kg) und die Kapazitäten werden zu 68 % ausgeschöpft.
75 Vgl. EHO (2024a), S. 24.
76 Vgl. EHO (2024a), S. 25.
77 Vgl. EHO (2024a), S. 26–28.
78 Siehe EHO (2023b).

tor.[79] Daher wird im Folgenden die anteilsmäßige Verteilung des Verbrauchs hinsichtlich verschiedener Anwendungsbereiche betrachtet, um einen Überblick zur Wasserstoffnachfrage zu gewinnen. Soweit nicht anderweitig gekennzeichnet, basieren die folgenden Angaben auf der interaktiven Karte des EHO.[80]

Der Wasserstoffverbrauch lag insgesamt knapp unter der produzierten Menge von 7,44 Mt. Abweichungen ergeben sich durch den Import sowie Export und in die Atmosphäre entwichenen Wasserstoff. Anhand des Endverbrauchs lässt sich nachvollziehen, wie sich die Nachfrage aus den einzelnen Anwendungsbereichen zusammensetzt. Mehr als die Hälfte (ca. 57,1 %) des Wasserstoffs wird in Raffinerien für verschiedene Zwecke genutzt. Darunter fallen bspw. das Hydrotreating und Hydrocracken als bedeutende Prozesse bei der Raffinierung von Erdöl.[81] Als nächstes folgt die Ammoniakindustrie, welche über ein Viertel (ca. 26,4%) verbrauchte. Ammoniak ist u.a. für die Düngemittelproduktion von großer Bedeutung und birgt zugleich durch die Möglichkeit, chemisch gebundenen Wasserstoff zu speichern, Potenzial als zukünftiger Energieträger.[82] Ungefähr 10% des Wasserstoffs wurden bei der Methanolerzeugung und in übrigen Bereichen der chemischen Industrie eingesetzt. Ca. 3,1 % des Verbrauchs konnte keinem spezifischen Endnutzen zugeordnet werden. So entfielen lediglich knapp 3,4% auf den Bereich der aufstrebenden Wasserstoffanwendungen, wobei ungefähr 3,24% der Gesamtnachfrage der industriellen Wärmeerzeugung zuzuordnen waren. Das bedeutet, dass nur ein verschwindend geringer Anteil von unter 0,2% in den folgenden Bereichen eingesetzt wurde, deren Zukunftspotenzial sich noch beweisen muss: Beimischung in Erdgaspipelines, Herstellung von E-Fuels, Wärmeerzeugung für Haushalte, Stromerzeugung, Mobilitätsanwendungen und Stahlerzeugung. Zugleich waren diese aufstrebenden Wasserstoffanwendungen mit einem Anteil von ungefähr 54% Haupttreiber der Nachfrage nach erneuerbarem Wasserstoff, wobei die Gesamtnachfrage nach diesem auf 0,03 Mt geschätzt wurde.[83]

Außerdem lieferte das EHO eine Prognose für die Entwicklung der zukünftigen Wasserstoffnachfrage. Dafür wurde für die Jahre 2030, 2040 und 2050 jeweils ein Mittelwert anhand der von unterschiedlichen Organisationen entwickelten Szenarien gebildet.[84] Danach soll die jährliche Gesamt-

79 Siehe Unterabschn. 2.1.1.
80 Siehe EHO (o. D.-d).
81 Vgl. Jahn et al. (2022), S. 102 f.
82 Vgl. Jahn et al. (2022), S. 100.
83 Vgl. EHO (2024a), S. 49.
84 Für die einzelnen Szenarien siehe EHO (2023a).

nachfrage in Europa (inkl. Großbritannien und der Schweiz) bis 2030 um knapp 56% auf 12,35 Mt und bis 2050 sogar auf 45,55 Mt ansteigen.[85] Während für die Industrie bis 2050 mehr als eine Verdoppelung der Nachfrage (Anstieg auf jährlich 16,88 Mt) vorhergesagt wird, soll dazu insbesondere auch die Nachfrage im Transportsektor (16,83 Mt) beitragen, welcher im Jahr 2023 nahezu keine Rolle spielte.[86]

2.2.4 Kosten der Wasserstoffproduktion und Break-Even-Preis für erneuerbaren Wasserstoff

Abschließend werden die im Rahmen der Produktionsverfahren anfallenden Herstellungskosten gegenübergestellt. Diese beeinflussen maßgeblich, zu welchen Preisen Wasserstoff angeboten werden kann. Damit geben sie einen Einblick, wie sich der Markt rein aus ökonomischen Gesichtspunkten entwickeln würde. Es stellt sich insbesondere die Frage, inwieweit erneuerbarer Wasserstoff zu wettbewerbsfähigen Preisen hergestellt werden kann. Daher beschränkt sich die folgende Darstellung auf einen Vergleich zwischen der marktbeherrschenden Dampfreformierung und der Wasserelektrolyse zur Herstellung erneuerbaren Wasserstoffs. Bezüglich letzterer wird zudem am Beispiel der Stahlproduktion ein möglicher Break-Even-Preis betrachtet. Dieser zeigt für den Anwendungsbereich der Stahlherstellung, zu welchem Preis erneuerbarer Wasserstoff im Vergleich zu fossilem Wasserstoff wettbewerbsfähig wäre.

Das EHO stellt auf einer interaktiven Karte für das Jahr 2023 die Zusammensetzung der Herstellungskosten für die einzelnen Verfahren dar, wobei aufgrund teils starker Schwankungen zwischen den Staaten (inkl. Großbritannien und der Schweiz) jeweils Mittelwerte gebildet wurden.[87] Bei der Dampfreformierung ergaben sich somit gemittelte Gesamtkosten von 3,76 EUR/kg. Dagegen betrugen diese für die Herstellung erneuerbaren Wasserstoffs 6,61 EUR/kg. Mehr als die Hälfte dieser Kosten (3,79 EUR/kg) sind allerdings dem zu leistenden Kapitaleinsatz zuzuordnen. Da die Dampfreformierung bereits etabliert ist, liegt dieser hier deutlich niedriger bei 0,26 EUR/kg. Auf lange Sicht besteht also die Perspektive, die Herstellungskosten für erneuerbaren Wasserstoff deutlich zu senken. Dies wird auch notwendig sein, um einen wettbewerbsfähigen Preis bieten zu können.[88]

---

85 Vgl. EHO (2024a), S. 59 f.
86 Vgl. EHO (2024a), S. 61.
87 Siehe EHO (o. D.-c).
88 Siehe Kap. 4 hinsichtlich des derzeitigen Ansatzes zur Überbrückung der Kostendifferenz.

Gestützt wird dies durch eine Fallstudie für das Jahr 2023 zur Bestimmung eines Break- Even-Preises für erneuerbaren Wasserstoff zur Verwendung in der Stahlproduktion:[89] Dieser bezeichnet hier den Preis für erneuerbaren Wasserstoff, welchen die Endabnehmenden (hier: die Stahlwerke) zahlen, bei dem die Kosten der Nutzung von erneuerbarem Wasserstoff der anhand fossilen Wasserstoffs festgelegten Benchmark entsprechen. Der Preis für die Endabnehmenden umfasst dabei nicht nur die Herstellungskosten, sondern sämtliche weitere Kosten, welche für Transport, Lagerung etc. anfallen. Für die Stahlherstellung ergab sich im Rahmen der Fallstudie ein Preis in Höhe von 4,70 EUR/kg. Dieser liegt also deutlich unter den gemittelten Herstellungskosten für erneuerbaren Wasserstoff, zu denen noch die weiteren Kosten hinzuzuaddieren sind. Aufgrund dieser Stand 2023 nicht gegebenen Wettbewerbsfähigkeit erneuerbaren Wasserstoffs und dem generellen Entwicklungsstand des Marktes sind im nächsten Abschnitt die politischen Ambitionen hinsichtlich des Markthochlaufs zu betrachten.

2.3 Wasserstoffpolitischer Rahmen

Im Folgenden wird ein Überblick über die EU-Strategien gegeben, welche die Entwicklung des europäischen Wasserstoffmarktes betreffen und diesen aufgrund ihres Gewichts im EWR maßgeblich prägen. Dabei werden darin enthaltene Zielvorgaben, insbesondere hinsichtlich der Produktion von erneuerbarem Wasserstoff,[90] hervorgehoben. Abschließend wird ein kurzer Einblick gegeben, inwieweit sich aus dieser strategischen Ausrichtung entsprechende politische Maßnahmen auf nationaler Ebene ergeben.

2.3.1 Anfänge und internationaler Rahmen

Den Grundstein der strategischen Ausrichtung legte die Verkündung des europäischen Green Deals im Jahr 2019, der EU-Wachstumsstrategie für eine nachhaltige Zukunft.[91] Darin wurde das Ziel der Klimaneutralität bis 2050 bekräftigt und zugleich die Arbeit am „Fit für 55“-Paket angedeutet, welches bis 2030 zur Senkung der EU-Treibhausgasemissionen auf mindestens 50 % im Vergleich zu 1990 beitragen soll (dabei wird eine Reduktion auf 55 % an-

---

89 Vgl. EHO (o. D.-b).

90 Dieser wird in den Strategiepapieren zum Teil noch als sauberer Wasserstoff bezeichnet.

91 Vgl. Europäische Kommission (2019), S. 2.

gestrebt).[92] Wie bereits einleitend erwähnt, entstehen 75% dieser Treibhausgasemissionen durch die Erzeugung und den Verbrauch von Energie, weswegen der Dekarbonisierung in diesem Sektor zur Erreichung der Klimaziele eine entscheidende Rolle zugewiesen wurde.[93] (Erneuerbarer) Wasserstoff fand hier nur am Rande als Zukunftstechnologie explizite Erwähnung.[94] Der Green Deal ist zudem als europäische Antwort auf internationale Übereinkommen zu verstehen. So sieht die Europäische Kommission ihn als zentralen Bestandteil ihrer Strategie zur Umsetzung der Agenda 2030 der Vereinten Nationen und der damit verbundenen Ziele für nachhaltige Entwicklung.[95] Außerdem bekennt sie sich deutlich zum Übereinkommen von Paris als internationalen Rahmen zur Bekämpfung des Klimawandels,[96] in welchem das sogenannte 1,5-Grad-Ziel zur Begrenzung der globalen Erderwärmung festgelegt wurde.[97]

Im folgenden Jahr 2020 hob die neue Industriestrategie der EU den Begriff der wettbewerbsfähigen Nachhaltigkeit hervor und unterstrich die Bedeutung des Wettbewerbs im Europäischen Binnenmarkt.[98] Daher müssten die Beihilfevorschriften in zentralen Bereichen wie Energie und Umweltschutz überarbeitet werden,[99] woraus sich später die Leitlinien für staatliche Klima-, Umweltschutz- und Energiebeihilfen 2022 (KUEBLL) ergaben. Ein entscheidendes Ziel bei der Transformation der Industrie sei es, Leitmärkte für saubere Technologien zu schaffen.[100] Da die energieintensiven Industrien für Europa unverzichtbar seien, läge ein Hauptaugenmerk auf deren Dekarbonisierung (z.B. durch Zukunftstechnologien zur CO_2-freien Stahlerzeugung).[101] Generell sei die Dekarbonisierung nur mit einem stärker integrierten Energiesystem möglich, weswegen die Europäische Kommission mit der EU-Strategie zur Integration des Energiesystems einen Plan zur Beschleunigung dieser vorlegte.[102] Darin wird auch die zukünftige Rolle von Wasserstoff im integrierten Energiesystem dargelegt und zugleich auf die parallel verkündete EU-Wasserstoffstrategie verwiesen.[103]

---

92 Vgl. Europäische Kommission (2019), S. 5.
93 Siehe Abschn. 1.1.
94 Vgl. Europäische Kommission (2019), S. 8, 10 u. 22.
95 Vgl. Europäische Kommission (2019), S. 3.
96 Vgl. Europäische Kommission (2019), S. 24.
97 Nach Art. 2 Abs. 1 Buchst. a Übereink von Paris.
98 Vgl. Europäische Kommission (2020b), S. 3.
99 Vgl. Europäische Kommission (2020b), S. 7.
100 Vgl. Europäische Kommission (2020b), S. 4.
101 Vgl. Europäische Kommission (2020b), S. 9.
102 Vgl. Europäische Kommission (2020a), S. 1 f.
103 Vgl. Europäische Kommission (2020a), S. 2.

2.3.2 EU-Wasserstoffstrategie

Die EU-Wasserstoffstrategie hebt dessen maßgebliche Rolle bei der Dekarbonisierung hervor und verweist auf die Vielzahl möglicher Anwendungen, insbesondere auch auf das Potenzial als Speicher- und Transportmedium für erneuerbare Energien.[104] Dabei wurde erneuerbarer Wasserstoff aufgrund der Herstellungskosten als aktuell nicht wettbewerbsfähig, aber zugleich als die Option identifiziert, welche langfristig am besten mit der Vision von Klimaneutralität und den damit verbundenen Zielen vereinbar sei.[105] Investitionszyklen im Bereich der sauberen Energie würden ungefähr 25 Jahre betragen, weshalb die Wasserstoffstrategie zu diesem Zeitpunkt einen strategischen Fahrplan als konkreten politischen Rahmen zur Erzeugung von erneuerbarem Wasserstoff liefere.[106] Als Übergangslösung sei jedoch auch kohlenstoffarmer Wasserstoff nötig, um möglichst schnell die durch fossile Wasserstofferzeugung verursachten Emissionen zu vermindern.[107]

Der strategische Fahrplan ist dafür in folgende drei Phasen gegliedert:[108] In der ersten Phase (2020 bis 2024) sollten Elektrolyseure mit einer Leistung von mindestens 6 GW in Betrieb genommen werden, um bis zu eine Mt erneuerbaren Wasserstoffs herzustellen. Das Ziel war also insbesondere, die Installation von Elektrolyseuren voranzutreiben. Diese sollten zunächst primär nahe den Endabnehmenden errichtet werden und zugleich sollte angesichts der angestrebten Entwicklung des Marktes mit der Planung der Fernleitungsinfrastruktur begonnen werden. Zur Entwicklung des Marktes sei zudem das Schaffen eines adäquaten Rechtsrahmens und das Setzen von Angebots- sowie Nachfrageanreizen notwendig. In der zweiten Phase (2025 bis 2030) müsse (erneuerbarer) Wasserstoff zu einem bedeutenden Bestandteil eines integrierten Energiesystems heranwachsen. Dies wurde mit dem ambitionierten Ziel unterstrichen, bis 2030 Elektrolyseure mit einer Leistung von mindestens 40 GW zu errichten, um damit jährlich bis zu 10 Mt erneuerbaren Wasserstoffs zu produzieren. Um auf die allmähliche Wettbewerbsfähigkeit der erneuerbaren Wasserstofferzeugung hinzuarbeiten, werden auch gezielte nachfrageseitige Maßnahmen in Betracht gezogen, wodurch neue Anwendungsbereiche wie der Mobilitätssektor[109] und die Stahlerzeugung erschlos-

104 Vgl. Europäische Kommission (2020d), S. 1.
105 Vgl. Europäische Kommission (2020d), S. 6.
106 Vgl. Europäische Kommission (2020d), S. 4.
107 Vgl. Europäische Kommission (2020d), S. 6.
108 Vgl. Europäische Kommission (2020d), S. 6–9.
109 Dieser ist im Fokus der ebenfalls 2020 mitgeteilten Strategie für nachhaltige und intelligente Mobilität. Siehe dafür Europäische Kommission (2020c).

sen sowie ausgebaut werden könnten. Auch die Rolle von Wasserstoff beim Ausgleich des verstärkt auf erneuerbaren Energieträgern basierenden Stromversorgungssystems soll sukzessive gestärkt werden. Insgesamt wird der Aufbau einer EU-weiten Logistikinfrastruktur thematisiert, was teilweise mittels Umwidmung des bestehenden Gasnetzes gelingen soll. Letztendlich soll in der dritten Phase (2030 bis 2050) die erreichte Marktreife von Technologien für erneuerbaren Wasserstoff dafür sorgen, dass diese in großem Maßstab Anwendung finden.

An diesen Fahrplan schließen sich Ausführungen zur möglichen Finanzierung dieser Vorhaben an.[110] Die gemeinsame grenzüberschreitende Arbeit entlang der gesamten Wertschöpfungskette soll insbesondere durch sogenannte „wichtige Vorhaben von gemeinsamem europäischem Interesse" (IPCEI) gelingen.[111] Diese IPCEI sollen explizit die Möglichkeit bieten, durch staatliche Beihilfen einem Versagen des Marktes entgegenzuwirken.[112] An dieser Stelle wurde also deutlich der politische Regelungswille unterstrichen.

2.3.3 Bekräftigung des strategischen Kurses angesichts neuer Herausforderungen

Infolge des russischen Angriffskriegs auf die Ukraine wurde 2022 der REPowerEU-Plan verkündet. Dieser soll aufbauend auf dem „Fit für 55"-Paket die grüne Transformation des Energiesektors beschleunigen und den Aufbau eines resilienteren integrierten Energiesystems fördern, um auch die Abhängigkeit von fossilen Energieträgern aus Russland zu reduzieren.[113] Im Sinne der Dekarbonisierung wurde die maßgebliche Rolle von erneuerbarem Wasserstoff sowie das 10 Mt-Ziel der Wasserstoffstrategie bekräftigt; zusätzlich sollen bis 2030 die jährlichen Importe von erneuerbarem Wasserstoff auf ebenfalls bis zu 10 Mt gesteigert werden.[114] Damit einher geht eine entsprechende Anregung der Nachfrage, sodass sich bis 2030 eine intendierte Steigerung des Verbrauchs durch europäische Endabnehmende auf bis zu 20 Mt erneuerbaren Wasserstoffs ergibt. In dem Sinne sind die angebotsbezogenen Zielvorgaben auch als Nachfrageziele zu verstehen.[115] Zur Beschleunigung der Wasserstoffstrategie zielte der REPowerEU-Plan zudem auf eine möglichst baldige Finalisierung des überarbeiteten Wasserstoff- und Gasmarktpa-

110 Vgl. Europäische Kommission (2020d), S. 9–11.
111 Vgl. Europäische Kommission (2020d), S. 10 f.
112 Vgl. Europäische Kommission (2020d), S. 11.
113 Vgl. Europäische Kommission (2022), S. 1.
114 Vgl. Europäische Kommission (2022), S. 8 f.
115 Vgl. ACER (2024), S. 4.

kets sowie den Erlass zweier delegierter Verordnungen[116] über die Definition und Erzeugung von erneuerbarem Wasserstoff.[117]

Zudem wurde im Jahr 2023 das Festhalten am Kurs Richtung Klimaneutralität durch einen neuen Industrieplan zum Green Deal bestätigt.[118] Teil dieses Plans war es, erstmals auf Grundlage der überarbeiteten Emissionshandelsrichtlinie durch Auktionsverfahren Mittel des Innovationsfonds zur Förderung der Erzeugung von erneuerbarem Wasserstoff bereitzustellen.[119] Daraus folgte dann im selben Jahr die erste Pilotauktion der neu gegründeten Europäischen Wasserstoffbank.[120] Wie bereits einleitend erwähnt,[121] scheint sich auch mit dem zuletzt veröffentlichten „Clean Industrial Deal" die strategische Ausrichtung hinsichtlich des Wasserstoffs nicht zu ändern:[122] Die zentrale Rolle bei der Dekarbonisierung des Energiesystems wird weiterhin bekräftigt. Allerdings werden nur wenige konkrete Maßnahmen genannt, darunter der Erlass eines delegierten Rechtsaktes zur Erzeugung von kohlenstoffarmem Wasserstoff und das nächste Auktionsverfahren im Rahmen der Europäischen Wasserstoffbank.

2.3.4 Nationale Ebene und Gesamtbetrachtung

Der strategische Kurs der Europäischen Kommission überträgt sich auch auf die nationale Ebene des EWR:[123] Stand Mai 2024 hatten exakt zwei Drittel der Staaten (20 von 30) eine nationale Wasserstoffstrategie veröffentlicht. In drei weiteren Staaten befand sich eine in Arbeit und somit hatten lediglich sieben Staaten noch gar nicht damit begonnen.

Insgesamt wird in der strategischen Ausrichtung ein politischer Regelungswille deutlich. Angesichts der politischen Ambitionen hinsichtlich der Entwicklung des europäischen Wasserstoffmarktes wurde ein Marktversagen identifiziert, das u.a. durch staatliche Beihilfen ausgeglichen werden soll. Gleichzeitig wurde die zentrale Bedeutung des Wettbewerbs mehrfach hervorgehoben. Die wettbewerbsorientierte Förderung infolge der Auktionsverfahren der Europäischen Wasserstoffbank soll beides miteinander vereinen,

116 Dies sind die deleg. Verordnung zur RFNBO-Produktion und die deleg. Verordnung über Treibhausgaseinsparungen.
117 Vgl. Europäische Kommission (2022), S. 9.
118 Vgl. Europäische Kommission (2023c), S. 3.
119 Vgl. Europäische Kommission (2023c), S. 15.
120 Siehe dazu Kap. 4.
121 Siehe Abschn. 1.1.
122 Vgl. Europäische Kommission (2025), S. 8 f.
123 Vgl. EHO (2025), S. 36 f.

was daher im Kern dieser Arbeit zu untersuchen ist. Dafür wird zunächst im folgenden Kapitel der rechtliche Rahmen des europäischen Wasserstoffmarktes betrachtet, welcher die rechtliche Grundlage der sich aus dem Regelungswillen ergebenden Markteingriffe bildet.

3. Rechtlicher Rahmen des europäischen Wasserstoffmarktes

Beim Aufbau eines neuen Marktes ist für sämtliche Akteur:innen wie Unternehmen und Investor:innen die Rechtssicherheit von großer Bedeutung.[124] Dies ist insbesondere der Fall, wenn im Rahmen der ambitionierten Ziele und daraus folgenden tiefgehenden Transformationsprozesse enorme Anschubfinanzierungen zu leisten sind, wie im vorangegangenen Kapitel deutlich wurde. Damit ist der rechtliche Rahmen auch von zentraler Bedeutung für die Unternehmen, welche eine Teilnahme an den Auktionsverfahren der Europäischen Wasserstoffbank in Erwägung ziehen.

3.1 Funktionsweise des europäischen Mehrebenensystems im EWR

Im europäischen Mehrebenensystem sind dabei insbesondere die relevanten Richtlinien und Verordnungen zu betrachten. Diese werden im Rahmen der Zuständigkeiten erlassen, welche der Union im AEUV zugewiesen wurden.[125] Eine Verordnung hat allgemeinen Geltungscharakter und ist in ihrer Gänze unmittelbar in den Mitgliedsstaaten anzuwenden.[126] Dagegen ist in einer Richtlinie ein an die Mitgliedsstaaten gerichtetes verbindliches Ziel formuliert, wobei die Wahl der Form und Mittel zur Zielerreichung den jeweiligen Mitgliedsstaaten überlassen ist.[127] Richtlinien erfordern folglich eine Umsetzung in nationales Recht. Dadurch soll eine Harmonisierung des mitgliedsstaatlichen Rechts, also eine Rechtsangleichung, erreicht werden, wobei im Gegensatz zu einer Rechtsvereinheitlichung die Möglichkeit besteht, die jeweiligen nationalen Besonderheiten und Voraussetzungen zu berücksichti-

---

124 Vgl. Burmeister et al. (2024), S. 307.

125 Im Sinne von Art. 2 AEUV wird unterschieden zwischen einer ausschließlichen Zuständigkeit der Union in den Bereichen nach Art. 3 AEUV, einer mit den Mitgliedsstaaten geteilten Zuständigkeit der Union in den Bereichen nach Art. 4 AEUV und letztendlich den Bereichen nach Art. 6 AEUV, in welchen die Union für die Durchführung von Maßnahmen zur Unterstützung, Koordinierung oder Ergänzung der mitgliedsstaatlichen Maßnahmen zuständig ist.

126 Nach Art. 288 Abs. 2 AEUV.

127 Nach Art. 288 Abs. 3 AEUV.

gen. Außerdem kann im Rahmen dieser Gesetzgebungsakte der Kommission die Befugnis übertragen werden, zur Ergänzung oder Änderung nicht wesentlicher Vorschriften des betreffenden Gesetzgebungsaktes, sogenannte delegierte Rechtsakte zu erlassen, welche als Rechtsakte ohne Gesetzescharakter mit allgemeiner Geltung definiert sind.[128] Dies ist insbesondere für die Ausführungen zur Regulierung des Wasserstoffangebots relevant.[129]

Generell ist allerdings fraglich, wie die zuvor beschriebene EU-Gesetzgebung Wirkung auf den in dieser Arbeit betrachteten EWR entfaltet. Das zentrale Organ ist dabei der Gemeinsame EWR-Ausschuss, bestehend aus Vertreter:innen der EU-Kommission und der drei EWR-EFTA-Staaten.[130] Durch Beschluss kann der Gemeinsame EWR-Ausschuss gem. Art. 98 EWR-Abk die dem Abkommen beigefügten Anhänge und Protokolle ändern, um Rechtsakte der EU in dieses Verzeichnis aufzunehmen. Die Beschlussfassung[131] erfolgt dabei nach Art. 93 Abs. 2 EWR-Abk im Einvernehmen zwischen der Kommission und den mit einer Stimme sprechenden EWR-EFTA-Staaten. Nach erfolgter Aufnahme eines Rechtsaktes in das oben erwähnte Verzeichnis, wird dieser im Falle einer EU-Verordnung direkt in das nationale Recht der EWR-EFTA-Staaten übernommen,[132] während ihnen bei der Umsetzung einer EU-Richtlinie in nationales Recht die Wahl der Form und Mittel überlassen ist.[133] Auf diesem Weg entfalten die den EWR betreffenden Rechtsakte der EU auch Wirkung auf die EWR-EFTA-Staaten.

Nach dieser grundlegenden Einleitung zur Funktionsweise des europäischen Mehrebenensystems im EWR sind in den folgenden Abschnitten die zentralen Regelungsinhalte der relevanten EU-Rechtsakte entlang der Wertschöpfungskette dargestellt. Dabei werden zunächst im Rahmen des Wasserstoffangebots Zertifizierungsvorgaben für Wasserstoff betrachtet, gefolgt von der Regulierung der Infrastruktur in einem leitungsgebundenen Markt und zuletzt verbindlichen Zielvorgaben bezüglich der Endabnahme von Wasserstoff (Wasserstoffnachfrage). Ziel ist es, sowohl die Regelungsdichte als auch den Grad der Harmonisierung herauszuarbeiten und dadurch aus rechtlicher Perspektive die Marktsituation zu verdeutlichen, in welcher die zu untersu-

128 Nach Art. 290 Abs. 1 Unterabs. 1 AEUV.

129 Siehe Abschn. 3.2.

130 Nach Art. 93 Abs. 1 EWR-Abk, wobei hier unter Anwendung des Art. 2 Buchst. c EWR-Abk zum einen die EU und zum anderen die drei EWR-EFTA-Staaten im Sinne des Art. 2 Buchst. b EWR-Abk als Vertragsparteien zu verstehen sind. Die EU wird gem. Art. 94 Abs. 1 EWR-Abk durch die Kommission vertreten.

131 Das Beschlussfassungsverfahren richtet sich nach Maßgabe der Art. 99 f. u. 102 f. EWR-Abk.

132 Nach Art. 7 Buchst. a EWR-Abk.

133 Nach Art. 7 Buchst. b EWR-Abk.

chenden Auktionsverfahren stattfinden. Außerdem ist insbesondere im Rahmen der Wasserstoffinfrastruktur[134] zu untersuchen, wie erst durch Regulierung wettbewerbliche Verhältnisse sichergestellt werden.

3.2 Regulierung des Wasserstoffangebots durch Zertifizierung

Wie bereits dargestellt, sollen vor allem erneuerbarer Wasserstoff und als Übergangslösung auch kohlenstoffarmer Wasserstoff zum Erreichen der Dekarbonisierungsziele beitragen.[135] Dabei stellt sich die Frage, wie gewährleistet wird, dass im EWR angebotener Wasserstoff tatsächlich dem Regelungswillen des Gesetzgebers entspricht und mit den politischen Zielen vereinbar ist. Der europäische Gesetzgeber wählt dabei den Ansatz einer Zertifizierung, die auf rechtlich festgelegten Definitionen basiert. Im Sinne der Rechtssicherheit ist die Schaffung eines einheitlichen Rahmens für alle Marktakteur:innen von großer Bedeutung. Denn ohne Klarheit darüber, was in diesem Kontext unter den Begriffen „erneuerbar" und „kohlenstoffarm" zu verstehen ist, wäre ein funktionierender Binnenmarkt nicht vorstellbar und auch der Beitrag zur Dekarbonisierung gefährdet. Im Folgenden wird dargestellt, wozu die Mitgliedsstaaten bezüglich der Zertifizierung verpflichtet werden und nach welchen Rechtsvorschriften sowie Legaldefinitionen sich die Ausgestaltung eines Zertifizierungssystems richtet.

Unter Maßgabe des Art. 9 Gas- und Wasserstoffrichtlinie werden die Mitgliedsstaaten zur Einführung eines Zertifizierungssystems verpflichtet, wobei ihnen die Umsetzung in nationales Recht obliegt. Erneuerbare Gase sind dabei nach den Vorgaben der Art. 29 ff. der überarbeiteten Erneuerbare-Energien-Richtlinie (RED III) zu zertifizieren.[136] Allerdings erfassen die Zertifizierungsvorgaben nach RED III keine kohlenstoffarmen Brennstoffe. Deswegen wurde diese Regelungslücke mit Erlass der Vorgaben in Art. 9 Abs. 2 bis 12 Gas- und Wasserstoffrichtlinie geschlossen.[137] Dabei soll die Zertifizierung kohlenstoffarmer Brennstoffe im Einklang mit der Zertifizierung erneuerbare Gase erfolgen und die Regelungen der RED III seien daher analog anzuwenden.[138] Außerdem finden die jeweiligen Zertifizierungsvorgaben sowohl bei der heimischen Erzeugung als auch bei Importen Anwendung.[139]

---

134 Siehe Abschn. 3.3.

135 Siehe Unterabschn. 2.3.2.

136 Nach Art. 9 Abs. 1 Satz 1 Gas- und Wasserstoffrichtlinie.

137 Nach Art. 9 Abs. 1 Satz 2 Gas- und Wasserstoffrichtlinie.

138 Vgl. ErwG 14 Gas- und Wasserstoffrichtlinie.

139 Nach Art. 30 Abs. 3 Unterabs. 2 Satz 1 RED III u. Art. 9 Abs. 4 Satz 1 Gas- und Wasserstoffrichtlinie.

Im Rahmen der Zertifizierung sind also insbesondere die bereits thematisierten Begriffe „erneuerbar“ und „kohlenstoffarm“ von Bedeutung.[140] Diese sind im Sinne der Dekarbonisierungsziele als Abgrenzung zum Begriff „fossil“ zu verstehen. Im Gas- und Wasserstoffpaket sind „erneuerbare Gase“ als u.a. erneuerbare Kraftstoffe nicht biogenen Ursprungs (RFNBO) definiert.[141] Zunächst nur für den Verkehrssektor vorgesehen,[142] umfassen die RFNBO nach RED III allgemein flüssige oder gasförmige Kraftstoffe, deren Energiegehalt aus erneuerbaren Energiequellen mit Ausnahme von Biomasse stammt.[143]

Hinsichtlich des Wasserstoffmarktes und auch der zu untersuchenden Auktionen der Europäischen Wasserstoffbank[144] ist fraglich, unter welchen Kriterien erneuerbarer Wasserstoff den RFNBO zuzuordnen ist. Dafür entscheidend sind die damit verbundenen Treibhausgaseinsparungen[145] und insbesondere der Strombezug der Anlagen zur Erzeugung erneuerbaren Wasserstoffs. In Art. 27 Abs. 6 RED III finden sich Regelungen dazu, wann und in welchem Umfang bezogener Strom erneuerbaren Energiequellen zuzurechnen ist. Mit der delegierten Verordnung zur RFNBO-Produktion[146] wurden diese Regelungen detaillierter ausgestaltet sowie um die drei Kriterien der Zusätzlichkeit, der zeitlichen Korrelation und der geografischen Korrelation ergänzt. Beim Strombezug der Produktionsanlagen wird unterschieden zwischen Strom,[147] welcher über einen Direktanschluss an eine Anlage zur Erzeugung von erneuerbarem Strom bezogen wird, und Strom,[148] welcher indirekt aus dem Netz bezogen wird. Auch eine Kombination beider Alternativen zu unterschiedlichen Zeiten ist möglich.[149] Das Kriterium der Zusätzlichkeit soll den Ausbau erneuerbarer Energien vorantreiben, indem die

140 Siehe Unterabschn. 2.1.2.

141 Nach Art. 2 Nr. 2 Gas- und Wasserstoffrichtlinie sowie Art. 2 Nr. 41 Gas- und Wasserstoffverordnung.

142 Nach Art. 2 Satz 2 Nr. 36 RED II.

143 Nach Art. 2 Satz 2 Nr. 36 RED III.

144 Nach Kap. 2 Abschn. 2.1 Nr. 1.1 Terms and Conditions 2024. Beim auktionierten Gut handelt es sich um RFNBO-Wasserstoff.

145 Eine einheitliche Methode zur Berechnung der Treibhausgaseinsparungen wurde in der deleg. Verordnung über Treibhausgaseinsparungen festgelegt.

146 Diese delegierte Verordnung wurde im Sinne des Art. 27 Abs. 6 Unterabs. 4 RED III bereits gem. Art. 27 Abs. 3 Unterabs. 7 RED II erlassen.

147 Dieser Strom ist als vollständig erneuerbar anrechenbar unter Maßgabe des Art. 3 deleg. Verordnung zur RFNBO-Produktion.

148 Dieser Strom ist als vollständig erneuerbar anrechenbar unter Maßgabe des Art. 4 deleg. Verordnung zur RFNBO-Produktion.

149 Nach Art. 3 Satz 2 deleg. Verordnung zur RFNBO-Produktion.

Produzierenden erneuerbaren Wasserstoffs Verträge über den Bezug von erneuerbarem Strom abschließen müssen, welcher mit frühestens vor 36 Monaten in Betrieb genommenen und grundsätzlich nicht-geförderten Kapazitäten generiert wurde.[150] Weiter sollen die Korrelationskriterien sicherstellen, dass erneuerbarer Wasserstoff abhängig davon produziert wird, wann (zeitlich)[151] und wo (geografisch)[152] erneuerbarer Strom verfügbar ist, damit durch eine verstärkte Nachfrage nach erneuerbarem Strom für die Wasserstoffproduktion nicht zugleich Anreize für die Deckung des Strombedarfs in anderen Bereichen durch fossile Stromerzeugung geliefert werden.

Wie bereits dargestellt, soll zudem kohlenstoffarmer Wasserstoff als Übergangslösung zur Dekarbonisierung beitragen.[153] Dieser zählt wie auch unter bestimmten Voraussetzungen synthetische gasförmige Brennstoffe mit einem aus kohlenstoffarmem Wasserstoff stammenden Energiegehalt zu den kohlenstoffarmen Gasen.[154] Unter denselben Voraussetzungen wird Wasserstoff als „kohlenstoffarm" bezeichnet, dessen Energiegehalt aus nicht erneuerbaren Quellen stammt und der in Bezug auf die Verringerung von Treibhausgasemissionen einen Mindestschwellenwert von 70% des Vergleichswerts für RFNBO erreicht.[155]

Insgesamt besteht somit aufgrund der Zertifizierungsvorgaben insbesondere hinsichtlich der Erzeugung erneuerbaren Wasserstoffs eine hohe Regelungsdichte mit komplexen Anforderungen, welche den Markthochlauf von erneuerbarem Wasserstoff erschweren könnte. Lediglich für kleine und mittlere Wasserelektrolyseure (Produktionskapazität von höchstens 50 t pro Tag) wurden mit der neuen Industrieemissionsrichtlinie administrative Hürden abgebaut, indem diese nicht mehr in den Anwendungsbereich der Richtlinie fallen.[156] Dadurch entfallen sich aus der Umsetzung auf nationaler Ebene ergebende Regelungen und eine schnellere Inbetriebnahme ist möglich. Im Gesamteindruck der Regelungen wird das Streben nach Harmonisierung hinsichtlich der Erzeugung von erneuerbarem und kohlenstoffarmem Wasserstoff deutlich, um Rechtssicherheit innerhalb des EWR zu gewährleisten. Dennoch wurde darauf verzichtet, ein einheitliches Zertifizierungssystem

---

150 Nach Art. 5 deleg. Verordnung zur RFNBO-Produktion.

151 Nach Art. 6 deleg. Verordnung zur RFNBO-Produktion.

152 Nach Art. 7 deleg. Verordnung zur RFNBO-Produktion.

153 Siehe Unterabschn. 2.3.2.

154 Nach Art. 2 Nr. 12 Gas- und Wasserstoffrichtlinie.

155 Nach Art. 2 Nr. 11 Gas- und Wasserstoffrichtlinie. Eine entsprechende Methode zur Bestimmung der Treibhausgaseinsparungen wurde im Sinne des Art. 29a Abs. 3 RED III bereits in der deleg. Verordnung über Treibhausgaseinsparungen gem. Art. 28 Abs. 5 RED II festgelegt.

156 Nach Art. 10 iVm Anhang I Nr. 6.6 Industrieemissionsrichtlinie.

einzuführen, denn die Umsetzung der Zertifizierungsvorgaben aus Art. 9 Gas- und Wasserstoffrichtlinie obliegt den Mitgliedstaaten. So äußern auch *Burmeister et al.* überzeugende Bedenken hinsichtlich der Möglichkeit eines Flickenteppichs unterschiedlicher mitgliedsstaatlicher Regelungen,[157] was wiederum die Rechtssicherheit mindern und den Markthochlauf im Binnenmarkt erschweren würde.

3.3 Regulierung der Wasserstoffinfrastruktur

Für einen funktionierenden Wasserstoffmarkt ist die entsprechende Infrastruktur von zentraler Bedeutung, um Angebot und Nachfrage miteinander zu verknüpfen. Mit dem Gas- und Wasserstoffpaket wurde ein erster Rechtsrahmen geschaffen, um diese im Aufbau befindliche Infrastruktur von Beginn an zu regulieren. Da viele Fragen hinsichtlich der Entwicklung des Marktes noch nicht geklärt sind, bspw. in welchen Formen und auf welchen Wegen Wasserstoff künftig transportiert werden wird, wurde dieser Rechtsrahmen bezüglich eines Marktes für gasförmigen Wasserstoff festgelegt.[158] Dabei wird der Transport perspektivisch überwiegend mittels Wasserstoffnetzen erfolgen. Somit ist davon auszugehen, dass vergleichbar zu anderen leitungsgebundenen Energien auch ein leitungsgebundener Markt im Aufbau begriffen ist, wie ihn *Konstantin & Konstantin* beschreiben.[159] Die Teilnahme an diesem Markt setzt dann Netzzugang voraus, was im Zuge der im folgenden Unterabschnitt betrachteten Regelungen näher erläutert wird.

Außerdem ist fraglich, ob die Wasserstoffinfrastruktur ein natürliches Monopol bilden wird, also die gesamte Wertschöpfungskette von vertikal integrierten Versorgungsunternehmen beherrscht würde.[160] *Reinecke & Scholz* sehen zumindest bezüglich des deutschen Wasserstoff-Kernnetzes gegenwärtig und auch in naher Zukunft noch keinen Grund zu dieser Annahme, da die Wasserstoffnetze noch nicht durch unüberwindbare Marktbarrieren dem Wettbewerb entzogen wären.[161] Dagegen stellen *Burmeister et al.* überzeugend dar, dass die Monopolbildung perspektivisch abzusehen sei und der europäische Gesetzgeber deswegen von Beginn an eine Regulierungsnotwendigkeit sehe.[162] Dabei stützen sie sich auch auf den Gesetzesentwurf der deut-

157 Vgl. Burmeister et al. (2024), S. 301.
158 Vgl. ErwG 86 Gas- und Wasserstoffrichtlinie.
159 Vgl. Konstantin & Konstantin (2023), S. 476 f.
160 Vgl. Konstantin & Konstantin (2023), S. 476.
161 Vgl. Reinecke & Scholz (2024), S. 120.
162 Vgl. Burmeister et al. (2024), S. 300.

schen Bundesregierung bezüglich des Wasserstoff-Kernnetzes, aus welchem diese Regulierungsnotwendigkeit ebenso hervorgeht.[163]

Aus einem natürlichen Monopol wäre eine marktbeherrschende Stellung abzuleiten, deren missbräuchliche Ausnutzung nach Maßgabe des Art. 102 AEUV mit dem Binnenmarkt unvereinbar und verboten ist. Allerdings stellt das Wettbewerbsrecht lediglich eine ex-post- Kontrolle dar, wie auch *Jones et al.* in ihrem Grundlagenwerk zum Wettbewerbsrecht der EU darlegen.[164] Das bedeutet, dass im Nachhinein geprüft wird, ob das Agieren von Unternehmen einer missbräuchlichen Ausnutzung ihrer marktbeherrschenden Stellung entspricht. Die Schwächung des Wettbewerbs ist aber zu diesem Zeitpunkt bereits erfolgt und kann folglich nur im Nachhinein sanktioniert werden. Im gleichen Zug beschreiben *Jones et al.* den ex-ante-Ansatz, welcher berechtigterweise im Sekundärrecht zu finden ist. Danach sollen – im Gegensatz zur ex-post-Kontrolle – durch Regulierung im Vorhinein, also präventiv, missbräuchliches Verhalten verhindert und somit diskriminierungsfreie Wettbewerbsverhältnisse gewährleistet werden. Im Folgenden wird daher aufgezeigt, welche Aspekte der Infrastruktur im Sinne dieses ex-ante-Ansatzes reguliert werden.

3.3.1 Netzanschluss und -zugang

Zentrale Voraussetzung der Teilnahme an einem leitungsgebundenen Markt ist der sogenannte Netzzugang. Fraglich ist, was genau unter Netzzugang zu verstehen ist. So unterscheidet die deutsche Bundesnetzagentur zwischen dem Netzanschluss als rein technischer Anbindung an das Netz und dem Netzzugang als dem Recht der Netzeinspeisung und -entnahme.[165] Dem Wortlaut nach folgt der europäische Gesetzgeber in der Gas- und Wasserstoffrichtlinie dieser Unterscheidung, wie im Folgenden verdeutlicht wird.

Zunächst ist in dem Sinne die Regulierung des Netzanschlusses sowie dessen Verweigerung zu betrachten. Maßgeblich für die Regulierung sind die technischen Vorschriften nach Art. 10 Gas- und Wasserstoffrichtlinie. Die Mitgliedsstaaten werden zu diesem Zweck verpflichtet, technische Vorschriften für den Anschluss an das Wasserstoffsystem auszuarbeiten und zu veröffentlichen, welche die Interoperabilität der Netze sicherstellen sowie objektiv und nichtdiskriminierend sind.[166] Außerdem tragen die Mitgliedsstaaten

163 Vgl. BT-Drs. 20/10014, S. 56.
164 Vgl. Jones et al. (2023), S. 68.
165 Vgl. Bundesnetzagentur (o. D.).
166 Nach Art. 10 Abs. 1 Satz 1 u. 2 Gas- und Wasserstoffrichtlinie.

Sorge dafür, dass die Netzbetreibenden in ihrem Hoheitsgebiet im Einklang mit den oben erwähnten Vorschriften ihrerseits technische Vorschriften veröffentlichen.[167]

Nach Art. 38 Abs. 1 Gas- und Wasserstoffrichtlinie können Netzbetreibende den Netzanschluss dann verweigern, wenn sie nicht über die nötige Kapazität verfügen oder es einer Netzverbindung ermangelt. Wird aus diesen Gründen ein Netzanschluss verweigert, sind die Mitgliedsstaaten verpflichtet, geeignete Maßnahmen zu ergreifen, um zu gewährleisten, dass die Netzbetreibenden für den erforderlichen Ausbau Sorge tragen, soweit dies wirtschaftlich vertretbar ist oder potenzielle Kund:innen für die Kosten aufkommen.[168] Hieraus ergibt sich zudem die Notwendigkeit einer regulierten Netzplanung, welche im Anschluss an die folgenden Ausführungen zum Netzzugang thematisiert wird.

Sobald ein Netzanschluss besteht, stellt sich die Frage, inwiefern der Netzzugang reguliert ist, also unter welchen Voraussetzungen die Möglichkeit besteht, Wasserstoff einzuspeisen oder zu entnehmen. Im ersten Schritt nimmt der europäische Gesetzgeber dabei eine Unterscheidung zwischen Wasserstoffnetzen, -terminals und -speicheranlagen vor. Der Zugang Dritter zu Wasserstoffnetzen ist in Art. 35 Gas- und Wasserstoffrichtlinie geregelt und die Mitgliedsstaaten werden nach Abs. 1 zur Einführung eines Systems des regulierten Netzzugangs verpflichtet, welches auf veröffentlichten Netzentgelten basiert und diskriminierungsfrei nach objektiven Kriterien Anwendung findet. Allerdings können sich die Mitgliedsstaaten mittelfristig entscheiden, bis zum 31. Dezember 2032 stattdessen ein System für den Zugang Dritter auf Vertragsbasis einzuführen, wobei die zuständigen nationalen Regulierungsbehörden sicherstellen, dass die Nutzenden der Wasserstoffnetze den Zugang tatsächlich aushandeln können.[169] Da die Kapazitäten zur Wasserstoffspeicherung begrenzt und ungleich verteilt sind, soll der Zugang zu diesen ebenfalls reguliert werden, um gleiche Wettbewerbsbedingungen zu gewährleisten.[170] Dabei wird in Art. 37 Gas- und Wasserstoffrichtlinie der gleiche Ansatz wie bei der Regulierung der Wasserstoffnetze verfolgt. Bezüglich des Zugangs Dritter zu Wasserstoffterminals ist generell ein System auf Vertragsbasis einzuführen.[171]

In Art. 38 Gas- und Wasserstoffrichtlinie ist dann die Verweigerung des Netzzugangs geregelt. Die Voraussetzungen dafür entsprechen den obigen

167 Nach Art. 10 Abs. 2 Satz 1 Gas- und Wasserstoffrichtlinie.
168 Nach Art. 38 Abs. 2 Gas- und Wasserstoffrichtlinie.
169 Nach Art. 35 Abs. 4 Gas- und Wasserstoffrichtlinie.
170 Vgl. ErwG 85 Gas- und Wasserstoffrichtlinie.
171 Nach Art. 36 Abs. 1 Satz 1 Gas- und Wasserstoffrichtlinie.

Ausführungen hinsichtlich der Verweigerung des Netzanschlusses. Allerdings darf der Zugang von erneuerbarem Gas und kohlenstoffarmem Gas zum Wasserstoffnetz nur unter Vorbehalt der Art. 20 u. 36 Gas- und Wasserstoffverordnung verweigert werden.[172] Diese verpflichten Netzbetreibende dazu, den Produktionsanlagen für erneuerbaren und kohlenstoffarmen Wasserstoff verbindliche Kapazitäten bereitzustellen. Nur aus Gründen der Infrastruktursicherheit und der wirtschaftlichen Effizienz dürfen diese betrieblichen Beschränkungen unterliegen.[173] Insgesamt ist somit gem. Art. 38 Gas- und Wasserstoffrichtlinie ein Einspeisevorrang erneuerbarer und kohlenstoffarmer Gase vorgesehen.

3.3.2 Netzplanung

Die Verpflichtung der Netzbetreibenden zur Bereitstellung verbindlicher Kapazitäten verweist zudem auf den nächsten Regelungsinhalt, und zwar die Netzplanung. Denn nur durch die Bereitstellung genügender Kapazitäten infolge einer entsprechenden Netzplanung kann der Anspruch auf diskriminierungsfreie Teilnahme am Markt sichergestellt werden. In dem Sinne muss eine regulierte Netzplanung auf europäischer wie nationaler Ebene erfolgen.

Im Rahmen des nach Art. 57 Gas- und Wasserstoffverordnung geschaffenen Europäischen Netzwerks der Wasserstoffnetzbetreiber (ENNOH) sollen Wasserstofffernleitungsnetzbetreibende auf Unionsebene zusammenarbeiten, um u.a. die Entwicklung und das reibungslose Funktionieren des Wasserstoffbinnenmarkts zu gewährleisten.[174] Eine zentrale Aufgabe des ENNOH ist die Annahme und Veröffentlichung eines allerdings nicht bindenden EU- Netzentwicklungsplans für Wasserstoff im Sinne des Art. 60 Gas- und Wasserstoffverordnung.[175] Dieser Plan hat u.a. auf den nationalen Fernleitungsnetzentwicklungsplänen[176] aufzubauen und Investitionslücken insbesondere hinsichtlich der Realisierung der angestrebten Elektrolysekapazitäten aufzuzeigen.[177] So soll im Einklang zwischen Union und Mitgliedsstaaten eine vollständig integrierte Netzplanung gelingen. Die zehnjährigen nationalen Entwicklungspläne für Fernleitungsnetze müssen dabei u.a. umfassend darstellen, welche wichtigen Infrastrukturen errichtet oder ausgebaut

172 Nach Art. 38 Abs. 3 Gas- und Wasserstoffrichtlinie.

173 Nach Art. 36 Abs. 2 Satz 2 Gas- und Wasserstoffverordnung.

174 Nach Art. 57 Abs. 1 Gas- und Wasserstoffverordnung.

175 Nach Art. 59 Abs. 1 Buchst. c Gas- und Wasserstoffverordnung.

176 Im Sinne des Art. 55 Gas- und Wasserstoffrichtlinie.

177 Nach Art. 60 Abs. 1 Unterabs. 2 Buchst. a u. c Gas- und Wasserstoffverordnung.

werden müssen, insbesondere mit Blick auf den Anschluss von Anlagen zur Erzeugung von erneuerbaren Gasen und kohlenstoffarmen Gasen.[178] Zudem werden auch die Wasserstoffverteilernetzbetreibende verpflichtet, einen Netzentwicklungsplan im Sinne des Art. 56 Gas- und Wasserstoffrichtlinie zu erstellen, dessen Überprüfung[179] der zuständigen nationalen Regulierungsbehörde obliegt.

3.3.3 Entflechtung

Einleitend zu diesem Abschnitt wurde bereits thematisiert, dass infolge einer möglichen Monopolstellung vertikal integrierte Versorgungsunternehmen die gesamte Wertschöpfungskette beherrschen und ihre Stellung missbräuchlich ausnutzen könnten. Daher sieht der europäische Gesetzgeber bezüglich des Netzbetriebs eine wirksame Entflechtung, also eine Trennung des Netzbetriebs von der Erzeugung und Versorgung, als notwendig an, um eine diskriminierungsfreie Ausübung des Netzgeschäfts zu gewährleisten.[180] Dabei soll ein transparenter sowie wirksamer Rechtsrahmen Interessenskonflikte, die einem Ausbau der Netzinfrastruktur und dem Funktionieren des Marktes entgegenstehen könnten, lösen und auch die Teilnahme von Markteinsteigenden gewährleisten.[181] Insbesondere hinsichtlich vertikal integrierter Unternehmen müssten Anreize beseitigt werden, Wettbewerbende bezüglich Netzzugang und Investitionen zu benachteiligen.[182] Aufgrund der Kostspieligkeit einer möglichen nachträglichen Entflechtung seien daher dementsprechend erlassene Regelungen im Wasserstoffsektor unverzüglich anzuwenden, bevor dieser eine starke vertikale Integration entwickele.[183]

Im Sinne der Entflechtung wird im Rahmen des Gas- und Wasserstoffpakets zwischen Wasserstoffverteilernetzen und Wasserstofffernleitungsnetzen unterschieden. Erstere sind für den örtlichen oder regionalen Transport von Wasserstoff vorgesehen und dienen in erster Linie der Lieferung an direkt an das Netz angeschlossene Kund:innen.[184] Dagegen ist zwar nicht die Möglichkeit auszuschließen, dass auch Wasserstofffernleitungsnetze zur direkten Lieferung an Kund:innen dienen, allerdings wird mittels dieser primär Wasser-

178 Nach Art. 55 Abs. 2 Unterabs. 1 Buchst. a Gas- und Wasserstoffrichtlinie.
179 Nach Art. 56 Abs. 4 Gas- und Wasserstoffrichtlinie.
180 Vgl. ErwG 61 Gas- und Wasserstoffrichtlinie.
181 Vgl. ErwG 63 Gas- und Wasserstoffrichtlinie.
182 Vgl. ErwG 62 Gas- und Wasserstoffrichtlinie.
183 Vgl. ErwG 66 Gas- und Wasserstoffrichtlinie.
184 Nach Art. 2 Nr. 24 Gas- und Wasserstoffrichtlinie.

stoff zu anderen Wasserstoffnetzen, -speicheranlagen oder -terminals transportiert.[185] Diese Unterscheidung wird für die Netzbetreibenden von großer Bedeutung sein, da sich aus ihr im Sinne der Gas- und Wasserstoffrichtlinie unterschiedlich strenge Anforderungen ergeben. So fallen die entflechtungsrechtlichen Vorgaben für Wasserstoffverteilernetze nach Art. 46 Gas- und Wasserstoffrichtlinie weniger streng aus, da diese in der Regel keine direkte Verbindung zu wichtiger Infrastruktur darstellen.[186]

Dagegen werden die Mitgliedsstaaten bezüglich Wasserstofffernleitungsnetzbetreibenden verpflichtet, die in Art. 60 Gas- und Wasserstoffrichtlinie für Erdgasfernleitungsnetzbetreibende festgelegten Vorschriften zur eigentumsrechtlichen Entflechtung anzuwenden.[187] Eigentumsrechtliche Entflechtung bedeutet hier im Kern u.a., dass nicht ein und dieselbe Person berechtigt ist, Kontrolle über ein Unternehmen auszuüben, welches Funktionen der Erzeugung oder Versorgung wahrnimmt, und zugleich direkt oder indirekt Kontrolle über ein Fernleitungsnetz auszuüben.[188] Außerdem gelten die Vorgaben zur horizontalen Entflechtung nach Art. 69 Gas- und Wasserstoffrichtlinie. Diese betreffen den Fall, dass Wasserstofffernleitungsnetzbetreibende Teil eines Unternehmens sind, welches im Bereich der Übertragung oder Verteilung von Erdgas oder Strom tätig ist, und verpflichten diesbezüglich zur Sicherstellung derer Unabhängigkeit zumindest hinsichtlich der Rechtsform.[189]

3.3.4 Netzentgelte

Ein letztes Instrument zur Verhinderung des Missbrauchs einer marktbeherrschenden Stellung ist die Netzentgeltregulierung. Die Regulierung der nach Art. 35 Abs. 1 zu veröffentlichenden Netzentgelte ist in Art. 17 bis 19 Gas- und Wasserstoffverordnung festgelegt. Entscheidend ist dabei u.a. die nichtdiskriminierende Anwendung der Netzentgelte sowie der Methoden zu ihrer Berechnung.[190] Eine Festlegung der Netzentgelte durch marktorientierte Verfahren wie Auktionen ist unter Maßgabe des Art. 17 Abs. 1 Unterabs. 2 Gas- und Wasserstoffverordnung auch möglich. Hier zeigt sich wie bei den zu untersuchenden Auktionsverfahren der Europäischen Wasserstoffbank

185 Nach Art. 2 Nr. 23 Gas- und Wasserstoffrichtlinie.
186 Vgl. ErwG 80 Gas- und Wasserstoffrichtlinie.
187 Nach Art. 68 Abs. 1 Gas- und Wasserstoffrichtlinie.
188 Nach Art. 60 Abs. 1 Buchst. b Gas- und Wasserstoffrichtlinie.
189 Nach Art. 69 Abs. 1 Gas- und Wasserstoffrichtlinie.
190 Nach Art. 17 Abs. 1 Unterabs. 1 Satz 2 Gas- und Wasserstoffverordnung.

der Wille, die Regulierung des Marktes mit dem Wettbewerbsgedanken zu vereinbaren.

An Einspeisepunkten von Erzeugungsanlagen ist für erneuerbares Gas und kohlenstoffarmes Gas ein Nachlass auf die Netzentgelte zu gewähren.[191] Dieser Nachlass beträgt bei erneuerbarem Gas 100% und bei kohlenstoffarmem Gas 75%.[192] Dadurch sollen Anreize für die Erzeugenden gesetzt und die Einspeisung von erneuerbarem Gas priorisiert werden. Weitere Regelungen zu Nachlässen finden sich in Art. 18 Abs. 4 Gas- und Wasserstoffverordnung.

Außerdem können die nationalen Regulierungsbehörden beschließen, Nachlässe nicht anzuwenden oder niedrigere Nachlässe festzulegen, wenn die Voraussetzungen des Art. 18 Abs. 5 Gas- und Wasserstoffverordnung erfüllt sind. Ein mögliches Szenario ist dabei, dass die Anwendung von Nachlässen aufgrund der Fortschritte bei der Einführung von erneuerbarem Gas und kohlenstoffarmem Gas in dem jeweiligen Mitgliedsstaat oder aufgrund bestehender alternativer Fördermechanismen nicht erforderlich ist.[193]

3.3.5 Gesamtbetrachtung

Insgesamt ergibt sich somit bei der Regulierung der Wasserstoffinfrastruktur im Großen und Ganzen ein Zusammenspiel der Gas- und Wasserstoffrichtlinie sowie -verordnung. Die Richtlinie ist bis zum 05. August 2026 in nationales Recht umzusetzen.[194] Daher bleibt abzuwarten, wie die jeweilige Ausgestaltung sowie letztendliche Anwendung der Regelungen aussehen wird und inwieweit dies den Markthochlauf insbesondere von erneuerbarem Wasserstoff fördert. Dennoch ist im Gas- und Wasserstoffpaket ein deutlicher Wille zur Harmonisierung zu erkennen, um frühzeitig rechtssichere Rahmenbedingungen für den Aufbau und Betrieb von Wasserstoffnetzen zu schaffen. Damit geht eine hohe Regelungsdichte einher, welche komplexe Anwendungsfragen aufwirft, bspw. hinsichtlich der entflechtungsrechtlichen Vorschriften. Hierbei sind die nationalen Gesetzgebenden in der Verantwortung, bei der jeweiligen Umsetzung in nationales Recht einen klaren Rahmen zu setzen.

---

191 Nach Art. 18 Abs. 1 Unterabs. 1 Buchst. a Gas- und Wasserstoffverordnung.

192 Nach Art. 18 Abs. 1 Unterabs. 2 Gas- und Wasserstoffverordnung.

193 Nach Art. 18 Abs. 5 Buchst. b Gas- und Wasserstoffverordnung.

194 Nach Art. 94 Abs. 1 Unterabs. 1 Satz 1 Gas- und Wasserstoffrichtlinie.

3.4 Regulierung der Wasserstoffnachfrage

Relevante Regelungen hinsichtlich der Wasserstoffnachfrage und des Endverbrauchs bestehen zum einen als Verbraucherrechte und zum anderen als eine Vielzahl an Zielvorgaben, welche u.a. Nachfrageanreize zu einer verstärkten Nutzung von Wasserstofftechnologien und insbesondere von erneuerbarem Wasserstoff setzen sollen. Letztere sind im Folgenden nur auszugsweise dargestellt und sollen die dahinterstehende Logik verdeutlichen.

Durch das Inkrafttreten der Gas- und Wasserstoffrichtlinie werden die Mitgliedsstaaten verpflichtet, dass sie bezüglich vertraglicher Verhältnisse zwischen Endabnehmenden und Versorgern sowohl die Wahrung grundlegender vertraglicher Rechte nach Art. 11 Gas- und Wasserstoffrichtlinie als auch das Recht auf Wechsel des Versorgers nach Art. 12 Gas- und Wasserstoffrichtlinie sicherstellen. Diese Vorschriften sind also ins jeweilige nationale Vertragsrecht umzusetzen.

Als ein entscheidender Sektor bei der Dekarbonisierung wurde vom europäischen Gesetzgeber die Industrie ausgemacht,[195] weswegen im Zuge der RED III eine Industrieunterquote zur Nutzung erneuerbaren Wasserstoffs festgelegt wurde. Danach müssen die Mitgliedsstaaten sicherstellen, dass in der Industrie bis spätestens 2030 mindestens 42% und bis 2035 60% des genutzten Wasserstoffs erneuerbar ist.[196] Außerdem führte die RED III sektorspezifische RFNBO-Ziele ein, welche von den Mitgliedsstaaten umzusetzen sind. So müssen diese bspw. Kraftstoffanbietende verpflichten, dafür zu sorgen, dass 2030 der RFNBO-Anteil an der Energieversorgung des Verkehrs mindestens 1% beträgt.

Bezüglich des Verkehrssektors besteht eine Vielzahl an Vorschriften in unterschiedlichen Verordnungen und Richtlinien, so bspw. in der FuelEU-Verordnung für den Seeverkehr und in der ReFuelEU-Verordnung für den Luftverkehr. Erstere legt einen Grenzwert für die Treibhausgasintensität der an Bord verbrauchten Energie fest.[197] Zusätzlich werden Zielvorgaben zur Verwendung von RFNBO formuliert.[198] Dies könnte Anreize zur Verwendung von E-Fuels zur Dekarbonisierung der Schifffahrt setzen, welche u.a. basierend auf erneuerbarem Wasserstoff hergestellt werden. In der ReFuelEU-Verordnung für den Luftverkehr werden Mindestverpflichtungen für alle Flugkraftstofflieferanten festgelegt, um den Anteil der an Flughäfen der Union verfügbaren nachhaltigen Flugkraftstoffe schrittweise zu erhö-

195 Vgl. ErwG 59 RED III.
196 Nach Art. 22a Abs. 1 Unterabs. 5 Satz 1 RED III.
197 Nach Art. 4 FuelEU-Verordnung für den Seeverkehr.
198 Nach Art. 5 FuelEU-Verordnung für den Seeverkehr.

hen.[199] Zur Erfüllung dieser Verpflichtung können explizit auch erneuerbarer Wasserstoff und kohlenstoffarme Flugkraftstoffe verwendet werden.[200] Auch hier könnte also der gesetzliche Rahmen zu einer gesteigerten Nachfrage beitragen.

Inwieweit diese und ähnliche Vorgaben in weiteren Sektoren tatsächlich zur Steigerung der Nachfrage sowie zum Markthochlauf beitragen, bleibt abzuwarten. Vieles hängt von der mitgliedsstaatlichen Umsetzung sowie der Klärung auftretender Anwendungsfragen ab. Mehrfach zeigte sich in diesem Kapitel bei der Schaffung eines rechtssicheren Rahmens der Balanceakt zwischen staatlichen Eingriffen zur Verwirklichung der politisch intendierten Marktentwicklung und der Wahrung des für den Binnenmarkt zentralen Wettbewerbsgedankens. Dabei wurde auch die Notwendigkeit von Regulierung zur Wahrung fairer Wettbewerbsbedingungen deutlich. Daran anschließend widmen sich die folgenden Kapitel der Frage, wie eine angebotsseitige Förderung des Markthochlaufs von erneuerbarem Wasserstoff im Sinne des Wettbewerbsgedanken zu bewerten ist. Dafür ist zunächst die Ausgestaltung dieser Förderung im Rahmen der Europäischen Wasserstoffbank zu betrachten.

4. Förderung des Markthochlaufs von erneuerbarem Wasserstoff

In Unterabschnitt 2.2.4 wurde hinsichtlich des Preises die fehlende Wettbewerbsfähigkeit von erneuerbarem Wasserstoff und dementsprechend das mangelnde Angebot deutlich, was aller bereits thematisierten politischen Ziele und Ambitionen[201] zum Trotz dem intendierten Markthochlauf entgegensteht. Darauffolgend stellte Kapitel 3 den europäischen Regelungswillen und dessen rechtliche Ausgestaltung dar, welche den Markthochlauf rahmt, sowie den Ansatz der Regulierung zur politisch gesteuerten Entwicklung des Marktes und insbesondere zur Wahrung wettbewerblicher Verhältnisse. Vor allem in Anbetracht des Ziels eines heimischen Produktionsvolumens von bis zu 10 Mt erneuerbaren Wasserstoffs im Jahr 2030[202] ergibt sich daraus die Frage, auf welche Art und Weise die Europäische Kommission das Angebot an erneuerbarem Wasserstoff fördert.

---

199 Nach Art. 4 Abs. 1 Unterabs. 1 Satz 1 iVm Anhang I ReFuelEU-Verordnung für den Luftverkehr.

200 Nach Art. 4 Abs. 1 Unterabs. 2 ReFuelEU-Verordnung für den Luftverkehr.

201 Siehe Abschn. 2.3.

202 Vgl. Europäische Kommission (2020d), S. 7.

Bei der Ausgestaltung der Förderung gibt es eine Vielzahl potenzieller Instrumente, Regelungen und Mechanismen, wie bereits das Recht der erneuerbaren Energien zeigt. So findet sich in Art. 2 Satz 2 Nr. 5 RED III eine nicht abschließende Auflistung verschiedener Instrumente zur Förderung der Nutzung von Energie aus erneuerbaren Quellen, indem die Kosten der Energie gesenkt, ihr Verkaufspreis erhöht oder ihre Absatzmenge gesteigert wird. Zu diesen Zwecken sind z. B. Investitionsbeihilfen, steuerliche Maßnahmen, Verpflichtungen zur Nutzung erneuerbarer Energiequellen und direkte Preisstützungssysteme vorgesehen. Letztere umfassen nach Art. 2 Satz 2 Nr. 5 RED III die Anwendung von Einspeisetarifen und Verträge über gleitende oder feste Prämien. Wie bereits einleitend erwähnt, entschied sich die Kommission zur Vergabe von festen Prämien, um die heimische Erzeugung von erneuerbarem Wasserstoff zu fördern.[203] Die Begründung der Wahl einer Output-basierten Förderung mittels der Zahlung fester Beträge pro Einheit wird in Unterabschnitt 4.1.2 näher erläutert und die konkrete Ausgestaltung der Finanzhilfevereinbarungen (engl.: Grant Agreements) wird in Unterabschnitt 4.3.2 dargestellt.

Zunächst stellt sich die Frage, auf Grundlage welcher Mechanismen die festen Prämien vergeben werden. Schon im Rahmen der RED II wurden Überlegungen angestellt, wie die wettbewerbsverzerrende Wirkung einer Förderregelung auf ein Mindestmaß reduziert werden kann, und in dem Zuge marktbasierte Mechanismen wie bspw. Ausschreibungsverfahren diskutiert.[204] Diesem Gedanken folgend und aufgrund des signifikanten Erfolgs solcher wettbewerblicher Mechanismen bei der Förderung erneuerbarer Energien in vielen Staaten des EWR wurde die Entscheidung getroffen, die festen Prämien in dem hier untersuchten Fall durch Auktionsverfahren im Rahmen der u. a. dafür gegründeten Europäischen Wasserstoffbank zu vergeben.[205]

4.1 Grundlagen des Fördermechanismus

4.1.1 Zielsetzung und Aufbau der Europäischen Wasserstoffbank

Als überliegende Ebene des Fördermechanismus ist im ersten Schritt die Europäische Wasserstoffbank hinsichtlich ihrer Zielsetzung und ihres Aufbaus zu betrachten. Dabei handelt es sich um ein von der Europäischen Kommis-

203 Siehe Abschn. 1.1.
204 Vgl. ErwG 16 u. 19 RED II.
205 GD Klimapolitik (o. D.-a), Abs. 4.

sion umgesetztes gebündeltes Förderinstrument,[206] welches erst seit 2023 etabliert wurde.[207] Mittels der Europäischen Wasserstoffbank soll auf die Schließung der hinsichtlich erneuerbarer Wasserstoffprojekte identifizierten Investitionslücke hingearbeitet sowie eine stärkere Verknüpfung zwischen dem ins Ziel genommenen künftigen Angebot und den bereits thematisierten Nachfragezielen[208] bezüglich erneuerbaren Wasserstoffs hergestellt werden.[209] Nur durch diese Verknüpfung einer geförderten Versorgung durch sowohl heimische Erzeugung als auch Importe mit der entstehenden Nachfrage der europäischen Endabnehmenden könne ein Markt für erneuerbaren Wasserstoff geschaffen und damit auch die zusätzlich nötigen privaten Investitionen entlang der gesamten Wertschöpfungskette mobilisiert werden.[210]

Zur Erreichung dieser Ziele sind in der Mitteilung über die Europäische Wasserstoffbank mögliche Tätigkeiten skizziert, welche auf vier Säulen fußen:[211] Die erste Säule soll mittels Auktionen im Rahmen des EU-Innovationsfonds der Schaffung eines heimischen Marktes für erneuerbaren Wasserstoff dienen. Da die Förderung im Sinne der ersten Säule der Untersuchungsgegenstand dieser Arbeit ist, sind die Auktionsverfahren nach einem grundlegenden Überblick zur Europäischen Wasserstoffbank näher zu beleuchten. Mit der zweiten Säule wird ein weiterer neuer Finanzierungsmechanismus eingeführt, um auch die internationale Erzeugung von erneuerbarem Wasserstoff zu fördern. Mittels Auktionen zu grünen Prämien für Wasserstoffeinfuhren soll somit ein Beitrag zur Erreichung des bereits erwähnten Importziels[212] geleistet werden. In der dritten Säule sammeln sich transparenzfördernde und koordinative Tätigkeiten, welche zur oben beschriebenen Verknüpfung von Angebot und Nachfrage sowie allgemein zum Markthochlauf beitragen sollen. Letztendlich betrifft die vierte Säule das Ausschöpfen bereits bestehender Finanzierungsinstrumente auf europäischer und internationaler Ebene.

Im Rahmen der ersten Säule wird die Zielsetzung der Europäischen Wasserstoffbank mit Blick auf die Auktionsverfahren noch konkretisiert:[213] So werden die hier bereits dargestellten Aspekte der Verknüpfung von Angebot

---

206 Vgl. Europäische Kommission (2023a), S. 3.
207 Siehe Europäische Kommission (2023a). Die Kommission informierte in ihrer entsprechenden Mitteilung vom 16. März 2023 über die Gründung der Europäischen Wasserstoffbank.
208 Siehe Unterabschn. 2.3.2 u. 2.3.3.
209 Vgl. Europäische Kommission (2023a), S. 2.
210 Vgl. Europäische Kommission (2023a), S. 6.
211 Vgl. Europäische Kommission (2023a), S. 7.
212 Siehe Abschn. 2.3.3.
213 Vgl. Europäische Kommission (2023a), S. 8.

und Nachfrage bezüglich erneuerbaren Wasserstoffs sowie der Mobilisierung von privatem Kapitel durch Leisten einer Startfinanzierung aus dem EU-Innovationsfonds als zwei zentrale Ziele unterstrichen. Insbesondere soll außerdem die bereits thematisierte Kostendifferenz[214] zwischen erneuerbarem und fossilem Wasserstoff überbrückt sowie verringert werden. Der Ansatz wettbewerbsorientierter Förderung durch Auktionen habe bereits im Bereich der Stromerzeugung aus erneuerbaren Quellen sehr erfolgreich zu solchen Kostensenkungen beigetragen. Letztendlich sollen durch ein einfaches und transparentes Auktionsdesign die Preisfindung und die Marktbildung angestoßen werden, indem private Kosten offengelegt und vergleichbare Preispunkte geschaffen werden.

Neben diesen Auktionen soll außerdem ein „Auctions-as-a-Service"-Mechanismus etabliert werden; interessierte Mitgliedsstaaten können nach Anmeldung die im Rahmen der Auktionen bereits etablierte Plattform nutzen, um zusätzliche Vorhaben zu identifizieren und nach Ausschöpfung der Mittel aus dem EU-Innovationsfonds mit nationalen Mitteln zu unterstützen.[215] Diese Arbeit beschränkt sich allerdings auf die Förderung nach dem grundlegenden Auktionsmechanismus, zumal „Auctions-as-a-Service" auf dessen Design aufbaut.

Insgesamt ist am Ende dieser grundlegenden Einführung zur Europäischen Wasserstoffbank wichtig zu beachten, dass diese keine neue Institution mit eigener Rechtsgrundlage darstellt, sondern es sich dabei, wie bereits erwähnt, um ein von der Kommission umgesetztes gebündeltes Förderinstrument handelt.[216] Also ist jeweils der rechtliche Rahmen der einzelnen Fördermechanismen zu beachten, im Folgenden somit die Rechtsgrundlagen der Förderung infolge von Auktionsverfahren.

4.1.2 Rechtlicher Rahmen

Der hier angewendete Fördermechanismus wurde im Rahmen der überarbeiteten Emissionshandelsrichtlinie eingeführt, welche CDs, CCDs und Verträge über feste Prämien als neue Förderinstrumente definiert.[217] Wie bereits einleitend in diesem Kapitel erwähnt, wird das Angebot an erneuerbarem Wasserstoff mittels Verträgen über feste Prämien gefördert.[218] Dabei handelt

214 Siehe Unterabschn. 2.2.4.
215 Vgl. Europäische Kommission (2023a), S. 10.
216 Vgl. Europäische Kommission (2023a), S. 3.
217 Nach Art. 3 Doppelbuchst. ab-ad Emissionshandelsrichtlinie.
218 Nach Kap. 2 Abschn. 2.1 Nr. 1.5 Terms and Conditions 2024.

es sich um einen Vertrag zwischen der Europäischen Kommission (hier: der Europäischen Exekutivagentur für Klima, Infrastruktur und Umwelt; kurz: CINEA)[219] und dem Erzeuger eines CO_2-armen oder CO_2-freien Produkts (hier: dem Erzeuger erneuerbaren Wasserstoffs), der im Rahmen eines Ausschreibungsmechanismus (hier: im Rahmen eines Auktionsverfahrens) ausgewählt wurde, und bei welchem dem Erzeuger gemäß dem Vertrag eine Unterstützung in Form eines festen Beitrags pro Einheit des hergestellten Produkts gewährt wird.[220]

So erfolgt auch im Falle der hier zu untersuchenden Förderung eine Output-basierte Unterstützung; es wird also ein Beitrag pro Einheit geprüften und als RFNBO zertifizierten[221] Wasserstoffs ausgezahlt.[222] Die Auszahlung von Beiträgen pro Einheit ist gem. Art. 125 Abs. 1 Unterabs. 1 Buchst. c Haushaltsordnung 2018[223] möglich, welche bezüglich der ersten Pilotauktion anzuwenden ist. Diese Beiträge werden im Falle direkter Mittelverwaltung[224] gem. Art. 181 Haushaltsordnung 2018[225] oder sektorspezifischer Vorschriften festgelegt. In dem Sinne ist vor der Festlegung eine Genehmigungsentscheidung nach Art. 181 Abs. 3 Haushaltsordnung 2018 erforderlich, welche der Maßgabe des nachfolgenden Abs. 4 unterliegt.[226]

Die erforderliche Genehmigung zur Anwendung von Beiträgen pro Einheit bei Auktionen im Rahmen des EU-Innovationsfonds, in deren Folge feste Prämien ausgezahlt werden, wurde mit dem entsprechenden Genehmigungsbeschluss erteilt.[227] Im zugehörigen Anhang wurde die Angemessenheit dieser Form der Output-basierten Förderung im Rahmen eines Auktionsverfahrens, bei dem Preis, Mengen und Begünstigte wettbewerblich

---

219 Nach Art. 5 Buchst. a iVm Art. 6 Abs. 1 Buchst. a Durchführungsbeschluss wurde der CINEA die (teilweise) Durchführung von Programmen im Rahmen des EU-Innovationsfonds übertragen.

220 Nach Art. 3 Doppelbuchst. ad Emissionshandelsrichtlinie.

221 Die Zertifizierung erfolgt im Rahmen des durch die Mitgliedsstaaten unter Umsetzung des Art. 9 Gas- und Wasserstoffrichtlinie eingeführten Zertifizierungssystems. Zur näheren Ausgestaltung siehe Abschn. 3.1.

222 Nach Kap. 2 Abschn. 2.1 Nr. 1.3 Terms and Conditions 2024.

223 Soweit nicht anderweitig spezifiziert, gab es keine Änderungen in der neuen Haushaltsordnung 2024, welche bezüglich des zweiten Auktionsverfahrens anzuwenden ist.

224 Sowohl die Pilotauktion als auch das zweite Auktionsverfahren unterliegen der direkten Mittelverwaltung durch die Kommission und die CINEA. Vgl. Anhang zum Finanzierungsbeschluss 2023, S. 6; Anhang zum Finanzierungsbeschluss 2024, S. 7.

225 Entsprechend Art. 184 Haushaltsordnung 2024.

226 Entsprechend Art. 184 Abs. 3 u. 4 Haushaltsordnung 2024.

227 Nach alleinigem Art. Genehmigungsbeschluss zur Anwendung von Beiträgen pro Einheit.

festgelegt werden, folgendermaßen begründet:[228] Beiträge pro Einheit seien besonders geeignet, da der geförderte Output (hier: die erzeugte Menge erneuerbaren Wasserstoffs) auf einfache Art und Weise gemessen, zertifiziert und überprüft werden könne. Außerdem würde dies unmittelbare Anreize für die Produktion schaffen, um zur Erreichung der bereits dargestellten Ziele[229] hinsichtlich des Markthochlaufs beizutragen. Der Markthochlauf würde auch dadurch unterstützt, dass die Förderung nur für hergestellte Einheiten ausgezahlt werde und somit eine zusätzliche Einnahmequelle in Verbindung mit der tatsächlichen Produktion biete.

4.1.3 Mittelherkunft

Als nächstes stellt sich bezüglich der Förderung die Frage nach der Mittelherkunft. Wie bereits verdeutlicht,[230] wird das Grant Agreement zwischen den Begünstigten und der CINEA geschlossen, welche für die Vergabe der festen Prämien infolge der durchgeführten Auktionsverfahren zuständig ist.[231] Dabei stammen die Mittel aus dem EU-Innovationsfonds, mittels welchem u.a. Projekte zur Förderung der Dekarbonisierungsziele durch preisorientierte Ausschreibungen unterstützt werden, die wie in diesem Fall zur Vergabe von Verträgen über feste Prämien führen.[232] Bei der Förderung infolge von Auktionsverfahren werden dann bis zu 100% der relevanten Projektkosten aus dem EU-Innovationsfonds finanziert.[233] Dieser wiederum ist gespeist aus den Einnahmen des EU-Emissionshandels bzw. aus der Versteigerung der Zertifikate, welche dem Fonds im Sinne des Art. 10a Abs. 8 Unterabs. 1 Emissionshandelsrichtlinie zugeteilt wurden.

Die Zuweisung der Mittel aus dem EU-Innovationsfonds hinsichtlich der durchzuführenden Auktionsverfahren erfolgt dann auf der Grundlage sogenannter Finanzierungsbeschlüsse. In dem Sinne bildete der Finanzierungsbeschluss 2023 (inkl. Anhang) die Grundlage für die Pilotauktion.[234] Darin wurde die Mittelbindung festgelegt[235] und er ist somit hinsichtlich der Mit-

---

228 Vgl. Genehmigungsbeschluss zur Anwendung von Beiträgen pro Einheit, S. 2.

229 Siehe Abschn. 2.3.

230 Siehe Unterabschn. 4.1.2.

231 Nach Kap. 2 Abschn. 2.5 Nr. 5.3 Terms and Conditions 2024.

232 Nach Art. 10a Abs. 8 Unterabs. 11 Emissionshandelsrichtlinie.

233 Nach Art. 10a Abs. 8 Unterabs. 17 Satz 6 Emissionshandelsrichtlinie.

234 Dieser Beschluss wurde unter Maßgabe des Art. 110 Haushaltsordnung 2018 am 22. November 2023 verabschiedet.

235 Nach Art. 1 Finanzierungsbeschluss 2023 iVm Anhang zum Finanzierungsbeschluss 2023.

telverwendung als Arbeitsprogramm bezüglich des EU-Innovationsfonds zu verstehen. Im Anhang[236] des Beschlusses sind die Grundzüge des Auktionsmechanismus dargestellt, welche im Rahmen der Einleitung des Verfahrens noch zu konkretisieren waren.[237] Diese konkrete Ausgestaltung wird im Abschnitt 4.2 dargestellt.

Für die erste Pilotauktion wurde somit aus dem EU-Innovationsfonds ein maximales Fördervolumen in Höhe von 800 Mio. EUR bereitgestellt.[238] Im Zuge des zweiten Auktionsverfahrens[239] wurde das maximale Fördervolumen auf 1 Mrd. EUR erhöht sowie in einem zweiten Topf zusätzliche 200 Mio. EUR für Projekte im maritimen Sektor bereitgestellt.[240] Dies kann nicht als die vom Bundesverband der Energie- und Wasserwirtschaft e.V. (BDEW) geforderte deutliche Erhöhung des Budgets bezeichnet werden, die in der Hochlaufphase des Wasserstoffmarktes nötig sei, damit eine möglichst große Anzahl an Projekten davon profitieren und zur Entwicklung des Marktes beitragen könne.[241] Auch Hydrogen Europe[242] sah das maximale Fördervolumen der Pilotauktion kritisch, auf dessen Grundlage nur sechs von 132 Projekten mit einem Gesamtproduktionsvolumen von jährlich knapp 152 kt erneuerbaren Wasserstoff subventioniert wurden.[243] Das ist weit entfernt von der ambitionierten Zielvorgabe in Höhe von 10 Mt heimischer Erzeugung bis 2030. Daher forderte Hydrogen Europe für das zweite Auktionsverfahren ein weit höheres Budget und flexiblere Regeln, um das aus ihrer Sicht durchaus vorhandene Potenzial (Projekt-Pipeline mit einem potenziellen Gesamtvolumen von bis zu 8,8 Mt bis 2030) auszunutzen.[244]

---

236 Siehe Kap. 2 Abschn. 2.2 Anhang zum Finanzierungsbeschluss 2023.

237 Nach Kap. 2 Abschn. 2.2 Abs. 6 Unterabs. 7 Anhang zum Finanzierungsbeschluss 2023.

238 Nach Art. 1 Finanzierungbeschluss 2023 iVm Kap. 2 Abschn. 2.2 Abs. 2 Anhang zum Finanzierungsbeschluss 2023.

239 Die Grundlage bildet der Finanzierungsbeschluss 2024 (inkl. Anhang), welcher unter Maßgabe des Art. 110 Haushaltsordnung 2024 am 25. November 2024 verabschiedet wurde.

240 Nach Kap. 2 Abschn. 2.1 Nr. 1.2 Terms and Conditions 2024.

241 Vgl. BDEW (2024), S. 3.

242 Die Position von Hydrogen Europe, der bereits in Unterabschn. 2.2.1 erwähnten Interessensvertretung der europäischen Wasserstoffwirtschaft, ist von außerordentlicher Relevanz, da diese im direkten Austausch mit vergangenen, gegenwärtigen und künftigen Auktionsteilnehmenden steht.

243 Vgl. Hydrogen Europe (2024), Nr. 1.2 Spalte 5 Abs. 2 u. 4. Aufgrund des in Unterabschn. 4.2.3 dargestellten Rückzugs eines Proposals waren die Angaben von Hydrogen Europe auf Grundlage von GD Klimapolitik (o. D.-b) anzupassen.

244 Vgl. Hydrogen Europe (2024), Nr. 1.2 Spalte 4 Abs. 1 u. Spalte 5 Abs. 3.

Auch die im Zuge des zweiten Auktionsverfahrens vorgenommene Unterteilung in mehrere Töpfe wird von Hydrogen Europe kritisiert, da somit erst recht bei einem relativ niedrigem Gesamtbudget die ökonomische Optimierung verhindert werde und zudem nach den Erfahrungen der Pilotauktion die meisten Projekte auf mehrere Abnehmende in verschiedenen Sektoren angewiesen seien.[245] Ein eigener Fördertopf mit Beschränkung auf den maritimen Sektor könne somit insbesondere unter Berücksichtigung des geringen Fördervolumens zu weniger kompetitiven Geboten führen.

4.2 Festlegung der Begünstigten, Mengen und Preise

Vor der Ausarbeitung und Unterzeichnung der Grant Agreements ist zunächst festzulegen, welche Begünstigten eine Förderung zur Produktion welcher Mengen erneuerbaren Wasserstoffs zu welchen Preisen[246] erhalten. In diesem Fall erfolgt die Festlegung durch Anwendung eines Auktionsmechanismus, welcher den generellen Regelungen der delegierten Innovationsfondsverordnung hinsichtlich der Durchführung von Ausschreibungsverfahren[247] unterliegt. Die folgenden Unterabschnitte stellen die Ausgestaltung des Auktionsmechanismus überwiegend anhand der bereits abgeschlossenen Pilotauktion dar, um die grundlegende Funktionsweise des Fördermechanismus zu verdeutlichen. Außerdem werden jeweils kurz relevante Änderungen am Fördermechanismus sowie der aktuelle Stand des zweiten Auktionsverfahrens hervorgehoben. Anschließend werden die Rechtsnatur der Grant Agreements sowie zentrale Punkte derer Ausgestaltung beleuchtet, bevor dann in Kapitel 5 die Förderung angesichts der primärrechtlichen Bedeutung des Wettbewerbsbegriffs bewertet wird.

4.2.1 Einleitung der Auktionsverfahren

Zentral für die Einleitung eines Auktionsverfahrens ist die Veröffentlichung der sogenannten Aufforderung zur Einreichung von Vorschlägen (engl.: Call for Proposal; kurz: Call), welche sich an potenzielle Begünstigte richtet und diese auffordert, einen Antrag zwecks Teilnahme am Auktionsverfahren

245 Vgl. Hydrogen Europe (2024), Nr. 1.2 Spalte 5 Abs. 5.

246 Der Preis bezeichnet hier die Höhe der festen Prämie in EUR pro kg erneuerbaren Wasserstoffs.

247 Im Sinne von Art. 2 Nr. 6 deleg. Innovationsfondsverordnung hier anzuwenden auf die Auktionsverfahren.

(engl. kurz: Proposal) einzureichen.[248] Zur Ermöglichung eines wirksamen Wettbewerbs ist das Design des Auktionsverfahrens rechtzeitig vor der Veröffentlichung des Calls bekanntzugeben.[249] Dies erfolgt durch die Veröffentlichung der „Terms and Conditions", welche später im Call wieder aufgegriffen werden.

In dem Sinne wurden am 29. August 2023 die „Terms and Conditions" der Pilotauktion veröffentlicht,[250] bevor der entsprechende Call[251] das Auktionsverfahren unter Management der CINEA am 23. November 2023 einleitete.[252] Der Call unterlag dabei den Vorschriften des Art. 13b Abs. 2 u. 3 deleg. Innovationsfondsverordnung und konkretisierte das im Anhang zum Finanzierungsbeschluss 2023 festgelegte Design des Auktionsverfahrens. Als Frist zur Einreichung der Proposals wurde der 08. Februar 2024 festgesetzt.[253]

Unter Anwendung derselben Vorschriften wurde nach Bekanntgabe der „Terms and Conditions" am 27. September 2024[254] das zweite Auktionsverfahren durch den entsprechenden Call[255] am 03. Dezember 2024[256] eingeleitet, welcher das im Anhang zum Finanzierungsbeschluss 2024 festgelegte Auktionsdesign konkretisierte. Daraufhin konnten bis zum Fristende am 20. Februar 2025 Proposals eingereicht werden.[257]

4.2.2 Prüfung der Proposals auf Zulässigkeit und Förderfähigkeit

Im weiteren Auktionsverfahren waren nur die Proposals zu berücksichtigen, welche die im Einklang mit Art. 13c deleg. Innovationsfondsverordnung festgelegten Qualifikationsanforderungen erfüllen.[258] Mit diesen sollte zum einen im Sinne des Art. 13c Abs. 2 deleg. Innovationsfondsverordnung sichergestellt werden, dass die potenziellen Begünstigten das von ihnen vorge-

---

248 Nach Art. 13b Abs. 1 deleg. Innovationsfondsverordnung.
249 Nach Art. 13a Abs. 4 deleg. Innovationsfondsverordnung.
250 Siehe S. 1 Terms and Conditions 2023.
251 Ermöglicht wurde der Call durch Verabschiedung des Art. 1 Finanzierungsbeschluss 2023 iVm Kap. 2 Abschn. 2.2 Anhang zum Finanzierungsbeschluss 2023.
252 Nach Kap. 0 Abs. 3 u. Kap. 4 Zeile 1 Call 2023.
253 Nach Kap. 4 Zeile 2 Call 2023.
254 Vgl. GD Klimapolitik (2024a), Abs. 1.
255 Ermöglicht wurde der Call durch Verabschiedung des Art. 1 Finanzierungsbeschluss 2024 iVm Kap. 2 Abschn. 2.3 Anhang zum Finanzierungsbeschluss 2024.
256 Nach Kap. 4 Zeile 1 Call 2024.
257 Nach Kap. 4 Zeile 2 Call 2024.
258 Nach Art. 13c Abs. 1 deleg. Innovationsfondsverordnung.

schlagene Projekt tatsächlich umsetzen können, und zum anderen das Risiko von Geboten mit spekulativem Charakter[259] möglichst gering gehalten werden.[260] Die Anforderungen waren dabei auf ein erforderliches Maß zu beschränken, sodass die bereits beschriebenen Ziele des Auktionsverfahrens[261] erreicht werden sowie zugleich ein Höchstmaß an Wettbewerb und Qualität der eingereichten Proposals gewährleistet ist.[262] Insgesamt wurden im Call-Dokument Qualifikationsanforderungen in den beiden Bereichen „Zulässigkeit" und „Förderfähigkeit" sowie als Gewährungskriterien[263] im Bereich „Relevanz und Qualität" festgelegt. Die Gewährungskriterien fanden allerdings erst Anwendung infolge des in Unterabschnitt 4.2.3 dargestellten Einstufungsverfahrens. Somit sind hier lediglich die Anforderungen hinsichtlich der Zulässigkeit und der Förderfähigkeit zu betrachten.

Die Zulässigkeit umfasste eine Vielzahl formaler Anforderungen inkl. einzureichender Dokumente; insbesondere waren die zentralen Bestandteile des Gebots anzugeben:[264] Diese waren erstens der Gebotspreis in EUR pro kg erneuerbaren Wasserstoffs, zweitens das erwartete durchschnittliche Jahresproduktionsvolumen in kg pro Jahr über eine Zeitspanne von zehn Jahren und drittens die Elektrolyseurkapazität in MW, welche zum Zeitpunkt des Produktionsstarts als installiert und betriebsbereit zu verifizieren ist.

Hinsichtlich der Förderfähigkeit wurden zahlreiche weitere Anforderungen festgelegt, wovon im Folgenden die zentralen Aspekte dargestellt sind:[265] Eingereichte Proposals mussten Projekte innerhalb des EWR betreffen, wobei die Herkunft der Projekttragenden keiner geografischen Beschränkung unterlag, und die gesamte Elektrolyseurkapazität an einem Standort errichtet werden. Weiter durfte die auf Grundlage des Gebots zu gewährende Förderung maximal ein Drittel des verfügbaren Budgets (insgesamt: 800 Mio. EUR) betragen und der eingereichte Projektvorschlag musste mindestens 5 MW neu zu installierende Elektrolyseurkapazität umfassen.[266] Außerdem durften die Gebote den bezüglich der zu zahlenden festen Prämie festgelegten Höchstpreis[267] in Höhe von 4,50 EUR pro kg hergestellten Was-

259 Nach Art. 13a Abs. 2 deleg. Innovationsfondsverordnung.
260 Nach Kap. 2 Abschn. 2.2 Abs. 2 Terms and Conditions 2023.
261 Siehe Unterabschn. 4.1.1.
262 Nach Art. 13c Abs. 3 deleg. Innovationsfondsverordnung.
263 Im Sinne des Art. 11 deleg. Innovationsfondsverordnung.
264 Nach Kap. 3 Abs. 2 Terms and Conditions 2023.
265 Nach Kap. 3 Abs. 3 Terms and Conditions 2023.
266 Nach Kap. 3 Abs. 3 iVm Kap. 2 Abschn. 2.2 Nr. 2.3 Terms and Conditions 2023.
267 Nach Kap. 2 Abschn. 2.3 Nr. 3.6 Terms and Conditions 2024 wurde für das zweite Auktionsverfahren ein Höchstpreis in Höhe von 4 EUR pro kg erzeugten Wasserstoffs festgelegt.

serstoffs nicht überschreiten.[268] Letztendlich waren mehrere Selbstauskünfte einzureichen, welche u.a. darlegen, dass die beabsichtigte Wasserstoffproduktion den bereits erläuterten RFNBO- Kriterien[269] für erneuerbaren Wasserstoff entspricht, es sich bei der im Gebot angegebenen Kapazität tatsächlich um neue Kapazität (d.h. die Installationsarbeiten haben zum Zeitpunkt der Einreichung des Proposals noch nicht begonnen) handelt, keine Gefahr der Quersubventionierung von fossilem Wasserstoff besteht und die Vorschriften[270] über die Kumulierung von Förderung im Rahmen des Auktionsverfahrens mit anderer öffentlicher Förderung eingehalten werden.[271]

Unter Anwendung des Auswahlverfahrens für einstufige Antragsverfahren gem. Art. 12a deleg. Innovationsfondsverordnung wurden die eingereichten Proposals dann durch die CINEA hinsichtlich ihrer Zulässigkeit sowie Förderfähigkeit geprüft und die Anforderungen jeweils als erfüllt oder nicht erfüllt beurteilt.[272] Infolge dieser Prüfung wurden lediglich 13 der insgesamt 130 eingereichten Proposals wegen Nichterfüllung entsprechender Kriterien auf Grundlage des Art. 13c Abs. 1 deleg. Innovationsfondsverordnung vom anschließenden Einstufungsverfahren ausgeschlossen.[273]

Hinsichtlich des zweiten Auktionsverfahrens wurden ein paar Anpassungen an den Förderfähigkeitskriterien vorgenommen. Entgegen der von Hydrogen Europe geäußerten Kritik wurde die Beschränkung der maximalen Fördersumme je Proposal leicht verschärft und beträgt 250 Mio. EUR im Falle des allgemeinen Fördertopfs[274] sowie 200 Mio. EUR im Falle des maritimen Sektors.[275] Diese Beschränkung habe bereits bei der Pilotauktion die Teilnahme der größten Projekte verhindert, welche in der Theorie hinsichtlich der Kosten die größte Wettbewerbsfähigkeit aufweisen würden.[276] Aus Sicht des BDEW seien außerdem klarere Vorgaben und flexiblere Regelungen hinsichtlich der Kumulierung mit nationalen Fördermaßnahmen erforderlich, um eine Förderung über verschiedene Instrumente zu ermöglichen und

---

268 Nach Kap. 3 Abs. 3 iVm Kap. 2 Abschn. 2.3 Nr. 3.7 Terms and Conditions 2023.

269 Siehe Abschn. 3.2.

270 Siehe Kap. 4 Terms and Conditions 2023.

271 Nach Kap. 3 Abs. 3 Terms and Conditions 2023.

272 Nach Kap. 2 Abschn. 2.2 Abs. 3 u. Nr. 2.1 Terms and Conditions 2023.

273 Vgl. GD Klimapolitik (o.D.-d), Folie 2. Die Gesamtzahl der eingereichten Proposals betrug eigentlich 132, allerdings wurden davon zwei Proposals im Vorhinein aus anderen Gründen vom Auktionsverfahren ausgeschlossen und daher in den veröffentlichten Daten nicht weiter berücksichtigt.

274 Bei der Pilotauktion betrug diese ein Drittel des verfügbaren Budgets in Höhe von 800 Mio. EUR, also knapp 267 Mio. EUR.

275 Nach Kap. 2 Abschn. 2.2 Nr. 2.3 Terms and Conditions 2024.

276 Vgl. Hydrogen Europe (2024), Nr. 1.2 Spalte 5 Abs. 3.

trotzdem zugleich eine Überkompensation zu vermeiden.[277] Dahinter steckt der Gedanke, verstärkte Anreize für die Teilnahme von Projekten zu setzen, die ansonsten aufgrund der nationalen Gegebenheiten preislich wenig kompetitiv wären. Die CINEA formulierte im Zuge der Anpassungen zwar klarere Regeln zur Kumulierung mit anderen Fördermaßnahmen, allerdings ohne die Einführung von mehr Flexibilität oder anderer inhaltlicher Änderungen.[278]

Im Rahmen des zweiten Auktionsverfahrens wurde unverändert das Auswahlverfahren für einstufige Antragsverfahren[279] angewendet und die eingereichten Proposals hinsichtlich ihrer Zulässigkeit und Förderfähigkeit geprüft.[280] Infolge dieser Prüfung wurden hinsichtlich des allgemeinen Fördertopfs 11 von 53 Proposals und hinsichtlich des maritimen Sektors 3 von 8 Proposals wegen Nichterfüllung entsprechender Kriterien auf Grundlage des Art. 13c Abs. 1 deleg. Innovationsfondsverordnung vom folgenden Einstufungsverfahren ausgeschlossen.[281]

4.2.3 Einstufungsverfahren und finale Auswahl

Als nächstes erfolgte dann im Rahmen der Pilotauktion die Einstufung der übrigen 117 Proposals unter Anwendung eines Kaskadenansatzes.[282] Als alleiniges Einstufungskriterium wurde im Sinne des Art. 13d Abs. 1 deleg. Innovationsfondsverordnung der Gebotspreis festgelegt und somit keine zusätzlichen Kriterien gem. Abs. 2 angewandt.[283] Also wurde eine Rangfolge vom niedrigsten bis zum höchsten Gebotspreis gebildet,[284] wobei der Gebotspreis in EUR pro kg der auszuzahlenden festen Prämie entspricht, welche jeweils aus Sicht der potenziell Begünstigten zur Förderung des Angebots an erneuerbarem Wasserstoff nötig ist.[285] Für den Fall, dass Proposals mit demselben Gebotspreis vorliegen, wurden zudem Tiebreaker-Vorschriften festgelegt, um diese nach Priorität einzustufen.[286]

277 Vgl. BDEW (2024), S. 4.
278 Nach Kap. 2 Abschn. 2.2 Nr. 2.8 Terms and Conditions 2024.
279 Nach Art. 12a deleg. Innovationsfondsverordnung.
280 Nach Kap. 2 Abschn. 2.2 Abs. 1 u. Nr. 2.1 Terms and Conditions 2024.
281 Vgl. GD Klimapolitik (o. D.-c), Folien 2–4.
282 Nach Kap. 8 Abs. 3 Call 2023.
283 Nach Kap. 2 Abschn. 2.1 Nr. 1.7 Terms and Conditions 2023.
284 Nach Kap. 8 Abs. 3 Unterabs. 1 Call 2023.
285 Nach Kap. 2 Abschn. 2.1 Nr. 1.8 Abs. 1 Terms and Conditions 2023.
286 Nach Kap. 2 Abschn. 2.3 Nr. 3.9 Terms and Conditions 2023.

Als nächstes wurden entlang der Rangfolge die Fördersummen der Proposals[287] aufaddiert, bis das maximale Fördervolumen erreicht war, und nur diese Proposals anhand der festgelegten Gewährungskriterien „Relevanz und Qualität“ geprüft.[288] Durch die Festlegung eines maximalen Fördervolumens als begrenzender Faktor sollte Übersubventionierung vermieden werden; zusätzlich soll die Aufrechterhaltung wettbewerblicher Bedingungen durch Beobachtung der Marktentwicklung und einem Feedbackmechanismus zum Grad des Wettbewerbs von einer Auktion zur nächsten sichergestellt werden.[289]

Alle übrigen Proposals wurden abgelehnt und nicht auf Erfüllung der Gewährungskriterien geprüft.[290] Die Gewährungskriterien sollten sicherstellen, dass mit den eingereichten Projekten tatsächlich ein Beitrag im Sinne der Ziele des Auktionsverfahrens und auch der überliegenden Dekarbonisierungsziele geleistet werden kann:[291] So musste u. a. eine glaubwürdige Strategie zum Bezug von Strom aus erneuerbaren Quellen vorgelegt werden, mit dem die im Proposal angegebene Menge erneuerbarer Wasserstoff produziert werden kann. Außerdem war eine Strategie hinsichtlich der Wasserstoffabnahme zu erstellen; also es musste anhand zu erwartender Endabnehmender dargelegt werden, dass eine dem zu fördernden Angebot entsprechende Nachfrage bestehen wird. Weitere Dokumente sollten den Fortschritt bezüglich einzuholender Genehmigungen sowie die technische, finanzielle und operationelle Reife des Projekts belegen, um innerhalb von fünf Jahren nach Unterzeichnung des Grant Agreements in Betrieb zu gehen.[292]

Im Rahmen des Einstufungsverfahrens wurden letztendlich sieben Proposals mit einem Fördervolumen von insgesamt knapp 720 Mio. EUR ausgewählt, wobei der Gebotspreis bezüglich der zu erhaltenden festen Prämie zwischen 0,37 und 0,48 EUR pro kg erneuerbaren Wasserstoffs lag.[293] Das sogenannte „marginale Gebot“, welches das maximale Fördervolumen in

---

287 Die Fördersumme der Proposals wurde dafür jeweils anhand der Gebotskomponenten berechnet: [Gebotspreis in EUR/kg] * [erwartetes durchschnittliches Jahresproduktionsvolumen in kg/Jahr] * 10 Jahre; nach Kap. 2 Abschn. 2.1 Nr. 1.8 Abs. 2 Unterabs. 2 Terms and Conditions 2023.

288 Nach Kap. 8 Abs. 3 Unterabs. 2 Call 2023.

289 Nach Kap. 2 Abschn. 2.1 Nr. 1.2 u. 1.6 Terms and Conditions 2023.

290 Nach Kap. 8 Abs. 3 Unterabs. 3 Call 2023.

291 Nach Kap. 3 Abs. 4 Terms and Conditions 2023.

292 Nach Kap. 2 Abschn. 2.4 Nr. 4.1 Abs. 1 Terms and Conditions 2024 muss im Rahmen des zweiten Auktionsverfahrens zusätzlich innerhalb von zweieinhalb Jahren nach Unterzeichnung des Grant Agreements die Finanzierung des Projekts abschließend geklärt sein, was zu belegen ist.

293 Siehe GD Klimapolitik (o. D.-d), Folie 3.

Höhe von 800 Mio. EUR überschritt, wurde den im Call festgelegten Regeln folgend abgewiesen und das Gesamtvolumen der Auktion dementsprechend reduziert.[294] Insgesamt wurde die ausgeschriebene Fördersumme durch die eingereichten Proposals um das Fünfzehnfache übertroffen, wobei sich eine kontinuierlich bis zum festgelegten Höchstpreis ansteigende Gebotskurve ergab.[295]

Am 30. April 2024 wurde dieses Ergebnis offiziell verkündet und bezüglich der sieben ausgewählten Proposals startete die Vorbereitung der individuellen Grant Agreements,[296] wobei im Sinne des Calls letzte Feinabstimmungen im Dialog zwischen den Projektträgern und der CINEA vorgenommen werden sollten.[297] Im Ergebnis der Dialoge wurde ein Proposal zurückgezogen, sodass letztendlich am 07. Oktober 2024 die Unterzeichnung von sechs Grant Agreements über ein Fördervolumen von insgesamt knapp 695 Mio. EUR verkündet wurde.[298]

Im Rahmen des zweiten Auktionsverfahrens wurde die bereits dargestellte Zielsetzung[299] erweitert und schließt nun einen Beitrag zur Führungsrolle und Wettbewerbsfähigkeit Europas im Wasserstoffsektor sowie die Förderung der Versorgungssicherheit ein.[300] Aus diesem Grund wurde im Bereich „Relevanz“ bezüglich der Resilienz ein weiteres Gewährungskriterium eingeführt, welches insbesondere die Diversifizierung der Lieferketten hinsichtlich der Beschaffung und Produktion der benötigten Elektrolyseure betrifft.[301] Die Einführung eines solchen Kriteriums wurde von Hydrogen Europe zwar als prinzipiell sinnvoll erachtet,[302] erhöht allerdings wiederum die Anzahl der einzureichenden Dokumente und den damit verbundenen organisatorischen Aufwand. So forderte der BDEW im Nachgang der Pilotauktion eine Beschränkung der Anforderungen des Calls auf weniger und genau definierte Unterlagen, um den Aufwand für die potenziellen Begünstigten bei der Antragstellung zu reduzieren.[303] Vereinfachungen der Antragstellung sind im Call 2024 jedoch nicht ersichtlich.

Ansonsten wurde das oben beschriebene Einstufungsverfahren ebenso beim zweiten Auktionsverfahren angewendet. Dies resultierte in der Aus-

294 Vgl. GD Klimapolitik (o. D.-d), Folie 3; auf Grundlage von: Kap. 8 Abs. 5 Call 2023.
295 Vgl. GD Klimapolitik (o. D.-d), Folie 4.
296 Vgl. Europäische Kommission (2024a), Abs. 5.
297 Nach Kap. 8 Abs. 6 Unterabs. 3 Call 2023.
298 Vgl. GD Klimapolitik (2024b), Abs. 9 u. 10.
299 Siehe Unterabschn. 4.1.1.
300 Nach Kap. 2 Abschn. 2.1 Nr. 1.0 Terms and Conditions 2024.
301 Nach Kap. 2 Abschn. 2.1 Nr. 1.15 Terms and Conditions 2024.
302 Vgl. Hydrogen Europe (2024), Nr. 1.15 Spalte 4 Abs. 4.
303 Vgl. BDEW (2024), S. 5.

wahl von zwölf Proposals (allgemeiner Topf) mit einem Fördervolumen von insgesamt knapp über 895 Mio. EUR, wobei der Gebotspreis bezüglich der zu erhaltenden festen Prämie zwischen 0,20 und 0,60 EUR pro kg erneuerbaren Wasserstoffs lag.[304] Zusätzlich wurden hinsichtlich des Fördertopfs für den maritimen Sektor drei Proposals mit einem Fördervolumen von insgesamt knapp 97 Mio. EUR ausgewählt, wobei der Gebotspreis von 0,45 bis 1,88 EUR pro kg reichte.[305] Das verbliebene Budget in Höhe von ca. 208 Mio. EUR wird wieder dem EU-Innovationsfonds zugeführt und die Unterzeichnung der Grant Agreements ist für den Zeitraum September bis November 2025 vorgesehen.[306]

4.3 Vertragliche Umsetzung der Förderung (Grant Agreements)

4.3.1 Rechtsnatur

Vor der Betrachtung der vertraglichen Ausgestaltung stellt sich zunächst die Frage nach der Rechtsnatur der Grant Agreements, also ob es sich dabei um privatrechtliche oder öffentlich- rechtliche Verträge handelt. Die Abgrenzung wird dabei im Sinne der deutschen Rechtsprechung anhand des Vertragsgegenstandes vorgenommen.[307] Bei einem öffentlich-rechtlichen Vertrag müsste der Vertragsgegenstand somit dem öffentlichen Recht zuzuordnen sein.

Zuvor ist allerdings zu klären, inwieweit ein vertragliches Verwaltungshandeln der EU-Organe bzw. ihrer Vertretungen (hier: der CINEA) in Form eines öffentlich-rechtlichen Vertrages überhaupt vorgesehen ist. Im Primärrecht, insbesondere im zentralen Art. 288 AEUV, findet das vertragliche Verwaltungshandeln keine explizite Erwähnung. Allerdings weist *Stelkens* berechtigterweise darauf hin, dass die Bestimmungen des Art. 272 AEUV[308] und des Art. 340 Abs. 1 AEUV[309] diese Möglichkeit voraussetzen.[310] Zudem finden sich Regelungen zum vertraglichen Handeln im Sekundärrecht, so bspw. hinsichtlich der Gewährung von EU-Finanzhilfen mittels entsprechender

---

304 Vgl. GD Klimapolitik (o. D.-c), Folie 5.

305 Vgl. GD Klimapolitik (o. D.-c), Folie 6.

306 Vgl. GD Klimapolitik (o. D.-c), Folien 5 f.

307 Vgl. Huck, in: Huck/Müller, VwVfG § 54 Rn. 1.

308 Art. 272 AEUV betrifft die Zuständigkeit des EuGH bei Entscheidungen aufgrund einer Schiedsklausel, welche in einem von der Union oder für ihre Rechnung abgeschlossenen öffentlich-rechtlichen oder privatrechtlichen Vertrag enthalten ist.

309 Art. 340 Abs. 1 AEUV betrifft die vertragliche Haftung der Union.

310 Vgl. Stelkens, in: Stelkens/Bonk/Sachs, VwVfG § 54 Rn. 173.

Verträge.[311] In diesem Zusammenhang verweist Stelkens auf Muster-Finanzhilfevereinbarungen (engl.: Model Grant Agreements) der Kommission, welche für verschiedene Förderinstrumente erarbeitet werden.[312] Dabei ist die Rechtsnatur dieser Verträge jedoch nicht konkretisiert, wobei insbesondere im Bereich der EU-Finanzhilfen öffentlich-rechtliche Verträge Anwendung finden.[313] Hinsichtlich öffentlich-rechtlicher Verträge wird in der Rechtsliteratur eine Abgrenzung zwischen völkerrechtlichen Verträgen und Verwaltungsverträgen vorgenommen, welche im Zuge der Umsetzung einer Unionspolitik geschlossen werden und z.B. die Forschungsförderung oder die Vergabe von Finanzhilfen betreffen.[314] Den Verwaltungsvertrag definiert *Karpenstein* dabei als einen Vertrag, welcher zwischen der Union oder einem für ihre Rechnung tätigen Organ und einer natürlichen oder juristischen Person auf dem Gebiet des öffentlichen Rechts geschlossen wird.[315] Wie bereits einleitend erwähnt, ist also die Natur des Vertragsgegenstandes entscheidend.

Folglich ist zu prüfen, ob der Vertragsgegenstand der hier zu untersuchenden Grant Agreements dem öffentlichen Recht zuzuordnen ist. Mit dieser Frage wurde sich bereits bezüglich der Forschungsförderung befasst, und zwar hinsichtlich der Rechtsnatur von Verträgen, welche im Rahmen von indirekten Maßnahmen zur Umsetzung des mehrjährigen Forschungsrahmenprogramms nach Art. 183 AEUV mit den Teilnehmenden geschlossen werden. Diese Verträge werden nach *Eikenberg* vorwiegend als dem öffentlichen Recht zugehörige Verwaltungsverträge eingestuft, da die Kommission als juristische Person des öffentlichen Rechts zur Umsetzung der im Primärrecht festgelegten Förderziele[316] handelt.[317] *Eikenberg* führt zu Recht weiter aus, dass die Verträge vorrangig auf die Zuwendung von Fördermitteln im Sinne der Förderziele und nicht auf einen Leistungsaustausch abzielen. Dabei lägen diese Förderziele, welche sich in den Finanzhilfevereinbarungen konkretisieren, zudem im öffentlichen Interesse.

---

311 Nach Art. 204 Abs. 1 Haushaltsordnung 2024 unterliegen Finanzhilfen einer schriftlichen Vereinbarung, welche mindestens die in Abs. 2 genannten Angaben enthält.

312 Vgl. Stelkens, in: Stelkens/Bonk/Sachs, VwVfG § 54 Rn. 173. Ein solches Model Grant Agreement wird bezüglich der Gewährung fester Prämien in diesem Abschnitt betrachtet.

313 Vgl. Athanasiadou (2016), S. 121–123.

314 Vgl. Ehricke, in: Streinz, AEUV Art. 272 Rn. 6; Karpenstein, in: Grabitz/Hilf/Nettesheim, AEUV Art. 272 Rn. 17.

315 Vgl. Karpenstein, in: Grabitz/Hilf/Nettesheim, AEUV Art. 272 Rn. 17.

316 Nach Art. 179 Abs. 1 AEUV sind dies u.a. die Stärkung der wissenschaftlichen und technologischen Grundlagen der Union sowie die Förderung ihrer Wettbewerbsfähigkeit einschließlich ihrer Industrie.

317 Vgl. Eikenberg, in: Grabitz/Hilf/Nettesheim, AEUV Art. 183 Rn. 33.

Fraglich ist also, ob sich diese Argumentation auf die hier zu untersuchenden Verträge über feste Prämien anwenden lässt. Wie bereits erwähnt,[318] werden die Grant Agreements zwischen den Begünstigten und der CINEA geschlossen, welche als Exekutivagentur im Auftrag der Kommission tätig wird. Dabei handelt es sich ebenso um eine juristische Person des öffentlichen Rechts, welche im Sinne der Förderziele[319] agiert. Diese sind nicht konkret im Primärrecht verankert, leiten sich aber daraus ab. Die Auktionen der Europäischen Wasserstoffbank sind auf die Förderung des Markthochlaufs von erneuerbarem Wasserstoff gerichtet.[320] Dadurch soll u. a. ein Beitrag zur Wettbewerbsfähigkeit Europas[321] im Sinne von Art. 173 AEUV sowie zum Erreichen der bereits erwähnten Dekarbonisierungsziele[322] geleistet werden. Diese stehen in direkter Verbindung mit der Bekämpfung des Klimawandels nach Art. 191 Abs. 1 Nr. 4 AEUV. Somit betreffen die Förderziele ohne Zweifel das öffentliche Interesse. Zudem steht bei den Grant Agreements die Vergabe von festen Prämien im Vordergrund, um die Kostendifferenz[323] zur fossilen Wasserstofferzeugung zu überbrücken, und nicht der Leistungsaustausch. Zwar erhalten die Begünstigten im Rahmen des Vertrags von der CINEA Zahlungen pro hergestellter Einheit erneuerbaren Wasserstoffs,[324] aber dabei überwiegt die Anreizwirkung zur Marktentwicklung einem möglichen Auftragscharakter. Folglich ist der Vertragsgegenstand dem öffentlichen Recht zuzuordnen und es handelt sich bei den Grant Agreements um öffentlich-rechtliche Verträge. Dafür spricht außerdem die Bezugnahme auf verwaltungsrechtliche Sanktionen im Model Grant Agreement,[325] dessen Ausgestaltung im folgenden Unterabschnitt zu betrachten ist.

4.3.2 Ausgestaltung

Bei der Betrachtung der vertraglichen Ausgestaltung wird hier Bezug auf das für die Pilotauktion vorgesehene Model Grant Agreement genommen, da auf dessen Grundlage im Jahr 2024 bereits die finalen Grant Agreements unterzeichnet wurden.[326] Im Grant Agreement war jeweils zwischen den Vertrags-

318 Siehe Unterabschn. 4.1.2.
319 Siehe Unterabschn. 4.1.1.
320 Siehe Unterabschn. 4.1.1.
321 Siehe Unterabschn. 4.2.3.
322 Siehe Abschn. 2.3.
323 Siehe Unterabschn. 2.2.4.
324 Siehe Unterabschn. 4.3.2 zur Logik des Zahlungsmechanismus.
325 Siehe Art. 43 Abs. 2 Unterabs. 4 MGA 2023.
326 Siehe Unterabschn. 4.2.3.

partner:innen (hier: zwischen der CINEA und den Begünstigten) der vertragliche Rahmen für die Vergabe der festen Prämien festzulegen, insbesondere auch hinsichtlich der Meilensteine und Liefergegenstände, der Berichterstattung sowie der Modalitäten der Auszahlungen.[327]

Als Startdatum des Projekts war ausgehend von der Unterzeichnung der erste Tag des folgenden Monats festzulegen, also hier der 01. November 2024.[328] Außerdem wurde anhand der Vorgaben des Calls individuell die Projektlaufzeit bestimmt. So muss spätestens fünf Jahre nach Unterzeichnung des Grant Agreements mit der Produktion begonnen werden und diese im Regelfall[329] über zehn Jahre die vereinbarte Menge erneuerbaren Wasserstoff bereitstellen, wodurch sich bis zur letzten Zahlung eine Laufzeit zwischen zehn und fünfzehn Jahren ergibt.[330] Die Vertragslaufzeit umfasst insgesamt 21 Arbeitspakete mit jeweils verpflichtenden Meilensteinen und Liefergegenständen:[331] Das erste Arbeitspaket betrifft die Zeit bis zur Inbetriebnahme der Produktion und endet mit der nachgewiesenen Inbetriebnahme der im Proposal angegebenen Kapazitäten. Bereits drei Monate zuvor ist dabei die Betriebsbereitschaft zu belegen. Die folgenden 20 Arbeitspakete umfassen jeweils halbjährlich nachzukommenden Berichtspflichten, insbesondere der jeweilige Bericht über die geprüfte und zertifizierte Produktion. Dieser soll belegen, dass im vergangenen Halbjahr die vereinbarte Menge Wasserstoff produziert und dieser den RFNBO-Kriterien[332] entsprechend zertifiziert wurde.

Anhand der somit nachgewiesenen Produktionsmengen soll dann die Auszahlung der Finanzhilfe erfolgen, welche auf Basis der im Gebot festgelegten festen Prämie (in EUR pro kg erneuerbaren Wasserstoff) zu berechnen ist.[333] Der detaillierte Berichts- und Zahlungsplan war im Grant Agreement festzulegen.[334] Entscheidend dabei ist, dass die Finanzhilfe somit keine Vorfinanzierungskomponente enthält, sondern erst nach Start der Produktion halbjährlich auf Grundlage des tatsächlichen Produktionsvolumens ausgezahlt wird.[335] Sollten Beiträge der Begünstigten, also erzeugte Einheiten Wasserstoff, insbesondere nach Prüfung gem. Art. 25 MGA 2023 als nicht-förderfähig im Sinne von Art. 6 Abs. 3 MGA 2023 gewertet werden, sind diese unter

327 Nach Kap. 10 Call 2023.
328 Nach Art. 4 iVm Data Sheet Abs. 1 MGA 2023.
329 Nach Kap. 2 Abschn. 2.1 Nr. 1.10 Terms and Conditions 2023 sind auf Grundlage der festgelegten Produk- tionsflexibilitätsregeln Abweichungen möglich.
330 Nach Kap. 6 Abs. 5 Call 2023.
331 Nach Kap. 10 Abs. 5 Call 2023.
332 Siehe Abschn. 3.2.
333 Nach Kap. 10 Abs. 7 Unterabs. 3 Call 2023.
334 Nach Art. 21 u. 22 iVm Data Sheet Abs. 4 Unterabs. 2 MGA 2023.
335 Nach Abs. 8 Unterabs. 2 u. 3 Call 2023.

Maßgabe des Art. 27 MGA 2023 zurückzuweisen.[336] Als nicht-förderfähige Beiträge gelten Einheiten, welche nicht den Vorgaben des Art. 6 Abs. 1 u. 2 MGA 2023[337] entsprechen, welche von einer Aussetzung des Grant Agreements im Sinne von Art. 31 MGA 2023 betroffen sind oder welche zu einer anderweitig geförderten Aktivität beitragen, sofern sie keinen Ausnahmetatbestand erfüllen.[338] Im Sinne des Art. 27 MGA 2023 zurückgewiesene Beiträge werden vom durch die Begünstigten erklärten Produktionsvolumen abgezogen und die durch die CINEA zu zahlende Fördersumme dementsprechend angepasst; sofern die Zahlung bereits zuvor erfolgt ist, ergibt sich unter Maßgabe des Art. 22 MGA 2023 eine entsprechende Rückforderung gegen die Begünstigten.[339]

Neben der Zurückweisung nicht-förderfähiger Beiträge leiten sich aus der Nichterfüllung der verpflichtenden Arbeitspakete zudem Gründe ab, auf deren Grundlage die CINEA das Grant Agreement auflösen oder die Fördersumme verringern kann. Sollte entgegen der Vorgaben des ersten Arbeitspakets die Inbetriebnahme der angegebenen Kapazitäten nicht innerhalb von fünf Jahren erfolgen, kündigt die CINEA das Grant Agreement auf und zieht die Fertigstellungsgarantie ein, welche die Begünstigten im Sinne des Calls bereitzustellen haben.[340] Der Vertrag kann außerdem vonseiten der CINEA aufgelöst werden, falls das Produktionsvolumen in drei aufeinanderfolgenden Jahren durchschnittlich unter 30% des im Gebot angegebenen Jahresdurchschnittsvolumens fällt.[341] Eine Minderung der Fördersumme kommt infrage, sofern die Begünstigten am Ende der Förderung nicht nachweisen können, dass im Rahmen der installierten Kapazitäten keine Quersubventionierung von kohlenstoffintensiven Produkten erfolgte.[342] Dafür müssen im

336 Nach Art. 6 Abs. 4 MGA 2023.

337 Diese betreffen u. a. die Zuordenbarkeit der Beiträge zu der entsprechenden Zahlungsperiode und die zu erbringenden Nachweise über die erzeugten Mengen Wasserstoff und ihrer Zertifizierung als erneuerbar.

338 Nach Art. 6 Abs. 3 MGA 2023.

339 Nach Art. 27 Abs. 3 MGA 2023.

340 Nach Art. 32 Abs. 3 Unterabs. 1 Buchst. m Doppelbuchst. ii Alt. 1 iVm Anhang 5 MGA 2023. Im Sinne von Kap. 10 Abs. 12 Unterabs. 2 Call 2023 deckt die Fertigstellungsgarantie 4% der vereinbarten maximalen Fördersumme ab. Im Rahmen des zweiten Auktionsverfahrens wurde die Fertigstellungsgarantie gem. Kap. 2 Abschn. 2.2 Nr. 2.2 Abs. 1 Terms and Conditions 2024 auf 8% der vereinbarten maximalen Fördersumme erhöht.

341 Nach Art. 32 Abs. 3 Unterabs. 1 Buchst. m Doppelbuchst. ii Alt. 2 MGA 2023 iVm Kap. 10 Abs. 6 Unterabs. 6 Call 2023.

342 Nach Art. 28 Abs. 1 Buchst. a Doppelbuchst. ii MGA 2023 iVm Kap. 10 Abs. 6 Unterabs. 7 Call 2023.

Zusammenhang mit dem Gesamtproduktionsvolumen der geförderten Elektrolyseurkapazitäten Treibhausgaseinsparungen von mindestens 70% nachgewiesen werden.[343] Diese Auflistung an Gründen ist bei weitem nicht abschließend, sondern beschränkt sich auf die Szenarien, welche speziell im Zusammenhang mit der Vergabe einer festen Prämie infolge eines Auktionsverfahrens Anwendung finden.

Zuletzt stellt sich die Frage, welches Recht im Zusammenhang mit den Verträgen Anwendung findet und welcher Rechtsweg den Vertragsparteien offensteht. Die Grant Agreements unterliegen dem geltenden EU-Recht, welches gegebenenfalls durch das belgische Recht ergänzt wird.[344] Bei Streitigkeiten über die Auslegung, Anwendung oder Gültigkeit des Vertrags müssen die Parteien gem. Art. 272 AEUV das EuG oder im Berufungsfall den EuGH anrufen.[345] Wenn die Streitigkeit andere Aspekte wie verwaltungsrechtliche Sanktionen betrifft, müssen die Begünstigten gem. Art. 263 AEUV Klage beim EuG oder im Berufungsfall beim EuGH erheben.[346] Dabei ist die Klage nicht gegen die EU-Exekutivagentur (hier: die CINEA) zu richten, sondern gegen die Kommission.[347]

5. Förderung des Markthochlaufs im Lichte des europäischen Wettbewerbsgedankens

Im vorherigen Kapitel wurde die Zielsetzung des Mechanismus zur Förderung des Markthochlaufs von erneuerbarem Wasserstoff erläutert und anschließend dargestellt, wie im Sinne dieser Ziele feste Prämien infolge von Auktionen der Europäischen Wasserstoffbank vergeben werden. Dabei wurde insbesondere verdeutlicht, wie im Rahmen der Auktionsverfahren sowohl die Auswahl der Begünstigten als auch die Festlegung der Mengen sowie Preise erfolgt und wie letztendlich die Förderung in Grant Agreements vertraglich umgesetzt wird. Nun stellt sich die Frage, wie dieser Fördermechanismus angesichts des europäischen Wettbewerbsgedankens zu bewerten ist. Den Maßstab dafür bildet das primärrechtliche Wettbewerbsverständnis, wel-

343 Nach Art. 2 deleg. Verordnung über Treibhausgaseinsparungen. Die Berechnung der Einsparungen erfolgt nach der im Sinne von Art. 3 deleg. Verordnung über Treibhausgaseinsparungen festgelegten unionseinheitlichen Methode.

344 Nach Art. 43 Abs. 1 Unterabs. 1 MGA 2023. Dies folgt aus Art. 201 Abs. 2 Buchst. i Haushaltsordnung 2018.

345 Nach Art. 43 Abs. 2 Unterabs. 1 MGA 2023.

346 Nach Art. 43 Abs. 2 Unterabs. 4 MGA 2023.

347 Nach Art. 43 Abs. 2 Unterabs. 5 MGA 2023.

ches dem Wettbewerbsrecht zugrunde liegt und im folgenden Abschnitt zu untersuchen ist. Dabei ist zu beachten, dass es sich hier um ein allgemeines Wettbewerbsverständnis handelt und nicht eines, welches in den Beihilferegelungen gem. Art. 107 ff. AEUV zum Ausdruck kommt.

5.1 Der Wettbewerbsbegriff im europäischen Primärrecht

Zur Herleitung der primärrechtlichen Bedeutung ist im ersten Schritt der Stellenwert des Wettbewerbs im Primärecht der EU und anschließend die Anwendbarkeit dieses Wettbewerbsgedankens bezüglich des EWR zu betrachten. Unter Berücksichtigung von relevanter Rechtsprechung und wettbewerbsrechtlicher Fachliteratur werden dann die Eigenschaften herausgearbeitet, welche diesem Wettbewerbsverständnis zuzuordnen sind.

5.1.1 Stellenwert des Wettbewerbs

Wie bereits erwähnt wurde[348] und im Folgenden verdeutlicht wird, ist die Wettbewerbspolitik der EU eng mit dem primärrechtlich verankerten Binnenmarktziel[349] verbunden. Die Errichtung des Binnenmarkts steht hierbei an der Spitze des Zielkatalogs,[350] was seine Bedeutung unterstreicht.[351] Zwar lässt die Formulierung „errichtet“ in diesem Zusammenhang auf die Möglichkeit der vollständigen Zielerreichung schließen, doch *Terhechte* weist berechtigterweise darauf hin, dass die Verwirklichung des Binnenmarkts als eine Daueraufgabe zu verstehen ist.[352] Der Binnenmarkt ist dabei legaldefiniert als ein Raum ohne Binnengrenzen, in welchem die vier Grundfreiheiten[353] gewährleistet sind.[354] Anhand der Entstehungsgeschichte des Art. 26 AEUV lässt sich dies als die Beseitigung aller markrelevanter Schranken zwischen den Mitgliedsstaaten interpretieren, um einen die EU umfassenden

348 Siehe Unterabschn. 2.3.1.

349 Siehe Art. 3 Abs. 3 Unterabs. 1 EUV.

350 Siehe Art. 3 Abs. 3 Unterabs. 1 Satz 1 EUV.

351 Vgl. Terhechte, in: Grabitz/Hilf/Nettesheim, EUV Art. 3 Rn. 38; Becker, in: Schwarze/Becker/Hatje/Schoo, EUV Art. 3 Rn. 13.

352 Vgl. Terhechte, in: Grabitz/Hilf/Nettesheim, EUV Art. 3 Rn. 39.

353 Die vier Grundfreiheiten umfassen die Warenverkehrsfreiheit (gem. Art. 28 ff. AEUV), die Personenfreizügigkeit (gem. Art. 45 ff. AEUV), die Dienstleistungsfreiheit (gem. Art. 56 ff. AEUV) und die Kapitalverkehrsfreiheit (gem. Art. 63 ff. AEUV).

354 Nach Art. 26 Abs. 2 AEUV.

Wirtschaftsraum zu schaffen, welcher keinen Unterschied mehr zu einem innerstaatlichen Wirtschaftsraum aufweist.[355]

Trotz seiner Bedeutung wird dem Binnenmarktziel jedoch nach herrschender Meinung kein rechtlicher Vorrang gegenüber anderen vertraglichen Zielen eingeräumt. Diese Auffassung wird zu Recht anhand der Systematik des Art. 3 Abs. 3 Unterabs. 1 EUV begründet, in welchem zwar die Errichtung des Binnenmarktes als einleitendes Ziel formuliert wird, nachfolgend allerdings andere Werte wie u.a. der Umwelt- und Sozialschutz gleichgeordnet daneben aufgeführt werden.[356] In diesem Sinne sind hoheitliche Eingriffe in den Binnenmarkt nicht generell verboten, aber unter Abwägung der betroffenen Schutzgüter und Interessen so wettbewerbsschonend wie möglich vorzunehmen.[357]

Der Wettbewerbsgedanke ist dabei so eng mit dem Binnenmarkt und seinen Grundfreiheiten verbunden, da diese erst den Marktzugang und damit transnationalen Wettbewerb ermöglichen.[358] Im gleichen Zuge sind Regeln zur Wahrung eines unverfälschten Wettbewerbs notwendig, um den Binnenmarkt zu verwirklichen.[359] *Ruffert* bezeichnet daher zu Recht den Binnenmarkt mit seinen Grundfreiheiten sowie das Wettbewerbsrecht als zentrale Pfeiler des Primärrechts, welche maßgeblich zur europäischen Integration und zur Sicherstellung des Wohlstands in den Mitgliedsstaaten beitragen.[360] Umso verwunderlicher ist es, dass das Binnenmarktziel in Art. 3 Abs. 3 Unterabs. 1 EUV im Gegenzug zu Art. 3 Abs. 1 EGV nicht mehr die Errichtung eines Systems umfasst, welches den Wettbewerb innerhalb des Binnenmarkts vor Verfälschungen schützt. Eine entsprechende Verpflichtung wurde dem EUV erst mittels des Protokolls (Nr. 27) über den Binnenmarkt und den Wettbewerb angehängt. Dieser Ansatz geht auf eine französische Initiative zurück und wird in der Kommentarliteratur als rechtlich unerheblich gewertet, da die dem EUV angehängten Protokolle primärrechtlichen Charakter aufweisen[361] und der Grundsatz des unver-

---

355 Vgl. Schröder, in: Streinz, AEUV Art. 26 Rn. 20.

356 Vgl. Korte, in: Calliess/Ruffert, AEUV Art. 26 Rn. 16; Bast, in: Grabitz/Hilf/Nettesheim, AEUV Art. 26 Rn. 7.

357 Vgl. Korte, in: Calliess/Ruffert, AEUV Art. 26 Rn. 15; Bast, in: Grabitz/Hilf/Nettesheim, AEUV Art. 26 Rn. 7.

358 Vgl. Müller-Graff, in: Pechstein/Nowak/Häde, EUV Art. 3 Rn. 35.

359 Vgl. Müller-Graff, in: Pechstein/Nowak/Häde, EUV Art. 3 Rn. 35; Terhechte, in: Grabitz/Hilf/Nettesheim, EUV Art. 3 Rn. 41.

360 Vgl. Ruffert, in: Calliess/Ruffert, EU-Vertrag (Lissabon) Art. 3 Rn. 22.

361 Nach Art. 51 EUV sind die angehängten Protokolle Bestandteil der Verträge, also des Primärrechts.

fälschten Wettbewerbs als konstitutiver Teil des Binnenmarkts bestehen bleibt.[362]

Für diese Auffassung spricht außerdem, dass der Union in Art. 3 Abs. 1 Buchst. b AEUV die ausschließliche Zuständigkeit hinsichtlich der Festlegung von Wettbewerbsregeln zugewiesen wird, welche für das Funktionieren des Binnenmarkts erforderlich sind. Die Reichweite dieser Kompetenz wird allerdings in Abgrenzung zur geteilten Zuständigkeit im Bereich des Binnenmarktes[363] diskutiert. Dabei herrscht Einigkeit darüber, dass die ausschließliche Zuständigkeit nicht den gesamten Binnenmarkt im Sinne von Art. 26ff. AEUV und insbesondere nicht die Regelung der wirtschaftlichen Tätigkeiten umfasst, sondern nur das Wettbewerbsrecht in Art. 101ff. AEUV.[364] Umstritten ist, welche Teile des Wettbewerbsrechts von der ausschließlichen Zuständigkeit erfasst sind. Vorwiegend wird dabei die vorzugswürdige enge Auffassung vertreten, welche sich auf den Wortlaut der Norm[365] stützt.[366] Danach betrifft die ausschließliche Zuständigkeit lediglich das Festlegen der Wettbewerbsregeln, also eine Rechtsetzungskompetenz, welche von der materiellen Kompetenz zur Beseitigung von Wettbewerbsverfälschungen im Binnenmarkt, also der Anwendung und Durchführung von Wettbewerbsregeln, abzugrenzen ist. Dagegen sind nach Auffassung von *Nettesheim* auch das Kartellrecht gem. Art. 101 AEUV und das Verbot des Missbrauchs marktbeherrschender Stellungen gem. Art. 102 AEUV Gegenstand ausschließlicher Unionszuständigkeit, da die Kompetenzzuweisung[367] auf ein für das Funktionieren des Binnenmarktes erforderliche Maß beschränkt sei und damit die Kompetenz der Mitgliedsstaaten zum Schutz des Wettbewerbs weiter bestehen würde.[368]

Unabhängig von der vertretenen Auffassung unterstreicht dies insgesamt die Bedeutung des unverfälschten Wettbewerbs und der damit verbundenen

---

362 Vgl. Terhechte, in: Grabitz/Hilf/Nettesheim, EUV Art. 3 Rn. 41; Heintschel von Heinegg, in: Vedder/Heintschel von Heinegg, EUV Art. 3 Rn. 10; Becker, in: Schwarze/Becker/Hatje/Schoo, EUV Art. 3 Rn. 13.

363 Nach Art. 4 Abs. 2 Buchst. a AEUV.

364 Vgl. Häde, in: Pechstein/Nowak/Häde, AEUV Art. 3 Rn. 5; Kotzur, in: Geiger/Khan/Kotzur/Kirchmair, AEUV Art. 3 Rn. 3.

365 Gemeint ist Art. 3 Abs. 1 Buchst. b AEUV.

366 Vgl. Calliess, in: Calliess/Ruffert, AEUV Art. 3 Rn. 9; Häde, in: Pechstein/Nowak/Häde, AEUV Art. 3 Rn. 6; Kotzur, in: Geiger/Khan/Kotzur/Kirchmair, AEUV Art. 3 Rn. 3; Pelka, in: Schwarze/Becker/Hatje/Schoo, AEUV Art. 3 Rn. 9f.; Vedder, in: Vedder/Heintschel von Heinegg, AEUV Art. 3 Rn. 6.

367 Nach Art. 3 Abs. 1 Buchst. b AEUV.

368 Vgl. Nettesheim, in: Grabitz/Hilf/Nettesheim, AEUV Art. 3 Rn. 14.

Wettbewerbsregeln. Diese stellen einen Ordnungsrahmen[369] im Sinne von Art. 119 Abs. 1 AEUV dar, welcher den für die Wirtschaftspolitik der EU verpflichtenden Grundsatz einer „offenen Marktwirtschaft mit freiem Wettbewerb“ beinhaltet.[370] Der normative Gehalt dieses Grundsatzes ist allerdings fraglich. *Häde* sieht darin zwar ein deutliches Bekenntnis zur vom Wettbewerb geprägten Marktwirtschaft, aber zugleich keine Grundlage eines generellen Verbots nicht marktkonformer Eingriffe.[371] Dagegen beschreibt der „freie Wettbewerb“ nach *Schröder* einen Leistungswettbewerb, bei dem einzig die unternehmerische Leistung über den wirtschaftlichen Erfolg entscheiden soll, sodass ökonomische Ressourcen möglichst effizient verwendet werden.[372]

Allerdings wird dieser in Art. 119 Abs. 1 AEUV festgehaltene Grundsatz einer Wirtschaftsordnung in der Rechtskommentierung überwiegend zu Recht als bewusst vage gehalten eingeordnet, sodass die normative Wirkung gering ist.[373] Vielmehr ist er im Lichte des bereits thematisierten Zielkatalogs aus Art. 3 Abs. 3 Unterabs. 1 EUV zu betrachten, in welchem explizit sozialmarktwirtschaftliche Prinzipien mit der Wettbewerbsfähigkeit der Union verknüpft werden. In dem Sinne bleibt offen, inwieweit staatliche Markteingriffe zulässig oder sogar notwendig sind, was sich in der unionsrechtlichen Praxis zeigt, die auch stark geplante und regulierte Märkte (z.B. im Agrarsektor) kennt.[374]

Außerdem ist nach *Terhechte* im Bereich des Wettbewerbsrechts ein allgemeiner Wandel der Unionsteleologie zu erkennen, da eine alleinige Fokussierung auf ökonomische Prinzipien angesichts der tiefgreifenden wirtschaftlichen Transformationsprozesse nicht mehr zeitgemäß erscheint.[375] Letztendlich sind die Wettbewerbsregeln nach Auffassung des EuGH nicht allein dazu bestimmt, die unmittelbaren Interessen einzelner Verbraucher:innen oder Wettbewerber:innen zu schützen, sondern auch die Marktstruktur und der Wettbewerb als solches stellen ein Schutzgut

---

369 Im Sinne dieses Ordnungsrahmens adressieren Art. 101 u. 102 AEUV privatrechtliche Verhaltensweise, während Art. 107 ff. AEUV staatliche Beihilfen der Mitgliedsstaaten betreffen.

370 Vgl. Müller-Graff, in: Pechstein/Nowak/Häde, EUV Art. 3 Rn. 35.

371 Vgl. Häde, in: Calliess/Ruffert, AEUV Art. 119 Rn. 8 f.

372 Vgl. Schröder, in: Streinz, AEUV Art. 26 Rn. 24.

373 Vgl. Dornacher/Thiele, in: Pechstein/Nowak/Häde, AEUV Art. 119 Rn. 50; Khan/Richter, in: Geiger/Khan/Kotzur/Kirchmair, AEUV Art. 119 Rn. 7.

374 Vgl. Khan/Richter, in: Geiger/Khan/Kotzur/Kirchmair, AEUV Art. 119 Rn. 7.

375 Vgl. Terhechte, in: Grabitz/Hilf/Nettesheim, EUV Art. 3 Rn. 42.

dar.[376] Dies dient im Endeffekt wiederum dem Schutz des Verbrauchernutzens.[377]

5.1.2 Anwendbarkeit auf den EWR

Vor der näheren Analyse des hier verwendeten Wettbewerbsbegriffs ist zunächst zu klären, inwieweit die obigen Ausführungen auf den EWR zu übertragen sind bzw. inwiefern der im EWR verwendete Wettbewerbsbegriff auf denselben Grundlagen fußt. Schon in der Präambel des EWR-Abkommens werden mit dem oben erläuterten Binnenmarkt vergleichbare Ziele formuliert. Diese umfassen die Errichtung eines Europäischen Wirtschaftsraums auf der Grundlage gemeinsamer Regeln und gleicher Wettbewerbsbedingungen sowie das Erreichen einer Gleichbehandlung von Einzelpersonen und Marktteilnehmenden hinsichtlich der vier Grundfreiheiten.[378] Das Errichten eines homogenen EWR, welches direkt in Art. 1 Abs. 1 EWR-Abk als Ziel des Assoziierungsabkommens verankert ist, ist somit als eine Ausweitung des Binnenmarkts auf die EWR-EFTA-Staaten zu verstehen.[379] Zur Verwirklichung dieses Ziels umfassen die Bestimmungen des Abkommens u. a. die Einrichtung eines Systems, das den Wettbewerb vor Verfälschungen schützt.[380] In dem Sinne wurden die zentralen Wettbewerbsregeln aus Art. 101 u. 102 AEUV nahezu wortgleich in das EWR-Abkommen übernommen.[381] Es ist also davon auszugehen, dass der im Primärrecht der EU verwendete Wettbewerbsbegriff auch bezüglich des EWR Anwendung findet.

5.1.3 Eigenschaften des Wettbewerbs

Wie bereits erläutert, ist der freie und unverfälschte Wettbewerb ein zentrales Prinzip im Primärrecht der EU und des EWR.[382] Dabei ist allerdings fraglich,

---

376 Vgl. Urteil des EuGH v. 4.6.2009, T-Mobile Netherlands und andere, C-8/08, ECLI: EU:C:2009:343, Rn. 38.

377 Vgl. Jones et al. (2023), S. 55.

378 Vgl. Abs. 5 u. 16 Präambel EWR-Abk.

379 Vgl. Jones et al. (2023), S. 107.

380 Nach Art. 1 Abs. 2 Buchst. e EWR-Abk.

381 Art. 53 EWR-Abk beinhaltet das Kartellrecht und Art. 54 EWR-Abk das Verbot des Missbrauchs einer marktbeherrschenden Stellung. Der einzige Unterschied ist, dass sich das EWR-Abk hinsichtlich der Eignung zur Beeinträchtigung auf den Handel zwischen den Vertragsparteien bezieht und nicht wie im AEUV die Formulierung „Handel zwischen den Mitgliedsstaaten" verwendet.

382 Siehe Unterabschn. 5.1.1 u. 5.1.2.

welche Eigenschaften diesem angestrebten Wettbewerbszustand zuzuordnen sind. Dies wird im Folgenden mit dem Ziel untersucht, einen Maßstab zu bilden, mit welchem sich der Eingriffscharakter der angebotsseitigen Förderung von erneuerbarem Wasserstoff bewerten lässt.

In der Ökonomie existiert als Idealbild die Theorie des vollständigen Wettbewerbs:[383] Sie beschreibt die Annahme eines Marktes mit maximaler Effizienz, welche durch die Anwendung von Wettbewerbsregeln nicht weiter gesteigert werden kann. Die Produkte werden zu den minimal möglichen Kosten produziert und die Ressourcen mit maximalem Nutzen für die Gesamtgesellschaft verteilt. Grundlage dafür ist ein homogenes Produkt sowie eine Vielzahl von Anbietenden und Nachfragenden, welche jederzeit über Änderungen in Preis oder Nachfrage informiert sind und unverzüglich darauf reagieren. Zugleich bestehen keine Marktschranken, welche den Markteintritt oder -austritt erschweren könnten, und keine Transaktionskosten beim Agieren auf dem Markt. Außerdem existieren keine externalisierten Kosten, die Unternehmen tragen also die vollen Kosten ihrer Produktion. Insgesamt führen diese Bedingungen dazu, dass die einzelnen Anbietenden in Relation zum gesamten Markt jeweils unbedeutend sind und daher keinen Einfluss auf den Preis ausüben können.[384] Im bestehenden Gleichgewicht stellt sich ein sogenannter „Zero-Profit-Markt“ ein, in welchem der Preis nicht die marginalen Kosten übersteigt, wobei diese auch die Kapital- und Opportunitätskosten beinhalten. Das bedeutet, dass die anbietenden Unternehmen im Endeffekt genau so viel Profit machen, dass es sich anhand der Rendite auf das eingesetzte Kapital lohnt, im Markt zu verbleiben.

Dieses Ideal eines vollständigen Wettbewerbs ist allerdings gewöhnlicherweise unmöglich zu erreichen, weswegen Wettbewerbspolitik darauf abzielen sollte, die bestmögliche Wettbewerbslage zu schaffen, welche praktisch zu erreichen ist.[385] Auch aus diesem Grund hat sich das Prinzip des wirksamen Wettbewerbs als grundlegendes Konzept des europäischen Wettbewerbsrechts etabliert. So bestätigte der EuGH bereits im Jahr 1973, dass die zentralen Bestimmungen des Wettbewerbsrechts in Art 101 u. 102 AEUV auf die Aufrechterhaltung eines wirksamen Wettbewerbs gerichtet sind.[386] Zudem umfasst die marktbeherrschende Stellung im Sinne des Art. 102 AEUV nach Auffassung des EuGH die Macht eines Unternehmens, die Aufrechterhaltung eines wirksamen Wettbewerbs auf dem relevanten Markt zu beeinträchti-

383 Vgl. Jones et al. (2023), S. 11 f.

384 Die Anbietenden werden in diesem Zusammenhang als „Price-Taker“ bezeichnet.

385 Vgl. Jones et al. (2023), S. 29.

386 Vgl. Urteil des EuGH v. 21.2.1973, Europemballage Corporation und Continental Can Company/Kommission, C-6/72, ECLI:EU:C:1973:22, Rn. 25.

gen.[387] Mit der EG-Fusionskontrollverordnung erhielt der Tatbestand des wirksamen Wettbewerbs dann Einzug in das Sekundärrecht.[388] Auch in der Rechtsgrundlage des hier zu untersuchenden Fördermechanismus wird auf den Begriff des wirksamen Wettbewerbs verwiesen,[389] was dessen Eignung als Bewertungsmaßstab unterstreicht.

Dabei ist allerdings fraglich, anhand welcher Eigenschaften das Vorliegen eines wirksamen Wettbewerbs bestimmt wird, da es sich um einen unbestimmten Rechtsbegriff handelt. Nach der bereits in den 1940er-Jahren von J.M. Clark entwickelten Theorie kann die Wirksamkeit des Wettbewerbs anhand von Struktur-, Verhaltens- und Leistungskriterien beurteilt werden, wobei die Beurteilung des Erfüllens einzelner Kriterien in einer bestimmten Branche schwerfallen kann und zudem bei Erfüllung nur eines Teils der Kriterien eine abschließende Bewertung ohne subjektive Werturteile nur schwierig zu treffen ist.[390]

Dagegen konkretisierte der EuGH den Begriff des wirksamen Wettbewerbs erstmals im Zuge des *Metro*-Urteils:[391] Entscheidend sei ein solches Maß an Wettbewerb, dass die im Primärrecht festgelegten Grundanforderungen eingehalten sowie die dort verankerten Ziele erreicht werden, insbesondere die Verwirklichung des Binnenmarkts und die Gewährleistung seines Funktionierens.[392] Damit vereinbar sei eine unterschiedliche Art und Intensität des Wettbewerbs, abhängig von den betrachteten Waren oder Dienstleistungen und der wirtschaftlichen Struktur des jeweiligen Marktsektors. Dabei sei der Preiswettbewerb zwar von Bedeutung für den Binnenmarkt, aber nicht die einzige wirksame Form des Wettbewerbs, sodass er daher nicht unter allen Umständen den absoluten Vorrang erhalten müsse. Eine Schwächung des Preiswettbewerbs sei umso mehr dann möglich, wenn in dem Zuge der Wettbewerb in anderen Bereichen gestärkt würde.

---

387 Vgl. Urteil des EuGH v. 14.2.1978, United Brands/Kommission, C-27/76, ECLI:EU:C:1978:22, Rn. 65; Urteil des EuGH v. 13.2.1979, Hoffmann-La Roche/Kommission, C-85/76, ECLI:EU:C:1979:36, Rn. 38.

388 Nach Art. 2 Abs. 3 EG-Fusionskontrollverordnung sind Unternehmenszusammenschlüsse als mit dem Binnenmarkt unvereinbar zu erklären, sofern sie den wirksamen Wettbewerb erheblich behindern würden.

389 Nach Art. 13a Abs. 4 deleg. Innovationsfondsverordnung ist das Auktionsdesign rechtzeitig vor dem Call bekanntzugeben, um einen wirksamen Wettbewerb zu ermöglichen.

390 Vgl. Jones et al. (2023), S. 29.

391 Vgl. Urteil des EuGH v. 25.10.1977, Metro/Kommission, C-26/76, ECLI:EU: C:1977:167, Rn. 20 f.

392 Siehe Unterabschn. 5.1.1.

Auch die Rechtsprechung des EuG stützt sich auf dieses Verständnis eines wirksamen Wettbewerbs, allerdings ohne den Begriff weiter zu konkretisieren.[393] Erst in den Richtlinien zur Anwendung des Art. 101 AEUV auf horizontale Kooperationsvereinbarungen führte die Kommission die Zielbestimmung eines wirksamen Wettbewerbs weiter aus. Dieser fördere danach Innovation, erhöhe die Auswahl und Qualität der Produkte, gewährleiste eine effiziente Ressourcenallokation, senke die Produktionskosten und trage somit insgesamt zum Verbrauchernutzen bei.[394] Dabei bleibt allerdings weiterhin offen, was genau einen wirksamen Wettbewerb auszeichnet.

Dies zeigt sich ebenfalls in der Kommentarliteratur, welche nach herrschender Meinung zu Recht wenig Konkretisierung in dem sowohl vonseiten des EuGH als auch vonseiten der Kommission verfolgten Wettbewerbskonzept sieht.[395] Der verwendete Wettbewerbsbegriff erschließt sich also nicht direkt aus ökonomischen Denkmodellen (wie z.B. der Theorie des vollständigen Wettbewerbs),[396] sondern ist vielmehr im Lichte der bereits dargestellten Grundsätze und Ziele des Primärrechts,[397] insbesondere des Binnenmarktziels, zu betrachten, was auch der EuGH im oben thematisierten *Metro*-Urteil feststellte.[398] Dem hier vertretenen Marktmechanismus liegt nach herrschender Meinung die Entscheidungsfreiheit der Marktteilnehmenden zugrunde, mittels welcher Geschäftspolitik sie zum Ergreifen welcher Chancen unter Eingehen welcher Risiken bereit sind, was auch als Selbständigkeitspostulat bezeichnet wird.[399] Dies führt zu einem Produkt- oder Dienstleistungswettbewerb auf der Grundlage ihrer Leistungen, also ihrem Bemühen, sich mittels verschiedener Mittel gegenüber anderen Marktteilnehmenden zu behaupten.[400] Dabei ist eine formale Einschränkung der

---

393 Vgl. Urteil des EuG v. 27.9.2006, GlaxoSmithKline Services/Kommission, T-168/01, ECLI:EU:T:2006:265, Rn. 109.

394 Vgl. Europäische Kommission (2023b), Rn. 518.

395 Vgl. Weiß, in: Calliess/Ruffert, AEUV Art. 101 Rn. 79; Schuhmacher, in: Grabitz/Hilf/Nettesheim, AEUV Art. 101 Rn. 11; Zimmer, in: Immenga/Mestmäcker, AEUV Art. 101 Abs. 1 Rn. 117; Müller-Graff, in: Vedder/Heintschel von Heinegg, AEUV Art. 101 Rn. 19.

396 Siehe Unterabschn. 5.1.3.

397 Siehe Unterabschn. 5.1.1.

398 Vgl. Urteil des EuGH v. 25.10.1977, Metro/Kommission, C-26/76, ECLI:EU:C:1977:167, Rn. 20f.

399 Vgl. Müller-Graff, in: Vedder/Heintschel von Heinegg, AEUV Art. 101 Rn. 19; Khan, in: Geiger/Khan/Kotzur/Kirchmair, AEUV Art. 101 Rn. 19; Schuhmacher, in: Grabitz/Hilf/Nettesheim, AEUV Art. 101 Rn. 9; Zimmer, in: Immenga/Mestmäcker, AEUV Art. 101 Abs. 1 Rn. 117.

400 Vgl. Weiß, in: Calliess/Ruffert, AEUV Art. 101 Rn. 78; Müller-Graff, in: Vedder/Heintschel von Heinegg, AEUV Art. 101 Rn. 19.

wirtschaftlichen Handlungsfreiheit möglich, ohne direkt den Wettbewerb zu beschränken, wobei im Sinne des AEUV insbesondere die Marktintegration und die effiziente Ressourcenverteilung schutzwürdige Funktionen des Wettbewerbs darstellen.[401] In den letzten Jahren hat sich die Wettbewerbspolitik der Kommission allerdings vermehrt auf die Steigerung des Verbrauchernutzens fokussiert, wobei jedoch kurzfristige Vorteile, insbesondere hinsichtlich der Preise, mit den langfristigen Auswirkungen auf die Wettbewerbsbedingungen abzuwägen sind.[402]

Fraglich bleibt nach dieser Analyse weiterhin, anhand welchen Maßstabs der hier zu untersuchende Fördermechanismus wettbewerbsrechtlich zu bewerten ist. *Immenga et al.* liefern dafür einen Anhaltspunkt auf Grundlage ihrer Auswertung der Rechtsprechung des EuGH bezüglich wettbewerbsbeschränkenden Verhaltens: In seiner Urteilsfindung habe dieser wiederholt die Bedeutung des oben bereits beschriebenen Selbständigkeitspostulats hervorgehoben, also an die Entscheidungsfreiheit der Marktteilnehmenden bzw. deren Beschränkung angeknüpft.[403] Dies spricht für eine Bezugnahme auf marktwirtschaftliche Prinzipien und ist mit der bereits thematisierten Festlegung einer Wirtschaftsordnung[404] in Verbindung zu setzen. Obwohl der normative Gehalt des betreffenden Art. 119 Abs. 1 AEUV überwiegend als gering eingeschätzt wird,[405] zeigt sich in der Rechtspraxis die Festlegung auf eine marktwirtschaftliche Wirtschaftsordnung, wie *Hoffmann* überzeugend darlegt:[406] Danach soll der Wettbewerb auf Grundlage autonomer unternehmerischer Entscheidungen die Entwicklung des Binnenmarktes bestimmen, also ohne eine Einflussnahme durch willkürliche staatliche oder private Eingriffe. Vor allem die zentralen Wettbewerbsregeln in Art. 101 u. 102 AEUV sind daher auf den Schutz dieses Wettbewerbszustandes vor private Beschränkungen gerichtet, welche dieselbe Wirkung wie die im Binnenmarkt abgeschafften staatlichen Handelsschranken entfalten können.

Aus den dargelegten marktwirtschaftlichen Prinzipien lässt sich ein Wettbewerbsverständnis herleiten, wie es auch von *Kersting* beschrieben wird. Zentral für den Wettbewerb ist danach die Festsetzung von Preisen durch das Zusammenwirken von Angebot und Nachfrage unter Beteiligung einer Vielzahl unabhängiger Akteur:innen, welche aktuell oder potenziell am Markt

---

401 Vgl. Schuhmacher, in: Grabitz/Hilf/Nettesheim, AEUV Art. 101 Rn. 10 f.
402 Vgl. Zimmer, in: Immenga/Mestmäcker, AEUV Art. 101 Abs. 1 Rn. 117.
403 Vgl. Zimmer, in: Immenga/Mestmäcker, AEUV Art. 101 Abs. 1 Rn. 117.
404 Siehe Unterabschn. 5.1.1.
405 Siehe Unterabschn. 5.1.1.
406 Vgl. Hoffmann, in: Dauses/Ludwigs, H. I. § 1 Rn. 1 u. 3 f.

teilnehmen.[407] Auch dies ist mit dem zuvor dargestellten Selbständigkeitspostulat in Verbindung zu setzen.[408] Neben der wettbewerblichen Preisfestsetzung lässt sich ein wirksamer Wettbewerb zudem anhand der Realisierung von Effizienzgewinnen charakterisieren, die auch dem Verbrauchernutzen zugutekommen, insbesondere durch die Entwicklung neuer Produkte und der bestehenden Möglichkeit eines nachstoßenden Wettbewerbs.[409] Dem Wettbewerb ist also auch eine Innovationsfunktion zuzuschreiben.[410] In dem Sinne können

Eingriffe in den Markt mit den primärrechtlichen Zielen vereinbar sein, solange dynamische Effizienz sichergestellt ist, wirksame Anpassungsmechanismen auf dem Markt bestehen bleiben und dies letztendlich zu einer Steigerung des Verbrauchernutzens führt.[411] Insgesamt bilden folglich die wettbewerbliche Preisfestsetzung durch Angebot und Nachfrage unter Einwirken einer Vielzahl an Marktakteur:innen sowie die Innovationsfunktion einen angemessenen Maßstab für die folgende Bewertung der Förderung.

5.2 Wettbewerbsrechtliche Bewertung der Förderung

5.2.1 Eingriffscharakter

Im ersten Schritt ist der Eingriffscharakter der Förderung zu bewerten. Wie bereits verdeutlicht, ist die wettbewerbliche Preisfestsetzung eine maßgebliche Eigenschaft des wirksamen Wettbewerbs.[412] Das bedeutet, dass im Sinne eines unverfälschten Wettbewerbs die Preisfestsetzung auf dem europäischen Wasserstoffmarkt allein anhand des Zusammenwirkens von Angebot und Nachfrage erfolgen dürfte, welche sich aus dem autonomen Handeln der Marktteilnehmenden ergeben. Eine politische Maßnahme zur Förderung des Angebots an erneuerbarem Wasserstoff[413] stellt somit grundsätzlich einen wettbewerbsverfälschenden Eingriff in den Markt dar.

Erneuerbarer Wasserstoff wurde dabei von der Kommission als die wasserstoffbasierte Lösung identifiziert, welche langfristig am besten mit ihrer Vision von Klimaneutralität und den damit verbundenen Dekarbonisie-

407 Vgl. Kersting, in: Kersting/Meyer-Lindmann/Podszun, Einl. Rn. 7 u. 10.
408 Siehe Unterabschn. 5.1.1 u. 5.1.3.
409 Vgl. Kersting, in: Kersting/Meyer-Lindmann/Podszun, Einl. Rn. 11.
410 Vgl. Ewald, in: Wiedemann, § 7 Rn. 1.
411 Vgl. Schuhmacher, in: Grabitz/Hilf/Nettesheim, AEUV Art. 101 Rn. 14 u. 16.
412 Siehe Unterabschn. 5.1.3.
413 Siehe Unterabschn. 4.1.1.

rungszielen vereinbar ist.[414] Zugleich wurde aufgrund der im Vergleich zu fossilem Wasserstoff bestehenden Kostendifferenz dessen mangelnde Wettbewerbsfähigkeit betont, was auch im Rahmen dieser Arbeit festgestellt wurde.[415] Dies zeigt sich auch darin, dass das Angebot an erneuerbarem Wasserstoff im entstehenden Wasserstoffmarkt vergleichsweise verschwindend gering ist.[416] Im Rahmen der Förderung zahlt die CINEA nun den begünstigten Erzeugern erneuerbaren Wasserstoffs eine feste Prämie als Beitrag zu den Herstellungskosten pro hergestellter Einheit, um die Kostendifferenz zur fossilen Wasserstoffproduktion zu überbrücken.[417] Diese Begünstigten gewinnen also einen

Wettbewerbsvorteil und können den erzeugten Wasserstoff zu kompetitiveren Preisen anbieten. Somit erfolgt die Preisfestsetzung nicht allein anhand der Kräfte des Marktes.

Gleichzeitig ist die bereits beschriebene Innovationsfunktion des Wettbewerbs[418] zu beachten. Die Kommission hatte in dieser Hinsicht ein Marktversagen identifiziert und ihren strategischen Kurs auch auf die Förderung von Zukunftstechnologien im Bereich der sauberen Energien gerichtet, um somit Europas Wettbewerbsfähigkeit zu stärken und in diesem Sektor die Führungsrolle zu behaupten.[419] Dieser Aspekt wurde insbesondere im Rahmen des zweiten Auktionsverfahrens noch bekräftigt.[420] Zudem sind die besonderen Gegebenheiten eines leitungsgebundenen Marktes zu beachten, welcher erst im Aufbau begriffen ist. So demonstrierte Abschnitt 3.3 die zentrale Bedeutung der Wasserstoffinfrastruktur für die Verknüpfung von Angebot und Nachfrage sowie das damit verbundene Marktgeschehen. Ebenso wurde die Notwendigkeit der Regulierung zur Gewährleistung gleicher Wettbewerbsbedingungen deutlich. In diesem Konstrukt sind marktfähige Innovationen ohne politische Einflussnahme nur schwer vorstellbar, sodass ein gewisser initialer Anstoß notwendig erscheint, wobei die Möglichkeit des nachstoßenden Wettbewerbs[421] zu wahren ist. Nichtsdestotrotz erfolgt hier ein wettbewerbsverfälschender Eingriff in den Markt.

---

414 Siehe Unterabschn. 2.3.2.
415 Siehe Unterabschn. 2.2.4.
416 Siehe Unterabschn. 2.2.2.
417 Siehe Unterabschn. 4.1.2 u. 4.3.2.
418 Siehe Unterabschn. 5.1.3.
419 Siehe Abschn. 2.3.
420 Siehe Unterabschn. 4.2.3.
421 Siehe Unterabschn. 5.1.3.

5.2.2 Wettbewerbliche Gestaltung des Fördermechanismus

Schon bei der Analyse der primärrechtlichen Bedeutung des Wettbewerbsbegriffs wurde allerdings deutlich, dass hoheitliche Eingriffe in den Binnenmarkt nicht generell ausgeschlossen sind, sondern Markteingriffe vielmehr so wettbewerbsschonend wie möglich vorzunehmen sind.[422] Daher ist im Folgenden zu untersuchen, inwieweit der Fördermechanismus wettbewerblich gestaltet ist und wie die Intensität des zuvor dargestellten Eingriffs[423] angesichts dessen zu bewerten ist.

Wie bereits dargestellt, wurde die Vergabe von Verträgen über feste Prämien infolge von Auktionsverfahren durch die überarbeitete Emissionshandelsrichtlinie ermöglicht.[424] Die Einführung solcher marktbasierter Mechanismen begann im Rahmen der Förderung erneuerbarer Energien und hat dort zu signifikanten Erfolgen geführt.[425] Diesem Ansatz liegt der Gedanke zugrunde, eine Förderregelung so zu gestalten, dass deren wettbewerbsverzerrende Wirkung auf ein Mindestmaß reduziert werden kann. Am Beispiel der in Abschnitt 4.2 dargestellten Auktionsverfahren wird hier im Weiteren die Umsetzung dieses Gedankens wettbewerbsrechtlich bewertet. Dabei werden insbesondere das grundlegende Auktionsdesign und die damit verfolgten Ziele berücksichtigt. Für eine detaillierte Bewertung des Designs, auch hinsichtlich möglicherweise darin immanenter Schwächen, wäre bspw. eine komparative Analyse durchzuführen, welche den Rahmen dieser Arbeit überschreitet.

Im Folgenden ist also grundlegend zu bewerten, wie nah am wettbewerblichen Gedanken die Förderung infolge von Auktionsverfahren erfolgt. Bereits bezüglich des Einleitungsprozesses wird dieser Gedanke dem Wortlaut nach berücksichtigt. So ist das Auktionsdesign rechtzeitig vor der Veröffentlichung des Calls bekanntzugeben, um im anschließenden Verfahren einen wirksamen Wettbewerb zu ermöglichen.[426] Der Gedanke dahinter ist also, die potenziell teilnehmenden Unternehmen frühzeitig über die Voraussetzungen und den Ablauf des Auktionsverfahrens zu informieren, sodass diese mit genügend Vorlauf entsprechende Proposals erstellen können. Infolgedessen sind qualitativ hochwertigere Proposals und eine größere Anzahl an Teilnehmenden zu erwarten, was wiederum den Grad des Wettbewerbs fördert.

---

422 Siehe Unterabschn. 5.1.1. Bezüglich der Rechtfertigung des Eingriffs siehe Abschn. 5.3.

423 Siehe Unterabschn. 5.2.1.

424 Siehe Unterabschn. 4.1.2.

425 Siehe Kap. 4 Einl.

426 Nach Art. 13a Abs. 4 deleg. Innovationsfondsverordnung.

Diesbezüglich hob der BDEW positiv hervor, dass die Bekanntgabe der „Terms and Conditions“ im Zuge der Pilotauktion sehr frühzeitig[427] erfolgte und durch Informationsveranstaltungen vonseiten der Kommission ergänzt wurde.[428] Auch im Rahmen des zweiten Auktionsverfahrens betrug die Vorlaufzeit zumindest noch etwas über zweite Monate,[429] zumal der grundlegende Mechanismus durch die Pilotauktion bekannt war. Außerdem setzt die Kommission auf Marktbeobachtung und einen Feedbackmechanismus zum Grad des Wettbewerbs, um die Aufrechterhaltung wettbewerblicher Bedingungen im Laufe künftiger Auktionsverfahren sicherzustellen.[430]

Zentral für die Auktionsverfahren ist die Art und Weise, wie die Begünstigten ausgewählt und in dem Zuge die Mengen sowie Preise festgelegt werden.[431] Der einleitende Call stellt dabei eine Aufforderung an die potenziellen Teilnehmenden dar, den Anforderungen des Calls entsprechende Proposals einzureichen. Diese Proposals werden im weiteren Verlauf auf Erfüllung der vorher festgelegten Qualifikationsanforderungen geprüft.[432] Die Teilnahme am wettbewerblichen Verfahren ist also an hoheitlich bestimmte Bedingungen geknüpft. Dies ist gesetzlich so vorgesehen, um insbesondere das Risiko von Geboten mit spekulativem Charakter möglichst gering zu halten.[433] Außerdem ist auf diesem Wege zu belegen, dass die Teilnehmenden das von ihnen vorgeschlagene Projekt tatsächlich umsetzen können.[434] Somit wird die Teilnahme am Bieterwettbewerb berechtigterweise eingeschränkt, um dadurch faire Wettbewerbsbedingungen zu gewährleisten. Dafür spricht auch die Beschränkung der Anforderungen auf ein erforderliches Maß, um die Ziele des Auktionsverfahrens zu erreichen sowie zugleich ein Höchstmaß an Wettbewerb und Qualität der eingereichten Proposals sicherzustellen.[435] Allerdings wurde, wie bereits dargestellt aus praxisnaher Perspektive die Kritik geäußert, dass bspw. die Beschränkung der maximalen Fördersumme je Proposal die Teilnahme besonders kompetitiver Projekte verhindert hätte.[436] Viele der Anforderungen stehen im Zusammenhang mit der Regulierung des Wasserstoffangebots durch Zertifizierung und der regulierten Wasserstoffin-

427 Siehe Unterabschn. 4.2.1. Die Bekanntgabe erfolgte ca. drei Monate vor der Veröffentlichung des Calls.
428 Vgl. BDEW (2024), S. 3.
429 Siehe Unterabschn. 4.2.1.
430 Siehe Unterabschn. 4.2.3.
431 Siehe Abschn. 4.2.
432 Siehe Unterabschn. 4.2.2.
433 Nach Art. 13a Abs. 2 deleg. Innovationsfondsverordnung.
434 Nach Art. 13c Abs. 2 deleg. Innovationsfondsverordnung.
435 Nach Art. 13c Abs. 3 deleg. Innovationsfondsverordnung.
436 Siehe Unterabschn. 4.2.2.

frastruktur. Diese sollen im Sinne des Binnenmarkts Rechtssicherheit schaffen und zur Verwirklichung der Dekarbonisierungsziele beitragen, aber zum derzeitigen Stand bleibt noch fraglich, inwiefern diese den Wettbewerb einschränken und auch den Markthochlauf erschweren könnten.[437]

Zunächst ist allerdings das Auswahlverfahren zu bewerten, welches im Rahmen der Auktionen Anwendung findet. Die CINEA legte im Vorfeld der Auktionen ein maximales Fördervolumen[438] sowie einen Höchstpreis[439] bezüglich der abzugebenden Gebote fest. Anhand des Gebotspreises wurde dann eine Rangfolge aller sowohl zulässigen als auch förderfähigen Proposals gebildet.[440] Wie im Regelfall vorgesehen, wurde also der Gebotspreis als alleiniges Einstufungskriterium angewandt.[441] Beginnend mit dem niedrigsten Gebotspreis wurden die Fördersummen der Proposals infolge der Einstufung bis zur Erreichung des maximalen Fördervolumens aufaddiert, sodass nur diesen Proposals nach erfolgreicher Prüfung auf Erfüllung der Gewährungskriterien eine Förderung gewährt wurde.[442] Folglich wurden die Begünstigten anhand eines Preiswettbewerbs ausgewählt. Die Festlegung der Mengen und Preise ergab sich dann aus den Angaben der Proposals,[443] wobei der Preis die feste Prämie pro hergestellter Einheit erneuerbaren Wasserstoffs bezeichnet. Im Sinne eines wirksamen Wettbewerbs[444] behaupten sich also die Teilnehmenden gegenüber ihren Mitbewerbenden, indem sie hier einen möglichst niedrigen Gebotspreis abgeben. Es ergibt sich somit für die Teilnehmenden eine Anreizwirkung, ihre Herstellungskosten durch Innovationen und nach ökonomischen Prinzipien zu senken, sodass sie auf eine niedrigere Prämie angewiesen sind, um die Kostendifferenz zur fossilen Wasserstoffproduktion zu überbrücken. Die Anwendung eines Höchstpreises bezüglich der abzugebenden Gebote wird hier aus praxisnaher Perspektive als unbedenklich gewertet, da dieser das Niveau des Wettbewerbs sowie das marginale Gebot[445] nicht beeinflussen würde.[446]

---

437 Siehe Abschn. 3.2 u. 3.3.

438 Siehe Unterabschn. 4.1.3.

439 Siehe Unterabschn. 4.2.2.

440 Siehe Unterabschn. 4.2.3.

441 Nach Art. 13d Abs. 1 deleg. Innovationsfondsverordnung.

442 Siehe Unterabschn. 4.2.3.

443 Siehe Unterabschn. 4.2.2.

444 Siehe Unterabschn. 5.1.3.

445 Siehe Unterabschn. 4.2.3. Das marginale Gebot bezeichnet hier das Proposal, welches das maximale Fördervolumen überschreitet und somit entlang der gebildeten Rangfolge das erste der abgelehnten Gebote darstellt.

446 Vgl. Hydrogen Europe (2024), Nr. 3.7 Spalte 5 Abs. 3.

Insgesamt betrachtet stellt die Förderung somit zwar einen Eingriff in die freien Kräfte des Wettbewerbs dar; allerdings erfolgt dieser auf Grundlage eines wettbewerblich ausgestalteten Fördermechanismus, sodass die Eingriffsintensität als durchaus gering zu bewerten ist.

5.3 Rechtfertigung des Eingriffs

Wie in Abschnitt 5.1 deutlich wurde, ist dem Binnenmarktziel und dem damit verbundenen Prinzip eines wirksamen Wettbewerbs kein rechtlicher Vorrang gegenüber anderen primärrechtlich verankerten Zielen einzuräumen. So werden schon im Art. 3 Abs. 3 Unterabs. 1 EUV neben dem Binnenmarktziel andere Zielbestimmungen wie u. a. der Umwelt- und Sozialschutz sowie die Wettbewerbsfähigkeit der Union gleichrangig daneben aufgeführt. Daher ist auch die bereits diskutierte Festlegung[447] einer marktwirtschaftlichen Wirtschaftsordnung nach Art. 119 Abs. 1 AEUV im Lichte dieses Zielkatalogs zu betrachten. Die Aufrechterhaltung eines wirksamen Wettbewerbs ist also auch mit der Wahrung anderer primärrechtlicher Ziele abzuwägen. Bei sich daraus ergebenden Zielkonflikten ist dann im Sinne praktischer Konkordanz ein Ausgleich herzustellen, sodass die gleichrangigen Ziele weitestgehend erhalten bleiben.[448] Im Falle des hier untersuchten Eingriffs sind dabei insbesondere die Ziele des Umweltschutzes und der Wettbewerbsfähigkeit aus Art. 3 Abs. 3 Unterabs. 1 Satz 2 EUV zu berücksichtigen. Für den zuvor festgestellten, wenn auch durchaus geringen Eingriff[449] stellt sich somit die Frage nach einer Rechtfertigung aus Gründen des Umweltschutzes und der Wettbewerbsfähigkeit.

Die bereits thematisierten Dekarbonisierungsziele,[450] insbesondere hinsichtlich des Energiesektors, stehen in direkter Verbindung mit dem primärrechtlich verankerten Ziel[451] des Umweltschutzes. Im Zuge des anthropogenen Treibhauseffekts[452] betonte die Kommission die Dringlichkeit der Dekarbonisierung, zumal Investitionszyklen im Bereich der sauberen Energien schätzungsweise 25 Jahre betragen würden.[453] Ebenso hob die Kommission in ihrer Wasserstoffstrategie diesbezüglich die maßgebliche Rolle von Was-

447 Siehe Unterabschn. 5.1.1.
448 Vgl. Hoffmann, in: Dauses/Ludwigs, H. I. § 1 Rn. 6.
449 Siehe Abschn. 5.2.
450 Siehe Unterabschn. 2.3.1.
451 Nach Art. 3 Abs. 3 Unterabs. 1 Satz 2 EUV.
452 Siehe Unterabschn. 2.1.1.
453 Siehe Unterabschn. 2.3.2.

serstoff bei der Dekarbonisierung hervor, wobei erneuerbarer Wasserstoff als die Option bestimmt wurde, welche langfristig am besten mit der Vision von Klimaneutralität und den oben erwähnten Zielen vereinbar sei.[454] Dass die Kommission in diesem Sinne hinsichtlich des Markthochlaufs von erneuerbarem Wasserstoff ein Marktversagen identifizierte,[455] ist dabei ein zentraler Punkt der vorgenommenen Abwägung.

Außerdem sollen die hier untersuchten Auktionsverfahren nicht allein der Förderung ausgewählter Begünstigter dienen. Denn durch das Auktionsdesign sowie infolge weiterer Mechanismen der Europäischen Wasserstoffbank soll die Preisfindung und die Marktbildung hinsichtlich erneuerbaren Wasserstoffs überhaupt erst angestoßen werden, indem private Kosten offengelegt und vergleichbare Preispunkte geschaffen werden.[456] In diesem Zusammenhang sind auch die Verknüpfung von Angebot und Nachfrage sowie die Mobilisierung von privatem Kapital entlang der gesamten Wertschöpfungskette von zentraler Bedeutung.[457] Dass der Markthochlauf im Mittelpunkt der Förderung steht, zeigt sich auch darin, dass die feste Prämie nur für tatsächlich erzeugte Einheiten ausgezahlt wird.[458] Der Markthochlauf soll dabei einen Beitrag zur Wettbewerbsfähigkeit der Union leisten, welche ebenfalls als gleichrangiges Ziel in Art. 3 Abs. 3 Unterabs. 1 Satz 2 EUV verankert ist. Dieser Aspekt wurde im Zuge des zweiten Auktionsverfahrens noch unterstrichen, dessen Zielsetzung nun auch explizit einen Beitrag zur Führungsrolle und Wettbewerbsfähigkeit Europas im Wasserstoffsektor umfasst.[459] Gleichzeitig wurden in dieser Arbeit anhand der vom BDEW und von Hydrogen Europe geäußerten Kritik auch Zweifel deutlich, wie effektiv das derzeitige Auktionsdesign inkl. der bereitgestellten Budgets tatsächlich zur Förderung des Markthochlaufs beitragen kann.[460] Dies wird allerdings erst die Marktentwicklung der nächsten Jahre zeigen.

Insgesamt stehen der Aufrechterhaltung eines wirksamen Wettbewerbs folglich die zwei gleichrangigen Ziele des Umweltschutzes und der Wettbewerbsfähigkeit gegenüber, welchen ebenso maßgebliche Implikationen für den Verbrauchernutzen innewohnen. Der festgestellte Eingriff in den Wettbewerb[461] ist somit auch mit Blick auf dessen durchaus geringe Intensität

---

454 Siehe Unterabschn. 2.3.2.
455 Siehe Unterabschn. 2.3.4.
456 Siehe Unterabschn. 4.1.1.
457 Siehe Unterabschn. 4.1.1.
458 Siehe Unterabschn. 4.1.2 u. 4.3.2.
459 Siehe Unterabschn. 4.2.3.
460 Siehe Unterabschn. 4.1.3., 4.2.2 u. 4.2.3.
461 Siehe Abschn. 5.2.

aus Gründen des Umweltschutzes und der Wettbewerbsfähigkeit zu rechtfertigen.

6. Fazit und Ausblick

Ziel dieser Arbeit war es, die politisch motivierte Förderung des Markthochlaufs von erneuerbarem Wasserstoff innerhalb des EWR angesichts des primärrechtlich verankerten und für den Binnenmarkt zentralen Wettbewerbsgedankens zu bewerten. Die Vergabe von festen Prämien an ausgewählte Begünstigte stellt dabei grundsätzlich einen wettbewerbsverfälschenden Eingriff in den Markt dar.[462] Allerdings wurde bereits im Bereich der erneuerbaren Energien eine möglichst wettbewerbsschonende Gestaltung solcher Fördermechanismen erfolgreich umgesetzt.[463] Diese Prämisse findet sich auch im wettbewerbsorientierten Design der hier untersuchten Auktionen der Europäischen Wasserstoffbank wieder. Dadurch ist die Eingriffsintensität der Förderung anhand des gebildeten Maßstabs[464] als durchaus gering zu bewerten.[465] Außerdem enthält das Primärrecht neben dem Binnenmarktziel und dem damit verbundenen Prinzip des unverfälschten Wettbewerbs weitere gleichrangige Ziele, welche im Sinne praktischer Konkordanz einen solchen Eingriff rechtfertigen könnten.[466] Eine Rechtfertigung aus Gründen des Umweltschutzes und der Wettbewerbsfähigkeit wurde im vorangegangenen Abschnitt aufgezeigt. An dieser Stelle wurde zudem besonders deutlich, wie im Spannungsfeld zwischen Klimaschutz und Wettbewerb ein Ausgleich konkurrierender Interessen herzustellen ist.

Außerdem zeigte diese Arbeit, dass ein Herleiten zentraler Merkmale des europäischen Wettbewerbsverständnisses zwar möglich ist, aber dies keine abschließende Definition darstellt. Vielmehr setzt sich der Wettbewerbsbegriff aus ökonomischer Theorie, primärrechtlichen Prinzipien und der letztendlichen Rechtspraxis zusammen.[467] Die dynamische Entwicklung dieses Begriffs wäre, insbesondere mit Blick auf aktuelle Transformationsherausforderungen, in weiterer Forschung zu untersuchen. Ebenso ließe sich der in dieser Arbeit betrachtete Fördermechanismus aus weiteren Perspektiven näher analysieren. Wie bereits erwähnt, wäre bspw. eine komparative Analyse

462 Siehe Unterabschn. 5.2.1.
463 Siehe Kap. 4 Einl.
464 Siehe Unterabschn. 5.1.3.
465 Siehe Unterabschn. 5.2.2.
466 Siehe Abschn. 5.3.
467 Siehe Unterabschn. 5.1.3.

des Auktionsdesigns denkbar, um möglicherweise systemimmanente Schwächen in der wettbewerblichen Ausgestaltung zu identifizieren.[468]

Auch eine beihilferechtliche Bewertung der Förderung im Sinne der Art. 107 ff. AEUV könnte die Erkenntnisse dieser Arbeit sinnvoll ergänzen, denn das Beihilfenrecht stellt einen weiteren bedeutsamen Teil des Wettbewerbsrechts dar und das hier untersuchte Wettbewerbsverständnis ist diesem dementsprechend ebenso immanent. Dabei wäre u.a. zu prüfen, inwieweit die aus dem Innovationsfonds bereitgestellten Mittel[469] als staatliche Mittel im Sinne des Art. 107 Abs. 1 AEUV zu werten sind. Zudem wäre der Eingriffscharakter der Förderung hinsichtlich der wettbewerbsverfälschenden Wirkung einer Begünstigung ausgewählter Unternehmen näher zu untersuchen. So verdeutlichte diese Arbeit bereits, wie für die final ausgewählten Begünstigten ein Wettbewerbsvorteil entsteht, welcher die wettbewerbliche Preisfestsetzung verfälscht.[470] Sofern die im Rahmen der Auktionen vergebenen festen Prämien staatliche Beihilfen darstellten, wäre dann fraglich, inwiefern diese im Sinne der Ausnahmen[471] vom Beihilfenverbot als mit dem Binnenmarkt vereinbar angesehen werden könnten. Dabei wären zudem die bereits erwähnten KUEBLL anzuwenden.[472]

Letztendlich wird der Markthochlauf von (erneuerbarem) Wasserstoff in den kommenden Jahren noch viele Fragen aufwerfen. So verdeutlichte Kapitel 3 die Bedeutsamkeit eines klaren Rechtsrahmens und welche Herausforderungen in dieser Hinsicht insbesondere bei einem leitungsgebundenen Markt bestehen, welcher noch im Aufbau begriffen ist. In diesem Sinne ist vor allem zu beobachten, inwieweit der Regulierungsansatz zur Wahrung gleicher Wettbewerbsbedingungen den Markthochlauf auch erschweren könnte, wenn sich daraus komplexe Anwendungsfragen ergeben oder eine unterschiedliche mitgliedsstaatliche Umsetzung, bspw. bei der Zertifizierung, die Rechtssicherheit mindert. So wurde in dieser Arbeit bereits darauf hingewiesen, dass auf die Einführung eines unionseinheitlichen Zertifizierungssystems verzichtet wurde.[473] Zwar wurden mit dem Gas- und Wasserstoffpaket zumindest einheitliche Standards bezüglich der Definition von erneuerbarem sowie kohlenstoffarmem Wasserstoff eingeführt, doch auch eine unterschiedliche Ausgestaltung des Zertifizierungssystems in den einzelnen Mitgliedsstaaten könnte zu Marktverzerrungen führen und den Wettbewerb

468 Siehe Unterabschn. 5.2.2.

469 Siehe Unterabschn. 4.1.3.

470 Siehe Unterabschn. 5.2.1.

471 Nach Art. 107 Abs. 2 u. 3 AEUV.

472 Siehe Unterabschn. 2.3.1.

473 Siehe Abschn. 3.2.

verfälschen. Wie bereits thematisiert, wird die europäische Rechtsprechung zudem zeigen, inwiefern hier in konkreten Sachverhalten eine Abgrenzung des relevanten Marktes vorzunehmen ist.[474]

Literaturverzeichnis

ACER (2024). *European hydrogen markets 2024 Market Monitoring Report.* https://www.acer.europa.eu/sites/default/files/documents/Publications/ACER_2024_ MMR_Hydrogen_Markets.pdf

Athanasiadou, N. (2016). *Der Verwaltungsvertrag im EU-Recht.* In: Kahl, W., Schneider, J. P. & Wollenschläger, F. (Hrsg.). *Beiträge zum Verwaltungsrecht (BVwR).* Mohr Siebeck, Heidelberg.

BDEW (2024). *Diskussionspapier – Erfahrungen zur Pilotauktion der Europäischen Wasserstoffbank und Forderungen an die weitere Ausgestaltung* [Version 1.0]. https://www.bdew.de/media/documents/2000_Diskussionspapier_Pilotauktion_Europ%C3%A4ische_Wasserstoffbank.pdf

Binnewies, M., Finze, M., Jäckel, M., Schmidt, P., Willner, H. & Rayner-Canham, G. (2016). *Allgemeine und Anorganische Chemie* (3. Aufl.). Springer Spektrum, Berlin, Heidelberg. https://doi.org/10.1007/978-3-662–45067-3_14

Bockelmann, M., Becker, M., Stypka, S., Bauer, S., Minke, C. & Turek, T. (2024). *Erzeugung von Wasserstoff durch Elektrolyse.* Chemie in unserer Zeit, 58 (1), 29–45. https://doi.org/10.1002/ciuz.202300024

Bundesnetzagentur (o. D.). *Netzzugang und Messwesen.* Abgerufen am 21.6.2025 von https://www.bundesnetzagentur.de/DE/Fachthemen/ElektrizitaetundGas/Netzzugang Messwesen/start.html

Burmeister, T., Kistner, P. & Sievert, K. (2024). *Das Hydrogen and Decarbonised Gas Market Package.* Recht der Energiewirtschaft, 8, 296–307. https://research.wolterskluwer-online.de/document/004ed3cf-ad40-389c-8f2d- c3c202513ffd

Calliess, C. & Ruffert, M. (2022). *EUV/AEUV* (6. Aufl.). C.H. Beck, München. Chatenet, M., Pollet, B.G., Dekel, D.R., Dionigi, F., Deseure, J., Millet, P., Braatz, R.D., Bazant, M.Z., Eikerling, M., Staffell, I., Balcombe, P., Shao-Horn, Y. & Schäfer, H. (2022). *Water electrolysis: from textbook knowledge to the latest scientific strategies and industrial developments.* Chem. Soc. Rev., 52, 4583–4762. https://doi.org/10.1039/d0cs01079k

CHJU (o. D.). *Who we are.* Abgerufen am 21.6.2025 von https://www.clean- hydrogen.europa.eu/about-us/who-we-are_en

Dauses, M. A. & Ludwigs, M. (2024). *Handbuch des EU-Wirtschaftsrechts* (61. EL September 2024). C.H.Beck, München.

Deutscher Bundestag (2024). Gesetzesentwurf der Bundesregierung – Entwurf eines Dritten Gesetzes zur Änderung des Energiewirtschaftsgesetzes. BT-Drs. 20/10014 v. 11.01.2024.

EHO (o. D.-a). *About Us.* Abgerufen am 21.6.2025 von https://observatory.clean- hydrogen.europa.eu/about-us

474 Siehe Unterabschn. 2.2.1.

EHO (o. D.-b). *Break-even price of renewable hydrogen.* Abgerufen am 21.6.2025 von https://observatory.clean-hydrogen.europa.eu/hydrogen-landscape/end-use/break-even- price-of-renewable-hydrogen

EHO (o. D.-c). *Cost of hydrogen production* [Interaktive Karte]. Abgerufen am 21.6.2025 von https://observatory.clean-hydrogen.europa.eu/hydrogen-landscape/production- trade-and-cost/cost-hydrogen-production

EHO (o. D.-d). *Hydrogen Demand* [Interaktive Karte]. Abgerufen am 21.6.2025 von https://observatory.clean-hydrogen.europa.eu/hydrogen-landscape/end-use/hydrogen- demand

EHO (o. D.-e). *Hydrogen Production* [Interaktive Karte]. Abgerufen am 21.6.2025 von https://observatory.clean-hydrogen.europa.eu/hydrogen-landscape/production-trade- and-cost/hydrogen-production

EHO (o. D.-f). *Partners and Contributors.* Abgerufen am 21.6.2025 von https://observatory.clean-hydrogen.europa.eu/about-us/partners-and-contributors

EHO (2023a). *Hydrogen demand forecasts 2023.xlsx* [EXCEL-Tabelle]. https://observatory.clean-hydrogen.europa.eu/tools-reports/datasets

EHO (2023b). *Hydrogen trade 2023.xlsx* [EXCEL-Tabelle]. https://observatory.clean-hydrogen.europa.eu/tools-reports/datasets

EHO (2024a). *The European hydrogen market landscape November 2024.* https://observatory.clean-hydrogen.europa.eu/sites/default/files/2024- 11/The%20European%20hydrogen%20market%20landscape_November%202024.pdf

EHO (2024b). *Hydrogen production and consumption projects Dec2024.xlsx* [EXCEL- Tabelle]. https://observatory.clean-hydrogen.europa.eu/tools-reports/datasets

EHO (2025). *The European hydrogen policy landscape January 2025.* https://observatory.clean-hydrogen.europa.eu/sites/default/files/2025- 01/The%20European%20hydrogen%20policy%20landscape-%20January%202025.pdf

Erbach, G. & Svensson, S. (2023). *Briefing: EU rules for renewable hydrogen – Delegated regulations on a methodology for renewable fuels of non-biological origin. European Parliamentary Research Service.* https://www.europarl.europa.eu/RegData/etudes/BRIE/2023/747085/EPRS_BRI (2023) 747085_EN.pdf

EUR-Lex (o. D.). *Glossary of summaries – Europäischer Wirtschaftsraum (EWR).* Abgerufen am 21.6.2025 von https://eur-lex.europa.eu/DE/legal- content/glossary/european-economic-area-eea.html

Europäische Kommission (2019). *Der europäische Grüne Deal.* COM(2019) 640 final.

Europäische Kommission (2020a). *Förderung einer klimaneutralen Wirtschaft: Eine EU- Strategie zur Integration des Energiesystems.* COM(2020) 299 final.

Europäische Kommission (2020b). *Eine neue Industriestrategie für Europa.* COM(2020) 102 final.

Europäische Kommission (2020c). *Strategie für nachhaltige und intelligente Mobilität: Den Verkehr in Europa auf Zukunftskurs bringen.* COM(2020) 789 final.

Europäische Kommission (2020d). *Eine Wasserstoffstrategie für ein klimaneutrales Europa.* COM(2020) 301 final.

Europäische Kommission (2021). *„Fit für 55": auf dem Weg zur Klimaneutralität – Umsetzung des EU- Klimaziels für 2030.* COM(2021) 550 final.

Europäische Kommission (2022). *REPowerEU-Plan.* COM(2022) 230 final.

Europäische Kommission (2023a). *Die Europäische Wasserstoffbank.* COM(2023) 156 final.

Europäische Kommission (2023b). *Guidelines on the applicability of Article 101 of the Treaty on the Functioning of the European Union to horizontal co-operation agreements.* C(2023) 3445 final.

Europäische Kommission (2023c). *Ein Industrieplan zum Grünen Deal für das klimaneutrale Zeitalter.* COM(2023) 62 final.

Europäische Kommission (2024a, 30.4.). *Auktion der Europäischen Wasserstoffbank bringt 720 Mio. EUR für die Erzeugung von erneuerbarem Wasserstoff in Europa.* https://ec.europa.eu/commission/presscorner/detail/de/ip_24_2333

Europäische Kommission (2024b, 3.12.). *Kommission stellt im Rahmen des Innovationsfonds 4,6 Mrd. EUR zur Förderung von Netto-Null-Technologien, der Herstellung von Batteriezellen für Elektrofahrzeuge und erneuerbarem Wasserstoff bereit.* https://ec.europa.eu/commission/presscorner/detail/de/ip_24_6184

Europäische Kommission (2024c). *Bekanntmachung der Kommission über die Abgrenzung des relevanten Marktes im Sinne des Wettbewerbsrechts der Union.* C/2024/1645 (ABl. (EU) C v. 22.2.2024).

Europäische Kommission (2025). *The Clean Industrial Deal: A joint roadmap for competitiveness and decarbonisation.* COM(2025) 85 final.

Farchmin, F. (2017). *Die Entwicklung von Großelektrolyse-Systemen: Notwendigkeit und Herangehensweise.* In: Töpler, J. & Lehmann, J. (Hrsg.). *Wasserstoff und Brennstoffzelle.* Springer Vieweg, Berlin, Heidelberg. https://doi.org/10.1007/978-3-662–53360-4_12

Fraunh. ISE (2025). *Öffentliche Nettostromerzeugung in der europäischen Union 2024* [Diagramm]. https://energy- charts.info/charts/energy_pie/chart.htm?l=de&c=EU&year=2024&interval=year

Fritsch, M. (2018). *Marktversagen und Wirtschaftspolitik – Mikroökonomische Grundlagen staatlichen Handelns* (10. Aufl.). Verlag Franz Vahlen, München. https://doi.org/10.15358/9783800656448-I

GD Klimapolitik (o. D.-a). *Auctions in the Innovation Fund – Why does the Innovation Fund use auctions.* Abgerufen am 21.6.2025 von https://climate.ec.europa.eu/eu- action/eu-funding-climate-action/innovation-fund/competitive-bidding_en

GD Klimapolitik (o. D.-b). *IF23 Auction for renewable hydrogen production – Awarded projects.* Abgerufen am 21.6.2025 von https://climate.ec.europa.eu/eu-action/eu- funding-climate-action/innovation-fund/calls-proposals/if23-auction-renewable- hydrogen-production_en#awarded-projects

GD Klimapolitik (o. D.-c). *Results of the IF24 RFNBO Hydrogen Auction* [Slides]. https://climate.ec.europa.eu/eu-action/eu-funding-climate-action/innovation-fund/calls- proposals/if24-auction_en

GD Klimapolitik (o. D.-d). *Results of the Pilot Auction for Renewable Hydrogen* [Slides]. https://climate.ec.europa.eu/eu-action/eu-funding-climate-action/innovation-fund/calls- proposals/if23-auction-renewable-hydrogen-production_en

GD Klimapolitik (2024a, 27.9.). *Second renewable hydrogen auction: European Commission publishes Terms and Conditions.* https://climate.ec.europa.eu/news-your- voice/news/second-renewable-hydrogen-auction-european-commission-publishes- terms-and-conditions-2024-09-27_en

GD Klimapolitik (2024b, 7.10.). *Winners of first EU-wide renewable hydrogen auction sign grant agreements, paving the way for new European production.* https://climate.ec.europa.eu/news-your-voice/news/winners-first-eu-wide-renewable- hydrogen-auction-sign-grant-agreements-paving-way-new-european-2024-10-07_en

Geiger, R., Khan, D.E., Kotzur, M. & Kirchmair, L. (2023). *EUV AEUV* (7. Aufl.). C.H. Beck, München.

Geißelbrecht, M., Auer, F., Kiermaier, S. & Wasserscheid, P. (2024). *Wasserstofflogistik: flüssige organische Wasserstoffträger.* Chemie in unserer Zeit, 58(1), 52–60. https://doi.org/10.1002/ciuz.202300017

Grabitz, E., Hilf, M. & Nettesheim, M. (2025). *Das Recht der Europäischen Union* (84. EL Januar 2025). C.H. Beck, München.

Hilgedieck, J., Kaltschmitt, M., Lange, J. & Streicher, W. (2020). *Speicher.* In: Kaltschmitt, M., Streicher, W. & Wiese, A. (Hrsg.). *Erneuerbare Energien.* Springer Vieweg, Berlin, Heidelberg. https://doi.org/10.1007/978-3-662–61190-6_14

Huck, W. & Müller, M (2025). *Verwaltungsverfahrensgesetz* (4. Aufl.). C.H. Beck, München.

Hydrogen Europe (o. D.). *The Colors of Hydrogen.* Abgerufen am 21.6.2025 von https://hydrogeneurope.eu/in-a-nutshell/

Hydrogen Europe (2024). *Stakeholder consultation on draft of economic Terms and Conditions (T&C) of the 2024 Innovation Fund Auction for RFNBO hydrogen production – Feedback table.* https://hydrogeneurope.eu/wp-content/uploads/2024/06/ Public-consultation_Final_TC_-2nd-Auction-Hydrogen-Bank_Hydrogen-Europe.pdf

Immenga, U. & Mestmäcker, E. J. (2025). *Wettbewerbsrecht* (7. Aufl.). C.H. Beck, München.

IPCC (2021). *Zusammenfassung für die politische Entscheidungsfindung.* In: Masson- Delmotte, V., Zhai, P., Pirani, A., Connors, S. L., Péan, C., Berger, S., Caud, N., Chen, Y., Goldfarb, L., Gomis, M.I., Huang, M., Leitzell, K., Lonnoy, E., Matthews, J. B. R., Maycock, T.K., Waterfield, T., Yelekçi, O., Yu, R. & Zhou, B. (Hrsg.). *Naturwissenschaftliche Grundlagen. Beitrag von Arbeitsgruppe I zum Sechsten Sachstandsbericht des Zwischenstaatlichen Ausschusses für Klimaänderungen.* In Druck. Deutsche Übersetzung auf Basis der Druckvorlage, Oktober 2021. Deutsche IPCC-Koordinierungsstelle, Bonn; Bundesministerium für Klimaschutz, Umwelt, Energie, Mobilität, Innovation und Technologie, Wien; Akademie der Naturwissenschaften Schweiz SCNAT, ProClim, Bern, Februar 2022. https://www.de-ipcc.de/media/content/AR6-WGI-SPM_deutsch_barrierefrei.pdf

Jahn, M., Herz, G., Deerberg, G., Glasner, C., Kraft, A., Menne, A., Müller, T., Seifert, U., Stahl, E., Ilse, K., Spohn, U., Schattauer, S. & Tümmler, M. (2022). *Einsatz von Wasserstofftechnologien in der Industrie.* In: Neugebauer, R. (Hrsg.). *Wasserstofftechnologien.* Springer Vieweg, Berlin, Heidelberg. https://doi.org/10.1007/978-3-662–64939-8_5

Jones, A., Sufrin, B. & Dunne, N. (2023). *Jones & Sufrin's EU Competition Law – Text, Cases, and Materials* (8. Aufl.). Oxford University Press, Oxford.

Kersting, C., Meyer-Lindmann, H. J. & Podszun, R. (2025). *Kartellrecht* (5. Aufl.). C.H. Beck, München.

Konstantin, P. & Konstantin, M. (2023). *Praxisbuch Energiewirtschaft – Energieumwandlung, -transport und -beschaffung, Übertragungsnetzausbau und Kernenergieausstieg* (5. Aufl.). Springer Vieweg, Berlin. https://doi.org/10.1007/978-3-662–67335-5

Lillich, K.H. (2024). *Eine Bilanz zum anthropogenen Klimawandel für das Studium Generale.* Springer Vieweg, Wiesbaden. https://doi.org/10.1007/978-3-658-44200-2_9

Lodhi, S.K., Hussain, H.K. & Gill, A.Y. (2024). *Renewable Energy Technologies: Present Patterns and Upcoming Paths in Ecological Power Production.* Global Journal of Universal Studies, 1(1), 108–131. https://doi.org/10.70445/gjus.1.1.10

Ludwig, R. (2024). *Wasser, Wasserstoff, Wasserstoffbrücke und mehr.* Chemie in unserer Zeit, 58(1), 10–19. https://doi.org/10.1002/ciuz.202300023

Nationaler Wasserstoffrat (2022). *Einordnung verschiedener Pfade der Herstellung von Wasserstoff („Farbenlehre").* https://www.wasserstoffrat.de/fileadmin/wasserstoffrat/media/Dokumente/2022/2022- 04-01_NWR-Grundlagenpapier_Farbenlehre.pdf

Ocenic, E.L. & Tanţău, A. (2023). *Redefining the Hydrogen "Colours" based on Carbon Dioxide Emissions: A New Evidence-Based Colour Code.* Proceedings of the International Conference on Business Excellence, The Bucharest University of Economic Studies, 17(1), 111–121. https://doi.org/10.2478/picbe-2023-0013

Odenweller, A. & Ueckerdt, F. (2025). *The green hydrogen ambition and implementation gap.* Nature Energy, 10, 110–123. https://doi.org/10.1038/s41560-024–01684-7

Pechstein, M., Nowak, C. & Häde, U. (2023). *Frankfurter Kommentar zu EUV, GRC und AEUV* (2. Aufl.). Mohr Siebeck, Tübingen.

Reinecke, P. & Scholz, U. (2024). *Deutschlands Wasserstoff-Kernnetz: A Highway for Hydrogen?* InfrastrukturRecht, 5, 114–136. https://beck-online.beck.de/Bcid/Y-300-Z-IR-B-2024-S-119-N-1

Schwarze, J., Becker, U., Hatje, A. & Schoo, J. (2019). *EU-Kommentar* (4. Aufl.). Nomos, Baden-Baden.

Smil, V. (2017). *Energy and Civilization: A History.* The MIT Press, Cambridge. https://doi.org/10.7551/mitpress/9780262035774.001.0001

Stelkens, P., Bonk, H.J. & Sachs, M. (2022). *Verwaltungsverfahrensgesetz* (10. Aufl.). C.H. Beck, München.

Streinz, R. (2018). *EUV/AEUV* (3. Aufl.). C.H. Beck, München.

Vedder, C. & Heintschel von Heinegg, W. (2018). *Europäisches Unionsrecht* (2. Aufl.). Nomos, Baden-Baden.

Wesselak, V., Schabbach, T., Link, T. & Fischer, J. (2017). *Handbuch Regenerative Energietechnik* (3. Aufl.). Springer Vieweg, Berlin, Heidelberg. https://doi.org/10.1007/978-3-662–53073-3_2

Wetterau, J. (2024). *Alkalische Elektrolyse oder Anionenaustauschermembran.* CITplus, 27(6), 58–61. https://doi.org/10.1002/citp.202400619

Wiedemann, G. (2020). *Handbuch des Kartellrechts* (4. Aufl.). C.H. Beck, München.

Yue, M., Lambert, H., Pahon, E., Roche, R., Jemei, S. & Hissel, D. (2021). *Hydrogen energy systems: A critical review of technologies, applications, trends and challenges.* Renewable and Sustainable Energy Reviews, 146. https://doi.org/10.1016/j.rser.2021.111180

Zwaan, F., Brune, S., Glerum, A.C., Vasey, D.A., Naliboff, J.B., Manatschal, G. & Gaucher, E.C. (2025). *Rift-inversion orogens are potential hot spots for natural H_2- generation.* Science Advances, 11(8), eadr3418. https://doi.org/10.1126/sciadv.adr3418